INTELLIGENCE, STATECRAFT
AND INTERNATIONAL
POWER

HISTORICAL STUDIES

The Irish Committee of Historical Sciences inaugurated a series of biennial conferences of historians in July 1953. Since then the 'Irish Conference of Historians' has circulated among the Irish universities and university colleges and the papers read since 1955 have been published as *Historical Studies*. Since 1975 the conferences have been devoted to a single theme. The full list is as follows:

T.D. Williams (ed.), *Historical Studies* I (London: Bowes & Bowes, 1958)

M. Roberts (ed.), *Historical Studies* II (London: Bowes & Bowes, 1959)

J. Hogan (ed.), *Historical Studies* III (London: Bowes & Bowes, 1961)

G.A. Hayes-McCoy (ed.), *Historical Studies* IV (London: Bowes & Bowes, 1963)

J.L. McCracken (ed.), *Historical Studies* V (London: Bowes & Bowes, 1965)

T.W. Moody (ed.), *Historical Studies* VI (London: Routledge and Kegan Paul, 1968)

J.C. Beckett (ed.), *Historical Studies* VII (London: Routledge and Kegan Paul, 1969)

T.D. Williams (ed.), *Historical Studies* VIII (Dublin: Gill and MacMillan, 1971)

J.G. Barry (ed.), *Historical Studies* IX (Belfast: Blackstaff, 1974)

G.A. Hayes-McCoy (ed.), *Historical Studies* X (Dublin: ICHS, 1976)

T.W. Moody (ed.), *Nationality and the Pursuit of National Independence: Historical Studies* XI (Belfast: Appletree, 1978)

A.C. Hepburn (ed.), *Minorities in History: Historical Studies* XII (London: Edward Arnold, 1978)

D.W. Harkness and M. O'Dowd (eds), *The Town in Ireland: Historical Studies* XIII (Belfast: Appletree, 1981)

A. Cosgrove and J.I. McGuire (eds), *Parliament and Community: Historical Studies* XIV (Belfast: Appletree, 1983)

P.J. Corish (ed.), *Radicals, Rebels and Establishments: Historical Studies* XV (Belfast: Appletree, 1985)

Tom Dunne (ed.), *The Writer as Witness: Literature as Historical Evidence: Historical Studies* XVI (Cork: Cork University Press, 1987)

Ciaran Brady (ed.), *Ideology and the Historians: Historical Studies* XVII (Dublin: Lilliput, 1991)

T.G. Fraser and Keith Jeffery (eds), *Men, Women and War: Historical Studies* XVIII (Dublin: Lilliput, 1993)

Mary O'Dowd and Sabine Wichert (eds), *Chattel, Servant or Citizen: Women's Status in the Church, State and Society: Historical Studies* XIX (Belfast: Institute of Irish Studies, 1993)

Judith Devlin and Ronan Fanning (eds), *Religion and Rebellion: Historical Studies* XX (Dublin: University College Dublin Press, 1997)

Jacqueline Hill and Colm Lennon (eds), *Luxury and Austerity: Historical Studies* XXI (Dublin: University College Dublin Press, 1999)

Hiram Morgan (ed.) *Information, Media and Power Through the Ages: Historical Studies* XXII (Dublin: University College Dublin Press, 2001)

Niall Ó Coisáin (ed.), *Explaining Change in Cultural History: Historical Studies* XXIII (Dublin: University College Dublin Press, 2005)

Keith Jeffery and Neal Garnham (eds), *Culture, Place and Identity: Historical Studies* XXIV (Dublin: University College Dublin Press, 2005)

INTELLIGENCE, STATECRAFT AND INTERNATIONAL POWER

Historical Studies XXV

Papers read before the
27th Irish Conference of Historians
held at Trinity College, Dublin
19–21 May 2005

Editors
Eunan O'Halpin, Robert Armstrong
and Jane Ohlmeyer

Foreword by
Christopher Andrew

IRISH ACADEMIC PRESS
DUBLIN • PORTLAND, OR

First published in 2006 by
IRISH ACADEMIC PRESS
44, Northumberland Road, Dublin 4, Ireland

and in the United States of America by
IRISH ACADEMIC PRESS
c/o ISBS, Suite 300, 920 NE 58th Avenue
Portland, Oregon 97213-3644

© 2006 Individual contributors

***WEBSITE*: www.iap.ie**

British Library Cataloguing in Publication Data
An entry can be found on request

ISBN 0 7165 2840 1 (cloth)
ISBN 978 0 7165 2840 1
ISBN 0 7165 2841 X (paper)
ISBN 978 0 7165 2841 8

Library of Congress Cataloging-in-Publication Data
An entry can be found on request

Typeset by FiSH Books, Enfield, Middx.
Printed by Antony Rowe Ltd., Chippenham, Wilts

Contents

Acknowledgements

The Irish Committee of Historical Sciences inaugurated a series of biennial conferences of historians in 1953, and since 1955 papers presented to each one have been published under the title or subtitle *Historical Studies*. In 2001 the Irish Committee of Historical Sciences came under the aegis of the Royal Irish Academy and is now the National Committee for History. Since 1975 the biennial conferences have been organised around a single theme, and that held in Trinity College, Dublin, from 19 to 21 May 2005 continued the practice.

The National Committee for History expresses its gratitude to Trinity College Dublin for its generous provision of services and facilities, and in particular to the Institute for International Integration Studies (IIIS) and the History Department for financial and administrative support. We would also like to thank the Royal Irish Academy which co-hosted Paul Kennedy's keynote address and generously provided a reception for delegates.

As organisers and editors, we have incurred a great many debts to individuals and institutions, which can be only briefly acknowledged here. We would like to thank Geoffrey Parker and Richard Ned LeBow for their insights as we planned the programme. Much of the conference organization fell to Adrienne Harten and particularly Gail Weadick from the IIIS and we are deeply grateful to them and their colleagues for their goodwill and practical support. We would also like to thank Pauric Dempsey from the RIA and the History postgraduate students at Trinity – Joanna Archbold, Lisa Griffith, Elaine Murphy, Kevin O'Sullivan, and Patrick Walsh – who worked so hard to ensure that the conference ran so smoothly. The success of the conference can be attributed to the quality of the papers and the ensuing discussions and we are particularly grateful to David Kahn, Paul Kennedy and Brian Stewart.

We are indebted to Christopher Andrew for writing the foreword to this volume and to our contributors for facilitating its timely appearance. Finally, we would like to thank Irish Academic Press – and especially Frank Cass and Lisa Hyde – for their assistance and professionalism throughout.

Robert Armstrong
Eunan O'Halpin
Jane Ohlmeyer
Trinity College, Dublin
July 2006

Conventions and Maps

CONVENTIONS

Unless indicated otherwise, and where appropriate, dates are given throughout according to the Old (Julian) Calendar which was used in Scotland, Ireland and England until 1752, but not in most of continental Europe. The beginning of the year is taken, however, as 1 January rather than 25 March.

Unless otherwise state all monetary values are sterling.

Spellings from contemporary sources have been modernised and with proper names (especially people and places) the modern spellings have been preferred.

LIST OF MAPS

List of Abbreviations

AC	Archivio di Concistero
AG	Archivio Gonzaga
AIDA	American Irish Defense Association
ANRW	*Aufstieg und Niedergang der römischen Welt*
APS	*Acts of the Parliaments of Scotland*
AS	Archivio Sforzesco
ASE	Archivio Segreto Estense
ASMa	Archivio di Stato di Mantova
ASMi	Archivio di Stato di Milano
ASMo	Archivio di Stato di Modena
ASSi	Archivio di Stato di Siena
BL	British Library
BMH	Bureau of Military History, Dublin
CDS	*Calendar of Documents relating to Scotland*
CID	Committee of Imperial Defence
CPGB	Communist Party of Great Britain
CPR	*Calendar of Patent Rolls*
CSIS	Center for Strategic and Intelligence Studies
CSP	*Calendar of State Papers*
DIB	Delhi Intelligence Bureau
DMO	Director of Military Operations
FCO	Foreign and Commonwealth Office
FO	Foreign Office
FRUS	*Foreign Relations of the United States*
GRU	Chief Intelligence Administration (Soviet)
HCA	High Court of Admiralty
HMC	Historical Manuscripts Commission

IISS	International Institute for Strategic Studies
IMC	Irish Manuscripts Commission
INA	Indian National Army
IOR	India Office Records
IPI	Indian Political Intelligence
IRB	Irish Republican Brotherhood
JIC	Joint Intelligence Committee
LAI	League Against Imperialism
LBJL	Lyndon Baines Johnson Library
NAI	National Archives of Ireland
NARA	National Archives and Records Administration
NIE	National Intelligence Establishment
NKGB	People's Commissariat of State Security
NKVD	People's Commissariat of International Security
NLF	National Liberation Front
NLI	National Library of Ireland
NSF	National Security File
ONA	Office of Net Assessment
PRONI	Public Record Office Northern Ireland
RE	*Real-Encyclopädie der klassischen Altertumswissenschaft*
RGASPI	Russian State Archive of Socio-Political History
RIC	*The Royal Imperial Coinage*
RS	*Rotuli Scotiae in Turri Londinensi et in Domo Capitulari Westmonasteriensi Asservati*
RUC	Royal Ulster Constabulary
SHA	*Scriptores Historiae Augustae*
SIS	Secret Intelligence Service
SOE	Special Operations Executive
TCD	Trinity College Dublin
TNA	The National Archives of the United Kingdom
TT	British Library, Thomason Tracts
UAR	United Arab Republic
UCDA	University College Dublin Archives
USNA	United States National Archives
YAR	Yemen Arab Republic

Notes on Contributors

Robert Armstrong is Lecturer in History at Trinity College, Dublin, and author of *Protestant war: the 'British' of Ireland and the wars of the three kingdoms* (Manchester, 2005).

Thomas Bartlett is Professor of modern Irish history at University College, Dublin. He has recently edited *Revolutionary Dublin, 1795–1801: the letters of Francis Higgins to Dublin Castle* (Dublin, 2004) and co-edited *1798: a bicentennial perspective* (Dublin, 2003).

Anne Dolan is Lecturer in History at Trinity College, Dublin, and author of *Commemorating the Irish civil war: history and memory, 1923-2000* (Cambridge, 2003).

Paul M. Dover is Assistant Professor of History at Kennesaw State University, Georgia, and has published a number of essays and articles on Renaissance diplomacy and cultural history. He is currently completing a book on the transformation of diplomatic practice and the role of the ambassador in fifteenth-century Italy.

Yee-Kuang Heng is Lecturer in Political Science at Trinity College, Dublin, and author of *War as Risk Management: Strategy and Conflict in an Age of Globalised Risks* (Oxford, 2006).

Keith Jeffery is Professor of British History at Queen's University, Belfast, and author, most recently, of *Field Marshal Sir Henry Wilson: a Political Soldier* (Oxford, 2006), and *The GPO and the Easter Rising* (Dublin, 2006). In 2005 he was appointed to write the Official History of the British Secret Intelligence Service (MI6), 1909-49.

Alastair J. Macdonald is Mackie Lecturer in History at the University of Aberdeen, and author of *Border Bloodshed: Scotland and England at War 1369-1403* (East Linton, 2000).

Robert McNamara is a civil servant in Dublin and occasional lecturer in the National University of Ireland, Maynooth. He is the author of *Britain, Nasser and the balance of power in the Middle East, 1952–1967: from the Egyptian revolution to the Six-Day War* (London, 2003), based on his doctoral research.

Elaine Murphy is a research student in Trinity College Dublin, currently completing her PhD dissertation on 'The war at sea in Ireland, 1641-53', funded by the Irish Research Council for the Humanities and Social Sciences.

Eunan O'Halpin is Bank of Ireland Professor of Contemporary Irish History at Trinity College, Dublin, where he is also Director of the Centre for Contemporary Irish History. His recent publications include (edited) *MI5 and Ireland, 1939–1945: the official history* (Dublin, 2003) and *Defending Ireland: the Irish state and its enemies since 1922* (Oxford, 1999).

Jane Ohlmeyer is Erasmus Smith's Professor of History at Trinity College, Dublin. Her most recent publications include as co-editor *British Interventions in Early Modern Ireland* (Cambridge, 2004) and *Irish and Scottish Mercantile Networks in Europe and Overseas in the Seventeenth and Eighteenth Centuries* (Ghent, 2006).

Kate O'Malley works for the Royal Irish Academy's *Documents on Irish Foreign Policy* series. She was awarded her Ph.D from Trinity College, Dublin in 2006. Her book *Ireland, India and Empire: Indo-Irish Radical Connections 1919–1964* is forthcoming.

Micheál Ó Siochrú is Lecturer in History at the University of Aberdeen, and author of *Confederate Ireland, 1642-1649: a Constitutional and Political Analysis* (Dublin, 1999). He is currently working on his next book, *God's Executioner: Oliver Cromwell in Ireland*.

Geoffrey Roberts is Associate Professor of History at University College, Cork. He has published extensively on modern Russian history including *Victory at Stalingrad* (London 2004) and *Stalin's Wars: from World War to Cold War, 1939–1953* (New Haven, 2006).

Rose Mary Sheldon is Professor of History and Head of the Department of History, Virginia Military Institute, Lexington, VA. Her recent books include *Espionage in the Ancient World: an Annotated Bibliography* (Jefferson NC, 2003), *Intelligence Activities in Ancient Rome: Trust in the Gods, But Verify* (London & New York, 2005) and *Spies in the Bible: Espionage in Israel from the Exodus to the Bar Kokhba Revolt* (London, 2007).

Joanna Waley-Cohen is Professor of History at New York University. Her books include *The Sextants of Beijing: Global Currents in Chinese History* (New York, 1999) and *The Culture of War in China: Empire and Military in the Eighteenth Century* (London, 2006).

Bernadette Whelan is Senior Lecturer in History at the University of Limerick. Her publications include *Ireland and the Marshall Plan, 1947–57* (Dublin, 2000) and, as editor, *Women and Paid Work in Ireland, 1500-1930* (Dublin, 2000).

Foreword

The first enthusiast for Intelligence recorded in world literature is God. In about 1,300 BC He told the Children of Israel, after their escape from Egypt, that if they were to reach the Promised Land they would need to an intelligence service 'to spy out the land of Canaan'. God emphasised the need to select high-quality recruits to carry out the mission. The Children of Israel, however, failed to make good use of their intelligence service and, as a result, spent the next forty years wandering in the wilderness. But Joshua, the man who eventually led them to the Promised Land, was one of the spies who had been sent to Canaan forty years before and realised that good intelligence was one of the keys to the conquest of Jericho. Walking round the walls of Jericho blowing trumpets is probably best interpreted as a successful distraction operation. Rather more important was the fact that Joshua had an agent, Rahab the Harlot, in the enemy camp. The entry into the Promised Land was thus made possible, in part, by probably the first combined operation between the world's two oldest professions.

Intelligence historians, however, tend to have shorter-term perspectives. Most concentrate overwhelmingly on the history of the last hundred years. One of the merits of this intriguing volume of essays, based on the 2005 Conference at Trinity College, Dublin, organised by Dr Robert Armstrong, Professor Eunan O'Halpin and Professor Jane Ohlmeyer, is that it takes a much longer view, with contributions spanning two millennia from the Ancient World to the twenty-first century. Rose Mary Sheldon makes some striking comparisons between the Roman and American combinations of 'shock and awe' and inadequate intelligence in the invasion of Iraq. Like the Emperor Trajan 1,900 years ago, the US-led coalition also failed to foresee that dealing with a widespread insurgency would prove more difficult than the initial military conquest.

One of the chief errors of Western intelligence analysis during the

Cold War was its frequent failure to take the long view. Had analysts remembered the tendency of autocrats through the ages to be told only what they are willing to hear, they would have found it less difficult to grasp the striking contrast between the frequent success of Soviet intelligence collection and the poor quality of Soviet intelligence analysis.[1] Because analysis in all one-party states is distorted by the insistent demands of political correctness, foreign intelligence reports do more to reinforce than to correct the regime's misconceptions of the outside world. Though the politicisation of intelligence sometimes degrades assessment even within democratic systems, it is actually built into the structure of all authoritarian regimes.

Looking back on the Cold War, Sir Percy Cradock, former Chairman of the British Joint Intelligence Committee and Margaret Thatcher's Foreign Policy Advisor, is surely right to identify 'the main source of weakness' in the Soviet intelligence system as 'the attempt to force an excellent supply of information from the multifaceted West into an over-simplified framework of hostility and conspiracy theory'.[2] The distortions which resulted were at their worst under Stalin, whose world-view was accurately summed up by the British diplomat, R. A. Sykes, as 'a curious mixture of shrewdness and nonsense'.[3] For an intelligence officer to have challenged the nonsense would have been to take an enormous personal risk. Before the Second World War, at a time when neither Britain nor the United States even had an intelligence station in Moscow, Stalin persuaded himself, as Geoffrey Roberts writes in his article in this volume, that 'foreign spies and saboteurs were ubiquitous and threatened the very foundations of the Soviet system'. The NKVD did not seek to disabuse him. Even under the far less conspiracy-minded Leonid Brezhnev, intelligence reports carefully avoided challenging the misconceptions of the Politburo. Nikolai Leonov, who became head of foreign intelligence assessment in 1973, recalls how 'All the filtration stages...were concerned with making sure that alarming, critical information did not come to the attention of the bosses'.[4]

Intelligence assessment in Saddam Hussein's Iraq reproduced many of the vices of the Soviet era. Saddam, indeed, had a personal admiration for 'the way [Stalin] governed the country'. An authoritative recent study of 'Saddam's Delusions', based on thousands of captured documents and numerous interviews with former members of his regime demonstrates how Iraqi intelligence reports were carefully tailored to conform to what the autocrat expected to hear. 'The evidence now clearly shows', the study concludes, 'that Saddam and those around him believed virtually every word issued by their own propaganda machine'. As late as 30 March 2003, with US tanks a hundred miles south of Baghdad and preparing for their final push, the Iraqi foreign minister was instructed to tell the French and Russian governments that Saddam would accept only an 'unconditional withdrawal' of US forces because 'Iraq is now winning and...the United States has sunk in the mud of defeat'. At one point during the Iraq-Iran War of the 1980s, a remarkably naïve Minister of Health responded frankly to Saddam's insincere request for candid advice. The next day a number of his body parts were delivered to his wife. No subsequent Iraqi minister made the same error of judgement.[5]

Yee-Kuang Heng's article on the Iraq War reminds us of the importance of the comparative as well as the long-term perspective in intelligence history. The US and British intelligence failures in Iraq cannot be adequately interpreted, as they often are, simply in a US and British context. The intelligence services of a number of countries opposed to the war, France and Germany among them, also believed that Saddam Hussein had hidden stocks of WMD—judgements which were not influenced by the attempt to make a case for war. These intelligence errors in some of the countries which opposed, as well as those which supported, the war in Iraq serve to emphasise the truth of President Dwight D. Eisenhower's often forgotten dictum that intelligence on what weapons the enemy does *not* have is often as important as intelligence on what they do possess.[6] That dictum will remain true in intelligence operations against twenty-first century transnational terrorist groups as some of them struggle to acquire various forms of WMD ('a religious duty', according to Usama bin Laden). Assessing how much progress they have made, and how serious their intentions are, will sometimes be as difficult a challenge as it was in the Iraq of Saddam Hussein.

Nations, institutions and individuals bring their distinctive presuppositions and priorities to the collection, interpretation and utilisation of intelligence, as the chapters which follow demonstrate. Joanna Waley-Cohen identifies the geopolitical priorities of the Qing emperors, including the significance attached to powers and territories subsequently incorporated into, or eliminated by, the empire. Kate O'Malley's chapter on Indian Political Intelligence (IPI) shows how an over-concentration on Indian Communism, reflecting exaggerated metropolitan fears of the Red Menace, initially distracted IPI from the much more serious threat posed to British rule by Indian nationalists. Keith Jeffery's study of Sir Henry Wilson shows how one remarkable individual was able to combine a responsibility for the collection of intelligence with a career as what Jeffery terms a 'successful "policy entrepreneur"', using his own intelligence assessments to influence government policy. Robert McNamara uses the example of British covert action in Nasser's Egypt, a folly comparable with US covert action in Cuba, to show the tendency of much covert action 'to blow up in the faces of their instigators'.

Intelligence (or the lack of it) has often mattered even when, as has been the case for most of human history, there were no professional intelligence services. Alastair Macdonald shows, for example, how poor Scottish intelligence helps to explain why, in the medieval wars between them, the English won far more battles than the Scots. Poor intelligence was also a serious problem for Cromwell's forces in Ireland, argues Micheál Ó Siochrú. The fact that military commanders thus felt themselves forced to rely instead on 'traditionally crude methods to obtain information and disrupt the enemy's communications networks' added to their brutality.

Paul Dover argues convincingly that, in the later Middle Ages, there was often a very fine distinction between the role of the ambassador and that of the spy: 'The line between legitimate and illegitimate information gathering was vague, subjective and movable. In fact, because of the courtesies extended to them, ambassadors were regarded as among the most useful potential spies.' One of the traditional barriers to the successful use of foreign intelligence until the twentieth century, however, was the absence of speedy methods of communication. Though seventeenth-century merchants and ships' officers, and nineteenth-century consuls, among others, as well as ambassadors, could sometimes supply accurate and detailed information, this had often lost much, if not all, of its significance by the time it reached metropolitan policy makers. Those on the spot, as the chapters by Elaine Murphy and Bernadette Whelan demonstrate, were thus frequently better able to put intelligence to good use.

Though this is a book with large geographical as well as chronological horizons, it makes a particularly impressive contribution to the history of intelligence in Ireland over the last four centuries, a theme to which seven of the articles which follow are devoted. A number of long-held Irish intelligence myths will not survive a reading of this volume: among them the supposed efficiency of the Dublin Castle intelligence system in the 1790s and of the IRA in Dublin on Bloody Sunday 1920, reassessed, respectively, by Thomas Bartlett and Anne Dolan. Eunan O'Halpin's impressive analysis of 'Intelligence and Anglo-Irish Relations, 1922-1973' is understandably sceptical of the claim by the British Ambassador in 1973 that the British 'were not conducting espionage activities against the Government of the Republic and had never done so', though he reminds us of occasions when Dublin has secretly collected intelligence in Northern Ireland and Britain. Professor O'Halpin arrives at the thought-provoking conclusion, on the basis of the admittedly incomplete available evidence, that 'since 1922 Britain has generally protected her security interests more effectively through cooperation with the independent Irish state than by clandestine operations against it'. That conclusion is capable of a larger application. During the twenty-first century states will continue, in their national interests, to collect intelligence even on some of the countries with which they share intelligence. But in the struggle against transnational terrorism, the protection of their national security will require wider intelligence collaboration than ever before.

Christopher Andrew
June 2006

NOTES

1 This contrast is a recurrent theme in Christopher Andrew and Vasili Mitrokhin, *The Mitrokhin Archive: The KGB in Europe and the West* (London: Allen Lane/Penguin, 1999) and *The Mitrokhin Archive II: The KGB and the World* (London: Allen Lane/Penguin, 2005).
2 Sir Percy Cradock, *Know Your Enemy: How the Joint Intelligence Committee Saw the World* (London: John Murray, 2002), ch.17.
3 Minute by R. A. Sykes, 23 Oct. 1952, TNA (formerly PRO), FO 371/100826 NS 1023/29/G.
4 N S Leonov, *Likholet'e* (Moscow: Mezhdunarodnye otnosheniia, 1995), pp.129-31.
5 Kevin Woods, James Lacey and Williamson Murray, 'Saddam's Delusions: The View from the Inside', *Foreign Affairs* 85, 3 (May/June 2006).
6 Christopher Andrew, *For the President's Eyes Only: Secret Intelligence and the American Presidency from Washington to Bush* (London/New York: HarperCollins, 1995), ch.6.

DIPLOMATS, SOLDIERS AND SPIES:
THIRTEENTH TO EIGHTEENTH CENTURIES

Did intelligence matter? Espionage in later medieval Anglo-Scottish relations[1]

Alastair J. Macdonald

Intelligence and the related topic of espionage offer a number of opportunities for the medieval historian. An investigation of spying can, for instance, throw light on the otherwise obscure activities of shady, marginal characters. Such, perhaps, was Robert Scort, arrested for passing information to the Scots in 1300 and said to have deserted the allegiance of Edward I three times. Whatever motivated his dangerous career in espionage, it was for robbery that he was hanged at Carlisle in the following year.[2] We know no more about this figure and even less about others, such as the six traitors executed on the Marches by Henry Percy, earl of Northumberland, for which a £30 exchequer payment was ordered in 1401.[3] We do not even know, of course, if these traitors were guilty of espionage. Later medieval record sources are replete with such tantalising hints – payments for services here, legal crackdowns on enemy spies there. The available evidence for an activity like spying is often very patchy, and governments were notably coy about recording their involvement in such matters.[4]

Where we do have more detail on the careers of spies the dangers of their occupation become abundantly clear. Such is the case for John Lambe, a Scottish operative in English employment in the reign of Richard II. In 1378 he was given the perilous task of assassinating Owain Lawgoch, a Welsh commander in French service whose chief danger to English interests lay in his claim to be the rightful Prince of Wales. According to the chronicler Jean Froissart, Lambe used his linguistic expertise in French and Welsh to infiltrate the Franco-Welsh camp as Owain lay siege to Mortagne-sur-Mer in Poitou. Froissart goes on to give a horrified account of Owain's subsequent murder at Lambe's hands.[5] As an agent undertaking tasks like this it is hardly surprising that Lambe was paid at double wage and bonus ('regard') rates for himself and his retinue in continental service for Richard II.

Lambe may also have been dispatched on a spying mission connected to the English invasion of Scotland in 1385; in June of that year he was about to go there on service that clearly entailed a significant risk of death.[6] The English spy, chronicler and forger John Hardyng, meanwhile, claimed to have been sorely maimed undertaking dangerous activities in Scotland on behalf of Henry V.[7]

As well as individual lives, intelligence and related activities can illuminate the circumstances pertaining in societies, like that of the Anglo-Scottish border, subject to frequent warfare. Both the individual and the societal are encapsulated in the well-known act of sabotage of Alice Emson. Of Scottish origin, but long – indeed forty years – resident in Cumberland, Alice lit a warning beacon in 1389 to alert the Scots of Galloway to an English raid imminently due to be launched across the Solway Firth. Arrested and tried, she was acquitted of treason due to her Scottish birth.[8] Difficult and dangerous choices clearly had to be made in a frontier war zone. The system of early-warning beacons, maintained in both England and Scotland, is itself a reflection of the need for this society to provide means for the rapid dissemination of that most crucial of intelligence, knowledge of impending enemy attack.[9] Watchers on the walls of castles, towns and ecclesiastical buildings were also intended to provide early notice of danger. At times of Anglo-Scottish tension such sentinels could be numerous on the walls of a frontier town like Berwick. Even the tiny monastic community on Farne, off the Northumberland coast, in 1380–1 felt the need to furnish a room for a sole watchman.[10] When an enemy approach was detected the local population and defensive forces would need to be informed. Such was clearly the purpose of the great bell in late fourteenth-century Berwick called the 'Wachebell'.[11] Intelligence mechanisms show this to have been a society always (although in varying measure depending on the character of the times) on the edge, poised to face attack.

The Anglo-Scottish frontier was clearly also a highly permeable region in which there were numerous ways for information to be gathered readily. Despite later medieval hostility, there was plenty of peaceful interchange across the border with merchants and pilgrims travelling in both directions and migrant Scottish labour a considerable presence in northern England.[12] It was in the guise of a merchant that Aeneus Silvius Piccolomini, the future Pope Pius II, attempted to pass secretly from Scotland to England in 1435. The ruse failed, Northumbrian locals crowding around Aeneus in wonder at his exotic appearance.[13] It seems, clear, though, that more normal trading links were an everyday aspect of life. Aristocratic contacts, even in times of high tension, were also able to prosper across the border line. Prior to 1400 the Scottish earl of March had clearly established ties of trust and perhaps affection with the earl of Westmorland and his brother, Lord

Furnivall.[14] A ballad culture also developed in the aristocratic households of the border region. Both English and Scottish versions of ballads celebrating the battle of Otterburn (1388) developed in the two realms. The similarities between these are such that they clearly had a common origin and minstrels obviously enacted performances of such works in both England and Scotland.[15]

Such interaction made the gathering of intelligence easier. This is one reason that both governments were so sensitive to 'intercommunance', peaceable intermingling for various reasons between English and Scottish borderers. Much of the concern about such contacts related to the activities of cross-border criminal networks.[16] But both governments were also aware that intelligence could be passed easily between the realms in such a permeable society. In troubled times Anglo-Scottish intermingling could raise issues of national security well beyond the sphere of low-level criminality. When Henry IV's son John of Lancaster was given the unenviable role of keeper of Berwick and the East March in the disturbed conditions of the early fifteenth century, one of his security concerns was unauthorised cross-border contacts. In time of war the Scots, for their part, regarded such interaction as treason.[17] In 1490, during another troubled period in Anglo-Scottish relations, Henry VII ordered the bailiff of Redesdale (Northumberland) to prohibit any 'conventicles or privy meetings' between the Scots and the English in his jurisdiction.[18] Concerns about such contacts would persist in the sixteenth century.

The role of the church establishment in the region also shows the importance of intelligence gathering in this society and indicates that, in some sense, there were no non-combatants in the war zone. A well-known case in point is the career of Robert Claxton, prior of Coldingham, an outpost of Durham Priory on Scottish soil. As violence increased in the borders in the 1370s the English monks were eventually expelled amid lurid allegations of misconduct. Prior Claxton himself was accused, among other things, of spying on the Scots and sending information on their movements across the border.[19] We should not be too sceptical of this suggestion: Durham lands, many of which lay close to the border, were being raided by the Scots at this time, and there was surely an expectation that the well-placed Scottish cell would provide early warning of attack. Institutions like Durham Priory regularly paid for scouts and watchers; it was vital that the monks should react as early as possible to danger. Claxton was, in any case, an enthusiastic warrior-monk. There is some support for the Scottish accusation that he plundered Berwickshire in the company of the earl of Northumberland, probably in 1377, in his subsequent military career. He campaigned against the Scots at least three times between 1384 and 1400 and carried out the traditional task of carrying the banner of St Cuthbert against them.[20]

At a local level, then, intelligence quite obviously did matter and could, indeed, be a case of life and death. A more complex issue, perhaps, is whether intelligence mattered in the broader political context of later medieval Anglo-Scottish conflict. Again, it may seem obvious that it did. It has been demonstrated amply that theorists on war regarded the gathering of intelligence as an important aspect of state activity, so important, according to the fifteenth-century writer Jean de Bueil, that prudent monarchs should spend a third of their income on it.[21] It has also been shown that in practice governments paid close attention to intelligence throughout the medieval period. The Anglo-Norman and Angevin kings in England and the competing parties in the Hundred Years War period were at pains to be well informed about their enemies' activities. From the late fifteenth century, meanwhile, it is clear that rulers devoted considerable efforts to sophisticated systems of information gathering and espionage.[22] It hardly seems surprising in this context that intelligence also seemed to matter to England and Scotland in the course of their long wars from 1296. Both regimes employed spies and both were at pains to prevent the espionage of the other realm.

Of the two regimes, intelligence gathering and counterespionage structures seem to have been less advanced in Scotland. Reference to explicit attempts to halt English spying are rare in medieval Scottish sources and, although a 'Master Spyar' was paid in the 1490s, evidence of regular payments to Scottish spies occurs mainly from the sixteenth century.[23] The Scots did, nevertheless, have some striking intelligence successes. The impact of accurate information is most obvious on the battlefield and the greatest battlefield victory of them all for the Scots, Bannockburn, may well have owed much to this factor. On the night of 23 June 1314 Sir Alexander Seton, previously in English service, defected to the Scots and brought with him a description of the low morale and disorganisation prevailing in Edward II's army. Robert I may have been persuaded by this intelligence to stand and fight, successfully as it turned out, the following day.[24] Fine judgement must have been applied by the Scottish king here; he could, after all, have been falling victim to a ruse. Another, rare, Scottish victory in the field was at the battle of Otterburn in 1388. Froissart provides us with a compelling image of border espionage in action in the prelude to this encounter. As the Scottish host prepared to invade Northumberland its camp was infiltrated by an English spy. Unfortunately for this individual his horse was stolen by the Scots (who, we are informed, were notorious thieves). Making off on foot in full riding attire, the spy's suspicious behaviour was noted and he was apprehended and forced to divulge information on English defensive preparations.[25] This was an intelligence coup for the Scots: it may (if we can trust Froissart's tale) have aided them in their successful invasion, leading to the victory at Otterburn a few days later.

The English perspective was certainly that Scottish espionage could be highly effective, and indeed that military failures could often be explained by treasonable collusion of English nationals with the Scots. In 1327, for instance, after a failed campaign against the Scots, it was believed that Roger, Lord Mortimer (widely unpopular head of the ruling faction in England along with Edward II's queen, Isabella) had been heavily bribed to impede the English war effort.[26] Frequently when war went badly there were suspicions that the Scots were receiving help from within England. Northerners in particular came under suspicion of aiding the enemy. At times, for instance in the 1330s and 1340s, both chronicle accounts and governmental sources suggest that they were not to be trusted, and might at worst be guilty even of sabotage on behalf of the Scots.[27] English border officers, meanwhile, could face prosecution if it was felt that they had done less than their duty in opposing the Scots. Such was the fate of William, Baron Greystoke, keeper of Berwick, who was sentenced to death for losing the town (briefly) to the Scots in 1355.[28] He was eventually pardoned. A lesser man, William Davison, was not so lucky. Having met certain Scots in Northumberland on 6 October 1408 he accepted payment to betray the English-held castle of Roxburgh to them. Found guilty of treason and felony, he was sentenced to execution in 1411.[29] There had previously been suspicion, in 1339, that attempts were being made to betray Roxburgh to the Scots, and as late as 1494 a friar in Berwick attempted to help them capture the castle there.[30]

The Scots were, then, certainly able to gather important intelligence in England. They had spies, both Scottish and English, in the northern counties. Official terminology could be very explicit on this: in 1428 two men of Newcastle were accused of being notorious receivers of Scottish 'spyers'. Robert Shortrede, also of Newcastle, was found in 1421 to have received and concealed in his house two Scots 'spyes' some eight years previously.[31] Espionage caused governmental authorities to have long memories. Beyond the occasional renegade northerner, the English government believed there was an elaborate Scottish espionage network spread throughout England, poised to reveal secrets and engage in sabotage behind the lines. Royal commissions were issued with some frequency specifically for the arrest of such operatives. There are many examples: in 1336 orders were given for the arrest of those who were buying up supplies in England preparatory to a feared Scottish invasion; in 1393, in a time of truce, a royal commission was appointed to arrest the suspicious Scots to be found hanging around the towns and castles of the North.[32]

Sometimes the grounds for these sorts of suspicions seem quite flimsy. On the front line during a state of war this is perhaps understandable. Four 'spies' were seized during Edward I's invasion of Scotland in 1296, one apparently for wandering abroad at night. All were eventually acquitted of any crime.[33] If some were held on tenuous grounds during campaigns, fears of espionage on the English home front seem more to do with xenophobia, perhaps paranoia, than a serious assessment of the Scottish threat. Are we really to believe that Scots – male and female – were wandering the Yorkshire countryside in 1477 setting buildings alight, miles from the border, at a time of Anglo-Scottish peace?[34] It seems unlikely and fits instead with broader trends of anti-Scottish sentiment, for instance the widespread legislation against Scots passed in northern communities in the fifteenth century.[35] The seizure of alien priories (ecclesiastical properties and institutions under foreign control) in England in the fourteenth century has similar roots in largely ungrounded fears of fifth-columnists, while the murder of a suspected Breton spy by London women in 1429 gives some indication of the strength of popular feeling inspired by suspect foreigners.[36] The widespread fear of Scottish espionage ultimately says less about the extent of a Scottish spying system in England than the hatred and mistrust spawned by years of war.[37]

Ultimately, in their intelligence endeavours the Scots seem to have had more failures than successes. Well informed before Bannockburn, Robert I had previously had difficult lessons to learn: his army was routed at Methven in 1306 by a surprise English attack. Robert's naval descent on Carrick (south-western Scotland) in 1307 was into a terrain overrun by more numerous enemies, despite Cuthbert, the king's spy, having been sent ahead to check the position there.[38] In numerous battlefield defeats of the Scots in the middle ages flawed intelligence can be regarded as having played a role. At Halidon Hill in 1333 the Scots failed to appreciate the strength of the English position until committed to a disastrous pitched battle.[39] Even more striking, perhaps, is the great Scottish defeat at Neville's Cross in 1346. With Edward III campaigning with a mighty host in France the Scots apparently believed that England had been emptied of fighting men. They were shown to be mistaken in this when – another intelligence misadventure – Sir William Douglas of Liddesdale blundered into English forces prior to the battle and was repulsed with heavy losses.[40]

Enormous mishaps for the Scots could occur in relation to non-military intelligence as well. In 1384 the Scots went to war, alone, against the might of the English state. This was precisely the circumstance their diplomacy was designed to prevent, the international nightmare the Scottish state always strove to avoid. It is well known that England and France agreed a truce in January 1384, the culmination of negotiations held at Leulinghen, near Calais, from the previous November. The Scots, though, were unaware of this development and took the path to war thinking that their French allies, as previously agreed between them, had done the same.[41] Not so well known is the fact that the senior Scottish herald, Lyon king of arms, was present at the Anglo-French negotiations, at least in their early stages, and presumably representing the Scottish Crown.[42] He should have been aware that international diplomacy, late in 1383 and early in the following year, was taking a turn precisely against current Scottish plans. If he tried to get an urgent message home about the direction Anglo-French talks had taken, he failed. This was a disastrous intelligence failure, although the war of 1384 went relatively well for the Scots in the end.[43] Ultimately, the relatively rudimentary intelligence mechanisms of the Scots did not matter, all that much, in the bigger picture of successful maintenance of Scottish independence.

The English state, though, had an altogether more sophisticated and extensive intelligence network at its disposal. It is unsurprising that we have much more evidence of English intelligence successes than Scottish ones and that the quality of English intelligence seems on the whole to have been much better.[44] Intelligence, then, would seem to have been a force tending more towards the destruction of the independent Scottish state than its survival. There are some obvious reasons for an English edge in the espionage war with the Scots. For one thing, many Scots, and many others who held lands in Scotland, were in the service of Edward I from the outbreak of war in 1296. Divided loyalties remained a significant factor in Scottish war with England until the middle of the fourteenth century. In this phase of Anglo-Scottish conflict there were plenty in Scotland who could, and were willing to, provide excellent intelligence for the English Crown. Even once national divides became more firmly entrenched from the mid-fourteenth century English kings were able to maintain fortified outposts on Scottish soil. Some of these, such as Lochmaben, in English hands until 1384, and Roxburgh, held until 1460, represented relatively deep intrusions into the Scottish borders.

The most crucial English advantage was, of course, financial. England could afford to pay for a military complex of far greater sophistication than the Scottish equivalent. English kings could even afford to hire naval vessels contracted specifically for espionage.[45] More prosaically, royal strongpoints in the Anglo-Scottish borders were permanently manned by paid watchers. Scottish dissidents were attracted to English service by the financial rewards on offer. In these circumstances it was commonplace for Scottish military planning to be compromised, and indeed for Scottish armies to be infiltrated, by informants willing to work for the English kings. This can be seen in action in an incident of 1299. The Scottish army, assembled in the Forest, a great tract of wild land in the south of the kingdom, contained at least one enemy spy. His report was conveyed to Edward

I, who must have been delighted by the agent's tale of violent disputes among the Scottish leadership there, with knives drawn and hands raised in anger.[46]

It is again on the battlefield that we see the clearest manifestations of intelligence in action to striking and obvious effect. And in the sphere of open battle the English advantage is obvious: they won far more such encounters than they lost. Edward I's victory at Falkirk in 1298 against William Wallace's Scottish host was a hugely significant triumph for a very embattled king. The road to success was paved by a spying report, giving details to Edward of the location and intentions of Wallace's army.[47] The English authorities also had early and accurate intelligence of the Scottish invasion of 1346 leading to Neville's Cross. Certain knowledge of preparations for the invasion had been acquired by August of that year. Only in October did the Scottish invaders finally trundle south and by then careful and effective defensive measures had been taken. The levies of the North had been gathered and were ready in good order to face the enemy and defeat them comprehensively.[48] Another great defeat of a Scottish invasion force was at the battle of Humbleton Hill in 1402. The imminence of a major Scottish incursion was known to the English government by 4 August and the mechanism of gathering suitable forces for defence was put into action. In the end it was on 14 September that the Scots were caught and totally defeated near Wooler in Northumberland by an army consisting of men from both the East and West Marches and as far south as Lincolnshire.[49]

It was one of the duties of border officers (captains of fortified points, wardens of the Marches) to gather reliable information on enemy activities. In 1322 Edward II was furious with his constable of Bamburgh, who was not active enough in the king's opinion in sending out spies and taking military action against the Scots on the basis of their reports.[50] In the early fifteenth century it is obvious from the conditions of service of English border officers that they were obliged to gather intelligence of Scottish activities as part of their duties. Successive keepers of Berwick and Roxburgh were obliged to reinforce their garrisons if they were credibly informed of an imminent attack by a Scottish royal host. If either place was besieged the English king undertook to bring relief within six weeks of having received the relevant information.[51] Such officers were assisted in their information-gathering activities by local Scots, a number of whom are to be found in, for instance, the garrison of Roxburgh in the early fifteenth century.[52] Presumably these men were attracted into service by the wages offered by the English Crown.

Beyond the sphere of local scouting, the English intelligence network also included paid operatives, centrally controlled and working directly for the Crown. It may be doubtful that one such – a woman or a friar, depending on the source – poisoned the Scottish guardian, Thomas Randolph, earl of Moray, in 1332, as alleged in Scottish accounts.[53] But there clearly were paid royal spies operating in Scotland, such as Lambe and Hardyng, who might be expected to provide valuable information. This was the purpose of dispatching Thomas de la Hawe to Scotland in 1399 to spy on Scottish war preparations. Although he seems to have accompanied a royal diplomatic mission north, his purpose was not to seek peace but to provide militarily valuable information in the context of extremely tense Anglo-Scottish relations. Henry IV was to invade Scotland in the following year and presumably found his agent's report informative.[54]

The English Crown also seems to have had advanced and successful mechanisms for gathering information on a continental scale. Intelligence coups from European sources frequently yielded valuable material relating to the Scottish theatre of war. In 1336, for instance, Edward III was able to gain minute detail about the war plans of the French king, Philip VI. This included information on intended operations in the Scottish theatre to be led by Scottish nobles then exiled in France. The quality of intelligence suggests an informant in French government circles.[55] Another great coup of English intelligence on the continental stage came in 1364 when an agent of the Black Prince, son of Edward III, gathered details of the long-term plans of the new French king, Charles V, who intended, when the time was right, to bring about the destruction of the English state. Among the allies he intended to recruit for his purpose, alongside the Castilians and the Danes, were the Scots.[56] Just as in Scotland, the English Crown possessed castles and towns on the continent useful for the collection of fresh and accurate intelligence. The mayor of Bordeaux was able to inform Henry V that a great company of Scottish men-at-arms and archers had landed at La Rochelle in March 1419. Sources in Bayonne informed Henry later in the year that Castilian vessels were attempting to transport a Scottish army to France. Acting on this intelligence, attempts to intercept the flotilla were made.[57]

It is clear that the English state enjoyed key advantages in the field of intelligence over its Scottish adversary in their later medieval conflicts. In the end, though, the wars between the two realms ended in stalemate. Intelligence, in this broad view, did not matter enough to give England a decisive edge in its conflict with the Scots. It is quite understandable that this should have been the case. Intelligence works only if acted upon before it is out of date. And in this sense the English government had major problems. It took time for news to travel from the border to Westminster, and time for orders to be conveyed back again. Mustering an army, if that was required, was expensive as well as time-consuming. It is telling that northern garrisons were expected to hold out against major Scottish attack for six weeks before they could hope for help to arrive from the South. Even with its relatively advanced intelligence-gathering systems, meanwhile, there were places the English government could not reach and information that it could not access easily. In the disturbed conditions of Scotland in the early fifteenth century normal English channels of communication seem to have been impeded. When James, heir to the Scottish throne, was captured at sea in March 1406 he was rightly referred to initially as the son of the king of Scots in English governmental sources. The captive (by now actually King James I) was still being referred to in that way, however, more than six months after the death of his father.[58] Sources of information on the latest developments in Scotland had clearly been badly disrupted.

When information took time to be conveyed south and reactions to it took even longer, there was an impetus on local officers to react appropriately to breaking news. John of Lancaster in his official capacity as keeper of the East March in the early fifteenth century kept close tabs on what the Scots were up to and regularly relayed this information south. He also sought permission to open letters (other than those addressed to the king) which came into his jurisdiction.[59] Starved of payments for his troops, however, his posting (judging by a series of letters he sent to the king) was a constant struggle just to ensure that his defensive responsibilities were adequately carried out.[60] Some decades later, little had changed. On the feast of St James (25 July) 1436 the former mayor of Berwick, Thomas Elwyk, arrived hot-foot in Durham bearing excellent, fresh intelligence from the border. The town of Berwick was in great jeopardy, the garrison either deserting or unsure of payment of their wages. Elwyk feared that great harm – a Scottish attack, no doubt – would occur. The assembled worthies of the North to whom this report was conveyed (the earl of Northumberland, the archbishop of York and the bishops of Durham and Carlisle were present) can have given him little comfort. He was sent back to reassure the garrison, and out of his own pocket paid to keep a watch on the town walls for eight days and nights, even this basic precaution having lapsed.[61] There was no mechanism in place, as this incident makes clear, for a truly swift and effective governmental response to fast-changing local circumstances. Eventually all of this information reached Westminster – but the necessary immediate response had perforce to be in the hands of the powerful local figures, whose help in this case seems to have been limited indeed. News might be fresh, but the reaction to it could be ponderous. Even when an English royal army was in the North, information could be too slow to be acted on effectively. This was the case for the Weardale campaign of 1327, when an English host attempted to track down a fast-moving Scottish invasion force but was reduced to following impotently the fires set alight in the devastated countryside by the elusive foe.[62] No matter how accurate the intelligence it was useless in this sort of scenario if even a few hours old.

Finally, the interpretation of intelligence could also be flawed. So sensitive was the English government to the threat of Scots and others that sometimes an unnecessary state of panic seems to have prevailed. In July 1403, for instance, the English government ordered the urgent dispatch of war materials to Pontefract in the face of an imminent and very dangerous Scottish invasion.[63] No such invasion occurred. There was no realistic threat to Pontefract; the Scots had not penetrated so far south for almost a century, and were not likely to do so a year after crushing defeat in battle at Humbleton Hill the year before. There was no realistic assessment of the Scottish threat in 1403. More generally, no matter how good the intelligence, there was a failure to understand the limits of the possible in the Anglo-Scottish dialectic. The Scots failed in this sense, unable to realise that military defeat of the English state was impossible. Similarly, the English Crown tenaciously held to its belief that the Scots could be subdued, long after this possibility had receded. So when the fruits of John Hardyng's espionage, accurate and detailed maps of Scotland, were provided to English kings in the fifteenth century he was offering them excellent intelligence. His depiction of towns, harbours and strongpoints was of pragmatic and concrete usefulness. Yet his analysis of his own findings was that the Scots could be subdued in a year of campaigning.[64] His interpretation was flawed, but so was that of successive English kings. Ultimately, the intelligence on Scotland gathered by the English Crown could not be used to its full capacity. In an Anglo-Scottish context an examination of intelligence, and its use, gives an indication of why the Scottish state survived in two centuries of conflict against its much more powerful neighbour.

NOTES

1 I am grateful to David Ditchburn for his comments on a draft of this paper.
2 Joseph Bain et. al. (eds), *Calendar of Documents relating to Scotland* (5 vols, Edinburgh, 1881–1986) [hereafter *CDS*], ii, no. 1152; G.W.S. Barrow, 'The Aftermath of War' in idem., *Scotland and its Neighbours in the Middle Ages* (London, 1992), pp. 177–200 at p. 191.
3 TNA, E404/16/695. £5 per head was clearly the going rate for exposing and apprehending traitors at this time: cf. Frederick Devon (ed.), *Issues of the Exchequer* (London, 1837), p. 229.
4 J.R. Alban and C.T. Allmand, 'Spies and spying in the fourteenth century', in C.T. Allmand (ed.), *War, Literature and Politics in the Late Middle Ages* (Liverpool, 1976), pp. 73–101 at pp. 74–5.
5 Jean Froissart, *Oeuvres*, ed. Kervyn de Lettenhove (27 vols, Brussels, 1867–77), ix, pp. 72-6. For Owain's career see: A.D. Carr, *Owen of Wales: The End of the House of Gwynedd* (Cardiff, 1991).
6 TNA, E101/38/12; *CDS*, iv, no. 337.

7   BL, MS Lansdowne 204, m. 3r. Hardyng's account of his sufferings cannot, though, be verified and he is a very untrustworthy source. For his career in a Scottish context see: A. J. Macdonald, 'John Hardyng, Northumbrian identity and the Scots', in C.D. Liddy and R.H. Britnell (eds), *North-East England in the Later Middle Ages* (Woodbridge, 2005), pp. 29–42.

8   TNA, JUST3/176, m. 28. The case is discussed in: Henry Summerson, 'Crime and society in medieval Cumberland', *Transactions of the Cumberland and Westmorland Antiquarian and Archaeological Society*, 82 (1982), pp. 111–24 at p. 114.

9   For the maintenance of warning beacons in Scotland see: Thomas Thompson and Cosmo Innes (eds), *Acts of the Parliaments of Scotland* (12 vols, Edinburgh, 1814–75) [hereafter *APS*], i, p. 716, ii, p. 44.

10 In Berwick in the late 1370s the number of watchers on the walls varied between twenty and thirty (TNA, E364/15, m. 6). For Farne see: Barrie Dobson, 'The Church of Durham and the Scottish Borders, 1387-88', in Anthony Goodman and Anthony Tuck (eds), *War and Border Societies in the Middle Ages* (London, 1992), pp. 124–54 at p. 142.

11 TNA, E101/41/13B. There was a warning bell of identical name in Roxburgh also: *CDS*, iv, no. 810.

12 David Ditchburn, *Scotland and Europe: The Medieval Scottish Kingdom and its Contacts with Christendom, c.1215–1545, vol. 1: Religion, Culture and Commerce* (East Linton, 2000), ch. 5.

13 F.A. Gragg (ed.) and L.C. Gabel (trans.), *Memoirs of a Renaissance Pope: The Commentaries of Pius II* (London, 1960), pp. 34–5.

14 BL, MS Cotton Vespasian FVII, fo. 22.

15 Minstrelsy has been described as the 'classic cover for the spy': J.C. Holt, *Robin Hood* (London, 1982), p. 139.

16 For the criminal aspect of intercommunance see: C.J. Neville, *Violence, Custom and Law: the Anglo-Scottish Borderlands in the Later Middle Ages* (Edinburgh, 1998), pp. 30–2, 60–1, 110–11, 114.

17 S.B. Chrimes, 'Some letters of John of Lancaster as warden of the East Marches towards Scotland', *Speculum*, 14 (1939), pp. 3–27 at p. 8; *APS*, i, p. 714, ii, p. 44.

18 *CDS*, iv, no. 1556.

19 A. L. Brown, 'The priory of Coldingham in the late fourteenth century', *Innes Review*, 23 (1972), pp. 91–101; Dobson, 'Church of Durham', pp. 144–5.

20 James Raine, *The History and Antiquities of North Durham* (London, 1852), Appendix, no. 591; J.T. Fowler (ed.), *Extracts from the Account Rolls of Durham Abbey* (3 vols, Surtees Society, Durham, 1898-1901), iii, pp. 593–4, 603; TNA, E101/42/35.

21 Philippe Contamine, *War in the Middle Ages* (trans. Michael Jones, Oxford, 1984), p. 226.

22 J.O. Prestwich, 'Military intelligence under the Norman and Angevin kings', in George Garnett and John Hudson (eds), *Law and Government in Medieval England and Normandy: Essays in Honour of Sir James Holt* (Cambridge, 1994), pp. 1–30; Christopher Allmand, 'Intelligence in the Hundred Years War' in Keith Neilson and B.J.C. McKercher (eds), *Go Spy the Land: Military Intelligence in History* (Westport, CT, 1992), pp. 31–47; Ian Arthurson, 'Espionage and intelligence from the Wars of the Roses to the Reformation', *Nottingham Medieval Studies*, 35 (1991), pp. 134–54.

23 *APS*, ii, 44–5; Thomas Dickson and J.B. Paul (eds), *Accounts of the Lord High Treasurer of Scotland* (11 vols, Edinburgh, 1877–1916), i, pp. 173, 305. For spying payments in the 1540s see vol. viii, pp. 270, 346, 399, 464–5, 483. (I am grateful to David Ditchburn for these references.)

24 *Scalacronica by Sir Thomas Gray of Heton, Knight*, ed. Joseph Stevenson (Maitland Club, Edinburgh, 1836), p. 142.

25 Froissart, *Oeuvres*, xiii, pp. 203–6.

26 Geoffrey Baker, *Chronicon*, ed. E.M. Thompson (Oxford, 1889), p. 47.
27 John Barnie, *War in Medieval English Society: Social Values in the Hundred Years War* (Ithaca, NY, 1974), pp. 32–3; Neville, *Violence*, p. 30.
28 *Calendar of Patent Rolls* (71 vols, London, 1901–74) [hereafter *CPR*], *1358–61*, p. 18; John Strachey et al. (eds), *Rotuli Parliamentorum* (6 vols, London, 1767), iii, pp. 11–12.
29 TNA, JUST3/191, m. 51; C.J. Neville, 'The law of treason in the English border counties in the later middle ages', *Law and History Review*, 9 (1991), pp. 1–30 at p. 27.
30 *CPR, 1338–40*, 275; *CDS*, v, no. 1107.
31 R.L. Storey, *Thomas Langley and the Bishopric of Durham, 1406–1437* (London, 1961), pp. 141–2.
32 David Macpherson et al. (eds), *Rotuli Scotiae in Turri Londinensi et in Domo Capitulari Westmonasteriensi Asservati* (2 vols, London, 1814–19) [hereafter *RS*], i, p. 463; *CPR, 1391–6*, p. 291.
33 C.J. Neville (ed.), 'A plea roll of Edward I's army in Scotland, 1296', in *Miscellany of the Scottish History Society*, xi (Edinburgh, 1990), pp. 7–133, nos 1, 40, 89, 118.
34 *CPR, 1476-85*, p. 50.
35 Margaret Bonney, *Lordship and the Urban Community: Durham and its Overlords, 1250–1540* (Cambridge, 1990), p. 187; C.M. Newman, *Late Medieval Northallerton: A Small Market Town and its Hinterland, c.1470–1540* (Stamford, 1999), pp. 134–6; Tim Thornton, *Cheshire and the Tudor State 1480–1560* (Woodbridge, 2000), p. 86.
36 Alison McHardy, 'The effects of war on the church: the case of the alien priories in the fifteenth century', in Michael Jones and Malcolm Vale (eds), *England and her Neighbours 1066–1453* (London, 1989), pp. 277–95; R.A. Griffiths, 'Un espion breton à Londres, 1425–1429', *Annales de Bretagne et des Pays de l'ouest*, 86 (1979), pp. 399–403.
37 For a divergent view placing more credence on English security fears see: Alban and Allmand, 'Spies and spying', pp. 87–97.
38 G.W.S. Barrow, *Robert Bruce and the Community of the Realm of Scotland* (3rd ed., Edinburgh, 1988), p. 154; John Barbour, *The Bruce*, ed. A.A.M. Duncan (Edinburgh, 1997), pp. 177–93.
39 *The Original Chronicle of Andrew of Wyntoun*, ed. F.J. Amours (6 vols, Scottish Text Society, Edinburgh, 1903–14), vi, pp. 10–11.
40 Alexander Grant, 'Disaster at Neville's Cross: the Scottish point of view', in David Rollason and Michael Prestwich (eds), *The Battle of Neville's Cross 1346* (Stamford, 1998), pp. 15–35 at pp. 19, 24–5.
41 Nigel Saul, *Richard II* (London, 1997), p. 135; A.J. Macdonald, *Border Bloodshed: Scotland and England at War, 1369–1403* (East Linton, 2000), pp. 72–4.
42 Charles Johnson, 'An abortive passage of arms in the late fourteenth century', *Speculum*, 2 (1927), pp. 107–12.
43 Macdonald, *Border bloodshed*, pp. 75–81.
44 For a general discussion of English intelligence mechanisms see: Michael Prestwich, *Armies and Warfare in the Middle Ages: The English Experience* (London, 1996), pp. 211–18.
45 J.W. Sherborne, 'English barges and balingers in the late fourteenth century', *Mariner's Mirror*, 63 (1977), pp. 109–14 at p. 113.
46 Cosmo Innes (ed.), *Facsimiles of the National Manuscripts of Scotland* (3 vols, London, 1867–71), ii, no. 8.
47 *Chronicle of Walter of Guisborough*, ed. Harry Rothwell (Camden Society, London, 1957), p. 326.
48 *RS*, i, pp. 673–4; James Campbell, 'England, Scotland and the Hundred Years War in the fourteenth century', in J.R. Hale et al. (eds), *Europe in the Later Middle Ages* (London, 1965), pp. 184–216 at pp. 192–3.
49 Thomas Rymer (ed.), *Foedera, Conventiones, Litterae et Cuicunque Generis Acta Publica* (20 vols, London, 1704–35), vii, pp. 272–3; *CDS*, iv, Appendix I, no. 19.
50 *CDS*, iii, no. 783.

51 TNA, E101/70/4/655, 656A; E101/71/3/869, 878; E101/71/4/905, 917; E101/73/3/44.
52 TNA, E101/42/38; E101/42/40.
53 Walter Bower, *Scotichronicon*, ed. D.E.R. Watt (9 vols, Aberdeen, 1987–99), vii, pp. 62–3, 72–3; James Raine (ed.), *The Correspondences, Inventories, Account Rolls and Law Proceedings of the Priory of Coldingham* (Surtees Society, London & Edinburgh, 1841), p. 251.
54 TNA, E403/564, m. 8; A.L. Brown, 'The English campaign in Scotland, 1400', in Harry Hearder and H.R. Lyon (eds), *British Government and Administration: Studies Presented to S.B. Chrimes* (Cardiff, 1974), pp. 40–54.
55 Prestwich, *Armies and Warfare*, pp. 212–13; Jonathan Sumption, *Trial by Battle: The Hundred Years War I* (London, 1990), p. 159.
56 J.J.N. Palmer, 'England, France, the Papacy and the Flemish succession, 1361–9', *Journal of Medieval History*, 2 (1976), pp. 339–64 at pp. 351–2.
57 BL, MS Additional 38,525, fo. 76; E.W.M. Balfour-Melville, *James I, King of Scots 1406–1437* (London, 1936), pp. 78–9.
58 TNA, E404/22/165 (24 October 1406). Robert III died on 4 April 1406: Stephen Boardman, *The Early Stewart kings: Robert II and Robert III* (East Linton, 1996), p. 297.
59 *CDS*, v, no. 930.
60 Chrimes, 'Letters', passim.
61 TNA, E404/53/131.
62 C.J. Rogers, *War Cruel and Sharp: English Strategy under Edward III, 1327–1360* (Woodbridge, 2000), pp. 17-18.
63 TNA, E404/18/599.
64 BL, MS Lansdowne 204, fo. 225v.

The resident ambassador and the transformation of intelligence gathering in Renaissance Italy

Paul M. Dover

Of all the cultural innovations and social transformations associated with the Italian Renaissance, one of the novel features that has perhaps not received enough attention is the degree to which attitudes towards the acquisition, archiving and dissemination of information changed.[1] Cultural and institutional attitudes toward the value and virtue of acquiring information underwent slow, yet important changes, prompting a significant increase in the volume of the 'circulation of information', in the words used recently by Isabella Lazzarini.[2] A range of pressures meant that Italian institutions and individuals expended increased energies on gathering information and then on creating mechanisms to keep and subsequently access it. There was power in having data recorded in written form. Thus, as Edward Muir has pointed out, 'notaries in Renaissance Italy were the priests of practical literacy, the professionals who held the reins of power over memory'.[3] Italians had long been known for their 'ink-stained fingers', but by the fifteenth century the ink was flowing in unprecedented volumes, onto countless reams of paper. This paper was consumed by the bureaucrats of Italy's many city-states, whose archives bulged with documentation in the years after 1450, fed by the activities of chanceries that sought to acquire information, and revenue, from the state's subjects;[4] by the merchants who adhered to the maxim that 'one should never stop using the pen' in cataloguing their commercial activity; by the printers who eagerly took the Rhineland invention of the printing press and made it their own, to the extent that there were already considerably more presses in Italy than in any region of Europe by the year 1480; and by the humanists who made Italy the intellectual core of a transnational Renaissance 'republic of letters', a 'chorus of muses' (to borrow Petrarch's phrase) that was also a chorus of scribblers.

All this writing was cataloguing what Francesco Senatore has called an 'intensification of contacts' in Italian society – a defining feature of modernity.[5] Fifteenth-century Italy was a society in love with paper and all of its preservative power. Nowhere is this more evident than in the realm of diplomacy and statecraft. The emergence of resident ambassadors, who wrote nearly daily dispatches, as an essential (but certainly not exclusive) means of diplomatic interface meant that diplomacy created more paper than ever before. Medieval European states and sovereigns had long sought to gather intelligence through a variety of channels, official and otherwise. The widespread use of resident ambassadors and the sheer volume of information that they generated, especially in the years after the middle of the fifteenth century, meant that the profile of intelligence gathering changed in the Italian political arena. Increasingly, the burden of intelligence gathering fell upon these resident ambassadors, who were tasked with identifying the useful information – the actionable intelligence – from amid all that they heard, from both official and informal interactions with the broad range of individuals who could be found at fifteenth-century courts. Like those in the intelligence community ever since, this meant sorting through the daily flow of rumour, innuendo and speculation, a buzz of white noise that could be fruitful, misleading and exasperating, all at the same time.

This essay will explore the contours of the shifts in intelligence gathering brought on by the changes in diplomatic practice and convention in the second half of the fifteenth century. The move toward residence in diplomatic representation and the accompanying increase in documentation of the activity of ambassadors, which was supported by the emergence of archives and chanceries, was fitful and uneven, and was certainly less than universal among the Italian states even by 1494 and the French invasion of the peninsula. But the changes were sufficiently widespread in Italy that they represented a fundamental shift in the nature of intelligence gathering. By the end of the fifteenth century, resident ambassadors had become the chief tools of state intelligence services. By the end of the sixteenth century, the same would be true for the rest of Europe as well.

We can capture an indirect glimpse of the new world of intelligence by looking at a remarkable manuscript, composed around the year 1470 by an Italian named Nicodemo Tranchedini da Pontremoli. By the time he wrote this work, the author had several decades of diplomatic service for the Milanese dukes behind him. He was among the first of what we might call 'career diplomats', serving initially as an extraordinary envoy on a large number of short-term missions, and later as a resident ambassador in Florence and Rome. A close associate of Francesco Sforza even before Francesco became Duke in 1450, Nicodemo was highly regarded as an ambassador and humanist in Sforza Milan and by his hosts in Florence and at the papal court. Sometime after his stint as the Milanese resident ambassador in Rome ended in 1472, Nicodemo completed this nearly two-hundred-page glossary of over 6,000 Italian words and expressions and their 23,000 Latin equivalents. Nicodemo called this massive lexicon a 'vocabulario'.[6] Housed in the Biblioteca Ricciardina in Florence, and recently edited and published by Federico Pelle, the work covers more than just diplomatic vocabulary – in fact, it seems to include virtually every word that Nicodemo might have used in his thousands of dispatches, written over a long diplomatic career. It is also likely that he availed himself of the expertise and libraries of the sizeable humanist communities in Florence and Rome – we know that he was a frequent guest of the papal librarian, Giovanni Andrea Bussi. He was also a humanist of some weight, a regular visitor to Marsilio Ficino's so-called Platonic Academy in Florence and a regular correspondent of the prominent humanist thinkers Pier Candido Decembrio, Francesco Filelfo and Antonio Cornazzano, among others. This work might be seen as just another somewhat self-indulgent exercise in humanist philology, an opportunity to show himself an accomplished Latinist, but what is striking about this list of words is how they reflect his experience as a resident ambassador in fifteenth-century Italy.[7]

By the time of the lexicon's writing, Italian diplomacy had become largely a conversation in the vernacular. Latin was still used in communication with extra-Italian correspondents and the papacy, and in treaties and statutory writing, but the vernacular was well suited for the primary task of most ambassadors: providing lengthy, matter-of-fact descriptions and considerations of information garnered and conversations held. The entries in the 'vocabulario' might consist of a single Latin equivalent. For certain frequently used words, he might provide as many as a dozen Latin equivalents, indicating a broadly ranging and flexible Latin and Italian vocabulary. Unsurprisingly, there are a large number of entries that concern areas such as diplomatic ceremonial, court life and institutions of state. But what is also notable is how many of his chosen words, and their many Latin equivalents, concern what had become the primary task of Nicodemo as a resident ambassador in Florence and then Rome, and indeed that of other resident ambassadors at the time: the acquisition of information. The amount of time and effort that the fifteenth-century Italian resident ambassador spent on intelligence gathering is reflected in the great diversity of words that Nicodemo found to describe such activities.

Nicodemo's list is vast, but we can take certain entries as demonstrative. Take the Italian word 'intendere', which in the fifteenth century, as now, means to listen or hear, but also to learn or understand. This was a word in fifteenth-century letters of instruction and in ambassadorial dispatches that was frequently used to indicate

efforts to acquire information and understand its meaning. Tranchedini provides no fewer than sixty Latin words and phrases that he
deems equivalent or comparable to 'intendere'.[8] This sampling of the
words contained in this entry indicate the broad range of ways that he
as an ambassador sought to fulfil the charge to 'intendere' – to listen,
hear, learn and understand.

Similarly, we can look to Tranchedini's entry on the word 'cavare',
which literally in Italian means 'to dig'. In the context of the service of
fifteenth-century Italian diplomacy, 'cavare' often came to denote the
process of seeking out information – ambassadors were deputised to
dig for useful information, the insinuation being that the acquisition
of such information took considerable effort, rather than being a
passive activity. For his entry on 'cavare', Tranchedini includes those
Latin words that imply the physical act of digging: 'haurio', 'eruo',
'fodio', 'fodico'; but he also includes those that better approximate the
meaning of cavare when applied to information gathering. He lists the
word 'excipio', which in classical Latin was used to describe picking
up news, ideas or gossip by listening. He also includes 'surripo',
meaning to acquire secretly; as well as 'extrico', to extricate or pull
something out.[9]

Or we might take 'intelligentia', the near-equivalent of a word
pertinent to so many of the essays in this volume. Among Renaissance
diplomats, 'intelligentia' was understood to mean both information
and informed understanding and awareness. But it also meant
harmony, agreement or friendship between parties or individuals. To
have 'intelligentia' meant to have a co-operative relationship, perhaps
something short of an alliance. When ambassadors spoke of the Pope
and the Republic of Venice having 'intelligentia' with one another, it
meant there was a suspicion that the two might be working together
for their mutual interests. There was also the implication that such co-
operation included sharing the other sort of 'intelligentia': information and its significance.

The course of Nicodemo's career is emblematic of the transformations that had reshaped diplomatic practice in his lifetime, and
the important role that Duke Francesco Sforza played in initiating
them. Nicodemo, by virtue of his long periods of service as resident
ambassador in both Florence and Rome between 1446 and 1473,
became synonymous with Milanese interests in those locales.[10] Via
Nicodemo, Florence became an important centre of information for
the Sforza – the ambassador relayed copious information garnered
from managers of the various branches of the Medici Bank and from
his intimate connections with an important cross-section of the
Florentine elite.[11] His long, continuous presence in the city meant a
wealth of connections in Florentine society, which served him as
political pressure points and as sources of information. Nicodemo

knew the workings of Florentine politics as well as most Florentine patricians. This inside knowledge put the Milanese ambassador in an advantageous position not only for managing the Sforzas' alliance with the Medici and for advocating for Milanese interests in Florence, but also for gathering information.

Long tenures like Nicodemo's in Florence, while a new phenomenon in diplomatic representation in the second half of the fifteenth century, was by no means unique. Towards the end of the Milanese ambassador's stay in Florence, Marino Tomacelli arrived as the resident ambassador of Ferrante d'Aragona, the king of Naples. Marino would remain in Florence for virtually all of the ensuing thirty years (1465–95), making him the longest-serving resident ambassador anywhere in Europe in the fifteenth century. Zaccaria Saggi da Pisa was in Milan for some twenty years (1468–88) as the Mantuan ambassador, and Jacopo Trotti was the ambassador of the Este of Ferrara at the same court for over a dozen (1482–95).[12] All these examples of very long-serving ambassadors (and there are others) come from princely states. Resident ambassadors from the republics in Florence, Venice and Siena tended to reside abroad for short periods only, as they were customarily elected to their offices and resisted lengthy absences from their commercial and political concerns at home.[13] But the fact remained that residence was becoming the most important feature of interstate relations in Italy in the second half of the fifteenth century. It was also the most important factor in the gathering of intelligence.

A significant body of historical scholarship has demonstrated that the decades after 1450 in Italy were a pivotal period of change in diplomatic practice.[14] Broadly speaking, we can identify three primary ways in which the new patterns of ambassadorial practice differed from the preceding medieval forms. First of all, to a much greater degree, the Renaissance model emphasised diplomatic representation with the interests of a particular state, a development closely related to the centralisation of state machinery that is a feature of Renaissance Italy.[15] Many non-state actors continued to send out and receive embassies – during the Barons' Revolt of the 1480s in Naples, for example, locally powerful nobles in rebellion conducted their own diplomacy.[16] Additionally, a number of prominent *condottiere* captains in Italy who did not possess their own states might send ambassadors to represent their interests.

This leads us to the second major transformation, the increased use of resident ambassadors, who now became the most important diplomatic actors within Italy. It was almost exclusively states that sent out resident ambassadors - the resident ambassador became a legitimating force, a representation of sovereignty.[17] 'The fundamental meaning of "ambassador" until the end of the Middle Ages' had been 'precisely "one sent on a mission".'[18] Ad hoc embassies still fulfilled such roles, to be sure – indeed, much of the important business of statecraft was still carried out by ambassadors who were not resident, who were charged with a specific task or purpose. Resident ambassadors, by contrast, were rarely sent out with a precise mission in mind – instead they were there to be a constant presence, a link with their host court, an advocate for their prince's interests and a listening post. They were thus there to pursue 'intelligentia' in both ways that Nicodemo Tranchedini understood it.

Residence is visible before 1450 but it becomes widespread only after that date. In the princely states in particular resident ambassadors like Nicodemo Tranchedini served at the same court for extended periods of time, accumulating contacts, connections and insights. This experience could prove invaluable – the presence, in Florence, of the likes of Marino Tomacelli, mentioned above, for thirty years became proverbial. While there is little statutory evidence of such positions becoming offices in their own right, in practice they became permanent offices that were left vacant only for very short periods.[19] The resident ambassador became a regular feature of Renaissance court life and an essential mechanism in Renaissance statecraft.

Thirdly, and finally, the types of individuals who were sent out on embassies changed markedly. Francesco Guicciardini reported that 'Ludovico Sforza used to say that the same rule applies to princes as to crossbows. Whether the crossbow is good or not, one judges from the arrows that it shoots; in the same way the worth of a prince one judges from the quality of the men that he sends out.'[20] The demands of the new diplomacy required individuals with a particular skill set – it was no longer satisfactory to send out someone whose primary qualification was being close to the prince. There was an acknowledgement that the demands of the residence required particular skills. The rhetorical ability and legal training that were essential in those tasked with short-term embassies remained useful, but were far less important than skills related to their essential role as information gatherers: the ability to forge relationships that produced useful intelligence and the writing of well-crafted and informative dispatches. Resident ambassadors were also sometimes instructed to raise loans, buy merchandise, advocate for offices or benefices and negotiate military contracts (although these were usually finalised by special envoys). Resident ambassadors in this period had broad job descriptions, but the gathering of information remained their chief task.[21]

The emphases of diplomacy as practiced in Renaissance Italy thus changed quite dramatically. As Michael Mallet has noted, 'a dramatic improvement in the quality and flow of information was one of the principal characteristics of Italian statecraft in the second half of the fifteenth century. The resident ambassadors, more informal spies and informers, and the development of patron–client relationships in which the main obligations on the client was to keep his patron informed, all contributed to this.'[22] The primary purpose of diplomatic correspondence, which now became almost daily, was to provide princes with a broad range of information. The duke of Milan once commended his ambassador for being 'informatissimo' – this, in truth, became the goal of every resident ambassador.[23] The ambassadors of John of Anjou in Naples once remarked that Francesco Sforza kept resident ambassadors there 'not to seek anything in particular but rather to find out what people were doing and what was going on in Naples'.[24]

Recently, Riccardo Fubini has sought to downplay these changes, and especially the novelty of residence in fifteenth-century Italy. Fubini is probably right in critiquing Mattingly's depiction of the new realities of interstate relations in Italy as a 'system' – the implementation of the new practices remained uneven for some time. He is also correct in questioning whether we can speak of the emergence of diplomatic 'offices' when speaking of the proliferation of resident ambassadors.[25] But, as Fubini concedes, if we look at the level of diplomatic and chancery praxis, the resulting impact is largely the same: 'There is no doubt . . . in the solemn arrogation of powers by the Lordship and in the relative dispositions regarding chancery registration, one discerns the origin of the new public physiognomy of the ambassador, who although not formally the incumbent of an "office", was effectively such.'[26] Whether these long-serving ambassadors envisioned themselves serving in the capacity of an 'office' is in the end not terribly important to our inquiry. Whether as office holders or not, the reality of the ambassadors' residence had considerable bearing on their roles as intelligence gatherers.

The existence of resident ambassadors tasked primarily with gathering information and reporting it in their dispatches, coupled with the determination to archive such material in diplomatic chanceries – a feature of several Italian states, big and small, in the fifteenth century – means that there was a veritable boom in the written record of diplomacy, a very large portion of which remains extant. The records we have for Italian states increase markedly after about 1450, a function of increased government activity and a commitment to systematic record keeping. The cataloguing of diplomatic material is perhaps the most important component of this explosion of paper. One of the notable results of the new diplomacy was the creation of chanceries that acted as both producers of correspondence and as archives (which kept not only letters but also copies of letters going out, such that we frequently have a two-way record of the correspondence). The statesmen who maintained such chanceries were applying the philosophy that the Venetian mathematician Luca Pacioli had applied to commerce in his famous treatise on double-entry bookkeeping: 'these written documents should be diligently kept for everlasting memory, on account of the dangers which may arise'.[27] What we have here is an institutionalised intelligence apparatus, one that appeared first in Milan, then in the princely states of Naples, Mantua and Ferrara, and eventually in Florence and Venice.

This was an intelligence apparatus that proved to have a voracious appetite. The notoriously hyperbolic Duke Galeazzo Maria Sforza of Milan once wrote his ambassador in France, Giovan Pietro Panigarola, that he should write at least a letter a day – if he did not, he warned, he risked having his head cut off.[28] This was so important, the duke added, because 'I ponder and turn over in my mind the content of your letters.'

Ermolao Barbaro, in perhaps the most famous of Renaissance tracts on the ambassador, instructed his reader to 'remember that you are an ambassador and not a spy.' He felt that ambassadors were more successful in acquiring information when they deliberately appeared not to be seeking it.[29] The best way to gain information was to listen, he suggested. Fifteenth-century ambassadors often spoke of having their ears pricked up or their eyes open. 'The ambassadors here in this court', wrote a Milanese ambassador at the papal court in 1467, 'all have their ears open to hear what will happen'.[30] The same ambassador wrote later that year: 'I write to you what I hear in good faith so that you will know everything'.[31]

Diplomatic instructions were full of such admonitions. 'With ears open and with eyes peeled', the Duke of Milan instructed his ambassador in Rome in November 1466, 'we want you to learn of all of the designs and movements and plans of Bartolomeo Colleone and of every other place in Italy... we want you to keep us informed of what you hear, from those who are at the court in Rome and whatever you hear that is new'.[32] Or as Ferrante, the King of Naples, instructed his resident ambassador in Venice in 1460: 'We want you to write to us more often, by as many routes as possible, because we are very interested in being advised continuously of the things that are happening in that city and the Signoria, especially those that have to do, or might have to do (directly or indirectly) with our state and affairs'.[36]

Fulfilling such orders by monitoring all conceivable avenues of information was an exacting and time-consuming task, especially in postings such as Milan and Rome. Milan was the centre of the extensive diplomatic network maintained by the Sforza dukes, who kept resident ambassadors at numerous courts throughout Italy and beyond. These ambassadors provided a steady flow of information coming into the chancery of the Sforza, and ambassadors resident in Milan positioned themselves to ascertain useful intelligence from among the incoming data. 'Today news from a variety of places has arrived', the Mantuan ambassador in Milan, Marsilio Andreasi, wrote in 1460. 'To my understanding some is true and another part lies.'[34]

In Rome, the Italian court with the greatest number and diversity of residents, the challenge was even greater. Ambassadors interacted with a wide range of cardinals and prelates, as well as fellow ambassadors and a host of other individuals attached to the papal court. Rome was the source and destination of correspondence with all of Christendom, communication that covered political as well as ecclesiastical affairs. As a Milanese ambassador once commented: 'at the court of Rome there are always envoys and ambassadors from the lords of the world, who on the face of it have nothing better to do than keep an eye on what papers are crossing the table'.[35] And ambassadors used more than just their eyes; instructed by King Ferrante to keep his ears open regarding the movements of the *condottiere* Bartolomeo Colleoni, the Neapolitan ambassador in Rome declared that he '[was] looking, listening and feeling with his hands' for applicable intelligence.[36]

The letters that we find in these diplomatic archives, the 'formal' communication we will call it, do not by any means represent the entirety of intelligence gathering. We know, for example, that in many cases ambassadors were given two set of instructions – one to share with their host and perhaps other ambassadors, and one, often oral, that indicated the true intentions of the prince. In the fifteenth century the Gonzaga of Mantua often sent out their ambassadors with two such sets of instructions.

There are other indications that in this official correspondence we are seeing only part of the story. Vincent Ilardi's insightful work on the coding system built into the patronage letters of Francesco Sforza and the Cardinal Guillaume d'Estouteville should give us pause when we too eagerly take official correspondence at face value.[37] We also know that Lorenzo de Medici maintained parallel streams of communication with his ambassadors, one for the consumption of his fellow patricians in the Florentine government and one for himself.[38] His personal correspondence inevitably contained politically sensitive information that was excluded from the 'official' Florentine correspondence, and his ambassadors customised the dispatches according to whom they expected to be reading them. Similar patterns emerged in Venice by the 1480s, when Venetian ambassadors started writing confidential dispatches to the tight decision-making circle of the Ten, alongside their more general correspondence to the doge and Senate.[39] And under the direction of the Milanese secretary Cicco Simonetta, letters from ambassadors were sometimes amended or even fabricated before being shared with others – meaning that there was an original correspondence and one expurgated for broader consumption.[40]

In the later middle ages, as Christopher Allmand has demonstrated, there was often an extremely fine distinction between the figure of herald and spy, of messenger and spy, and indeed of ambassador and spy. The line between legitimate and illegitimate information gathering was vague, subjective and moveable. In fact, because of the courtesies extended to them, ambassadors were regarded as among the most useful potential spies.[41] Observing the Italian practice of keeping resident ambassadors, the famous fifteenth-century chronicler Philippe de Commynes counselled that the movements of these men should be closely tracked in the interest of security and secrecy.[42] Commynes' admonition was an indication of a reality widely recognised in Italy by the second half of the century: that resident ambassadors were, for all intents and purposes, legalised spies.[43] And yet the resident ambassador had to toe a fine line, between the assiduous pursuit of useful information and being seen as intrusive or devious in his inquiries.

Ambassadors might learn a great deal from listening but they had to be pro-active as well – they had to 'cavare', or dig. How they were to do this was largely left to the ambassadors themselves, increasing numbers of whom had accumulated considerable experience in doing so. Guicciardini wrote in his *Ricordi* that 'it being impossible to give such detailed instructions to ambassadors that they are directed in all particulars: only discretion teaches them to accommodate themselves to their general purpose'.[44] Resident ambassadors were simultaneously envoys and independent actors. It was when the ambassadors went beyond merely listening that they might be deemed to transgress the line between legitimate information-gathering and espionage. Étienne Dolet, in his treatise *De officio legati* (1541), advised ambassadors to have one servant in his household who could walk about town, 'joining in conversations and courting familiarity with a large number of persons, to gather every breath of rumor, so that some conjecture can be drawn from them concerning the purposes of those with whom the ambassador is dealing. In this manner we often obtain much information which makes us more guarded in discussing and transacting business with members of the court to which we hold the ambassadorship.' He then suggests that the ambassador should not hesitate to 'inveigle with liberality' those who might have useful information, 'for liberality wins over even men of the greatest integrity'.[45] But this digging for information need not be as blatant as straightforward bribery. The resident ambassador might draw upon a vast array of people, inside and outside the court, for information, spending a good deal of his time quietly and unobtrusively cultivating useful contacts: the establishment of such a network of *amici* was among his most important tasks. In Florence, Nicodemo Tranchedini exploited his close relationship with the eminent Boccaccino Alamanni, among other patricians, to learn state secrets, in what Paolo Margaroli calls 'real espionage'.[46] In Rome, such *amici* might be friendly cardinals or other ecclesiastical officials. In Venice, they might be high-ranking senators. But useful contacts could extend well beyond 'official' figures. References to such sources, named and unnamed, are countless in the diplomatic correspondence of the period. During the Barons' Revolt in Naples, Lorenzo de Medici relied a great deal on the news provided to his ambassador from the Florentine business community in the kingdom.[47] The Sforza for many years had the Burgundian court doctor, Mattheo de Clarici, working for them as an informer.[48] Ambassadors spent much of their time exploiting such sources. As one Florentine ambassador once remarked: 'the job of the ambassador is day by day, to give notice of what he hears, and from whom, and in what fashion, to him who sent him'.[49]

The fear of spying by resident ambassadors, however it might be construed, was a real concern among sovereigns, frequently expressed outside Italy. Louis XI told Alberico Maletta, Francesco Sforza's ambassador in France, to tell the duke 'that the custom in France is different from that in Italy, because here the practice of keeping an ambassador continually is seen as suspect'.[50] In the 1480s, Ludovico Sforza destroyed the *coperti*, the covered places in Milanese neighbourhoods where citizens would come to chat and gossip, and where ambassadors could often be found.[51] Ludovico was particularly worried about ambassadors conversing with nobles inside Milan who were aligned with opposing factions. He once gave strict instructions to the ambassador of the Duke of Ferrara, Jacopo Trotti, as to who he should and should not talk to at the Milanese court. Jacopo, eager to learn as much as he could of goings-on in Milan, promptly ignored his warnings. His dispatches, stretching over more than a dozen years of residence in Milan, testify to a bewildering array of sources that encompassed every manner of individual at the Milanese court and beyond.[52] In Venice, the Senate had to introduce legislation to prevent spying by diplomats and their undue co-operation and plotting with Venetian patricians.[53] In Florence, resident ambassadors sought to cultivate connections with the Florentine nobles who were pro-Milanese, pro-Venetian or pro-Neapolitan – this was a way of gathering inside information but it could also be a form of subversion.[54] And in Milan, I have identified at least four separate occasions when Neapolitan ambassadors were asked to leave the Milanese court for allegedly subversive behaviour and unwelcome interaction with those in Milan hostile to the ducal regime.[55] The long-time Mantuan ambassador in Milan, Zaccaria Saggi, was also asked to leave Milan, when the Duke heard that he had been sharing information deemed sensitive with his Neapolitan counterpart.[56] Zaccaria defended himself by responding that he had not said anything that could not be heard by anyone walking around the Rialto in Venice.

Of course, walking around the Rialto, you were also bound to hear a great deal that was untrue. In the Renaissance, as now, statesmen could expect to receive intelligence that was false or deliberately misleading. Part of the 'discretion' that Guicciardini expected good ambassadors to display was the ability to validate or discount intelligence that they had received. Given the volume of information that a resident ambassador stationed at a post like Rome or Milan could expect to hear, this was no easy task. Sienese ambassadors in Naples in 1481, for example, recounted to the Consistory the difficulties of securing trustworthy information at the Neapolitan court, but asked that 'your lordships not blame it on us but on the nature of this court, where you can trust no one'.[57] These ambassadors no doubt exaggerated, but intelligence was only as reliable as the source from which it came, and resident ambassadors were careful to gauge their informants. A different Sienese ambassador in Naples, a few years earlier, told the consistory that 'your lordships know that I have not written anything without good foundation'. He insisted that most of what he had written had come either from the King himself, or his chief secretary and 'if they have told me lies, I have also told them to your lordships. But let God take my life along with your favour, if ever I have written anything that did not come from similar sources of authority...'. He then promised that he would not write anything without being confident of its veracity.[58]

It is quite clear that the statesmen of Italy felt that securing these flows of information and intelligence was valuable. Bianca Maria Sforza, the Duchess of Milan, expressed such sentiments to her ambassador in Rome: 'We are fully informed about exactly what has happened from your letters...and we say and insist that you continue to give us notice and warning of every event there...because knowing the things that happen there, we will be more knowledgeable about how to govern from here.'[59] But the extent to which the new and extensive efforts to maintain a regular flow of information actually made a measurable difference in the implementation of effective statecraft is difficult to gauge. How much of this information was in fact actionable intelligence? What value added was there for the Dukes of Milan, for example, in being able to call upon the fruits of an extensive diplomatic network? Did it make the state or its sovereign more powerful or secure? Louis XI once remarked that Francesco Sforza knew what was going on in France before he did – impressive, yes, but how exactly did this help him? In what ways was intelligence in Italian Renaissance statecraft a force equaliser or force multiplier?

Melissa Bullard has suggested that the proliferation of resident ambassadors created a surfeit of information, especially when states did not have the infrastructure to act on that information quickly. In fact she suggests that the unceasing flow of news and gossip served to reduce the sense of security felt by the Italian states: 'Too much scrutiny and too much reporting could be inflammatory in the already unstable political situation of late fifteenth-century Italy.'[60] Resident ambassadors, rather than allaying fears and building confidence, could just as easily fuel suspicion. Bullard writes 'whether or not the institutions of diplomacy unwittingly provoked war, they did vastly complicate contemporary perceptions of political circumstances and greatly sensitized political leaders and their agents to the fragility and fluidity of relations among states'.[61] In the final decade or so before Charles VIII's invasion of the peninsula turned Italy into the primary battlefield of Europe's dynastic conflicts, there is much evidence that the increased volume of information actually enhanced insecurity. Mutual suspicion increasingly led Italian states to seek support from outside Italy for political leverage in their intra-Italian squabbles. Such efforts led Ludovico Sforza into the dangerous business of encouraging Charles to press his claims against the Neapolitan kingdom.

But the new diplomacy and especially the emphasis on information gathering also may have led to another tendency in Italian statecraft, hinted at recently by Michael Mallett: the inclination to temporise. The increased anxiety and suspicion in Italian affairs at the end of the fifteenth century that Bullard has identified was wedded to an equally dislocating sense of confusion – over the intent of the various Italian states; over the designs of the French king; in sum, confusion as to what exactly was going on in the places that mattered. There was no shortage of intelligence surrounding these issues – it is just that it was confusing, contradictory and of uncertain veracity. In their desire to undermine their Italian rivals, princes such as Ludovico Sforza and Pope Alexander VI unleashed forces that they could no longer control.[62]

Access to such large quantities of intelligence, especially contradictory intelligence in such an uncertain international situation, frequently serves to slow down decision making at the highest levels. Such temporisation became a defining feature of early modern European international politics. The embryonic bureaucracies and institutions of the early modern state were slow-moving to begin with – communications were slow and spotty, few states had ready access to ample liquid assets, and armies took weeks and sometimes months to mobilise. Geoffrey Parker has shown masterfully in the case of Philip II that even a king consistently provided with information of superior quality could become bogged down in a torrent of human and paper intelligence. The *rey papalero*, as he became known, proved incapable of making prompt decisions. This, of course, was partly a function of a maniacal personality who refused to delegate.[63] But such temporisation was also a result of a fundamental imbalance between an intelligence apparatus's capacity to produce information and the state's inability to act on it promptly. This imbalance was a consistent reality of international relations in the early modern period and one that had its roots in the emergence of the new diplomatic institutions and practices of fifteenth-century Italy.

NOTES

1 There has recently been a treatment of similar changes in continental Europe in a slightly later time period, dealing specifically with the great increase in scientific information available. See A. Blair, 'Reading strategies for coping with information overload, 1550–1700', in *Journal of the History of Ideas*, 64, 1 (2003), pp. 11–28.

2 I. Lazzarini, *L'Italia degli Stati territoriali. Secoli XIII–XV.* (Rome, 2003), p. 142: 'Alla base di questo moltiplicarsi delle informazioni stanno dunque d'un lato – da parte del potere pubblico – la necessità di ottenere la volontà di utilizzare ogni sorte di notizie provenienti da ogni sorte di interlocutori, d'all altro – da parte di questi ultimi – la correspondente convenienza, in termini di influenza politica, di eminenza sociale, di costruzione identitaria, di raccogliere e fornire tali informazioni. In questo senso, il moltiplicarsi dei cittadini, mercanti, officiali, ecclesiastici che scrivono ai governi degli stati italiani e ai singoli grandi personaggi delle corti e dei reggimenti, è una manifestazione significativa del costruirsi minuto, quotidiano, traversale agli schieramenti politici locali e sovralocali, della simbiosi funzionale fra gli stati italiani.'

3 Muir writing in the introduction to D. Balestracci, *The Renaissance in the Fields* (University Park, PA, 1999), p. xiv.

4 The increasing demand at courts and in chanceries for 'reams of paper' ('risme di carta') is discussed, in the Milanese context, by A.G. Cavagna, 'Libri in Lombardia e alla corte sforzesca tra Quattro e Cinquecento', in A. Quondam (ed.), *Il libro a corte* (Rome, 1994), pp. 90–1.

5 Francesco Senatore, '*Uno mundo di carta*': *forme e strutture della diplomazia sforzesca* (Naples, 1998), p. 162: 'L'intensificarsi dei contatti – luogo comune della modernità – transformò prassi documentarie e archivistiche, modo di pensiero e di parola, rivoluzionando la struttura dei testi scritti e orali connessi all'azione politica e amministrativa a aprendo infine la strada all'evoluzione potente e sotterranea della burocrazia, elemento di continuità dell'intera storia pre-unitaria italiana.'

6 [Nicodemo Tranchedini da Pontremoli], *Vocabolario italiano-latino*, ed. F. Pelle (Florence, 2001).

7 A. Della Torre, *Storia dell'Accademia Platonica di Firenze* (Florence, 1902), p. 659. Marcello Simonetta makes note of the great variety of words that Nicodemo uses to denote the Italian word 'secreto', Simonetta, *Rinascimento Secreto* (Milan, 2004), p. 15. For a fuller biographical treatment of Nicodemo, see P. Sverzellati, 'Per la biografia di Nicodemo Tranchedini da Pontremoli, ambasciatore sforzesco', *Aevum*, 72 (1998), pp. 485–557. For more on Nicodemo's humanist inclinations, see P. Sverzellati, 'Il libro-archivio di Nicodemo Tranchedini da Pontremoli, ambasciatore sforzesco', *Aevum* 70 (1996), pp. 371–390; Sverzellati, 'Il carteggio di Nicodemo Tranchedini e le lettere di Francesco Filelfo', *Aevum*, 71 (1997), pp. 441–529.

8 Intelligo; intendo; attendo; teneo; cognosco; dignisco; cognitum habeo; percipio; excipio; accipio; recipio; concipio; sentio; presentio; audio; consequor; assequor; sapio; scio; disco; adisco; perdisco; condisco; perpendo; noto; annoto; habeo; comptum, *vel* exploratum, *vel* pro comperto, *vel* pro explorato; habeo; sumo; assumo; averto; animadverto; ausculto; haurio; admitto; conservo; prospicuo; perspicio; ingenio perspicio; interpetror; est animo; feriuntur aures; aures, *vel* aurem, adhibeo;

non me fallit, *vel* fugit, *vel* preterit; non sum expers, *vel* imprudens; bibo; ebibo; compactor; discerno; comprehendo; deprehendo; *et cetera ut in SAPERE et ODIRE*; conspiro; aures presto; cordi est, [Tranchedini], *Vocabulario*, ed. Pelle, p. 88.

9 The full list for 'cavare' is as follows: Cavo; haurio; exhaurio; eruo; obruo; subruo fodio; effodio; suffodio; infodio; defodio; fodico –as; excipio; traho; extraho; contraho; exceptuo; exprimo; depromo; eximo; exando –as; exedo; extirpo; emitto; effero; sinuo –as; detraho; scalpo –is; scalpurio –ris; extrico; evello; subigo; prosubigo; surripio; excucio; deprimo; perfodio; subago; subtraho; suburro –as, [Tranchedini], *Vocabulario*, ed. Pelle, p. 33.

10 He was resident in Florence 1440–50 (even before Francesco Sforza became Duke of Milan) and then again 1454–68, and was resident in Rome 1450–54 and 1469–72.

11 V. Ilardi, 'The Banker-Statesman and the Condottiere-Prince: Cosimo de' Medici and Francesco Sforza (1450–1464)', in S. Bertelli and C.H. Smyth (eds), *Florence and Milan: Comparisons and Relations* (Florence, 1989), p. 218.

12 For Marino Tomacelli, see P. Dover, 'Royal diplomacy in Renaissance Italy: Ferrante d'Aragona (1458–1494) and his ambassadors', in *Mediterranean Studies*, 14 (2005), pp. 57–94. For Zaccaria Saggi and Jacopo Trotti, see P. Dover, 'Letters, Notes and Whispers: Diplomacy, Ambassadors and Information in the Italian Princely State' (PhD dissertation, Yale University, 2003).

13 On Venice, see T. Beverly, 'Venetian Ambassadors, 1454–1494: An Italian Elite' (PhD dissertation, University of Warwick, 1999). For Florence, see R. Fubini, 'Classe dirigente ed esercizio della diplomazia nella Firenze quattrocentesca', in D. Rugiadini (ed.), *I ceti dirigenti nella Toscana del Quattrocento* (Florence, 1987), pp. 117–89, and his 'Diplomacy and government in the Italian city-states of the fifteenth century (Florence and Venice)', in D. Frigo (ed.), *Politics and Diplomacy in Early Modern Italy* (Cambridge, 2000), pp. 25–48.

14 The classic, and still useful, account is G. Mattingly's *Renaissance Diplomacy* (London, 1955). While Mattingly relies primarily on statutory material, rather than the actual diplomatic correspondence of fifteenth-century ambassadors, most of his arguments retain their validity. Mattingly echoed ideas suggested by R.A. Maulde de la Clavière, in his *Diplomatie au temps de Machiavel* (Paris, 1892), although Maulde de la Clavière was concerned primarily with sixteenth-century developments. A recent work of synthesis, M.S. Anderson, *The Rise of Modern Diplomacy 1450–1919* (New York, 1993), largely follows Mattingly's frame of analysis.

15 For a discussion of the limitations of such a generalisation, see A.K. Isaacs, 'Sui rapporti interstatali in Italia dal medievo all'età moderna', in G. Chittolini, A. Mohlo and P. Schiera (eds), *Origini dello Stato. Processi di formazione statale in Italia fra medioevo ed età moderna* (Bologna, 1994), pp. 113–132.

16 H. Butters, 'Politics and diplomacy in late Quattrocento Italy: the case of the Barons' War (1485–1486)', in F. Denley and C. Elam (eds), *Florence and Italy: Renaissance Studies in Honor of Nicolai Rubinstein* (London, 1998), p. 17.

17 D. Queller, *The Office of the Ambassador in the Middle Ages* (Princeton, 1967), p. 69: 'The modern notion that only a sovereign state could be represented by an ambassador was as inchoate in the Middle Ages as the concept of sovereignty itself.'

18 Ibid., p. 60.

19 For a fuller discussion of residence, and the office of 'permanent resident ambassador', see V. Ilardi, 'The First Permanent Embassy outside Italy: the Milanese Embassy at the French Court, 1464–1483', in M.R. Thorp and A.J. Slavin (eds), *Politics, Religion and Diplomacy in Early Modern Europe: Essays in Honor of Delamar Jensen* (Kirksville, MO, 1994), pp. 1–18.

20 *Ricordi*, no. 171: 'Diceva el duca Ludovico Sforza che una medesima regola serve a fare conoscere i prìncipi e le balestre. Se la balestra è buona o no, si conosce dale frecce che tira; così el valore de' principi si conosce dalla qualità degli uomini

mandano fuora', [Francesco Guicciardini], *Ricordi, Diari, Memorie*, ed. M. Spinella (Rome, 1981), pp. 223–4.

21 For a further discussion of the required skills, see M. Mallett, 'Ambassadors and their Audiences in Renaissance Italy', *Renaissance Studies*, 8, 3 (1994), pp. 232–3.

22 M. Mallett, 'Diplomacy and War in Later-Fifteenth-Century Italy', *Proceedings of the British Academy*, 67 (1981), p. 274.

23 Bianca Maria and Galeazzo Maria Sforza to Agostino Rossi, 19 Nov. 1466, Milan, Archivio di Stato di Milano (ASMi), Archivio Sforzesco (AS), Potenze Estere – Roma, cart. 61.

24 'non per requirere cosa alcuna ma per intendere quello che si fa ... et como passano le cose', quoted in Senatore, '*Uno Mundo di Carta*', p. 74.

25 Fubini, 'Diplomacy and government', pp. 27, 31.

26 Ibid., p. 37.

27 L. Pacioli, *Double-entry Book-keeping*, ed. and trans. P. Crivelli (Weston-super-Mare, 1966), p. 56.

28 F. Leverotti, *Diplomazia e governo dello stato: i "famigli cavalcanti" di Francesco Sforza (1450-1466)* (Pisa, 1992), p. 81.

29 'Legatum esse te non exploratorem memineris; alioquin rescire quid agatur facilius est his, qui negligere videntur, quam qui dissimulare curam talem haud possunt. Lustrare debent omnia non furtim, non latrunculorum more, sed interim simpliciter et aperte, interim per gradus et quodam quasi sensu, nec strepitu sed silentio', E. Barbaro, *De Coelibatu. De Officio Legati*, ed. V. Branca (Florence, 1969), p. 161.

30 'Li oratori soy che sono in questa corte stanno tutto'l dì con le orechie aperte per sentire che la pace habiy loco, de la quale mostrano havere molto più desyderio cha de guerra', Agostino Rossi to Galeazzo Maria Sforza, 1 Sept. 1467, Rome, ASMi, AS, Potenze Estere – Roma, cart. 63.

31 'Siche m'ha commisso ve prega per dio siati bene advertente de non ve fidare così liberamente de ogni covelle, benché se renda certo siati così prudente che bene intenderati il facto vero. Et io ve scrivo ciò che intendo a bona fede aciò che VS sapia il tuto', Agostino Rossi to Galeazzo Maria Sforza, 20 Aug. 1467, Ibid.

32 Instructions of Galeazzo Maria and Bianca Maria Sforza to Agostino Rossi, 25 November 1466, Milan, ASMi, AS, Potenze Estere – Roma, cart. 61: 'con le orrechie tese et con li occhi al penello per intendere tutti li disegni et movimenti et concepti del dixto Bartolomeo et ogni altro loco de Italia et de quanto sentiremo de tutto aviseremovi ... haverimo caro che ne avisati de quanto sentireti et similter como procedano le cose de quelle heresie così de verso Boemia, como de quilli se ritorovano li in corte di Roma et similiter de quanto sentireti di novo'.

33 Ferrante d'Aragona to Giovanni Zumbo, 20 Feb. 1460, Naples, in A. Messer (ed.), *Le codice aragonese* (Paris, 1912), p. 479: 'Vorriamo che più spesse volte ni scrivisseno, per queste vie potisseno, perché a nui ni è grande interesse non havere continue avisacione de le cose, che occorreno in questa citate et Signoria, maxime, che se sguardeno o squardare se possano (directe vel indirecte) a nostro stato et facende ...'.

34 Marsilio Andreasi to Ludovico Gonzaga, 24 Nov. 1460, Milan, Archivio di Stato di Mantova (ASMa), Archivio Gonzaga (AG), Affari Esteri – Milano, b.1621: 'Hozi sono venuto novelle per diverse vie, al comprendere mio parte ne sono pur vere et parte anche busie'.

35 Antonio Guidobono to Francesco Sforza, 7 Aug. 1457, quoted in E. Mahnke, 'The Political Career of a *Condottiere*-Prince: Ludovico Gonzaga 1444–1455' (PhD dissertation, Harvard University, 1974), p. 205.

36 Protonotary Rocca to Ferrante, 15 Nov. 1467, Rome (copy), ASMi, AS, Potenze Estere – Roma, cart. 63: '... de alcuni dì in qua me fo stare con le orecchie aperte et veda che dapoi che lo vescovo de Vicenza et cardinale quantunque in publicum per non approvare le cose de Bartolomeo et de la Sra tanto in honeste se mostre iusto

et equio nihilomente. *Vedo et sento et palpo con le manu* e dicto cardinale e dicti imbassatori fare se più guagliardi intermisti et domestici con altro modo che lo solito.' [Italics mine.]

37 V. Ilardi, 'Crosses and Carets: Renaissance Patronage and Coded Letters of Recommendation', *American Historical Review*, 92, 5 (Dec. 1987). I have recently discovered evidence that Ludovico Sforza also used a similar system of coding in his own letters. In a letter of 27 February 1489, the Ferrarese ambassador in Milan, Jacopo Trotti, reported that Ludovico Maria Sforza had written a favourable letter on behalf of his brother, the Cardinal Ascanio Sforza. Jacopo wrote that Ludovico had written this letter 'de sua mano sottoscripte cum il sigillo sella sua corniola secreta sotto la sua subscriptione, secondo la intelligentia ch'el ha cum il prefato monsignore [i.e. Ascanio] che è pur il modo soprasatto quando el desidera de obtenire cosse in corte da Roma che li siano a core', Jacopo Trotti to Ercole d'Este, Archivio di Stato di Modena (ASMo), Archivio Segreto Estense (ASE) – Cancelleria, Carteggio Ambasciatori–Milano, b.6.

38 N. Rubinstein, 'Lorenzo de' Medici: the Formation of his Statecraft', in C.C. Garfagnini (ed.), *Lorenzo de' Medici: Studi* (Florence, 1992), pp. 60–1.

39 M. Mallett, 'Renaissance Diplomacy', *Diplomacy and Statecraft*, 12, 1 (2001), p. 65.

40 F. Senatore, 'Falsi e "lettere reformate" nella diplomazia sforzesca', *Bollettino dell'Istituto Storico Italiano e Archivio Muratoriano*, 99 (1993), pp. 221–78

41 C.T. Allmand, 'Spies and Spying in the 14th Century', in Allmand (ed.), *War, Literature and Politics in the Late Middle Ages* (Liverpool, 1976).

42 P. de Commynes, *Mémoires*, ed. J. Calmette and G. Durville (3 vols, Paris, 1925), I, p. 219.

43 Queller, *The Office of the Ambassador*, p. 98.

44 *Ricordi*, no. 2: 'E non essendo quai possibile dare le instruzione agli imbasciadori suoi, sì particulari che lo indirizzino in tutti le particulari, se non in quanto la discrezione gli insegni accomodarsi a quello fine che ha in generale, chi non ha notizia non può fare questo, e però errarvi in mille modi'. Guicciardini says, however, that the prince must be able to trust the loyalty of his ambassadors in order to pursue such a policy: 'La opinione mia è che chi ha imbasciadori prudenti e integri, e che siano affezionati a sé, e dipendenti in modo che non abbino obieto di dipendere da altri, faccia meglio a communicare la mente sua; ma quando el prencipe non si risolve che siano totalmente di questa qualità, è manco pericoloso non si lasciare sempre intendere da loro e fare che el fondamento di persuadere una cosa a altri sia el fare persuasione del medesimo nel proprio ambiascadore', [Guicciardini], *Ricordi*, ed. Spinella, pp. 167–8.

45 'Étienne Dolet on the functions of the ambassador, 1541', trans. J. Dunlop, *American Journal of International Law*, 27,1 (Jan. 1933), p. 86.

46 P. Margaroli, *Diplomazia e stati rinascimentali: le ambascerie sforzesche fino alla conclusione della Lega Italica (1450–1455)* (Florence, 1992), p. 268.

47 H. Butters, 'Politics and Diplomacy', p. 24.

48 E. Sestan (ed.), *Carteggi Diplomatici fra Milano Sforzesca e la Borgogna, vol. II, 26 July 1475–19 October 1476* (Rome, 1987), p. 17.

49 'L'ufficio degli ambasciatori è giorno per giorno, secondo che intendono et da chi et in che modo, dare notitia a chi gli manda', G. Pandolfini to F. Sacchetti, 5 May 1450, quoted in Senatore, *'Uno mundo di carta'*, pp. 183–4.

50 'Voglio scrivati al vostro signore che la consuetudine de Franza non è simile a quella de Italia, perché in queste parte a tenere continuamente uno suo ambasadore pare una cosa de suspeto e non de tuto amore et a casa vostra hè il contrario', quoted in Margaroli, *Diplomazia e stati*, p. 273.

51 G.P. Bognetti, 'La città sotto i francesi', *Storia di Milano*, 8 (Milan, 1957), p. 6.

52 His letters, dating 1482–94 can be found in ASM, ASE, Carteggio Ambasciatori – Milano, b.2–b.8.

53 Queller, *The Office of the Ambassador*, p. 92.

54 Mallett, 'Diplomacy and War', p. 275

55 The removal of Turco Ciccinello from Milan is chronicled by the Venetian ambassador in Naples, Zaccaria Barbaro, in a series of letters of January–March 1472, *Dispacci di Zaccaria Barbaro. 1 novembre 1471–7 settembre 1473*, ed. G. Corazzol (Rome, 1994). On the dismissal of Fabrizio Caraffa, see R. Fubini (ed.), *Lorenzo de' Medici. Lettere* (11 vols, Florence, 1977–), I, p. 104. Giovan Battista Bentivoglio's dismissal was discussed by the Mantuan ambassador in Milan at the time: Zaccaria Saggi to Federico Gonzaga, 23 May 1480, ASMa, AG, Affari Esteri–Milano, b.1627. Zaccaria also remarked on Antonio del Gazzo's forced departure two years later: ibid., 30 Jan. 1482.

56 See P. Dover, 'Good Information, Bad Information and Misinformation in Fifteenth-Century Italian Diplomacy', in M. Crane, R. Raiswell and M. Reeves (eds), *Shell Games: Studies in Scams, Frauds and Deceits (1300–1650)* (Toronto, 2004), p. 87.

57 Lorenzo Latini and Placido Placido to the Consistory, 1 Feb. 1482, Archivio di Stato di Siena (ASSi), Archivio di Concistoro (AC), Carteggio, N. 2046, no. 1: 'Se qualche volta scriviamo alcuna cosa a V.M.S. doversi fare fra certo determinato tempo et non si fa così di punto, le Signorie Vostre non lo imputino noi ma a la natura di questa corte, che chi è stato qua, ne po far buona fede.'

58 Antonio Bicchi to the Consistory, ASSi, AC, Carteggio, N. 2040, no. 24: '…sappino le Signorie Vostre non lo scripto senza bono fondamento et tale che qui non si po havere miglior ne più degno…pur se sonno dette bugie ad me, io anco le dico a le Signorie Vostre. Ma Dio mi tolli la vita inseme con la gratia del vostro regimento, se mai ho scripto cosa alcuna se non quando la ho havuta da simili auctori, senza fidarmi a le parole del vulgo, a le quali havendo guardato mai mi sarebbe mancato che scrivere…Pure per lo advenire serò fatto più savio, et non scrivarò le cose se non quando le haverò vere; pensano havendole da tali auctori si dovesse credere. Spero però se verserà ho scripto lo vero come di qualche altra cosa che ei reuscita vera et non è stato creduta quando la ho scripto.'

59 'A pieno restamo advisate de quanto è successo per fino ad vostro di xxv, che multo ne è piazuto intendere et comendiamo la vostra dilìgentia. Et cossì ve dicemo et caricamo che continue ne vogliati continue dare notitia et adviso de tucte le occurentie de là et maxime perfino che Galeazo sta absente di qua; perché intendendo le cosse dellì, saperemo più consultamente governare de quà', instructions to Agostino Rossi, 14 August 1467, ASMi, AS, Potenze Estere–Roma, cart. 63.

60 M. Bullard, *Lorenzo il Magnifico: Image and Anxiety, Politics and Finance* (Florence, 1994), p. 95.

61 Ibid., p. 87.

62 Ludovico Sforza kept Ercole d'Este informed of the most recent news coming into the Milanese court in confidential letters, but was so worried about the information falling into the wrong hands that he instructed him to burn the letters as soon as he had read them. 'La riservatezza dei documenti fu tavolta si grande che il Moro raccomandò al venerato suocero di bruciarli appena letti', P. Negri, 'Studi sulla crisi italiana alla fina del secolo XV', *Archivio storico Lombardo*, 10 (1923), p. 12.

63 Philip was said to have looked at two thousand pieces of correspondence daily. The papal nuncio once remarked that 'his majesty wants to see and do every single thing himself'. See G. Parker, *The Grand Strategy of Philip II* (New Haven, 1998), especially pp. 13–45; and his *The World is Not Enough: the Imperial Vision of Philip II of Spain* (Waco, TX, 2001), especially pp. 9–28.

The English navy and intelligence in Ireland in the 1640s

Elaine Murphy[1]

With the onset of the English civil war in 1642 the contest for control of the English navy resulted in a rapid and clear-cut success for the parliamentary interest, at the expense of the king, Charles I. In the conflicts of the 1640s Parliament's navy gained and retained control of the coasts around Ireland. Parliamentary naval squadrons success-fully blockaded the city of Dublin and eliminated the threat posed by royalist forces there under the command of the Lord Lieutenant, the marquis of Ormond, and aligned with English supporters of the monarch against Parliament. The fleet supported the far flung and isolated parliamentary outposts in Munster, Ulster and Connacht. The dominance of the English navy also undermined the maritime abilities of the confederate Catholics, dominant over most of Ireland and, from 1643, locked into a succession of ceasefires and peace talks with the royalists built around a shared hostility to the English Parliament, its Scottish allies and its adherents in Ireland. Merchant-men trading to and from confederate ports were seized in greater numbers as the 1640s progressed. Privateers with confederate letters of marque were forced to operate further and further away from their home ports.

This paper will examine the role of intelligence in the war at sea in Ireland in the 1640s and the eventual domination of the parliamentary navy on the coasts around Ireland. It will focus on the capacity of the parliamentary navy around Ireland to acquire knowledge relating to the operations of the confederate and royalist forces. It will then examine the ability of the navy to apply that knowledge in the war at sea and on land. In order to do this it will concentrate on two aspects of intelligence in the war at sea: firstly the uses, and problems associated with the application, of information received from sources in Europe and in Ireland; secondly the role of the navy in gathering intelligence from the fleet on service in Ireland.

Intelligence and the navy in the seventeenth century is barely a consideration in most works covering the period. The standard work on the navy during the civil war remains J. R. Powell's *The Navy in the English Civil War*. This provides a narrative account of the navy and its operations from 1642 to 1648.[2] Most other works that examine the role of the navy in this period concentrate on narrating the events of the war or looking at aspects of the administration and personalities.[3] The seventeenth century saw a number of major transformations in naval warfare which greatly affected England. These changes included the large-scale expansion of the navy, the development of line-ahead battle tactics and the expansion of the overseas empire. Therefore most works that examine the navy in the seventeenth century concentrate on these areas or on narratives of the major events such as the wars with the Dutch.[4] In these works the role and use of intelligence tends to be touched on in passing. They do not analyse the function of the navy in gathering information or the value or use of material acquired at sea.

In the 1640s the interception of vessels going to and from Ireland became the primary function of the parliamentary navy on the Irish coast. These vessels included merchantmen trading with Irish ports, frigates serving as privateers and packet boats carrying letters to and from England. The problem facing the navy was how to effectively shut down all this traffic. The navy had two main sources of knowledge for the movement of confederate and royalist shipping on the Irish coast. The first of these was from the correspondence of English merchants and agents in the principal continental ports trading with Ireland. These included Dunkirk, Ostend, St Malo, St Sebastian and Bilbao. The merchants reported on the activities of vessels contracted to bring arms, munitions and soldiers to Ireland. They also detailed the fitting out of frigates to serve as men of war for the confederate association. These letters provided the admiralty in England with very detailed information regarding the activities of Irish rebels in European ports from the early months of the rebellion. In January 1642 Sir John Pennington wrote to the Lord High Admiral, the earl of Northumberland, that English merchants in Ostend and Dunkirk reported that many Irish commanders and arms came to those towns to make preparations to sail for Ireland, while in April the Lord Lieutenant, the earl of Leicester, received advice that Irish officers in France planned to take ship for Ireland with their arms.[5] English outposts on the Irish coast often heard about the expected arrival of ships from continental Europe to aid the rebels in their locality. Captain Willoughby, the governor of the fort at Galway, reported in July 1642 that he had been informed that three ships were *en route* to that town from St Malo.[6]

The second source of information relating to the movement of vessels going to and from Ireland came from the examinations of English and Irish merchant vessels on their return from continental ports. The questioning of the masters of these ships provided details about what they had seen and heard in various ports relating to Irish shipping. Captain John Bartlett examined William Law, the master of the *Alexander*, on his return from St Sebastian. Law deposed that a Galway ship laden with arms left that port on 3 July 1642 to rendezvous with two other Galway ships at San Antonio before heading for home. He also detailed the attempts of some English merchants in the town to have the ship searched and arms seized by the governor. However, they failed in this: the governor had an English ship there arrested so it could not pursue the Galway vessel and also imprisoned a number of the merchants. In September 1642 the mayor of Kinsale, Tristram Whetcombe, examined William Lake, the master of the *Hopewell of Foye*. Lake gave information relating to the Irish acquiring arms and ships at Bilbao and Nantes.[7] Intelligence available to the English navy and administration in Ireland on the movements of Irish shipping from Europe often proved to be quite detailed and accurate. Father Hugh Bourke, the Irish agent in Dunkirk, complained of the problems he faced in organising ships there. He grumbled that English spies found out his every move. Bourke believed that, if money was available, ships could be held in the name of a citizen of Dunkirk to try to prevent this.[8]

Although throughout the 1640s the navy often possessed this very detailed knowledge of the movements of Irish shipping from Europe, it often proved to be of limited use in preventing arms from reaching Ireland. Even with very specific information the time delay inherent in passing on material often made it worthless. In the case of the examination of William Law mentioned above John Bartlett reported the details of the deposition on 17 July to the Lords Justices in Dublin. Law had deposed that the Galway ship left St Sebastian on 3 July. Even allowing for its meeting with the other two Galway ships at San Antonio these vessels had a considerable head start on any attempt to catch them.[9] In many respects trying to find a ship at sea, even if its point of origin and destination were known, was akin to searching for a needle in a haystack. Too many variables hindered naval men-of-war trying to intercept shipping. These included wind and weather conditions, the exact route taken by the ship, the condition of the merchantman and the ability of her master and crew. The best utilisation of intelligence came only if a navy vessel was in the vicinity to act on it as, for example, in the case of the French ship the *Olive* in February 1642. Bad weather forced the vessel into Yarmouth, where local people suspected that she carried munitions for Ireland, but she managed to the leave the port before being searched. A ship in the vicinity, the *Rainbow*, received news of her departure and suspicions about her cargo. The *Rainbow* then overhauled and captured the *Olive* near Portsmouth.[10]

The interception of Irish vessels relied not so much on having good intelligence but on having sufficient men-of-war to effectively patrol the coasts around Ireland. Naval vessels stationed off the main ports in Irish control and off the coast of some of the major European ports like Dunkirk offered the best opportunity to seize the greatest number of ships. The bulk of military aid entering Ireland was due to a lack of shipping on the coast and not a lack of intelligence regarding arms shipments.[11] The administration in Dublin recognised this early in the rebellion. In February 1642 Sir William Parsons and Sir John Borlase, the Lords Justices in Dublin, wrote to the Lord High Admiral to stress the need for shipping on the coast to thwart the importation of arms and also for vessels to patrol the coast off Dunkirk. They recommended that Northumberland set out one ship each for guarding the harbours of Wexford, Waterford and Kinsale, while two ships were needed to patrol from Galway to Killybegs.[12] By September of that year they complained to the Commissioners for the Affairs of Ireland that Captain Thomas Kettleby, the admiral for the Irish Seas, had failed to leave sufficient shipping at Wexford and other ports and that this had allowed vessels carrying arms to enter Ireland freely. They also expanded the number of men-of-war needed to secure the coast to one ship at each of the following: Wexford, Waterford, Broadhaven, Sligo, Kinsale, Killybegs; and to two ships at Galway.[13]

From 1645 on, the success of the navy's Irish squadron in intercepting vessels going to and from Irish ports greatly increased. This can be attributed to a number of factors. The Irish squadron had been involved in helping to secure Wales for the Parliament. With the success of the parliamentary armies there and in England the navy refocused its attention on the war at sea on the coast of Ireland. The defection to Parliament of Lord Inchiquin, the royalist commander in Munster, in the summer of 1644 restored access for the navy to the important southern ports of Cork, Youghal and Kinsale. The increase in the level and strength of the fleet assigned to Ireland from 1645 proved to be the most important element in the success of the navy.[14] More men-of-war patrolling the coast resulted in more ships being taken as prizes. In December 1646 two newly built frigates – the *Assurance* under Captain William Penn and the *Nonsuch* under Captain William Thomas – received orders to ply off the coast of Wexford and Waterford.[15] They achieved immediate success on that station. The *Assurance* captured the *Catherine of Waterford* followed by the *Patrick of Waterford* in December 1646, while in January 1647 the *Nonsuch* took the *St Patrick of Ross*.[16] Parliamentary men-of-war on patrol seized most of the ships detained on the Irish coast. They usually had little specific information relating to the movements of vessels from Europe.

Information acquired from sources in Ireland came to be of more value to the parliamentary cause in Ireland. Overall, confederate ports offered little intelligence of significance: captured sailors might on their exchange convey details of ships or other military movements. The most useful information for the navy came from the city of Dublin. Following the cessation of September 1643 the city remained in royalist control. The Lord Lieutenant, Ormond, used the city as a base for the organisation and transport of soldiers to aid King Charles I in England. Many in Dublin supported the parliamentary cause and opposed the peace negotiations with the confederates. From mid-1644 on the navy began to blockade Dublin's harbour. A number of parliamentary men-of-war took up station there to search and seize any ships that attempted to enter or leave the harbour without permission. For example, in December 1646 the *Globe* under Captain Richard Willoughby detained the *Falcon* frigate belonging to the French agent to Ireland. Willoughby legitimised his actions on the basis that the French agent did not have the right to purchase the ship without parliamentary permission.[17]

The parliamentary squadron impeding Dublin harbour received information from within the city on the actions and intentions of the Lord Lieutenant. In May 1644 the arrival of two parliamentary ships and a frigate prevented an attempt to transport 300 men and arms across the Irish Sea to aid in the defence of Anglesey. Ormond complained that they had such good intelligence from their friends on shore that they thwarted his attempts to ship the men from elsewhere.[18] Preventing communication between people in the city and ships in the bay proved to be virtually impossible for Ormond. People regularly went out to visit and trade with the fleet and sailors sometimes came ashore to visit friends and relatives. In February 1646 a number of residents in the city took a boat out to two parliamentary ships anchored in the bay, the *Nicholas* and the *Swan*. They claimed on later examination that they went out to trade for tobacco and that they brought no messages or provisions for the ships, other than a bag of turnips. A boy and a mariner from the *Nicholas* came ashore when the boat returned to the city. The sailor, John Lambert, deposed that he had permission from Captain Bray to come ashore to visit his aunt and sister and that he brought no messages for anyone.[19] Many merchant ships that went to Dublin came under suspicion of spying for the Parliament. John Hay, the mayor of Wexford, arrested an unnamed vessel under the command of John Waterhouse. He suspected the ship intended going to spy on the royalists in Dublin. On searching her he found hidden passes and certificates from Captain Richard Swanley, the parliamentary admiral for the Irish Seas.[20] The fleet blockading Dublin remained well informed of the state of the city and its naval strength. Ormond tried to counter this problem by acquiring information about the parliamentary squadron. On one occasion in November 1644 he sent Mun Mathews on board the parliamentary warship in the bay to drink with her captain, an acquaintance of his. He was so successful that he was able to persuade the captain to come ashore. He failed to mention if Mathews found out any useful information.[21] However, as Ormond lacked the naval strength to challenge the parliamentary fleet any intelligence he received served little purpose.

The navy used its detailed knowledge of the city of Dublin and its naval defences to weaken and undermine the royalist position there. By 1645 only one strong warship, the *Swan*, remained at Ormond's disposal. She had been in service since the start of the rebellion in defence of the city,[22] and was commanded by the staunchly royalist John Bartlett. In 1644 it was complained that the men were near mutiny due to a lack of pay and in 1645 he sought a warrant to impress sailors.[23] The *Jocelyn* under Captain Robert Clark formed part of the parliamentary squadron blockading Dublin. On 5 November he sent the master of his ship with twelve men armed with muskets in his boat to seize the *Swan*. They accomplished this and also captured a small Flemish vessel called the *White Lamb*. Clarke sailed with the *Jocelyn* and his prizes to Liverpool and received command of the *Swan* for his efforts.[24] The ship then formed part of the blockading squadron at Dublin.[25]

The inquiry held in Dublin in the aftermath of the loss of the *Swan* illustrated the level of knowledge possessed by the parliamentary navy on the poor state of the defences of the ship. The captain, John Bartlett, did not go on board the *Swan* on the day of her loss as he had no money to pay the crew.[26] At the time of her seizure the crew on board consisted of approximately twenty sailors.[27] This means that, when she was taken about half the necessary crew were either ashore or no longer employed due to a lack of money to pay them. In the days leading up to the seizure the *Jocelyn* had a considerable amount of contact with people in the city. Captain Bartlett signed passes for three merchants to visit the *Jocelyn* to negotiate for permission to leave Dublin with their goods; they spent the night on board. The gunner from the *Swan* also sought a pass to visit a friend on the *Jocelyn*, though Bartlett denied this.[28] Examinations from Lewis Walcott and Thomas Warren both detailed the role in the events of John Andoe, a Dublin fisherman. Both testified that he had served in the parliamentary navy and knew Clarke and some of the men on his ship. They stated that, when the *Jocelyn* appeared in the bay, Andoe went out fishing and he received a bottle of strong water and a message from Captain Clarke. Warren also deposed that a man stayed at Andoe's house one night and that the next day said he intended going on board the parliamentary man-of-war. Andoe in his own deposition claimed that he had been pressed to serve as a pilot by Captains William Penn and Richard Swanley. He admitted to having spoken to Clarke when out fishing, but he denied having anything else to do with him.[29]

The boarding party from the *Jocelyn* met with virtually no resistance during their assault. Only one lieutenant was wounded in the attack. The crew of the *Swan* surrendered quickly and the gunner, possibly the same one who had wanted to visit the *Jocelyn* a few days earlier, handed over the keys to the gun room.[30] Most of the sailors joined the parliamentary navy. The exact information that Captain Clarke received and from whom it came remains unknown. However, the ease with which Parliament stole the *Swan* from Dublin Bay suggests Clarke knew fully about her vulnerabilities, in particular that her unpaid and unhappy crew were unlikely to put up much resistance, that she was poorly manned and that her captain was not on board. The loss of the *Swan* greatly weakened the royalist position in Dublin. Without a strong warship at his disposal Ormond lacked the ability to protect Dublin harbour and his lines of communication to England. The parliamentary situation before Dublin improved considerably by the capture of the *Swan*. The squadron blockading the city no longer faced the potential threat posed by the *Swan* and it became easier to intercept mail boats as the royalists used more unsuitable vessels after her loss. Intelligence received from parliamentary sympathisers in Dublin played a vital role in the success of the blockade. They kept the fleet informed on the movements of shipping and on the condition of the naval defences within the city. Ultimately the naval blockade played a key role in undermining the royalist position in Dublin and in forcing Ormond's eventual surrender of the city to Parliament in the summer of 1647.

The navy also played a major role in gathering intelligence concerning Ireland during the 1640s. The number of vessels seized by the navy on the Irish coast increased as the parliamentary squadron expanded. The primary source of material obtained by the navy came from captured ships: they examined the crews of captured vessels and sent any papers they found to London for closer study. In theory very few letters should have been found when the navy seized a prize. The standard procedure for disposing of papers in a ship which feared seizure involved weighing down any letters and throwing them overboard. Alexander Montgomery, the master of the *Alice of Londonderry*, ordered his crew to tear up all the letters on board upon her seizure sailing to Chester in March 1644.[31] Not all ships managed to destroy their papers before their apprehension. Samuel Allen, a mariner on the man-of-war the *Tiger* found letters for Wexford and Waterford hidden under a bag of hops in the *Swallow of Flushing* in 1649.[32] Even if correspondence was successfully disposed of, some or all of its contents might be revealed if someone in the ship's company talked, either voluntarily or under duress. Some parliamentary commanders tortured captured mariners and passengers for information when necessary. Captain Robert Gilson in the *Constant Warwick* allegedly tortured an Irish passenger for information when he took the *Charity of Flushing*. Her master claimed that Gilson placed a lighted match between the man's fingers and put a rope about his neck, threatening to throw him overboard.[33] At other times crew members revealed details of papers they had disposed of to a third party. John Taylor, the captain of the *King David of Rotterdam*, on being seized by the *Elizabeth* in 1649, claimed to be bound for Dublin. He later told John Mackey, a passenger on the parliamentary man-of-war, that he had thrown his papers overboard as they proved he was actually bound for a confederate port. Mackey promptly reported the conversation to the mayor of Kinsale.[34]

Ships going to and from Irish ports provided a considerable amount of information for the navy. However, much of this had quite limited military value. The navy mainly captured merchantmen, privateers and their prizes. The papers found on these ships included merchants' letters, bills of lading, commissions for privateers and other correspondence. The examinations of captured mariners concentrated on where they were coming from and going to, what goods they carried, what prizes they had taken and who owned the vessel. The depositions from sailors on prizes that the navy retook could be useful in providing information about the frigate that took them. In November 1649 Peter Toland, one of the crew of the privateer the *Cornelius of Wexford*, was taken by the *Tiger* as he brought a captured prize to Dunkirk. In his deposition he gave details about the captain of the *Cornelius*, his commission from Ormond, other prizes they had taken and that the frigate carried sixty-five men and mounted six pieces of ordnance.[35] Other prizes served useful propaganda purposes, especially if they contained some goods or passengers out of the ordinary. A pamphlet in 1642 featured the seizure of a ship going from Bilbao to Ireland contained 'an abundance of priests and Jesuits and others of their faction', as well as many relics, including the tears of Mary Magdalene collected in a bottle and a piece of Christ's cross.[36] These colourful accounts of the capture of vessels sailing to Ireland helped to justify the continued parliamentary involvement in the war in Ireland and boosted support for it. Overall, most ships captured by the navy provided little information of real value to the parliamentary cause.

Captured packet boats carrying letters between England and Ireland had much more significance. Parliamentary domination of the seas around Ireland removed secure lines of communication and freedom of action from the royalists in Ireland. Captured correspondence revealed the military plans and peace negotiations between Ormond and the confederate association. Packet boats could be of considerable military value if the letters they carried contained a large amount of intelligence on the military, political and economic situation in Ireland, though many of the letters found in these packet vessels tended to be of a quite mundane nature. In June 1644 the *Spy* frigate captured the Munster post bark the *Swallow of Youghal*. The bundle of letters found on board her included orders from the Lord Inchiquin, the military commander in the province, but most of the letters found on this ship contained private correspondence. For example, Margaret Nurse wrote to her mother in England about her inability to leave Munster due to the illness of her child.[37]

The navy gathered the most valuable intelligence in the war at sea from the royalists in Dublin, from where secure communications with England were essential for Ormond. From 1644 on, the naval blockade by Parliament became more effective and the Irish squadron intercepted large numbers of ships going to and from the city. In December 1644 Lord Brabazon, Sir Henry Tichborne and Sir James Ware, royalist commissioners to the king at Oxford, were taken at sea on their return voyage.[38] They were sent to London for interrogation by the Parliament. In February 1646 Captain Robert Clark and the *Swan* chased a packet boat leaving Dublin. She ran aground at Howth but, before she sank, Clarke managed to save the letters, which included some from Ormond and George Digby. Clarke then sent them on to the Committee of the Navy in London.[39]

The royalists were either particularly unfortunate or incompetent concerning the disposal of letters when a ship was in danger. In 1646 two vessels, both containing papers relating to the earl of Glamorgan's peace negotiations with the confederate Catholics were seized.[40] Documents found in these ships provided Parliament with a massive propaganda coup and greatly undermined the royalist position in England. In January Captain Robert Moulton in the *Lyon* seized a bark from Dublin near Milford Haven. He found letters on board relating to Glamorgan's dealings in Ireland. Moulton sent the letters to London and they were read in the House of Commons and ordered printed.[41] Then in March some dragoons at Padstow boarded a packet boat from Ireland. Captain Allen threw a packet and other loose letters overboard but he failed to weigh them down properly and the dragoons fished many of them out of the water. They included letters from Glamorgan and George Digby together with a copy of the articles of peace negotiated with the confederates. Writing to Ormond in early April Glamorgan noted the loss of the letters and that he expected to shortly see them in print. Both sets of letters duly appeared in a pamphlet entitled *The Earl of Glamorgans Negotiations and Colourable Commitment in Ireland Demonstrated*.[42] The capture and publication of these papers, which illustrated the king's willingness to reach a deal with the Irish, served to damage the royalist cause in England: as part of the agreement the confederates agreed to ship 10,000 troops across to England to serve Charles I. The papers' seizure enabled the navy to divert forces to hinder any attempt that might occur to transport those soldiers to England. Captain Robert Moulton, the admiral, left the siege of Bunratty and went to Wexford and Waterford to prevent any movement of forces across the sea.[43] The capture of royalist correspondence and commissioners gave a massive propaganda coup to parliament. The publication of the Glamorgan peace greatly undermined the king's integrity and forewarning of planned troop movements enabled the navy to divert ships to deal with the threat. The capture of so much correspondence by the navy also served to weaken the royalist position in Dublin. Without secure communications with England Ormond's freedom of action was limited and Parliament was aware of his weaknesses and intentions.

The main function of the navy in Ireland and England remained the same throughout the 1640s. The fleet patrolled the coast, intercepted enemy privateers and merchant traffic, blockaded opposition ports and supported loyal garrisons and shipping. With resources thinly stretched the gathering of intelligence never became a primary concern of the navy. The nature of the war at sea meant the navy acquired information of value to the parliamentary cause. Men-of-war captured ships which contained correspondence, parliamentary sympathisers on land passed on news and agents on the continent sent reports concerning enemy plans. Naval forces utilised the intelligence they received when possible. Parliamentary agents in Holland warned the earl of Warwick of the impending departure of the queen from that country, so Warwick unsuccessfully set out a number of ships to try to intercept her as she crossed over to England.[44] This situation is reflected in much of the literature concerning the navy as it focuses on the operations, administration and personalities of the navy.

In conclusion, most of the intelligence received by the navy concerning the movements of royalist and confederate shipping proved to be of limited use. Constraints of time and distance meant such information could rarely be operated on. The success of the navy in general on the Irish coast depended on the presence of a large fleet of warships. The exception to this was in the case of Dublin. With a blockade in effect and men-of-war on duty the navy was able to take advantage of information passed on from supporters within the city. Hence the fleet was able to hinder the Lord Lieutenant's attempts to ship troops and in November 1645 to steal the principal royalist warship from the bay with virtually no opposition. In the case of the navy's role in gathering intelligence much of the information it obtained was of limited military value, especially in relation to the war at sea. However, intelligence found on royalist packet boats was of huge propaganda importance to Parliament. It damaged the royalist cause in England and Ireland as well as providing useful information for the navy operating on the coast.

NOTES

1 The author wishes to acknowledge funding from the Irish Research Council for the Humanities and Social Sciences for this project.

2 J.R. Powell, *The Navy in the English Civil War* (London, 1962).

3 Michael Baumber, 'The navy and the civil war in Ireland, 1641–1643', *Mariner's Mirror* 57, 4 (Nov. 1971), pp. 385-97; Michael Baumber, 'The navy and the civil war in Ireland, 1643-46', *Mariner's Mirror*, 75, 3 (Aug. 1989), pp. 255–68; Bernard Capp, 'Naval operations', in Jane Ohlmeyer and John Kenyon (eds), *The Civil Wars: A Military History of England, Scotland and Ireland, 1638–1660* (Oxford, 1998), pp. 156–91; J.R. Powell, *Robert Blake: General at Sea* (London, 1972); Bernard Capp, *Cromwell's Navy: The Fleet and the English Revolution, 1648–60* (2nd ed., Oxford, 2001).

4 N.A.M. Rodger, *The Safeguard of the Sea: A Naval History of Britain, 660–1649* (London, 2004), pp. 411–26; N. A. M. Rodger, *The Command of the Ocean: A Naval History of Britain, 1649–1815* (London, 2004), pp. 1–64; Richard Harding, *Seapower and Naval Warfare 1650–1830* (London, 1999); Jeremy Black, *The British Seaborne Empire* (New Haven, CT, 2004); Brian Lavery, *Line of Battle: Sailing Warships 1650–1840* (London, 1992), pp. 182–3.

5 Sir John Pennington to earl of Northumberland, 4 Jan. 1641/2, *Calendar of State Papers* [hereafter *CSP*] *Domestic, 1641–3* (London, 1887), p. 236; Advice delivered to the Lord Lieutenant, 21 Apr. 1642, in James Hogan (ed.), *Letters and Papers relating to the Irish Rebellion between 1642–46* (IMC, Dublin, 1936), pp. 22–3.

6 Captain Willoughby to the Lords Justices, 12 July 1642, ibid., p. 80.

7 John Bartlett to the Lords Justices, 17 July 1642, in Hogan, *Letters and Papers*, pp. 82–3; TT E119(22), *A Most Exact Relation of a Great Victory Obtained by the Poor Protestants in Ireland* (London, 1642), p. 12.

8 Father Hugh Bourke to Luke Wadding, 12 Apr. 1642, HMC, *Report on the Franciscan Manuscripts Preserved at the Convent, Merchants Quay, Dublin* (Dublin, 1906), p. 132.

9 John Bartlett to the Lords Justices, 17 July 1642, in Hogan, *Letters and Papers*, pp. 82–3.

10 TT E137(18), *The Apprehending of Captayne Butler at Portsmouth in the County of Southampton and his Followers* (London, 1642), pp. 1–2.

11 Peter Edwards, *Dealing in Death: The Arms Trade and the British Civil Wars, 1638–52* (Stroud, 2000), pp. 216–7.

12 Lords Justices to earl of Northumberland, 12 Feb. 1642, HMC, *Calendar of the Manuscripts of the Duke of Ormonde*, new series (8 vols, London, 1902–20), i, p. 68.

13 Lords Justices for the Commissioners for the Affairs of Ireland, 1 Sept. 1642, ibid., pp. 185–9.

14 The summer guard lists show 10 ships in 1642, 11 in 1643, 24 in 1645, 18 in 1647 and 16 in 1648. In 1645 18 ships were assigned for the Irish squadron with a further 6 for the Scottish squadron. These Scottish ships, which included the *Jocelyn* and the *Fellowship*, were in reality active on the north and east coast of Ireland and I have included them in the Irish figure. In 1648 12 ships were allocated to the Irish squadron and a further 4 to patrol between Milford Haven and Land's End; as

these ships were essentially part of the Irish Guard I have included them in the total. TT 669f3 (50), *A List of His Majesties Navie Royall and Merchant Ships* (London, 1642), p. 1; TT 669f7 (7), *A List of his Majesties Royall and Merchant Ships* (London, 1643), p. 1; TT 669f9 (36), *A List of Such of the Navy Royall as also of the Merchant Ships* (London, 1645), p. 1; Granville Penn (ed.), *Memorials of the Professional Life and Times of Sir William Penn…* (2 vols, London, 1883), i, p. 236; Powell, *Navy in the English Civil War*, pp. 218–9.

15 Earl of Warwick to Captain Richard Swanley, 22 Dec. 1646, in Penn, *Memorials* i, p. 228.

16 Examination of Edward St Lawrence, master of the *Catherine of Waterford*, 28 Jan. 1646/7, (TNA, HCA 13/248); Penn, *Memorials*, i, p. 234; Petition of the owners of the *Love's Increase*, 11 Feb. 1646/7, (TNA, HCA 30/849, f. 653).

17 George Digby to Ormond, 31 Dec. 1646, in Thomas Carte (ed.), *The Life of James, Duke of Ormond: Containing an Account of the Most Material Affairs of his Time, and Particularly of Ireland under his Government; with Appendix and a Collection of Letters, Serving to Verify the Most Material Facts in the Said History* (2nd ed., 6 vols, Oxford, 1851), vi, pp. 487–8; Du Moulin to Captain Willoughby, 31 Dec. 1646, in J.T. Gilbert (ed.), *History of the Irish Confederation and War in Ireland 1641–53* (7 vols, Dublin, 1852), vii, pp. 304–5.

18 Ormond to Archbishop of York, 22 May 1644, in J.R. Powell and E.K. Timings (eds.), *Documents relating to the Civil War 1642–48* (Navy Records Society, London, 1963), p. 141.

19 Examinations of Jonathan Paley, Leonard Graves and Thomas Lowe, 12 Feb. 1645/6, (TCD Ms 810, fols 307–8v: Dublin depositions, vol. ii); Examinations of John Lambert, William Sheppard and Leonard Graves, 14 Feb. 1645/6, ibid., ff 329–32.

20 John Hay, Mayor of Wexford to Ormond, 2 June 1645, HMC, *Ormonde*, new series, i, pp. 93–4.

21 Ormond to Dr Gerald Fennell, 7 Nov. 1644, in Carte, *Ormond*, vi, p. 214.

22 Lords Justices to the earl of Northumberland, 12 Feb. 1641/2, HMC, *Ormonde*, new series, ii, pp. 68–9; Lords Justices to the Commissioners for the Affairs of Ireland, 21 Oct. 1642, ibid., p. 213; *Lords Journals*, vol. 5, pp. 379, 408. The *Swan* was a sixth-rate pinnace built in 1636. She originally carried twenty men and between twelve and twenty pieces of ordnance. This number was increased to forty in October 1642.

23 Captain John Bartlett to Ormond, 16 July 1644 (Bodleian Library, Oxford [hereafter Bodleian], Carte MS 11, f. 462: NLI microfilm p. 611); Captain John Bartlett to Ormond, 26 Mar. 1645 (Bodleian, Carte MS 14, f. 304: NLI microfilm p. 614).

24 A. Eames, 'The King's pinnace, the Swan, 1642–1645', *Mariner's Mirror* 47, 1 (Feb. 1961), pp. 52–4; Examination of Richard Dermot, 17 June 1650 (TNA, HCA 13/63, ff 267–267v).

25 C.J.M. Martin, 'The Cromwellian shipwreck off Duart Point, Mull: an interim report', *International Journal of Nautical Archaeology*, 24, 1 (Feb. 1995), pp. 15–32 suggests that it sank off Duart Point in 1653. Recent archaelogical findings indicate that this is not correct.

26 Examination of John Bartlett, 6 Nov. 1645, HMC *Ormonde*, new series, i, p. 101.

27 William Dalbie to Sir William Brereton, 7 Nov. 1645, HMC, *The Manuscripts of his Grace the Duke of Portland Preserved at Welbeck Abbey* (10 vols., London, 1891–1931), i, p. 305.

28 Examination of Abel Griffin, 7 Nov. 1645, HMC *Ormonde*, new series, i, p. 103.

29 Examinations of Lewis Walcot and Thomas Warren, 6 Nov. 1645, ibid., p. 102.

30 Examination of Thomas Suery, 8 Nov. 1645, ibid., p. 104.

31 Examination of Maurice Butler, 16 Oct. 1648 (TNA, HCA 13/61, ff 176–177). The *Alice* was arrested by Captain William Penn in the *Fellowship*. Chester was then under royalist control.

32 Examination of Samuel Allen, 12 April 1649, ibid., f. 401.
33 Examination of Adrian Bloc by the Aldermen and Council of Flushing, Feb. 1648/9 (TNA, HCA 13/249).
34 Examination of John Mackey, 26 Nov. 1649 (TNA, HCA 13/251, part ii).
35 Examination of Peter Toland, 3 Nov. 1649 (TNA, HCA 13/250, part i).
36 TT E135(5), *A True Relation of Certaine Passages which Captaine Basset Brought from the West Parts of Cornewall* (London, 1642), pp. 1–3.
37 Examination of Walter Quint, 29 June 1644 (TNA, HCA 13/246, no. 166); Lord Inchiquin to Sir Percy Smith, May 1644, ibid., no. 166; Margaret Nurse to her mother, 6 May 1644, ibid., no. 166.
38 Ormond to the earl of Clanricarde, 3 Feb. 1644/5 (Bodleian, Carte MS 14, f. 16: NLI microfilm p. 614).
39 Captain Robert Clarke to the Committee of the Navy, 13 Feb. 1645/6, in Powell and Timings, *Documents*, p. 231.
40 The first papers concerning Glamorgan's secret treaty with the confederates were found in late 1645 when the Archbishop of Tuam, Malachy O'Quelly, was killed near Sligo: Micheál Ó Siochrú, *Confederate Ireland 1642–1649: A Constitutional and Political Analysis* (Dublin, 1999), pp. 98–9.
41 TT E328(9), *The Earl of Glamorgans Negotiations and Colourable Commitment in Ireland Demonstrated* (London, 1646), p. 30; Order of the Commons, 17 Feb. 1646, *CSP, Domestic, 1645–7* (London, 1891), p. 346.
42 *The Earl of Glamorgans negotiations*, pp. 3–30; Captain John Crowther to the Committee of the Admiralty, 9 Mar. 1646, in Powell and Timings, *Documents*, p. 236; Earl of Glamorgan to Ormond, 3 Apr. 1646, in Gilbert, *Irish Confederation*, v, pp. 318–9.
43 Captain Robert Moulton to William Lenthall, 17 Mar. 1646, in Powell and Timings, *Documents*, p. 238; *The Earl of Glamorgans negotiations*, pp 3–6.
44 Powell, *Navy in the English Civil War*, pp. 35–7.

English military intelligence in Ireland during the Wars of the Three Kingdoms*

Micheál Ó Siochrú

In 1655, Giovanni Sagredo, Venetian ambassador to England, commented that 'no government on earth discloses its own acts less and knows those of others more precisely than that of England'.[1] He identified the determination of the English authorities to restrict sensitive information to a mere handful of individuals, and the use of spies rather than ambassadors for intelligence gathering, as the principal reasons for this success. Oliver Cromwell's secretary of state, John Thurloe, is usually credited with the growing professionalism of the English secret services, carrying on the pioneering work of Sir Francis Walsingham in the late sixteenth century.[2] However, Thurloe only assumed sole management of intelligence affairs only in the summer of 1653, by which time the war in Ireland had reached its bloody conclusion. In fact, prior to Thurloe's appointment, the English intelligence record in Ireland was far from impressive. In 1641, for example, despite increasingly alarming reports coming from Ulster during the summer, the authorities in Dublin failed to detect the plot of Sir Phelim O'Neill and his co-conspirators. They only discovered the plans to seize Dublin Castle from a self-appointed informer, Owen O'Connolly, and during the crucial early weeks of the rebellion they seriously underestimated the level of discontent throughout the kingdom. This intelligence failure helped transform a limited pre-emptive strike by a handful of Catholic Ulster landowners into a nationwide revolt. The causes and course of the 1641 rebellion have attracted extensive scholarly interest of late, so this essay will focus instead on intelligence matters during the final stages of the war, as the forces of the English Parliament completed the conquest of Ireland.[3]

I

On 4 July 1649, the English Council of State appointed the MP and regicide Thomas Scott 'to manage the business of intelligence both home and abroad for the State'.[4] Holding the post until the dissolution of the Rump Parliament in April 1653, Scott's tenure of office coincided almost exactly with the Cromwellian wars in Ireland, which began with Oliver Cromwell's expedition in August 1649, and concluded (officially at least) with the surrender of the Ulster forces under Colonel Philip MacHugh O'Reilly in April 1653. Over-shadowed by Thurloe, his more illustrious successor, Scott was in fact responsible for creating many of the structures of the Cromwellian intelligence system. Working on a budget, which he claimed never exceeded £2,500 per annum (including his own salary), Scott began establishing a network of overseas correspondents throughout Europe, who by the mid-1650s were located in places as diverse as Danzig, Hamburg, Paris, Madrid, Genoa and Rome.[5] On the domestic front, royalists claimed his informers swarmed 'over all England as Lice and Frogs did in Egypt', while Scott's enemies in the Republican camp similarly criticised his agents and their methods.[6] According to the radical army officer, Lieutenant-Colonel John Lilburne, Scott and his associates believed that one 'must do evil that good may come of it'. In this regard, Lilburne signalled out an Irishmen, 'Hugh Rily', whom he described as 'one of Mr Scott's great agents and negotiators beyond the seas'.[7] In a major intelligence coup, Scott obtained the services of Dr John Wallis, later professor of geometry at Oxford, who specialised in breaking substitution codes. Wallis's skills enabled the parliamentarians to read intercepted royalist corres-pondence as well as diplomatic mail, and Scott later described the art of cryptography as 'a jewel for a prince's use'.[8] Although involved in handling sensitive information for much of the 1640s, Scott claimed that on assuming sole control of intelligence matters in 1649 he received no assistance or briefing from those previously responsible for secret affairs, either on the Committee of Both Kingdoms or the Committee of Safety.[9] It was a thankless, lonely task in many ways, and Scott's assistant, Captain George Bishop, recorded how the job brought him

> little advantage except the loss of my calling, the prejudice of my estate, the wearing of my body, breaking of my health, neglect of my family, and encountering temptations of all sorts, prejudices, censures, jealousies, envies, emulations, hatreds, malice, and abuses, which the faithful discharge of my duties has exposed me to, in no small measure, besides the mischiefs designed on me by the enemy.[10]

Initially at least, Scott did not concern himself with Ireland, where he delegated his responsibilities to the commander-in-chief of the army there, Oliver Cromwell, a policy he repeated in 1650 when the English invaded Scotland. However, as soon as Cromwell left Ireland for Scotland, Scott established regular contact with Henry Jones, Protestant bishop of Clogher, and scoutmaster general of the parliamentary forces.[11] The role of the scoutmaster during much of the 1640s involved gathering military intelligence for the army in the field, but gradually expanded into more general espionage activities. Jones had gained valuable experience in intelligence matters during the early years of the Irish wars. In late December 1641, as Protestant refugees streamed into the city of Dublin, the Lords Justices, Sir William Parsons and Sir John Borlase, commissioned eight clergymen, including Jones, to collect witness statements from the traumatised settlers. Initially intended as an inventory of material losses, the authorities soon extended the scope of the commission as the rebellion intensified to include allegations of murders and massacres.[12]

The bulk of the statements were taken in 1642–3, but the commissioners continued their work until the end of the war in 1653. Irish Protestants quickly recognised the propaganda value of these testimonies, and Henry Jones skilfully exploited the harrowing accounts of death and destruction to construct a seemingly irrefutable case for the reconquest of Ireland by Protestant forces from England. From September 1652, the depositions began to be employed at the newly established High Court of Justice. The members of this court, including the ubiquitous Henry Jones, made systematic use of the original testimonies from 1641–2, to condemn scores of people to death for their alleged involvement in the initial months of the rebellion.[13] The intelligence collected in the depositions, therefore, not only played a key role in encouraging English military intervention against Irish Catholics during the 1640s and 1650s but also, in the words of the historian Walter Love, 'saved the [Cromwellian] settlement from moderation'.[14]

For much of the 1640s few English parliamentary troops were stationed in Ireland. Nonetheless, by exploiting contacts among the local Irish Protestant community, Parliament developed its own intelligence networks long before Cromwell's arrival in 1649. Large numbers of Protestants fled to England during the wars, including leading figures such as Sir Adam Loftus, Sir John Temple and Sir William Parsons. These men soon cultivated contacts with influential parliamentarians, and by 1645 they had become closely associated with the Independent faction at Westminster.[15] Loftus, Temple, Parsons and their supporters advocated a hard line against Irish Catholics, argued in favour of a total reconquest and provided invaluable intelligence on developments across the Irish Sea to their

English associates. The majority of Protestants who remained in Ireland proved equally sympathetic towards Parliament, and suspicious of Charles I's more lenient attitude towards Catholics. In Munster, Murrough O'Brien, Lord Inchiquin, controlled the coastal towns of Cork, Youghal and Kinsale, while Charles Coote commanded forces in north Connacht and west Ulster. Both men abandoned the king in 1644, and embraced the parliamentary cause. Dublin, under the command of James Butler, marquis of Ormond, remained in royalist hands until June 1647, when Ormond fled abroad and another Irish Protestant, Michael Jones, brother of Henry, took possession for Westminster. The parliamentarians, therefore, received vital military and political intelligence on each of the four Irish provinces from sympathetic local military commanders.[16]

The political and military balance changed dramatically in 1648 when Inchiquin switched sides once again to support the king. In January 1649, Ormond, who had returned to Ireland a few months earlier, signed a peace treaty with the Catholic confederates, which outraged many Irish Protestants. While the tide of war ran in favour of the royalists, both Ormond and Inchiquin managed to retain the loyalty of most of their Protestant supporters. Nonetheless, the political upheavals proved ideal for the extension of espionage activity, and Jones in particular took advantage of the confused circumstances in sending both 'cunning beggars' and soldiers to infiltrate royalist ranks and obtain valuable intelligence.[17] In April 1649, Sir Hardress Waller, keenly aware of Protestant discontent in Ireland, conferred with Cromwell about sending a person to Munster 'to do service there'. Secret contacts were maintained throughout the summer months as the parliamentary invasion force gathered in Milford Haven.[18] Following the battle of Rathmines in August, Cromwell dispatched Colonel Robert Phaier to negotiate with sympathisers in Cork, while the leading Munster Protestant magnate, Roger Boyle, Lord Broghill, played a key role in convincing the Protestant garrisons of Youghal, Kinsale and Bandon to surrender in November.[19] Indeed, the switch of allegiance by the Munster towns, the result of clandestine meetings and secret negotiations, may well have prevented the premature end of Cromwell's expedition. Following the storming of Drogheda and Wexford, the English army was reduced, mainly through disease, to as few as three thousand effective soldiers. With the town of Wexford uninhabitable, and Ormond in the vicinity with a large body of troops, Cromwell faced the prospect of a difficult retreat to Dublin. Instead, the defection of the Munster towns provided winter quarters for his depleted army, enabling his troops to rest and recover.

Crucially, Cromwell was also able to recruit replacements from among the local Protestant population. Following Ormond's crushing defeat at Rathmines by Michael Jones, just two weeks before Cromwell's arrival, the number of desertions from the royalist forces began to multiply. Munster Protestants taken prisoner at Rathmines joined the parliamentary army *en masse*, and by November Inchiquin had begun to execute deserters in a futile attempt to stem the flow.[20] As disease continued to ravage the invaders, Cromwell eagerly recruited local Protestants, each one of whom, according to a contemporary correspondent, was worth six soldiers from England.[21] Accustomed to Irish weather conditions, these new recruits also possessed valuable experience of fighting locally, and could provide vital intelligence to the parliamentary army.

II

While it might be expected that Irish Protestants would side with the English parliament, the role of Irish Catholics in providing the parliamentary forces with military and political intelligence is less well documented. During the course of 1648–9, the leader of the native Irish of Ulster, Owen Roe O'Neill, bitterly opposed the confederate leadership's plans for an alliance with the royalists, primarily over what he saw as a lack of significant concessions on religious and land issues. O'Neill, Randal MacDonnell, marquis of Antrim and some radical clerics believed they could make a deal with the Independent faction in England, based on religious toleration, a grant of indemnity for all acts committed during the rebellion and assurances about landholdings. After the signing of the peace treaty between Ormond and the confederates, O'Neill contacted the commanders of the three embattled parliamentary enclaves at Dublin, Dundalk and Derry – Michael Jones, George Monck and Charles Coote respectively. He sent a priest, Edmund Reilly (later archbishop of Armagh), to Dublin, supposedly to negotiate prisoner releases, though one hostile source described Reilly as 'Jones's inseparable confident and intelligencer'.[22] Desperately short of supplies, both Monck and Coote agreed to temporary ceasefires with the Ulster Irish, in order to exchange goods and information. They also forwarded O'Neill's demands on to London, where the parliamentary authorities not surprisingly rejected them, and publicly rebuked Monck on his return to England.[23]

Around this same time the marquis of Antrim developed his own lines of communication with Westminster. In late 1648, the marquis despatched Patrick Crelly, Cistercian abbot of Newry, to London, where he engaged in secret talks over the next six months with key figures in the new Commonwealth regime, such as Edmund Ludlow. Crelly offered Antrim's military support in return for concessions similar to those sought by O'Neill. Jane Ohlmeyer argues that the parliamentarians simply used these negotiations to sow divisions among their opponents in Ireland, while they prepared an invasion force, and the initiative did indeed collapse with news of Cromwell's departure for Ireland.[24] Crelly left England to petition the papacy for assistance, but he returned to London in the summer of 1650, and entered the service of Thomas Scott.[25] Crelly, who resided in the residence of the Spanish ambassador, Don Alonso de Cárdenas, and used the pseudonyms Mr Haley and Captain Holland, exploited his clerical contacts across Europe to obtain intelligence relating to Irish affairs in France, Flanders, Spain, Austria and Rome. He also kept Scott informed of the dealings between the Catholic Irish and Charles IV, duke of Lorraine, who between 1650 and 1653 seriously contemplated military intervention in Ireland. Indeed, Scott later claimed that Crelly played a role in ensuring that the papacy rejected Lorraine's request for financial support.[26]

In Ireland, Crelly's aristocratic benefactor entered parliamentary quarters in 1650 after almost two years of secret contacts. For the next twelve months Antrim concentrated on disrupting the royalist war effort in the MacDonald heartland of north-east Ulster and western Scotland. Antrim provided the parliamentarians with whatever intelligence he could, including information about the king's alleged involvement with Irish Catholics in the months leading up to the outbreak of rebellion in October 1641. However, many on the parliamentary side distrusted Antrim, a native Irish Catholic who had switched sides on a number of occasions during the 1640s. In March 1651, the authorities brought him to Dublin to keep a closer eye on his activities, and the marquis disappears from the official records shortly afterwards for the remainder of the war.[27]

Antrim and his agent Crelly have generally been dismissed as maverick operators, enjoying little support in the wider Catholic community, but surviving evidence presents a more complex picture. The levels of wastage in the parliamentary forces, ravaged by disease, desertions and combat deaths, could not be replaced solely from England, or from the relatively small Protestant population in Ireland. Moreover, the success of the parliamentary campaign further increased demands on manpower, as all the newly occupied towns and cities required garrisons. The startling solution favoured by the military leadership was to recruit from among the local Catholic population. Given the bitter antagonism displayed by English Protestants towards Irish Catholics from the outbreak of the rebellion in 1641, such a development hardly seems credible. Indeed, in anticipation of Cromwell's invasion of Ireland, propagandists in London had worked themselves into a frenzy of anti-Catholic and anti-Irish invective, while the authorities at Westminster authorised

Thomas Waring, formerly clerk of the commission taking statements from Protestant refugees in Ireland, to revisit in print the alleged massacre of settlers in 1641. Basing his account on the depositions of the survivors, Waring described the Catholic Irish as 'savages', 'cannibals', and concluded that Parliament could 'warrantably and righteously endeavour the extirpation of them'.[28] The English Parliament adopted a similar hard line towards the Irish during the 1640s. In October 1644 Westminster issued an ordinance of no quarter for any Irish Catholics captured while fighting for the king in England. A number of atrocities ensued, and it is remarkable how many of the documented massacres in the English civil war have an Irish connection, either directly or indirectly.[29]

The problems associated with campaigning in hostile territory, however, required pragmatic rather than idealistic solutions. Local Protestant commanders, such as Ormond and Coote, had recruited some Catholics into their forces during the 1640s, albeit with bad grace in the latter's case.[30] Arriving in Dublin towards the end of the campaign season in late August 1649, Cromwell desperately needed a co-operative local population to provide food and other vital supplies to his forces. From the outset of his campaign in Ireland, therefore, he developed a sophisticated propaganda strategy. While he condemned those 'barbarous and bloodthirsty Irish' who had planned and taken part in the rebellion, he publicly assured the lower social orders that he had no quarrel with them.[31] Cromwell hanged a handful of his own troops for unlicensed pillaging, and where possible insisted that his army pay for whatever goods they took.[32] This drive to win the hearts and minds of the local population floundered following the massacres at Drogheda and Wexford in the autumn. Yet, during the spring campaign in 1650, Cromwell adopted a more measured military approach, offering generous terms of surrender, and sparing the common soldiers at least, if not the officers.[33] His new tactics raised the possibility of recruiting local Catholic troops in significant numbers.

Writing after the war, an apologist for Ormond claimed that 'the Irish in all quarters of which the enemy were possessed not only submitted and compounded, but very many of them entered into their service and marched with them in their armies'.[34] Indeed, as early as March 1650, Donough Kelly, the Catholic governor of Ballyshannon in County Kildare, allegedly offered to join the parliament's forces in return for certain religious concessions.[35] Although his advances were rejected, that same month, James Tuchet, the Catholic earl of Castlehaven, complained to Ormond about increasing numbers compounding with the enemy, providing them with supplies, including manpower. The earl remarked incredulously how '[Cromwell's] army would soon be exhausted were it not daily supplied with the children and servants of contributors'. Castlehaven called on the Catholic bishops to excommunicate all those who assist 'or serve' the rebels.[36] The archbishops of Dublin and Tuam acknowledged that some did in fact contribute both 'persons and substance' to the enemy, but no clerical censures ensued, as the royalist alliance began to fracture under the pressure of successive military defeats.[37] By early August, Ormond noted how the loss of numerous towns and garrisons, 'and the lack of any visible power to protect them hath doubly induced many to contribute their subsistence and personal assistance to the rebels'.[38] However, not all of this recruitment was voluntary in nature. Following the fall of Wexford, Cromwell put Irish prisoners to work in his army as 'Pioneers', while Ulick Burke, marquis of Clanricarde, reported how the parliamentarians forced 'churles and garsons to march with them to make the greater show' of numbers.[39] More definitive proof of Catholic recruitment is provided by a Major Dongan, who reported to Ormond that after Carlow surrendered to the parliamentarians in July 1650 the majority of the garrison (exclusively Irish Catholics) took conditions 'to serve the rebels'.[40]

Not surprisingly, English sources for the period are completely silent on this issue, as army commanders might have found it difficult to justify accepting the very same blood-thirsty papists so effectively demonised by English propagandists into the ranks of the New Model Army. Similarly, after the restoration of the monarchy in 1660, neither Catholics nor Protestants in Ireland wished to be associated in any way with the Cromwellian regime, and subsequent accounts of the 1650s stressed the English nature of the invading army. Any Catholic complicity in the conquest appears to have been deliberately written out of history, or simply neglected over time. During the war, however, royalist and Catholic leaders were acutely aware of the threat posed by Catholic recruitment into parliamentary forces. In September 1650, Ormond issued a proclamation condemning those who consorted with the enemy, but the problem persisted.[41] A few months later, Ormond's deputy, the marquis of Clanricarde, warned anybody born in Ireland against collaborating with the parliamentarians, under pain of high treason. The marquis gave those already in service with enemy forces twenty-one days to defect.[42] Similarly, in December 1651, an assembly of leading Munster Catholics denounced their co-religionists who fought for the parliamentarians, while in May the following year, a congregation of Leinster clergymen pleaded with Irish Catholics not to support the English invaders.[43] In addition to these declarations, some military commanders resorted to more direct action. From early 1652, Catholic Irish troops who made separate terms with the parliamentarians, such as the group serving under Colonel John Fitzpatrick, were frequently attacked, maimed and in some instances killed.[44]

But what would induce an Irish Catholic to join the New Model Army and assist the English Parliament in the conquest of Ireland? The desire to support the winning side is one possible answer. As already mentioned, a number of Catholic leaders believed that their cause would best be served by an alliance with the Independent faction, which had emerged victorious in the English civil wars. They despised the royalist leadership, Ormond in particular and, as a consequence, the marquis of Antrim, and others, may well have encouraged their supporters to assist parliamentary forces. Economic imperatives also played a role, particularly as Catholic troops received little or no pay and were forced to live off the land, causing great hardship to the general population. Indeed, according to one contemporary commentator, the deprivations of the Catholic forces drove large numbers to turn to the parliamentarians for security.[45] In such straitened circumstances, the allure of secure employment may simply have proved too tempting. Indeed, the royalist Sir Lewis Dyve suggested as much, reporting how many 'for want of livelihood, having neither meat nor pay, flocked in unto the enemy'. Whatever their motivations, these locally recruited Catholic troops would have provided first-class, up-to-date intelligence to the parliamentary forces, through their own networks of personal contacts.[46]

As the war dragged on into 1652, the boundaries between the various antagonists became increasingly blurred. The author of the 'The Aphorismical Discovery' describes one prominent Catholic, Sir Richard Barnewall of Kirkstowne, as 'playing the ambo-dexter', switching from one side to the other as the situation dictated.[47] Similarly, soldiers often deserted from one army, only to re-enlist with their former opponents. As a consequence the parliamentarians began to specifically exclude from surrender terms those who had previously served in their armies.[48] Some resourceful commanders exploited the confusion to their own advantage. In early 1651, Colonel Richard Bourke entered into talks with the parliamentary governor of Birr, 'simulating to become of his party'. After resupplying his troops in parliamentary territory for a few days, Bourke revealed his true hand and promptly left the area.[49]

Despite some conspicuous success in recruiting local forces, both Catholic and Protestant, the English Parliament could not bring the war to a conclusion. They captured towns and castles but became increasingly isolated among a hostile population, while Tory bands operated almost with impunity behind enemy lines. According to one parliamentary source, these highly mobile guerrilla units had 'exact and constant intelligence from the natives...whereas our forces seldom or never have any intelligence of their motions'.[50] The authorities in Dublin introduced a number of measures to try to increase the flow of military intelligence, or at least prevent the enemy from receiving information from the local population. They offered bounties for private soldiers and officers as well as named individuals such as Viscount Muskerry (£500) and Colonel Richard Grace (£300), and those bringing in prisoners received protection and pardon for life.[51] Colonel John Hewson, governor of Dublin, introduced the concept of collective responsibility, whereby an entire community would be punished for attacks by 'tories or rebels' within the territory controlled by Parliament. For failing to warn the authorities of enemy raids, the colonel would fine the inhabitants of a barony £100 for every parliamentary officer killed, and £20 for all others, unless the murderers were handed over within ten days of the attack.[52]

The movement of the local population was also closely monitored. All people over the age of ten had to register with the authorities. They received a pass, which contained detailed data on the individual, such as name, place of abode, family, qualities or callings, age, sex, stature, colour of hair. Anybody who failed to apply for this seventeenth-century equivalent of the ID card would be accounted a spy, and treated accordingly.[53] In a move similar to US tactics in Vietnam during the 1960s, the parliamentarians established protected areas throughout the country, designating entire counties such as Wicklow as enemy territory. Anybody attempting to move into the parliamentary zones or found outside the line would be treated as an enemy, while those who had quit parliamentary protection since Cromwell's arrival in 1649 were to be 'deprived of the benefit of quarter'.[54] Colonel George Cooke in Wexford, however, often preferred to spare civilians in enemy territory, as they would continue to consume scare supplies of food, causing widespread starvation. This he believed was 'the only way to make a speedy end of these wars'.[55] Faced with such brutal tactics, the Irish grew increasingly desperate and divided, which greatly increased the flow of intelligence to the parliamentarians. For example, by 1652, the parliamentary commander in Ulster was 'promptly advised of all that is discussed in their [catholic] provincial council' by those hoping to ingratiate themselves with the new regime.[56] In addition to such freely offered information, the Dublin authorities also employed numerous spies to sow dissent and undermine the last vestiges of resistance.[57]

All sides in early modern conflict dealt harshly with those communicating with the enemy. The Swedish military manual, used as a guide all over Europe, stated simply that 'whosoever gives advice unto the enemy, any manner of way, shall die for it'.[58] Such strictures commonly applied to troops in service but, by early 1652, parliamentary commanders increasingly targeted the civilian population for maintaining contact with Catholic forces, or bands of Tories. A unique record of the minutes of a military court in Dublin over a two-month period, between February and April 1652, reveals that the authorities in the city sentenced over twenty people to death for spying, including five women.[59] By mid-March, a council of war granted Colonel Hewson the authority to impose the death sentence on his own in order to speed up the entire process. The figures from Dublin, if extended over a year, and applied across the country, suggest either a serious problem with civilian spies or wide-scale and indiscriminate retaliation against the general population by the parliamentary authorities. Although the number of capital cases decreased dramatically as the war reached its conclusion, the execution of alleged spies continued into 1653. The sentence on women was, however, increasingly commuted from death to transportation to Barbados.[60]

Spying, by its very nature, is a secretive business, and Marcus Nevitt argues that this fact, along with the patriarchal and discriminatory nature of early modern society, has obscured the role of women in intelligence affairs during the English civil war.[61] Women certainly featured prominently in contemporary accounts of the Irish wars from the outbreak of the rebellion in 1641. Lady Elizabeth Dowdall and the wives of other landowners helped co-ordinate the defence of family estates, while a number of Protestant deponents accused catholic women of instigating the violence against the settler community.[62] All sides in the conflict employed women as messengers, and they also appear now and again as major players in covert operations. As Cromwell approached the town of Drogheda in late August 1649, the royalist commander, Sir Arthur Aston, complained to Ormond about 'these female spies that are here', including his grandmother Lady Wilmot. The Lord Lieutenant replied sympathetically, remarking that women were indeed much inclined 'to make little factions', and he granted Aston powers of summary punishment to use against those giving intelligence to the enemy. Rather than execute or imprison his relative, however, Aston eventually forced Lady Wilmot to move to nearby Mellifont, to prevent her from causing any further trouble.[63] Despite Ormond's disparaging remarks, the royalists also employed female spies of a high social standing. In September 1651, for example, two daughters of Sir Nicholas White – Frances, wife of Thomas, Viscount Dillon of Costello-Gallen and Mary, wife of Theobald, Viscount Taaffe – became involved in a plot to retake Athlone castle from the parliamentarians. However, an informer warned the commander of the castle, who foiled the plot, killing fifty of the enemy in the process and imprisoning the two ladies.[64] Some women suffered the ultimate penalty, being executed for their espionage activities. On trial for his life in December 1653, Viscount Muskerry vigorously defended his decision to hang a number of spies, including a woman called Nora. The parliamentarians accepted that such actions were justified in times of war, and acquitted him on the charge of murder.[65]

III

According to the Venetian ambassador Sagredo, one of the most important maxims of government was to maintain spies everywhere, 'to be informed of what is happening in the world'.[66] On the military front, Henry Hexham's treatise on the art of war, published in 1642, argued that a general in the field 'should have good guides and spies about him, to get him intelligence of the state of an enemy, and ought to spare no money that way, for the breaking of an enemy's design, and for the advancing of his own'.[67] Espionage and intelligence gathering remained a high priority for English parliamentarians throughout the 1640s and 1650s, nowhere more so than across the Irish Sea. From 1649 to 1653 they spent over £70,000 on intelligence matters in Ireland, or 2 per cent of the total military budget for that country. In comparison, during the same four-year period, Thomas Scott claimed he only had £10,000 available to him to finance his domestic and continental activities.[68] Both figures are impressively high, but the former reflects the greater resources available to the military as distinct from the civil authorities, and also the scale of the problem facing the Commonwealth regime in Ireland. As foreign invaders, they relied heavily on local informers and recruits, both Protestant and Catholic, to provide them with vital military and political information, all of which cost a lot of money. By 1652, however, despite this heavy investment, the parliamentarians appeared to be losing the intelligence war. As a result, military commanders began to rely less on local co-operation, adopting instead traditionally crude methods to obtain information and disrupt the enemy's communication networks. While hangings, deportations and imprisonment proved brutally effective in the short term, success came at a heavy price. The increasingly indiscriminate targeting of civilians by the parliamentarian forces, much of it related to intelligence gathering, made a mockery of Cromwell's declaration on landing in Dublin that he had no quarrel with the ordinary people of Ireland, and left a bitter legacy for centuries to come.

NOTES

*   I would like to thank Jane Ohlmeyer, David Ditchburn, and my father Oisín Ó Siochrú for their detailed comments on earlier drafts.

1   26 Nov. 1655, Giovanni Sagredo, Venetian ambassador in England to the doge and Senate, *Calendar of State Papers* [hereafter *CSP*] ... *Venice...*, *1655–6* (London, 1930), pp. 142–3.

2   Richard Deacon, *A History of the British Secret Service* (London, 1969), pp. 9–15.

3   For some recent work on 1641 see Brian MacCuarta (ed.), *Ulster 1641: Aspects of the Rising* (Belfast, 1993); Michael Perceval-Maxwell, *The Outbreak of the Irish Rebellion*

of 1641 (Dublin, 1994); Pádraig Lenihan, *Confederate Catholics at War, 1641–49* (Cork, 2001), esp. pp. 1–72; Nicholas Canny, *Making Ireland British, 1580–1650* (Oxford, 2001), esp. pp. 461–550.

4   4 July 1649, Council of State, day's proceedings, *CSP, Domestic, 1649–50* (London, 1875), p. 221.

5   C.H. Firth (ed.), 'Thomas Scot's account of his actions as Intelligencer during the Commonwealth', *English Historical Review*, 12 (1897), pp. 116–26 at p. 124. Thurloe's papers reveal the extent of the English intelligence network overseas by the mid-1650s. See Thomas Birch (ed.), *A Collection of the State Papers of John Thurloe* (7 vols, London, 1742).

6   Clement Walker, quoted in David Underdown, *Royalist Conspiracy in England, 1649–1660* (New Haven, CT, 1960), p. 20.

7   Admittedly, Lilburne had an axe to grind with Reilly (and, by association, Scott), who presented a petition against the lieutenant colonel to the Council of State in 1653. See *A Defensive Declaration of Lieut. Col. John Lilburn* (London, 1653), p. 6. Unfortunately, the origins of this Hugh Reilly remain a mystery.

8   Firth (ed.), 'Thomas Scot's account', p. 121. See also Philip Aubrey, *Mr Secretary Thurloe: Cromwell's Secretary of State, 1552–1660* (London, 1990), pp. 28, 43.

9   Firth (ed.), 'Thomas Scot's account', pp. 118–9.

10 6 Sept. 1653, Captain George Bishop to the Council of State, *CSP, Domestic, 1653–4* (London, 1879), pp. 133–4.

11 Captain Matthias Rowe was originally appointed scoutmaster for the Irish expedition, but he died in Dungarvan at the end of 1649. See *CSP, Domestic, 1649–50*, p. 584; Denis Murphy, *Cromwell in Ireland: A History of Cromwell's Irish Campaign* (Dublin, 1883), p. 237. There are a number of references from 1652 in the Exchequer records in TNA, London, to a Charles O'Hara, 'Scoutmaster General to the Lord General Cromwell in Ireland deceased' (TNA, E315/483, fos. 47, 49). A Captain Charles O'Hara served in Colonel Hammond's regiment in 1647, and was promoted to colonel shortly afterwards, but does not appear in records elsewhere. See John Rushworth, *Historical Collections of Private Passages of State* (7 vols, London, 1659–1701), vi, p. 466; *CSP, Ireland 1647-1660* (London, 1903), p. 769. Thanks to David Ditchburn, Jane Ohlmeyer and David Worthington for assisting with this search.

12 Aidan Clarke, 'The 1641 Depositions', in Peter Fox (ed.), *Treasures of the Library: Trinity College Dublin* (Dublin, 1986), pp. 112–13.

13 Establishment of the High Court of Justice in Kilkenny, Marsh's Library, Dublin, MS Z2.1.7, f. 51.

14 Walter Love, 'Civil war in Ireland: appearances in three centuries of historical writing', *Emory University Quarterly*, 22 (1966), pp. 57–72 at p. 68.

15 See Patrick Little, 'The Irish "Independents" and Viscount Lisle's Lieutenancy of Ireland', *Historical Journal*, 44 (2001), pp. 941–61, for a discussion on the influence of these Irish Protestants at Westminster.

16 For the fluctuating political and military situation in Ireland during the 1640s, see Micheál Ó Siochrú, *Confederate Ireland, 1642–1649: A Constitutional and Political Analysis* (Dublin, 1999).

17 14 July 1649, Intelligence from London, Bodleian Library, Oxford [hereafter Bodleian], Carte MS 25, f. 37.

18 Three agents departed for Munster in May, Lieutenant-Colonel Pigot, Major Knight and a 'Mrs Foulkes' (presumably the wife of Major Francis Foulkes), with every care taken 'that they might not be suspected'. See *CSP, Domestic, 1649–50*, pp. 77, 112, 121, 530; 2 May 1649, Letter Book of the Council of State, TNA, SP 25/94 f. 129.

19 For detailed examination of Lord Broghill's role in these matters, including later fabricated claims that Cromwell forced Broghill to assist the parliamentarians, see

Patrick Little, *Lord Broghill and the Cromwellian Union with Ireland and Scotland* (Woodbridge, 2004), pp. 61–2.

20 4 November 1649, Inchiquin to Ormond, Bodleian, Clarendon MS 38, f. 109.

21 23 Jan. 1650, Sir Richard Fanshaw to George Lane, Bodleian, Clarendon MS 39, fos. 40–2.

22 'An Account of the war and rebellion in Ireland since the year 1641', NLI, MS 345, f. 1006.

23 Parliament published the correspondence between Coote, Monck and O'Neill to dispel rumours that major concessions had been offered to Irish Catholics. See *A True relation of the Transactions Between Sir Charls Coot Kt. Lord President of Connaught in Ireland, and Owen-Roe-O-Neal* (London, 1649); *Generall Owen Oneales Letter to Collonell Monck* (London, 1649). See also Jerrold Casway, 'George Monck and the controversial catholic truce of 1649', *Studia Hibernica* 16 (1976), pp. 54–72.

24 Jane Ohlmeyer, *Civil War and Restoration in the Three Stuart Kingdoms: The Career of Randal MacDonnell, Marquis of Antrim, 1609–1683* (Cambridge, 1993), p. 225.

25 According to one report, Crelly accompanied Cromwell to Dublin, and he may well have returned to Ireland before continuing on to Rome. See 24 Aug. 1649, John Dongan to Ormond, Bodleian, Carte MS 162, f. 46.

26 Crelly's relationship with Scott is described in Firth (ed.), 'Thomas Scot's account', pp. 119–21. Scott also mentions that Colonel Hugh Reilly provided him with information. For an analysis of Lorraine's engagement with the affairs of Ireland see Micheál Ó Siochrú, 'The Duke of Lorraine and the international struggle for Ireland, 1649-1653', *Historical Journal*, 48, 4 (2005), pp. 905–32.

27 Ohlmeyer, *Civil War and Restoration*, pp. 237–41, provides the best account of Antrim's activities during this period. See also 22 Aug. 1650, 'Declaration by Antrim re. 1641', Bodleian, Carte MS 28, fos. 365–6.

28 Thomas Waring, *A Brief Narration of the Plotting, Beginning & Carrying on of that Execrable Rebellion and Butcherie in Ireland* (London, 1650), pp. 30, 41–2, 64.

29 Will Coster, 'Massacre and codes of conduct in the English Civil War', in Mark Levene and Penny Roberts (eds), *The Massacre in History* (New York & Oxford, 1999), pp. 89–105.

30 Coote, for example, highly recommended Thomas Costello and his brother to Sir Philip Percivall in London. 'I confess they are Papists', Coote wrote, 'but such as never did any prejudice to the Protestants, but have constantly adhered to us and contribute much to our preservation'. See 4 June 1647, Coote to Percivall, in HMC, *Report on the Manuscripts of the Earl of Egmont* (2 vols, London, 1905–9), i, pp. 412–13.

31 W.C. Abbott (ed.), *The Writings and Speeches of Oliver Cromwell* (4 vols, Oxford, 1939, reprinted 1988) ii, pp. 107, 111–2.

32 The parliamentary expedition was well furnished with cash, which Ormond believed was 'more formidable' than any military strength Cromwell possessed, 22 Aug. 1649, Ormond to Clanricarde, Bodleian, Carte MSS, vol. 25, f. 321.

33 See Cromwell's letters describing the ongoing campaign in *Cromwelliana: A Chronological Detail of the Events in which Oliver Cromwell was Engaged from the Year 1642 to his Death 1658* (London, 1810), pp. 75–7; Abbott (ed.), *Writings of Oliver Cromwell*, ii, pp. 231–5; Thomas Carlyle (ed.), *The Letters and Speeches of Oliver Cromwell* (3 vols, London, 1904), iii, pp. 265–6, 420, 423.

34 'A short view of the state and condition of the kingdom of Ireland from the year 1640 to this time', Bodleian, Clarendon MS 121, f. 73v.

35 3 Mar. 1650, John Hewson to Speaker Lenthall, in J.T. Gilbert (ed.), *A Contemporary History of Affairs in Ireland from 1641 to 1652* (3 vols, Dublin, 1879–80), ii, pp. 370–2. A copy of the terms allegedly offered by Kelly was published in London. See *Several Letters from Ireland of the late Good Success of the Parliament Forces There* (London, 1649/50).

36 Castlehaven vowed to 'destroy all contributors with fire and sword'. See 28 Mar. 1650, Castlehaven to Ormond, Bodleian, Carte MS 27, fos. 217–8.

37 24 July 1650, Dublin and Tuam to Ormond, Royal Irish Academy, H.VI.I (collection of papers relating to Ireland), fos. 78–9.

38 2 Aug. 1650, Ormond to archbishops of Tuam and Dublin, Bodleian, Carte MS 28, fos. 259–60.

39 19 Aug. 1650, Clanricarde to Ormond, Bodleian, Carte MS 28, f.349; *A Perfect and Particular Relation of the Several Marches and Proceedings of the Armies of Ireland from the Taking of Drogheda to this Present* (London, 1649), p. 8.

40 Dongan claimed that many of those who had surrendered were further invited to serve in England, and although he personally refused the offer, the major feared that many would gladly accept. Once again, it hardly seems credible that the parliamentarians would employ Catholic Irish troops in England, unless perhaps to release more experienced soldiers for service in Ireland. See 3 Aug. 1650, Ormond to Clanricarde, Bodleian, Carte MS 28, f. 263.

41 10 Sept. 1650, 'Proclamation by Ormond', Bodleian, Carte MS 162, f. 331.

42 Clanricarde introduced further penalties for contributing to the enemy, either monetarily or with goods. [23 Dec.] 1650, 'Declaration by Clanricarde', Bodleian, Carte MS 27, fos. 217–8.

43 The two declarations appear in Gilbert (ed.), *Contemporary History*, iii, pp. 27, 111–12.

44 6 May 1652, Commissioners in Dublin to Council of State, in Charles McNeill (ed.), *The Tanner Letters* (IMC, Dublin, 1943), pp. 360–3; 'The Aphorismical Discovery', in Gilbert (ed.), *Contemporary History*, iii, p. 69.

45 'The Aphorismical Discovery', in Gilbert (ed.), *Contemporary History*, ii, p. 135.

46 According to one account, those in the countryside who compounded with the parliamentarians, corresponded with their friends in royalist-controlled towns, thus giving the enemy excellent intelligence. See 'A short view of the state and condition of the kingdom of Ireland', Bodleian, Clarendon MS 121, f. 76v.

47 'The Aphorismical Discovery', in Gilbert (ed.), *Contemporary History*, ii, pp. 136.

48 For an example of articles of surrender, including the exclusion clause, see Robert Dunlop (ed.), *Ireland under the Commonwealth* (2 vols, Manchester, 1913), i, p. 173.

49 'The Aphorismical Discovery', in Gilbert (ed.), *Contemporary History*, ii, pp. 131, 136.

50 [Jan. 1652], 'Some particulars to break the enemy's strength', in Dunlop (ed.), *Ireland under the Commonwealth*, i, pp. 119–20.

51 22 May 1652, 'Order by the Commissioners of Parliament', in Dunlop (ed.), *Ireland under the Commonwealth*, i, pp. 206–7; BL Egerton MS 1761, Orders of State (1650–4), 25 Nov. 1651, 22 May 1652, 14 July 1652, fos. 61v, 100–3, 108v–111. As early as November 1650, Evans Vaughan reported the offer by the parliamentary authorities of £20 for information leading to the capture of a priest. See 11 Nov. 1650, Evans Vaughan to ——, King's Inns, Dublin, Prendergast Papers, vol. 3, fos. 493–4.

52 25 Feb. 1650/1, 'Proclamation published by Colonel Hewson', King's Inns, Prendergast Papers, vol. 1, fos. 719–23.

53 29 April 1652, 'Order by the Commissioners of Parliament', in Dunlop (ed.), *Ireland under the Commonwealth*, i, p. 178. See also BL, Egerton MS 1761, Orders of State (1650–4), 29 April 1652, fos. 93–100. An order for 40,000 of these tickets of protection was issued on 5 May 1652. See King's Inns, Dublin, Prendergast Papers, vol. 1, f. 8.

54 Edmund Ludlow, *The Memoirs of Edmund Ludlow Esq.* (2 vols, Vivay, 1698), i, p. 391. See also Pádraig Lenihan, 'War and population, 1649-1652', *Irish Economic and Social History*, 24 (1997), pp. 1–21.

55 17 March 1651[2], Colonel Cooke to the commissioners of Parliament, in Henry

Cary (ed.), *Memorials of the Great Civil War in England from 1646–1652* (2 vols, London, 1842), ii, pp. 419–23.

56 11 April 1652, 'Advices from London', in *CSP, Venice, 1647–52* (London, 1927), p. 223.

57 'The Aphorismical Discovery' in Gilbert (ed.), *Contemporary History*, iii, p. 125–6.

58 [Watt, Wm.], *The Swedish Discipline, Religious, Civil and Military* (London, 1632), p. 54.

59 'Minutes of Court Martials held in Dublin, 1651/2', Marsh's Library, MS Z3.2.17[2]. Spying was a risky business, and during the 1640s spies in England were executed as publicly as possible, to deter others. See Charles Carlton, *Going to the Wars: The Experience of the English Civil Wars, 1638–1651* (London, 1992), p. 263.

60 'Minutes of Court Martials held in Dublin , 1651/2', Marsh's Library, Dublin, MS Z3.2.17[2].

61 Marcus Nevitt, 'Women in the business of revolutionary news: Elizabeth Alkin, "Parliament Joan", and the Commonwealth Newsbook', in Joad Raymond (ed.), *News, Newspapers, and Society in Early Modern Britain* (London, 1999), pp. 84–108 at p. 93.

62 For a description of the role in women in the Irish wars of the mid-seventeenth century see Mary O'Dowd, 'Women and war in Ireland in the 1640s', in Margaret MacCurtain and Mary O'Dowd (eds), *Women in Early Modern Ireland* (Dublin, 1991), pp. 91–111. For the situation in England, see Carlton, *Going to the wars*, pp. 150–79.

63 27 Aug. 1649, Aston to Ormond; 28 Aug. 1649, Ormond to Aston; 1 Sept. 1649, Aston to Ormond, all in Gilbert (ed.), *Contemporary History*, ii, pp. 236, 238, 246–7, 452. Ormond granted Aston the powers of 'martial law' to deal with 'several ill-affected persons'. See Bodleian, Carte MS 162, fos. 46–8.

64 18 Sept. 1651, Parliamentary Commissioners in Dublin to the Council of State, in Dunlop (ed.), *Ireland under the Commonwealth*, i, pp. 53–4.

65 For an account of Muskerry's trial, see Mary Hickson, *Ireland in the Seventeenth Century or the Irish massacres of 1641–2* (2 vols, London, 1884), ii, pp. 200–04.

66 26 Nov. 1655, Giovanni Sagredo, Venetian ambassador in England to the Doge and Senate, *CSP, Venetian, 1655–6*, pp. 142–3.

67 Henry Hexham, *The Second Part of the Principles of the Art Military, Practised in the Warres of the United Provinces* (London, 1642), p. 13.

68 'An abstract of all moneys received and paid for the public service in Ireland, July 1649–November 1656', Trinity College, Dublin, MS 650/7.

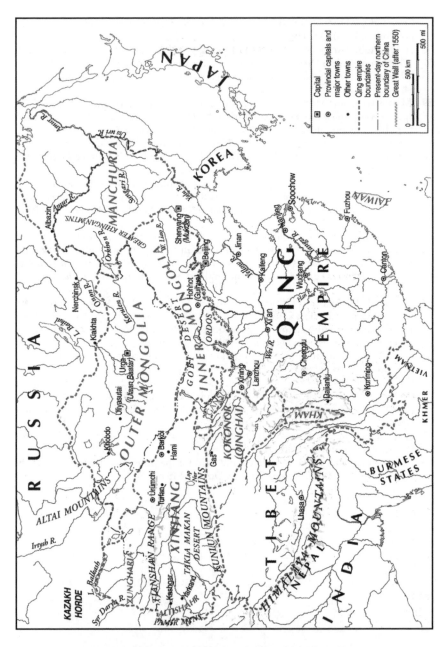

Reprinted by permission of the publisher from
China Marches West: The Qing Conquest of Central Eurasia
by Peter C. Perdue, p. 2, Cambridge, MA: Harvard University Press,
Copyright © 2005 by Peter C. Perdue.

The Qing empire and international power

Joanna Waley-Cohen[1]

In the eighteenth century, the empire ruled from Beijing was the most extensive in Chinese history, past or future. It encompassed not only China itself, but also Mongolia, Tibet, Taiwan, Xinjiang (Chinese Turkestan) and the north-eastern homelands of the Manchu ruling house of the Qing, whose rule over China lasted from 1644 to 1912. The Manchu Qing were the last conquest dynasty of imperial China, and despite sinocentric, and later Eurocentric, denigration of their skills and sophistication, were very serious contenders indeed in the world power stakes, at least until the early nineteenth century. The historian is not a clairvoyant able to predict the future, but with benefit of hindsight it does seem that China's past approximately two hundred years of weakness on the international scene may turn out to have been a protracted aberration rather than a normal state of affairs

In this essay I address two main questions: first, what did 'international power' mean to the Qing? And second, how did they both gain intelligence about others and disseminate information, accurate or misleading, about themselves, and what were some of their intelligence successes and failures?

First, what did 'international power' mean to the Qing? In one sense, of course, it had to do with, precisely, power: how could they make themselves more powerful than any of their competitors and reign supreme in East Asia? They were an expansionist state, but they also operated under an acute consciousness of history. This meant that, on the one hand, they hoped to emulate or surpass the reach of the great Chinese empires of the past, particularly the seventh–tenth century Tang, but on the other they were not particularly interested in the infinite possibilities offered by maritime expansion.[2] Their relations with others can be roughly divided into two categories, offensive and defensive; here it is important to note that they were very far from being solely reactive in those relations.

In the world of the eighteenth-century Qing there were four main groups who really mattered. First and foremost – and this is specifically in order of priority – international power referred to the Qing's Inner Asian neighbours, including the Mongols, Tibetans and Zunghars, whose empire stretched roughly from Hami in the east to Yarkand in the west and from the Kunlun mountains in the south up almost to Siberia in the north. The first two of these were effectively incorporated into the empire by the early eighteenth century through a combination of military conquest and marital alliance. The third, the Zunghars, were, after a series of wars, eventually eliminated altogether in the mid-eighteenth century. Until then, and well into the nineteenth century, these continental competitors were the ones whom Qing China took most seriously, not least because the Qing understood themselves to be striving for supremacy among near equals, people who operated according to roughly the same premises they did, with roughly the same goals in mind.[3]

Seven of the ten wars that the eighteenth-century Qianlong emperor claimed as his 'ten great victories' involved these groups – and the others might also be called 'international' in that they involved Burma, Vietnam, and Taiwan. These last are somewhat beyond the scope of this paper. In general terms, they fall into a category, also including Japan, which together constitutes the second group of states that may be categorised under the heading of 'international power'. With Japan the Qing had relatively little diplomatic contact – indeed the Japanese, like the Koreans, disdained the Qing as usurpers – but a fair amount of rather important commercial contact, since Japanese silver in particular was a major import. Japan was also of interest for security reasons, because it was a potential launching pad for anti-Qing activity and a base of operations for pirates raiding the China coast.

Third, for the Qing international power referred to the Russians, expanding eastwards as the Qing expanded westwards. In the seventeenth and eighteenth centuries the Qing and the Russians concluded a series of treaties that defined borders and established parameters for trade and other interactions. A Russian church and a language school were opened in Beijing, and a Russian division was added to the Manchu, Mongol and Han-martial divisions of the military-administrative system known as the Eight Banners that basically ran the empire. Finally, for the Qing international power referred to Europeans – and it is important to bear in mind that in the seventeenth and most of the eighteenth century Europe came last both temporally and in terms of perceived importance – first the Dutch in Taiwan and later as colonists in what is now Indonesia; the Portuguese, who with tacit Chinese consent used Macao as a commercial and missionary base from the mid-sixteenth century on; the Spanish, anchored in the Philippines after 1571, and later the British, based in India, not to mention such others as the Danes, who regularly traded through the sole Chinese port dedicated to Western commerce, namely, Canton on the south-east coast. All of these the Qing encountered not only as colonists around their own periphery but also as traders, diplomats and missionaries coming to China for various purposes, overt and covert, and often very evidently in competition with one another.

The conventional wisdom about China in general and Qing China in particular has been that it was unenthusiastic about war and not much good at it. This view, really a consequence of reading back from the mid-nineteenth century, prevailed for a long time without much serious interrogation. But lately scholars have completely debunked all the old assumptions about China's perennial reluctance to wage war and its supposed inability to do so effectively. When we look at the broad sweep of Chinese history, it is clear that, Sun Zi and the Confucian classical texts notwithstanding, China has never hesitated to use force when that seemed to be the most effective way of meeting its political goals. How could the empire possibly have lasted so long without a degree of force and of military sophistication?[4]

One of the most striking aspects about the Qing was the way in which they elaborated and fine-tuned existing traditions, taking them to new heights of sophistication. As noted, they were a conquest dynasty and, in fact, at least up to the end of the eighteenth century, war and imperial expansion were defining aspects of their rule. During this period, the Qing formulated a series of policies for the defence of the realm and its borders. Different agencies handled relations with different groups. In some ways this diffusion of foreign affairs institutions was a great strength, because it allowed for considerable flexibility, but on the other hand it made co-ordination and consistency difficult. Exactly the same was true of intelligence: the Qing do not appear to have had a specific intelligence agency to back up their military adventures, but that did not in any way mean that they had no interest in intelligence. On the contrary, they marshalled all the intelligence they could in a variety of different ways, some relatively formal, some more ad hoc.

Given the great importance of historical precedent to the self-consciousness of the Qing, we turn first with a brief overview of the ways in which China had gained intelligence about others in earliest times. As is by now well known, China's contacts with the outside world date back to time immemorial. Commercial exchange took place both along the transcontinental Silk Roads, which connected China indirectly to the Roman empire, and by sea, with maritime links with the Middle East since at least the third century and probably much earlier. Merchants going to and fro often conveyed information along with the goods they traded. Diplomatic exchange was also quite frequent, with foreign dignitaries coming to China, and Chinese emissaries visiting western and south0east Asia. The Han emperor's second-century BCE mission to obtain the blood-sweating horses of Ferghana, far to the west, is well known, as is the same emperor's dispatch of Zhang Qian in search of alliances against China's Xiongnu enemies. Captured by the Xiongnu *en route*, he spent ten years in captivity before continuing. He reached northern India, and although he failed in his mission to form alliances, he returned home with huge amounts of strategic, geographical and other information to report to the emperor.

Then as now, in other words, diplomacy included a strong element of intelligence gathering. Beginning at about the same time, a government agency was set up to supervise interpreters and liaison with foreign envoys. By no later than the seventh-century Tang, officials of this agency, in co-operation with military personnel, debriefed all foreign delegates immediately upon their arrival, interrogating them about the geography, living conditions and customs of their countries. They then had maps drawn on the basis of what they had learned, which they presented to the emperor, often with extensive annotation. It was a form of early ethnography that also served intelligence purposes. Foreign envoys also sometimes brought along local products and maps of their own territories as gifts to the Tang court, intended more or less to symbolise their submission to Tang authority. In exchange they would be sent home with Chinese goods to give their ruler or sell on the home market. In other words, from early times embassies were an instrument of both trade and the exchange of information, so they were a major means of obtaining information about the outside world. Moreover, it was entirely clear to Chinese officials and rulers that this was a two-way street, and they treated any foreigner found asking too many questions or drawing maps with the utmost suspicion.

Just as incoming embassies were extensively debriefed, so Chinese missions sent abroad were specifically expected to gather geographical and other information about the places they visited, on both land and sea. Thus in the seventh century the Tang emperor sent emissaries to Sogdiana and Tocharia, far to the west, to collect information on local customs and products and to draw detailed maps. Diplomacy, in short, was one major means of gathering intelligence. Other more ad hoc sources of information included travellers and war captives. For instance, a Tang officer captured near Samarkand in 751 eventually found his way back to China by way of what are now Eritrea and Iraq, bringing with him first-hand tales of these distant lands and their ways of life. We revert in a moment to this use of war captives.

The fairly regular traffic of religious pilgrims at this early date also provided a major source of information. When Xuanzang (?620–64), the monk who made an epic journey from Chang'an to India in search of

Buddhist scriptures in the eighth century, returned after a journey of several years' duration, Emperor Taizong (626–49) personally debriefed him in two audiences. It is clear that Taizong fully grasped the benefits of obtaining a first-hand account, for he questioned Xuanzang closely about Indian history, customs, geography, climate and products. All through the Tang, emperors continued to dispatch monks to India in search of information that was not limited to the acquisition of religious texts. In other words, it was normal practice, and the Qing knew that every Chinese empire had found ways to acquire intelligence about the peoples and territories beyond the imperial borders. The well-known early fifteenth-century treasure fleets that sailed through South-east Asia to India and the Persia Gulf, and as far as Malindi on the east coast of Africa, are one more example of this.[5]

In the use of monks as spies, if that's not putting it too strongly, we can see a kind of precedent for the exchange of information that in the seventeenth and eighteenth centuries was channelled through Jesuit missionaries resident at the Qing court. These men not only were the chief conduits of information about China to Europe, but also provided the Qing emperors, for whom they worked in a secular capacity, with detailed information about Europe, and how things were done there. The intense rivalry between the Catholic and Protestant nations spilled over into missionary reports, perhaps inadvertently enlightening the Qing about these kinds of disagreements between the various different Europeans they encountered.[6]

As is well known, intelligence about weaponry was a major factor in early European contacts in Asia. Knowledge about gunpowder had spread from China to Europe, where intense competition had led to major developments in gunnery. All that information filtered back east by multiple routes, including in particular via the Ottoman empire, as well as in more haphazard ways, for instance through the impressment by Korea of shipwrecked Dutchmen, who forged cannon for them and via the introduction by missionaries to the failing Ming of Portuguese artillerymen. Firearms played a significant role in the wars of the Ming–Qing transition, in the first half of the seventeenth century. In these wars the key Ming loss took place in 1619, despite their employment of firearms against Manchu mounted archers; thereafter the Manchus co-opted Chinese artillery experts for besieging Chinese cities in conjunction with their formidable cavalry. Subsequent defeats by better-armed Ming forces only prompted the Manchus to redouble their efforts to acquire more cannon. In the end their effective application of cannon against fortified cities was crucial to their victory, and one might say that they simply made extremely successful use of intelligence gained on the battlefield. After the Qing were established, Jesuit missionaries reluctantly forged new and lighter kinds of cannon for the Qing, helping them to victory in the series of campaigns of the later seventeenth and eighteenth centuries.[7]

In the Qing era, as earlier, diplomacy and embassies, both ingoing and outgoing, were very important. Best known in this connection, of course, was the Macartney embassy of 1792–3, notorious for the Qing emperor having, disingenuously, claimed that 'we have no need for foreign manufactures', but also highly significant for the enormous interest devoted by the emperor to military matters. That interest was epitomised by the Qianlong emperor's particular interest in gifts of a military nature: among the many offerings the British brought to impress the emperor, the single item to which Qianlong paid most attention was an exact model of a British 110-gun warship.[8]

The Macartney embassy was the first *British* embassy to China; there had been earlier Dutch and Portuguese ones, whose hopes of expanding trade met with success only in proportion to the amount of military aid they gave the early Qing against pockets of offshore resistance. Once those had been suppressed the Qing showed little interest in offering further concessions. This has led to the view of a lack of Qing interest in the outside world – the 'why didn't' version of history, which effectively belittles China for not having followed the same path as Western nations. But that view has failed to take into account a number of important missions sent out by the Qing, though not generally as far afield as Europe until matters took a sharp turn for the worse in the nineteenth century.

In 1712, for instance, the Qing sent Tulisen (1667–1741) on a mission to the Torghuts (or Kalmyks). The Torghuts were Mongol kin of the Zunghars, from whom they struggled to retain their autonomy, and had lived on the lower Volga since the early seventeenth century. Officially the purpose of the embassy was for Tulisen to seek permission from the Tsar to let the Torghut ruler's nephew return home; and, should the Torghuts propose an alliance against the Zunghars, to turn them down. To the contrary, however, the Manchus had quite other plans. To quote a nineteenth-century account: 'The embassy came to view the territory of the Russian people and moreover to try to perceive the nature and condition of the Russian government. If it were possible they would cause a quarrel between Ayuki, the Torghut leader, and Tsewang Rabtan, one of the Zunghar leaders.' Tulisen, indeed, returned with a detailed map of Siberia for the emperor, along with much other information, so his embassy was not much different from those sent by other world empires, such as the British and Russians, which combined strategic, geographical and commercial goals.[9]

War captives were a vital intelligence source for the Qing. After the great Qing victory over the Zunghars at the battle of Jao Modo in 1696, surrendering Zunghars told the Kangxi emperor (1662–1722) that the Dalai Lama, whom he supposed to be alive and active, had in fact died nine years earlier. It later transpired that the cleric had been dead even longer than that.

Kangxi presumed the Tibetan regent had issued proclamations in the Dalai Lama's name, encouraging the Zunghar leader, Galdan – Kangxi's great foe – to march against the Qing. Perhaps so, or perhaps the Qing did not understand Tibetan views of reincarnation. In other words, it may be that the Tibetans thought the Dalai Lama might return. In any event, it had been quite an intelligence failure, but this belated news enabled the Kangxi emperor to expose Galdan as having relied on the usurping regent to pursue a war that the Dalai Lama, it was claimed, would never have condoned. In this way the emperor was able to secure Tibet's at least temporary subordination, which he brought to completion in 1720.[10]

Tibet remained an important link to the outside world. In 1793, when General Fu Kang'an returned from successful campaigns against the Gurkhas there, he had heard about the presence in neighbouring India of the British, under Cornwallis, who had surrendered at Yorktown a decade or so earlier. Fu Kang'an feared they might have been helping the enemy, although in fact Cornwallis had not done so: he dared not offend China, because of the lucrative East India Company trade at Canton. Fu Kang'an's association with the most powerful minister at the Qing court was one reason that the members of the 1793 Macartney embassy met with what appeared to them to be great recalcitrance in China, because Fu Kang'an had told the court that the British were not to be trusted.[11]

Here we digress for a moment to mention important intelligence acquired by means of war captives on the other side, as it were. By 1711 several hundred Swedes captured by the Russians at Poltava had spread into Siberia. Some went to work for the Zunghars. One, a Lieutenant Renat, forged cannon and drew maps for them, and taught them how to smelt iron for bullets. The maps he drew, a hybrid of Swedish, Russian, Mongolian and Chinese cartographic techniques, were quite accurate, for he derived his information from interrogating the locals. These maps, now in the university library at Uppsala, were a major factor in spreading both cartographic and geographic knowledge of the region.[12]

Let me now turn to what was known about Europeans in Asia, other than the British in India. Most information about European colonial expansion into Asia came by way of internal communication channels, often reports from officials in south-east coastal China, which was closely linked to trading and diasporic communities all over South-east Asia, including areas that had fallen under European colonial power.

Within the empire, after the late seventeenth century there was a two-tier system of public and secret communications between the emperor and his provincial and metropolitan officials. Using the public system, officials sent in regular reports on both routine and exceptional matters. These were carried to the court by a relay system of government couriers and passed through the Grand Secretariat, then the top state agency, which made recommendations as to possible responses before the reports ever reached the emperor. So they were not at all confidential. By the end of the seventeenth century, the Kangxi emperor began to develop a second-tier, confidential system of communications in which the writers' private couriers would deliver reports to the palace, where they would be brought unopened to the emperor and then read, annotated and sealed by him in private before being sent back in the same way. This secret communications system functioned in various ways: apart from the obvious one of conveying information to the emperor from all over the empire, it also greatly strengthened links between the emperor and his officials, and it provided a whistle-blowing system, in which potential malfeasance, corruption and even sedition could be secretly reported to the emperor.[13]

> Thus in 1741 the emperor learned from senior officials in coastal Fujian province of a Dutch massacre of the rather considerable Chinese population then in Java: 'When the Dutch occupied Java, a barbarian chief was appointed to be stationed there. His appointment and replacement was to be decided by the king of Holland. The Chinese living in Java numbered several tens of thousand; some were born in Java...when the people were found guilty of a crime, the Dutch banished them to Sri Lanka, an old Dutch colony far distant in the western ocean. In the 6th year of QL (1741), Java was attacked by various aborigines. The Dutch could not resist them. Therefore, the chief sent Dutch convicts into the fight, promising that if they fought bravely and won, they would be allowed to return to Java. The convicts fought bravely and won so many victories that the aborigines finally retreated. The Dutch chief had promised they would be pardoned, but at the same time he feared that, after they left, Sri Lanka would be isolated and weakened. Several times he shifted innocent Chinese to replace the convicts. At that time a Chinese trade supervisor observed that the Chinese merchants paid silver for a trading license but had no obligation to be drafted to replace the convicts. So he refused to obey. The [Dutch governor] arrested him and other Chinese and murdered an unknown number. The Chinese then became frightened, set up an alarm, and suspended trade. The [governor], angered, ordered his soldiers to fire their cannon on the Chinese merchants, butchering them in great numbers.

The information came, evidently, from Chinese eyewitnesses, but whether by the sporadic and informal passing of information through relatives on the mainland, or more systematically, we do not know. The reporting official concluded by expressing concern that the Dutch would interfere with Chinese offshore trade; in the end the emperor decided that to ban the trade would cause too much of a hardship to coastal residents, and declined to do so, incidentally demonstrating the error of any assumption of Qing hostility towards trade.[14]

Other matters that came up fairly often in reports from the provinces included accounts of European missionary involvement in arms trading; and accounts of disputes between different Europeans, for instance during the many Anglo-French wars of the eighteenth century. In late 1745, for instance, they reported on British privateers chasing French ships outside the China Sea, lining up their own navy to guard the coast. This kind of spat was often repeated, notably in the Napoleonic wars; each incident was duly reported in detail to Beijing, which was increasingly unhappy about the presence of foreign warships in their waters, which the Europeans claimed to be necessary to protect trade.

As an occupying force bent on expanding imperial borders, the Qing went out of their way to make sure their subjects were aware that they were and continued to be a military force to be reckoned with. In part they did this by establishing garrisons across the empire as a permanent reminder, but conscious of the blunting of such garrisons' impact over the long term, they took other steps to make this point. Among their northern subjects, the main way in which they did so was through the institution of the annual hunts. Launched in 1681, these hunts took place regularly at least up to the end of the eighteenth century. Many imperial princes took part in the hunts, and troops from the capital were chosen to participate on the basis of such military skills as archery, that were tested earlier in the year. The emperor required Inner Asian lords to participate in rotation, making it possible both to cultivate important personal relationships and to assemble the desired audience for this implicitly intimidatory parade of military power. It was also, of course, a means of keeping track of what was going on in the outer territories. In the South, similarly, emperors undertook a series of imperial Southern Tours, major feats of logistics consciously conceived as peacetime counterparts to military campaigns and designed as a material allusion to Inner Asian martial prowess. Both the hunts and the tours were specifically seen as ways to propagate the notion of the Qing as a major military power: to spread information to those who needed to know.[15]

Who the Qing thought needed to know about their military power is also of interest, for that audience was both domestic and international. In 1761, following the final defeat of the Zunghars and the permanent elimination of the age-old nomadic threat to the inland frontiers, the emperor had four foreign Jesuit court artists execute a series of sixteen war illustrations, which he displayed in a pavilion in central Beijing purposely refurbished for the purpose. Foreign dignitaries were received there; they still are, although the war illustrations have long since left for the international art market. These paintings included scenes of battles, surrenders and triumphs. With a view to further broadcasting Qing military prowess, the Qianlong emperor decided in a manner worthy of the most far-seeing Disney executive to have mass reproductions of the war illustrations made, in the form of copper engravings. And, almost certainly because the Qing emperor wanted to impress his own military might on the great king of France about whom the missionaries at court had told him so much, copies of the sixteen war illustrations were sent to Paris on French East India Company ships, with orders for two hundred sets of copper engravings. These eventually returned to China, where many more were made. They bedecked public buildings all over the empire and were distributed to deserving officials as a mark of imperial favour. In addition to the originals and some sets of engravings, which are in Beijing, other sets were retained in France in disregard of the Qing emperor's perhaps provocative stipulation for exclusivity, and they can now be found all over the world.

Separate paintings were also made of some of the individual events depicted in the war illustrations, and here we slide into the realm of wishful disinformation. A painting of the ceremonial execution of war captives in 1760 not only shows large numbers of Qing officials in awestruck attendance, but also an astonishing range of tribute-paying foreign visitors bearing their national flags. According to the 1790 catalogue of the imperial art collection, these foreign visitors apparently included French, English, Dutch, Koreans and Japanese as well as representatives of numerous South-east Asian and Central Asian states. A number of other paintings from this period depicting imperial successes of one kind and another include legions of admiring foreigners apparently in attendance, to an extent that defies credibility. The impression is inescapable that the incorporation of these supposed audiences was to display them as consenting observers of his imperial successes.[16]

What does all this tell us? It reconfirms, I think, that the eighteenth-century Qing were as much a world empire as any of their contemporaries; that they took what they could when and as they found it; that, as an imperial prince once told a Jesuit missionary, in warfare they would stop at nothing to achieve their objectives; and that they were highly sophisticated in their understanding of the utility of disinformation as well as gaining intelligence. This use of what we would now call 'spin' – propaganda – is best understood in the context of their highly developed historical consciousness. I have mentioned their desire to surpass their predecessors; it is also important not to underestimate their wish to stake their own claim to a place in history. Their view of international power, in other words, took shape in not only a spatial framework, across territorial borders, but in a temporal framework, in which the past and the future formed part of a kind of continuum across which emperors considered that it was their responsibility to form a bridge.

NOTES

1 I am grateful to the American Council of Learned Societies, the National Endowment for the Humanities and the John M. Olin Foundation for funding; and to librarians and archivists at the First Historical Archives, Beijing; the National Library, Beijing; the Stone Carvings Museum, Beijing; the Cultural Relics Bureau, Beijing, the Institut de France, Paris; Yale University Library; and the Bobst Library, New York University. For comments on various versions of this work as it developed, I thank participants and audiences from the many different forums in the United States, Europe and New Zealand to whom I have presented it in different guises; and my colleagues and students, past and present, at New York University. Thanks also to Jane Ohlmeyer, Robert Armstrong and Eunan O'Halpin for inviting me to present a version of this paper at the Irish Conference of Historians' conference on 'Intelligence, Statecraft and International Power' in Dublin in May 2005.

2 They were also, as many scholars including myself have discussed, heirs to a historical legacy emanating from Inner Asia that derived from the Chinggissid tradition, and everything they did bore that legacy in mind as much as that inherited from China. See Joanna Waley-Cohen *The Culture of War in China: Empire and the Military under the Qing Dynasty* (London, 2006).

3 Peter C. Perdue, *China Marches West: The Qing Conquest of Central Eurasia* (Cambridge, MA, 2005).

4 See Alastair Iain Johnston, *Cultural Realism: Strategic Culture and Grand Strategy in Chinese History* (Princeton, 1995).

5 Louise Levathes, *When China Ruled the Seas: The Treasure Fleet of the Dragon Throne, 1400–1433* (New York, 1994).

6 See Joanna Waley-Cohen, *The Sextants of Beijing: Global Currents in Chinese History* (New York, 1999).

7 See Nicola di Cosmo, 'Did guns matter?: Firearms and the Qing formation', in Lynn A. Struve (ed.), *The Qing Formation in World-Historical Time* (Cambridge, MA, 2004).

8 See Joanna Waley-Cohen, 'China and Western technology in the eighteenth century', *American Historical Review*, 98, 5 (Dec. 1993), pp. 1525–44.

9 See Perdue, *China Marches West*, pp. 213–20.

10 Chinese claims on Tibet date back at least to this period, although contemporary accounts of official connections between the two often refer to a much earlier link in the form of a Chinese princess, Wencheng, who married the king of Tibet during the Tang dynasty (618–906).

11 In 1841 Yao Ying, a Qing official in Taiwan, noticed racial friction between British and Indian captives and interrogated one of the officers about the British empire in

India. What he learned convinced him that colonial overextension and racial tension would ultimately prove fatal to British imperial ambitions. See Waley-Cohen, *Sextants of Beijing*, p. 146.

12 See Perdue, *China Marches West*, p. 306–7.

13 On the secret palace memorial system, see Jonathan Spence, *Ts'ao Yin and the K'ang-hsi Emperor: Bondservant and Master* (New Haven, CT, 1966); Beatrice S. Bartlett, *Monarchs and Ministers: The Grand Council in Mid-Ch'ing China, 1723–1820* (Berkeley & London, 1991).

14 Fu Lo-shu, *A Documentary Chronicle of Sino-Western Relations, 1644–1820* (Tucson, 1966), pp. 172–3: 1741, citing *Qingchao Wenxian Tongkao* 297.

15 See Michael G. Chang, 'A Court on Horseback: Constructing Manchu Ethno-Dynastic Rule in China, 1751–1784' (PhD dissertation, University of California, San Diego, 2001).

16 See Waley-Cohen *The Culture of War in China*, ch. 2. For an example of such a painting, see the anonymous, undated hanging scroll of 'Envoys from Vassal States and Foreign Countries Presenting Tribute to the Emperor' illustrated in Jessica Rawson and Evelyn S. Rawski (eds), *China: The Three Emperors, 1662–1795* (exhibition catalogue, Royal Academy of Arts, London, 2005).

STRATEGY AND SUBVERSION: IRELAND, GREAT BRITAIN AND THE UNITED STATES

Three failures and a success: Dublin Castle's intelligence, 1796–1803[1]

Thomas Bartlett

Can I begin with a little vignette in which Dublin Castle, intelligence and failure figure prominently? It comes from the memoir composed by Arthur Hamilton Norway, secretary to the Irish Post Office, recounting his experiences of Easter Week 1916, in which of course his workplace, the GPO, figured prominently. On the afternoon of the first day of the Rising, Norway and Sir Mathew Nathan, under-secretary to the Irish Office, held an understandably fraught meeting in Dublin Castle. As the crackle of rifle fire and the crump of explosions reverberated around them, Norway drew attention to a captured copy of the rebels' Proclamation in which the Irish Republican Brotherhood (IRB) claimed responsibility for the planning and execution of the Rising. Norway then recalled how he drew Sir Mathew Nathan's attention to 'the latest report sent to me from the Intelligence Dept. in the Castle... and especially the assertion that the IRB was probably dormant and might be regarded as negligible'. Norway then put his finger on the passage in which the IRB claimed that it was behind the Rising and he 'passed it back to Sir Mathew with the remark, "It seems that the IRB is not so dormant after all." Sir Mathew smiled uncomfortably, but said nothing.'[2]

This paper addresses three earlier failures in intelligence which engulfed Dublin Castle, and which possibly provoked the Castle officials of that time – in this case Edward Cooke and William Wickham – to 'smile uncomfortably'. And it seeks to elucidate why it was that the famed intelligence system of Dublin Castle with its reputation for efficiency, with its large numbers of informers and with its penetration at the higher, if not highest, levels of the United Irishmen, fell down rather badly when put to the test. The three intelligence failures in question were the expedition of the French to Bantry Bay in late 1796, the outbreak of the rebellion in County Wexford in May 1798 and Robert Emmet's rebellion in Dublin in July

1803. But while my focus is on the shortcomings of the Castle intelligence apparatus in the 1790s, we need to remember that, as in 1916 – for the Easter Rising was of course suppressed – Dublin Castle did succeed in crushing the revolutionary movement in Ireland in the late eighteenth early nineteenth centuries. The Castle certainly had its failures but this success was ultimately what counted.

I

Let's look first at the attempted French invasion of December 1796. Unlike other *descentes en Irlande* in 1759 and 1798, this was no mere raid, but rather the largest amphibious operation attempted by the French since the 1690s. Some 15,000 men were mobilised and embarked on a fleet of some fifty warships bound for the south-west coast of Ireland. This French fleet under cover of appalling weather eluded the Royal Navy ships blockading Brest and made its way to Ireland. Many of the ships were scattered and blown far out to sea but a significant number did manage to reach Bantry, where they endured dreadful weather and huge seas for nearly two weeks before making their way back to Brest. Many French soldiers and sailors died on this expedition, for a number of ships foundered; but almost none were lost through enemy action. Had the French landed, almost certainly Cork would have fallen, and the invading force would then have gained shelter and supplies. Given that the raid by the elderly Colonel Tate and his band of French desperadoes on the coast of Wales two months later was sufficient to cause panic in British financial circles and take Britain off the gold standard, who knows what would have happened had a large body of French soldiers been put ashore in Ireland. In the gravest threat to the British state between the sailing of the Armada in 1588 and the planned invasion by Nazi Germany in 1940, British naval intelligence and Dublin Castle intelligence were badly caught out. Providence in the form of 'Protestant' winds, and possibly French incompetence, had saved the day, but not superior intelligence. What had gone wrong?

As is well known, Dublin Castle faced two security problems in the 1790s: the threat of invasion from abroad, and the threat of insurgency at home. No single security policy could address both, for a feared invasion demanded the concentration of soldiers in order to confront the enemy as soon as they landed, while a policy of counter-insurgency required the dispersal of forces in small detachments throughout the affected areas. From an early date, Dublin Castle decided that there was almost no possibility of the French effecting a landing in Ireland, and hence it prioritised a policy of counter-insurgency.

In deciding, in effect, to ignore the threat of a French invasion, Dublin Castle could call on history in its support, for while there had been many threats of invasion in the eighteenth century, in the end they had all come to nothing.[3] Moreover, if the French had proved singularly unsuccessful for over a hundred years in mounting a significant expedition to Ireland, there were good reasons for thinking that they could not be any more successful in the years after the outbreak of the French Revolution. It was, in fact, an article of faith that the French navy had noticeably declined in effectiveness since the Revolution, for executions, purges and flight had taken a heavy toll of that navy's most experienced officers. And the British victory on the 'Glorious First of June' [1794] and, even more, the treacherous surr-ender by disaffected members of the French navy of the important naval base at Toulon to the Royal Navy had confirmed a comfortable feeling of British naval superiority in contrast to French ineptitude and treason.[4] As well, it was axiomatic that seaborne invasions could not be successful without command of the sea and this the French palpably did not and would not have, given the perceived chaos into which the French navy had descended since 1793. From an early date in the war, the leading French naval ports had been blockaded, penning up the French sails of the line. By December 1796, Admiral Colpoys and his warships hovered off Brest, while his subordinate, Sir Edward Pellew, and his frigates tacked back and forth in the very mouth of this great natural harbour. Meanwhile at Spithead, sheltered by the Isle of Wight, a large reserve fleet under Admiral Bridport lay at anchor awaiting word of any French attempt to escape the blockade. Finally, off the south coast of Ireland, Admiral Kingsmill with a small squadron was stationed on convoy escort duty. For these compelling reasons, then, there was little or no fear of a French seaborne invasion: in fact, if anything, there was mounting frustration in naval and political circles that the cowardly French might continue to skulk in their ports and thus elude their fate. In the British Admiralty, the hope was openly expressed that the French would indeed attempt a break-out from Brest, for this would surely result in the destruction of their fleet and whatever troops it carried. No less a personage than the British home secretary, the duke of Portland, welcomed a French expedition to Ireland. In November 1796, he frankly declared that he hoped the French would launch an invasion of Ireland 'as it is hardly possible that it could escape the vigilance and superiority of the squadrons which are stationed to observe its motions'.[5] In retrospect, however, it is clear that by this date a healthy confidence with regard to the French threat had yielded to a dangerous complacency, and that this had fed through to intelligence gathering and processing. The French could not invade Ireland; therefore, all signals to the contrary were ignored and all information from spies, agents and informers that this was exactly what they were planning was discarded. Astonishingly, even though the French Admiral Richery and his commerce raiders had escaped out of Rochefort in early 1796, sailed to Newfoundland, plundered British possessions there and sailed back in triumph, no lessons had been learned by the Admiralty. It was this mindset that almost brought disaster to the British empire. And even when the French arrived in Bantry Bay there was a flat refusal to believe that the ships visible from land could be French. They must surely be Dutch or American merchantmen. Finally, on 26 December 1796, the penny dropped: Camden wrote that, taking into account information received from General Dalrymple in Cork, the opinion of Captain Boyle of the Royal Navy, observations from other witnesses (including Major Brown of the Engineers) and confirmation that the French fleet had indeed sailed out of Brest harbour and eluded its pursuers, he had reached a conclusion. These circumstances, he ended ponderously, 'leave me no room to doubt of the Fleet which has for some days appeared off Bantry Bay being hostile'.

II

If we turn to the Wexford rebellion we see an intelligence failure that had rather different roots. And here we need to remind ourselves that it was in Wexford that the 1798 rebellion was at its most formidable. Crown forces were routed in a number of engagements, rebel armies remained in the field for nearly a month, two thirds of the county was in rebel hands for a similar period, and of course there were very high casualties, combatant and non-combatant, and very great devastation in the areas affected by the conflict. It is not too much to say that if Wexford is removed from the picture very little of the 1798 rebellion would remain.[6]

And yet Dublin Castle was caught almost entirely unawares by rebellion in Wexford. Indeed, insurgency was so little anticipated in that county that the number of soldiers there had actually been reduced on the eve of the rebellion. Such complacency is very odd. Wexford, with its history of land confiscation and Cromwellian settlement, and its strong Catholic and Protestant communities, was a hot-bed of sectarian rancour. Moreover, the county's governing elite had been deeply divided for many years, and there had been a major disturbance, in which one hundred people may have died, as recently as 1793. Given the conflicted history and society of Wexford, surely the level of United Irish organisation there ought to have been high on the Castle's list of intelligence priorities in the months and years preceding the rebellion in May 1798? Recent research has painted a picture of Wexford as the Armagh of the South, and as a county in which the United Irishmen were very well organised. In particular, Louis Cullen has claimed that the strength of the United Irishmen in the county is revealed by the fact that the rebels were able to keep large numbers in arms for three weeks over two thirds of the county. How could Dublin Castle with its famed sources of information, and its ample resources for acquiring more, have failed to be apprised of all or any of this?

Dublin Castle's probable response to these questions tells us much about the way that information gathering and intelligence processing were organised in the revolutionary period. In the first place, the Castle might point to the small number of letters received from Wexford correspondents – magistrates, clergymen, gentry and village postmasters – relating to goings-on in that county in the 1790s. Among the Rebellion Papers, the chief archive for the revolutionary decade, there are, compared with other counties, very few letters concerning Wexford. Again, there was a marked absence of Wexford in the various United Irish documents, detailing numbers, leaders, funds and arms, which had been seized by the government in March 1798 at Oliver Bond's house in Dublin, and elsewhere.[7] In addition, Dublin Castle had been assured by Lord Mountnorris that the mass of the people in Wexford was law-abiding and loyal. He had been administering an oath of allegiance in those districts where loyalty was most in doubt in late 1797, and he was confident that that had done the trick, and that all danger had passed. His assurances were accepted by the Castle, and indeed by nervous Protestants.[8]

The conclusion seems inescapable: for the entire period of the 1790s, Dublin Castle relied on freelance correspondents to keep it apprised of developments within their county; but it did not see it as any part of its business to recruit agents in those counties where such informants failed to materialise. Note how many of the more success-ful informers had offered their services to the Castle; and note how few were actively recruited by it. Samuel Turner, a United Irishman deeply knowledgeable about their activities on the continent, simply turned up on Lord Downshire's doorstep in October 1797, and offered to tell all. Francis Higgins had long been a freelance informant for Dublin Castle and it was he who recruited Francis Magan, who would eventually reveal Lord Edward Fitzgerald's hideout. The amateur spy-ring in south Antrim headed by Captain Andrew MacNevin and Sergeant John Lee appears to have carried out its operations on its own initiative. Other Castle correspondents much cited by historians, for example George Holdcroft, postmaster of Kells, John Pollock who recruited Leonard MacNally ('JW'), Sir George Hill who was active in the North-west, and the Alexander brothers, Henry and Alexander, also active in Ulster, appear to have been equally self-selected and, indeed self-appointed. It was a clear weakness of the Castle's intelligence system that for most of the 1790s it relied almost entirely on 'walk-ins' or 'write-ins': where these were not forthcoming it appeared to be at a loss to know how to proceed.[9]

III

Lastly, we come to Emmet's insurrection in Dublin in July 1803. Why was Dublin Castle so completely taken unawares by this? There had been a premature explosion and fire in Emmet's depot in Thomas Street a week before the abortive rebellion got underway, but still Dublin Castle had remained oblivious to what was being planned in the Liberties of Dublin, barely half a mile from its (wide-open) gates. With the crushing of the 1798 rebellion the Castle had gained an enviable (or sinister) reputation for running informers, infiltrating agents into subversive organisations and general intelligence gathering. Yet in July 1803, contrary to the heated denials of the lord lieutenant, Lord Hardwicke, the lord chancellor, Lord Redesdale, and the chief secretary, William Wickham, it was evident to well-placed observers that Dublin Castle, 'lulled into a false sense of security', had been taken 'by surprise' by a rebellion that was 'certainly unexpected', and on which 'no intelligence' had been received beforehand.[10] How could this have happened?

One essential context within which to examine Dublin Castle's apparent intelligence failure in 1803 is that provided by the shattering defeat inflicted on the United Irish rebels in 1798. In addition, there was for the rebels the sickening realisation that their organisation had been from an early date beset by treachery and betrayal by those who were among the most trusted with its secrets. Moreover, the decision taken by the so-called State Prisoners, those leading United Irishmen in prison since before the rebellion, to reveal their plans to government in return for exile rather than execution had proved controversial and demoralising. Lord Cornwallis, the lord lieutenant, and Lord Clare, the lord chancellor (for once in agreement with each other), had calculated that if the State Prisoners, in return for their lives being spared, were to make a full statement of their subversive activities, such a disclosure would sow dissension and sap morale among their less elevated comrades, and so it had proved. After his capture in August 1803, Emmet was offered his life in return for a full statement of guilt along the lines of that agreed to by the State Prisoners of 1798, but he scorned the offer.

Two other developments since 1798 may also be noted as contributing to the initial context within which to view the Castle's 'intelligence failure' in 1803. The first of these was the dramatic turnaround in opinion among the Presbyterians in the North. Ulster, particularly east Ulster, had been the engine of disaffection in the 1790s, and there had been a creditable turnout in the summer of 1798, but thereafter radicalism, let alone disaffection, had cooled appreciably. Whether produced by disillusion at Bonaparte's treatment of Switzerland or driven by the attractions of a pan-Protestant Orangeism, or dictated by the absence through death, imprisonment or exile of the old radical leadership cadre, or by a combination of all three, radical Presbyterians and radical Presbyterianism had ceased to embrace disaffection in the aftermath of the 1798 rebellion. Reports of Catholic atrocities in Wexford and elsewhere, assiduously collected and published, also allegedly had a dramatic effect on Presbyterian opinion.

Second, the fundamental weakness of the United Irish–French alliance had been revealed by the extremely poor French performance at the time of the rebellion and after. A number of small raiding parties, dispatched after the rebellion was over, only one of which managed to get ashore (at Killala, under General Humbert), scarcely seemed an adequate recompense for all the promises of extensive French military assistance. And, of course, the ensuing negotiations between the French and the British, concluded at Amiens in March 1802, had offered precisely nothing to the United Irishmen; indeed, they had been fortunate not to be expelled by the French as part of the peace terms. To those in Dublin Castle charged with the defence of Ireland, the only conceivable danger after 1798 could come from a French expedition, and by 1802 there was no prospect of that.

A further context for understanding the Castle's apparent 'intelligence failure' in 1803 is that offered by the Act of Union and the new order which it promised to usher in. And here we must remember that, apart from its legislative details, and its economic and religious provisions, Union between Great Britain and Ireland was heralded as a major counterrevolutionary instrument. Just as the United Irishmen and their French allies had sought to prise Ireland and Great Britain apart, so Union was perceived as the prefect riposte to the separatists. There would henceforth be one kingdom, not kingdoms, separation would be impossible, it would disappear from the political agenda and, with it, any prospect of Irish revolution.

Moreover, the arguments that had been advanced in favour of Union, and the predictions made as to how Ireland would benefit from it, had been so categorical, so insistent and so optimistic, that that measure had, on the pro-Union side, become a panacea for all Irish ills. Those jealousies that had bedevilled Anglo-Irish relations would be removed at a stroke; English capital, English manners and English industry would flow into Ireland; talented Irishmen would find careers in the revitalised British empire; a new impartial legislature would convene in London and deal soberly and fairly with those knotty problems – of religion, education, tithes, even clerical salaries – that the old Irish parliament had been unable or unwilling to address. Above all, a mild government, resolutely embracing 'British standards' and acting on 'Union principles', a government that would be paternal, not repressive, acting in an even-handed, not one-sided way, would be instituted in post-Union Ireland.[11] In this way, the perceived evils of Ireland – endemic violence, sectarian divisions, chronic poverty, widespread disaffection and bankrupt institutions run by failed politicians – all of which were inextricably linked with *ancien régime* Ireland, would quickly fade from view under the new dispensation ushered in by Union.[12]

This new spirit infusing post-Union government in Ireland soon brought results. The draconian Insurrection Act of 1796, which had effectively abolished all rights at common law, was allowed to lapse, and so too was the act putting on hold habeas corpus: such legislation belonged to the repressive past, and was now out of place in that new country, post-Union Ireland. Charles Abbot, the first post-Union chief secretary, was determined to free Irish government from 'Irish animosities, prejudices and corruptions', and he grandly announced that the 'profligacy of Ireland before the Union', a condition he believed brought on by 'the looseness of Irish morals', was at an end.[13] What this meant in practice was that those who had formerly been key members of the viceroy's 'cabinet' at Dublin Castle – men such as John Beresford, Lord Clare and John Foster – now found themselves cold-shouldered. Bereford's conduct at the Revenue Board was investigated, Foster was kept at arms' length and Clare was ignored. Indeed, when he died in January 1802, Hardwicke's immediate reaction was one of good riddance.[14]

It was a similar story when Abbot was replaced as chief secretary by William Wickham in February 1802. Wickham immediately announced his intention of doing away 'with jobbery and the old system', and declared his conviction that no Irish politician, 'even the best', could be trusted, for they would 'one and all desert like rats in a sinking ship'.[15] He dismissed as exaggerated reports of agrarian disorder in Counties Limerick and Tipperary by claiming that 'there is nothing of rebellion in them nor even anything of religion', and he steadfastly resisted calls for the deployment of the Yeomanry on 'permanent duty, meaning only that they should receive permanent pay', for such a demand was an essential part of that 'system of jobbing' by local vested interests that he was determined to end.[16]

With such men at the helm in Dublin Castle, there was no disposition to accept and act on reports of subversion in the country, nor indeed to seek out intelligence on the disaffected. The rebels had been crushed in 1798, Great Britain was now at peace with France, and those Irish politicians sending in reports of disturbances, and darkly hinting at a wider conspiracy, could not be other than discredited alarmists playing their old game for their own purposes. Alexander Marsden, under-secretary in Dublin Castle, had little patience with them. Initially, he purported to be amused by such alarmist reports. For example, in January 1803, he ridiculed Prendergast Smith's warning that Tipperary town might be soon sacked by insurgents, and he rolled his eyes at the predicted consequences – 'his china would be broken and his favourite ladies all Lord knows what'.[17] Two months later, however, he was less indulgent: further reports of imminent disturbances led him to conclude that 'it is a sad thing that we are forever to be duped in this vile country'.[18]

In short, those in charge of government in post-Union Ireland were determined that there would be no going back to the bad old ways (as they saw them) of Ireland-before-the-Union. The principal features of that country – jobbery, corruption, sectarianism, repressive legislation and alarmist reports stressing the ineradicable nature of Irish disaffection and religious hatred – would steadily be eliminated as 'British standards' were relentlessly applied. Allegations of subversion, insurrection, popish plots, French emissaries, imminent massacres and the like, were to be treated with scepticism, if not incredulity, and regarded as a symptom of how much had yet to be done in healing the public mind in Ireland, rather than as evidence of a deep-laid conspiracy there. Given this mindset, and given their evident mistrust of all those who had been involved in pre-Union Irish politics, it was probably inevitable that the new men in Dublin Castle would miss some clues concerning the activities of Robert Emmet and his co-conspirators.

Emmet's rebellion constituted, in the final analysis, an intelligence failure on the part of Dublin Castle; and yet, on the face of it, this conclusion remains puzzling. We may remember that William Wickham, the chief secretary at the time of Emmet's rebellion, was no mere bureaucrat. *Au contraire*, he had been Pitt's spymaster in the 1790s, at the very centre of British counterintelligence in Europe, and he had been very well briefed on the continental plans of Irish subversives.[19] Surely he, of all people, would have been alert to the need for continued surveillance and intelligence gathering?

In fact, the reality was quite different for, in the years after 1798, the Castle's spy-network had undergone a huge reduction. Partly this was a result of what we may call natural wastage: a number of its key agents had died (Francis Higgins, Edward Newell), left Ireland (Thomas Collins, William Bird, possibly Captain Andrew MacNevin) or had had their cover blown through testifying in open court or otherwise (Nicholas Mageean, Thomas Reynolds, John Hughes). Again, its prime agent on the continent, Samuel Turner appears to have assumed that, with the signing of the Peace of Amiens, his services were no longer required. Similarly, Samuel Sproule, a very effective spy in Dublin from 1798 to 1800, subsequently took himself off to London where he dabbled in currency reform. Of the remaining agents who had been active in the pre-Union period, only Francis Magan, Leonard MacNally ('JW') and James McGucken continued to supply the Castle with intelligence. Magan, a Dublin barrister, became something of a recluse after the death of his handler, Francis Higgins, in January 1802, and largely confined his information to Catholic politics. MacNally, a barrister, continued to emphasise his connection with the long-standing radical, James Napper Tandy, then in Paris, and to ply the Castle with information gathered while he was out on the Munster circuit. McGucken, a solicitor based in Belfast, kept the Castle informed of developments among the remnants of the United Irish in the North-east.[20]

Those agents from the 1790s who for one reason or another stopped gathering information for Dublin Castle after 1800 were not replaced. Not only were substitutes not recruited, but there was a dramatic cutback in the amount of money paid out for information: a secret service bill that was running at around £13,000 per annum between 1797 and 1801, was ruthlessly pared back to just over £3,000 per annum (mostly for pre-Union commitments) between October 1801 and July 1803.[21] The inevitable result was that much of what passed for intelligence reports in the years before Emmet's rebellion were little more than angry, occasionally piteous, epistles from impoverished informers complaining of neglect, recalling past services and demanding adequate recompense.[22] In addition, just as the Castle apparently saw no need to recruit replacements, so too it seemed determined in the early years of the century to get rid of the agents that still remained on its books. The Boyle brothers, Thomas and Edward, had remained active after 1800, and two payments were made to them, one for 30 guineas in July 1800 and another for £200 in December 1802: but since the amounts were described in the ledger as 'in full discharge of services' and 'in full of all claims' respectively, we may surmise that these were seen as a final settling of their accounts.[23] Even the services of Samuel Turner, far and away the most valuable informer among the United Irishmen in France and Hamburg in the late 1790s, were dispensed with, and so too were those of Samuel Sproule. In post-Union Ireland, informers and spies were regarded as distasteful products of that inexhaustible Irish 'capacity for rapacity' held to have characterised pre-Union Ireland, and which, under the new dispensation, was no longer to be indulged but, rather, ruthlessly curtailed.

Moreover, if spies were in short supply after the Union, so too were spymasters. Edward Cooke had controlled the Castle's espionage network of the 1790s but, while he had been, as he modestly put it, 'not unsuccessful' in his efforts to gain intelligence on the United Irishmen, his sudden resignation and departure from Ireland in 1801 had thrown the entire information-gathering apparatus into disarray.[24] Agents felt abandoned by one to whom they had looked for reward, and because Cooke had kept so much intelligence in his head, rather than consign it to paper, there was to be no seamless transfer of office. Marsden, Cooke's successor, was criticised in the aftermath of Emmet's rebellion for being frankly 'incredulous' at reports of conspiracies. Admittedly, when war had resumed between Britain and France in March 1803, he had dismissed as bogus all 'reports of plots and meetings', explaining, 'I discover so many of these reports to be fabrications or upon insufficient surmises that it is impossible any evil of serious extent can be concealed'.[25] In addition, he had drawn further comfort from the fact that 'a separation has taken place between Catholics and Protestants which, however to be lamented in respect of the general welfare of this country, will work materially for us in case of Ireland becoming a seat of war'.[26] All in all, Marsden had concluded complacently, 'the cause of treason seems to have gone out of fashion in Ireland'.[27] And as we have seen, on ideological grounds, there had been little appetite for continuing, much less expanding, the 'dirty war' of the 1790s.

Again, the appointment of Pitt's spymaster, William Wickham, as Abbot's successor, in reality, had little impact on the Castle's intelligence gathering capacity. Wickham had not sought a position in Ireland, and had only taken the chief secretaryship (for which he was almost entirely unqualified)[28] because his activities in the 1790s had made him unwelcome in the major courts of Europe (neither Vienna nor Berlin would touch him). With hindsight, it may be suggested that Wickham was suffering from 'burn-out' as a result of his espionage operations on the continent, and that Ireland was attractive to him precisely because it appeared to offer him a quiet berth and a modest recompense rather than a scene for yet more cloak-and-dagger work.

To this picture of an administration which viewed with some distaste the grubbier features of British rule in Ireland, and which apparently believed that subversion and disaffection were almost entirely features of pre-Union Ireland, we may add the significant detail of strained relations between the London and Dublin governments in the early years of the Union. To an extent, problems of jurisdiction were inevitable, given that the Union had been put through with very little thought accorded to the administrative arrangements that would follow it. But Pelham, the former Irish chief secretary, appointed home secretary in July 1801, made matters worse by his domineering manner and, it seems, by his inefficiency.[29] Pelham had immediately clashed with Charles Abbot over their respective areas of authority, and he had continued the quarrel when Wickham was selected as Abbot's successor. Pelham's dilatory ways compounded the problem. The result was a frosty silence between London and Dublin in the years before Emmet's rebellion. Hardwicke was moved to complain of the 'very remarkable...want of efficiency and indeed of common attention in Lord Pelham's office',[30] while, revealingly, Wickham himself protested to Lord Eldon, the lord chancellor, at the lack of secret information coming into Dublin from 'your side of the water'. He revealed to Eldon in November 1802 that he had received almost no information on 'what our banished traitors are about in France and Germany, of all of which we used formerly to keep this government [Dublin] so very well informed', and he recalled that when he was in charge of espionage in the 1790s 'I never sat down to my dinner without fully informing Lord Castlereagh of everything that had passed that could in any way affect the cause of the disaffected in Ireland or throw the remotest light on their proceedings.'[31] In short, even if the Home Office had uncovered intelligence of Emmet's intentions, given the strained relations between it and the Castle, there could be no guarantee that this information would have been speedily passed on (or heeded). And of course, as was pointed out later, in these matters of foreign intelligence, Dublin Castle had no option but to rely entirely on London because 'the Irish government has no foreign ministers or foreign agents of any description and [has]...no means of obtaining intelligence of anything happening abroad'.[32]

Nor did the domestic information that the Castle did have coming in from its two prime agents, Leonard MacNally (JW) and James McGucken, give rise to any concern, much less alarm, for the letters and reports of both in the lead up to the rebellion were entirely reassuring. 'The spirit of disaffection sleeps' noted MacNally,[33] while McGucken claimed that nothing could go on without his knowledge.[34]

Lastly, Emmet conducted his affairs with the utmost secrecy. True, he was known to the authorities, but not nearly so well known as his brother, Thomas Addis Emmet, or James Napper Tandy, or Arthur O'Connor or the remaining leaders of the 1798 rebellion, and it was to these former chiefs that the Castle's attention was directed.[35] In its account of Emmet's rebellion, the Castle brushed away its failure to be forewarned by claiming that the conspiracy had 'received its chief protection from the insignificancy [sic] of the parties engaged in it', and from the fact that no more than eight persons had known about Emmet's arms depot, on which his 'whole game was staked'.[36] Nor had any correspondence been uncovered with France, which proved that the French authorities themselves had no idea what was going on.[37] Robert Emmet was, in the end, 'a general without an army'.[38]

If we put all of the foregoing together, the failure of Dublin Castle to discover in advance what Emmet had intended is readily understandable. The shattering defeat of the rebels in 1798 seemed to render inconceivable any resurgence, and divisions among the former rebels as to French objectives appeared to make this conclusion doubly secure. Post-Union government in its determination to put a distance between itself and the 'corrupt' pre-Union administration had wound down, or allowed to fall into disarray, its information-gathering network. New agents had not been recruited, and long-serving agents had not been adequately primed with fresh instruct-ions: more often, they had been given their marching orders. Cooke's resignation had been a huge blow to the Castle's spy-network, and Marsden, his replacement, was temperamentally averse to the work.[39] Nor was the appointment of Wickham as chief secretary an adequate answer. He had arrived in Dublin in August 1802, but had then left for London early in February 1803, and had not returned to Dublin until August 1803. Finally, Emmet's code of strict secrecy and his reliance only on tried and trusted men – no hint of mass participation here – effectively kept Dublin Castle in the dark concerning his plans.

IV

What conclusions can we draw from the preceding? It is hardly earthshaking to claim that governments everywhere and at all times relish the mystery and strive to protect the mystique of intelligence gathering and that, while keen to trumpet successes, or hint archly at them, they are much less keen to broadcast failures. The belief that Dublin Castle was omniscient and that its agents were ubiquitous was enormously serviceable to it in its war on subversion, real or imagined, in the nineteenth century. And its reputation for ubiquity and omniscience was nourished by writers such as Richard Robert Madden and William James Fitzpatrick, who wrote at length how the United Irishmen, and by implication later secret societies, were, indeed must be, riddled by informers, and that therefore it were best to stay out of them. A verdict heartily endorsed by the Catholic hierarchy. And of course, the Castle had its successes to support these claims; but it also had its failures; and perhaps living on its reputation would in the end contribute to that sick smile with which Nathan reacted to the IRB rebellion at Easter 1916.

NOTES

1 In this essay I have drawn on my 'The invasion that never was: naval and military aspects of the French expedition to Bantry Bay, 1796', in J.A. Murphy (ed.), *The French are in the Bay: The Expedition to Bantry Bay, 1796* (Cork, 1997), pp. 48–72; '"The cause of treason seems to have gone quite out of fashion in Ireland": Dublin Castle and Robert Emmet', in Patrick Geoghegan (ed.), *Robert Emmet* (Dublin, forthcoming); and lastly, 'Informers, informants and information: the secret history of the 1790s reconsidered', in T. Bartlett, D. Dickson, D. Keogh and K. Whelan

(eds), *1798, a Bicentennial Perspective* (Dublin, 2003), pp. 406–22.

2 Quoted in Keith Jeffery (ed.), *The Sinn Féin Rebellion as They Saw It* (Dublin, 1999), p. 114. In fact, British intelligence was quite aware of what the rebels were planning but chose not to alert Dublin Castle lest sources of information in Germany were compromised.

3 See the valuable survey of French invasion projects in M. de la Poer Beresford, 'Ireland in French Strategy, 1691–1789' (MLitt dissertation, Trinity College Dublin, 1975).

4 For an important reassessment of the French navy under the Revolution, see W.J. Cormack, *Revolution and Political Conflict in the French Navy, 1789–94* (Cambridge, 1995).

5 Portland to Camden, 29 November 1796 (TNA, 100/62/348-9)

6 For reassessments of the rebellion in Wexford see the essays in Bartlett et al., *1798: A Bicentennial Perspective.*

7 See the collection of reports into the United Irish conspiracy published in *Report from the Committee of Secrecy of the [Irish] House of Commons* (Dublin, 1798).

8 For Mountnorris's exertions, and for Wexford generally, see, L.M. Cullen, 'The 1798 rebellion in Wexford: United Irishman organisation, membership, leadership', in K.Whelan (ed.) *Wexford: History and Society* (Dublin, 1988), pp. 248–96.

9 For further discussion of this point see my introduction to Thomas Bartlett, *Revolutionary Dublin: The Letters of Francis Higgins to Dublin Castle, 1795–1801* (Dublin, 2004).

10 Edward Cooke to Buckingham, 28 July 1803, in Duke of Buckingham and Chandos, *Memoirs of the Court and Cabinets of George the Third* (4 vols, London, 1853–5), iii, pp. 316–17; Castlereagh to Melville, 1 Aug. 1803: W. L. Clements Library, Ann Arbor, MI, Melville MSS; Redesdale to Percival, 16 Aug. 1803: PRONI, T3030/7/7: Yorke to Hardwicke, 29 July 1803: BL, Add. MSS. 35702, fo. 281.

11 Charles Abbot to Charles Yorke, 28 Aug. 1801: BL, Add. MSS 35711/102.

12 For the classic statements of what Union would mean for Ireland, see Pitt's speeches on Union, especially those of 23 Jan. and 31 Jan. 1799: *Parliamentary History of England*, xxxiv, , pp. 242–9; *A Review of a Speech of the Rt. Hon. William Pitt* (Dublin, 1799).

13 Abbot to Yorke, 28 Aug. 1801: BL, Add MSS 35711/102. We may note that Abbot, when seeking to oblige Lord Rossmore was flexible enough to accept the fishing village of Arklow as eligible for a grant under a scheme to promote 'internal navigation': Abbot to Hardwicke, 13 July 1801: BL, Add. MSS. 35711/81.

14 Hardwicke to Yorke, and Yorke to Hardwicke, 18 Jan., 1 Feb. 1802: PRONI, Hardwicke–Yorke transcripts, T3451.

15 Wickham to Abbot, 15 Dec. 1802: PRONI, T2627/5/F/23; Wickham to Addington, 18 Dec. 1802: PRONI, T2627/5/D/34.

16 Wickham to Liverpool, 13 Dec. 1802: PRONI, T2627/5/O/36.

17 Marsden to Wickham, recvd. 10 Jan. 1803: PRONI, T2627/5/K/3.

18 Marsden to Wickham, 4 Mar. 1803: PRONI, T2627/5/K/58.

19 For Wickham's career in the 1790s, see Harvey Mitchell, *Underground War Against Revolutionary France: The Missions of W. Wickham, 1794–1800* (Manchester, 1965); see also R.G. Thorne, 'William Wickham', in idem (ed.), *The History of Parliament: The House of Commons, 1790–1820* (5 vols, London, 1986), v, pp. 549–53.

20 For details on Higgins, Magan, Sproule, Reynolds, Turner, McNevin and the others see Bartlett, *Revolutionary Dublin*, pp. 13–70.

21 Calculations based on the sums listed in 'Account of the Secret Service money', in J.T. Gilbert (ed.), *Documents relating to Ireland, 1795–1804* (Dublin, 1893), pp. 1–88.

22 See the lengthy letter from McGucken, entirely taken up with his pension: McGucken to [Marsden?], 2 Feb. 1802: NAI Rebellion Papers, 620/10/121/3.

23 Gilbert, 'Secret service accounts', pp. 44, 72.

24 Cooke's memorandum on his career [1801]; BL, Add. MSS 33107, fo. 165.
25 Addington to Wickham, 15 Aug. 1803: PRONI, T2627/5/D/17; Marsden to Wickham, 9 Apr. 1803: PRONI, T2627/5/K/117.
26 Marsden to Wickham, 16 Mar. 1803: PRONI, T2627/5/K/77.
27 Marsden to Wickham, 4 Apr. 1803: PRONI, T2627/5/K/108. In fairness, John Pollock, a level-headed loyalist who had played an important role in Irish espionage in the late 1790s, had written to Marsden shortly after he had succeeded Cooke, advising him 'be assured nothing can stir here without my knowing it instantly': Pollock to Marsden, 25 Sept. 1801, NAI Rebellion Papers, 620/49/55.
28 He had no parliamentary experience, and appears to have viewed the position (for which he was second choice and which he only obtained through his friendship with Abbot) as a recompense for his failure to obtain a diplomatic pension or posting. Thorne, 'William Wickham'.
29 D.R. Fisher, 'Thomas Pelham', in Thorne (ed.), *The History of Parliament: The House of Commons, 1790–1820* (5 vols, London, 1986), iv. Much to everyone's amusement, a letter from Lord Redesdale highly critical of Pelham's conduct and efficiency, was in error delivered to Pelham himself: Wickham to Marsden, 14 Feb. 1803: PRONI, T2627/5/K/23.
30 Hardwicke to Wickham, 3 May 1802: PRONI, T2627/5/E/35.
31 Wickham to Eldon, 23 Nov. 1802: PRONI, T2627/5/O/33.
32 Redesdale to 'my dear Sir', 14 Dec. 1803: PRONI, T3030/10/9.
33 JW to [Cooke?], 13 May 1801: NAI Rebellion Papers, 620/10/118/12.
34 McGucken to Pollock, 22 Sept. 1802: NAI Rebellion Papers 620/10/131/16.
35 Both T.A. Emmet and Arthur O'Connor were reported in Ireland in March 1803, but the sightings were pronounced 'vague': Marsden to Wickham, 11, 29 Mar. 1803: PRONI, T2627/5/K/75, 96
36 Marsden, 'General statement...relating to the insurrection of 23 July 1803', in *Memoirs and Correspondence of Viscount Castlereagh...*, ed. marquess of Londonderry (12 vols, 1848–53), iv, pp. 327–9.
37 Ibid., p. 330.
38 Redesdale to 'my dear sir', 14 Dec. 1803: PRONI, T3030/10/9; see also Hardwicke's comments along the same lines: 'The plan of rising in Dublin...was a perfect secret among the leaders themselves...[which]...at the same time that it diminishes our chance of procuring good information,...must greatly diminish their chance of success at any point': Hardwicke to Yorke, 11 Aug. 1803, BL, Add. MSS. 35702, fos. 300-5. I owe this reference to Dr Gillian O'Brien.
39 Marsden to Wickham, 16 Mar. 1803: PRONI, T2627/5/K/77.

The consuls who helped sink a fleet: Union consuls in Ireland, intelligence and the American civil war

Bernadette Whelan

In 1861, the American civil war broke out when the southern states seceded from the United States of America (the Union). There were many reasons but the most significant was the future status of the institution of slavery. The war would be a land and a sea conflict. The context to this study is the Union government's preservation of its naval blockade of the southern coastline from New Jersey to Florida and the Gulf of Mexico and the Confederate government's circumvention of it. The Union administration, led by Abraham Lincoln, started with the advantage of having a navy, money to expand it, yards for shipbuilding, skilled craftsmen, trained crews and unblockaded ports. The Confederate administration under the leadership of Jefferson Davis, had few, if any, of these advantages.[1] Consequently, from the beginning of the civil war one of the primary aims of the Confederate government was to create a modern navy, while its northern counterpart attempted to thwart this move.

Several European countries, despite their neutral positions, contributed to this naval build-up by selling arms, equipment and ships to the southern states. Consequently, the Confederate authorities enjoyed some success in obtaining foreign-built warships but their efforts could never match their plans. There were many reasons why the southern government did not get all of the ships that it wanted, or indeed was offered by private individuals. A combination of European neutrality and opposition to slavery, using inexperienced Confederate agents and diplomats abroad, uncertain credit, weak economic planning and competition for ships prevented the Confederate authorities from achieving what they wanted. But one of the most significant reasons was the work of Union consuls.[2] Depending on location, these men worked against Confederate efforts to build a modern naval force. During the period 1861–5, therefore, many consuls acquired new duties, including providing valuable intelligence and information on any unusual movements on land or sea in their districts. Written from a Union perspective, this chapter unravels the role of Union consuls based in Ireland in the efforts of their govermnent and specifically of the State Department's intelligence network, to prevent the Confederacy from building its navy and supplying its war effort.

UNION CONSULS IN IRELAND, 1861

In 1861, there were US consuls located in Belfast, Dublin, Queenstown, Londonderry and Galway, and commercial, also called consular, agents in Limerick, Athlone, Sligo, Ballymena, Newry, Lurgan and Waterford. They were responsible to the US consul general based in the London legation while the US minister to Britain exercised overall responsibility for Britain and Ireland. The consuls were US citizens, appointed as a result of the patronage system, who lived on salaries, fees or private incomes and had no pension. Their functions related largely to promoting trade and commerce between the United States and Ireland, dealing with emigration matters and protecting the interests of US citizens in their districts.[3] Their tenure was insecure and could be ended upon a change of US government.

Among the immediate tasks facing President Abraham Lincoln was to keep the Union together and, secondly, to repay political debts. Out of office since 1851, the Republican leadership spent the first days of office making appointments and the consular system was not excluded from their patronage. Beverly Tucker who was replaced in Liverpool as consul by Thomas H. Dudley, became a Confederate agent in Britain throughout the war. Patrick J. Devine replaced Robert Dowling in Cork. Devine described his predecessor 'as a most violent partisan, and advocate of the southern rebellion and equally violent in his abuse of the administration'. These suspicions were confirmed in June 1863 when Confederate President Jefferson Davis appointed Dowling commercial agent for the Confederate states in Cork.[4] Elsewhere in Ireland, Thomas McGinn replaced Alexander Henderson as consul in Londonderry in September 1861, John Young replaced Theodore Frean in Belfast and Henry B . Hammond replaced Samuel Talbot in Dublin. William Boxwell West owed his appointment as consul in Galway to the influence and friendship' of Secretary of State William Seward and Seward's 'sympathy for all foreigners and Irishmen'.[5] It fell to these men to protect Union interests during the civil war. Immediately after the war broke out Seward requested Union consuls to supply three categories of information detailing Confederate ship building and buying, cargoes carried by Confederate vessels and the routes they followed.[6]

INFORMATION ABOUT CONFEDERATE SHIPBUILDING

The key to Europe's response to the outbreak of the civil war was Britain. For economic and political reasons, she was unwilling to intervene on either side even though she was increasingly dependent on grain imports from the North and northern markets in which to sell British manufactures. Secretary Seward clarified Union–British relations on 27 April 1861, 'Great Britain cannot recognise the Confederate states and retain the friendship of the United States.[7] Britain did not recognise the Confederacy but her declaration of neutrality in May 1861 angered Seward and Lincoln because it implied recognition of the Confederacy's belligerent status. Charles Francis Adams, Union Minister to Britain, and Union consuls in Britain and Ireland diligently ensured that British neutrality was implemented. The policy also greatly complicated the work of Commander James Dunwoody Bulloch, the Confederate naval officer, who was in charge of acquiring and arming Confederate vessels in Europe and in late spring 1861 was on his way to Liverpool.

Liverpool was a convenient port for shipping supplies to the northern and southern states in addition to being a ship building centre and it quickly became an important centre of Confederate and Union intrigue. Bulloch arrived in the city on 3 June 1861 with a budget of one million Confederate dollars. He worked swiftly and succeeded in avoiding the Foreign Enlistment Act (1819) that forbade British subjects from 'equipping, furnishing, fitting out or arming, of any ship or vessel, with intent or in order that such ship or vessel shall be employed in the service' of a belligerent state. He circumvented British neutrality laws by contracting with British businesses to build unarmed vessels. Once built, the ships left the yards without armaments that were later fitted at sea outside British jurisdiction. Both the CSS *Florida* and CSS *Alabama* were built in Liverpool boat yards and were released to the Confederate side before sufficiently acceptable evidence could be presented to the British government by Thomas Haines Dudley, Union consul in Liverpool, and Adams, to have them seized. The onus was on the Americans to provide evidence of a violation of British law.

The CSS *Alabama* escaped on 28 July 1862, the day before the British government agreed that 'the vessel, cargo and stores may be properly condemned'.[8] Immediately Consul Dudley sent out a circular to all consuls warning them to be vigilant and to prevent the vessel from being 'armed or fitted out in your jurisdiction'.[9] A few days later Consul Devine in Queenstown had learnt from his informants and confirmed to Secretary Seward that 'a confederate privateer built and fitted up by Mr Laird of Birkenhead, sailed from Liverpool on, or about, the 29th ultimo, laden as it is believed with war material for the southern rebels'.[10] On 15 August, Consul Young in Belfast received a note from George Hill, one of his agents who lived in Ballycastle, County Antrim, on the north-east coast, that 'No. 290 [*Alabama*] passed this place on 31 July' and it took no notice of the coastguard's attempt to stop it.[11] Consul West in Galway on the west coast of Ireland seemed also to have knowledge of the *Alabama* building project in the Laird yard and reported to Seward on 16 August that this accounted for the delay in finishing two steamers for the Galway Line. West continued, 'I have had confidential agents on the western coast watching for her, and got inforrnation, I fear too late, of her being in Killary Harbour last Saturday night, and left in the morning westward, having, it now appears, taken in her guns...by previous arrangement offthat coast, the following day.' He was in no doubt but that the British authorities had turned a blind eye 'to the whole proceedings of this Rebel gun-boat!'[12] Collins suggests that it was possible for the Alabama to have come into Killary harbour and that it may have docked also in Kingstown, outside Dublin.[13] Hull no. 290 was met in the Azores by two supply boats, it was armed and commissioned as the CSS *Alabama* and it went on to sink many Union merchant vessels.[14]

Bulloch had circumvented a legal loophole in British legislation by having a private business house build the ship without armaments, recruit a crew from its own companies, sail the completed vessel outside British territory and then transfer it to a Confederate captain and crew for outfitting. Secretary Seward and Minister Adams in London had learned a valuable lesson. Subsequently, Secretary Seward developed an intelligence network based on consular inform-ation that supplied the State, War and Navy Departments with information on Confederate shipbuilding activity throughout Britain and Ireland.[15]

Every Union consul located in cities and ports where ships could be built and bought and cargoes bought and sold developed intelligence networks. Already many consuls received information from local contacts but, in the war situation, they needed regular and reliable information and used spies, informants and agents to gather intelligence. But, throughout the war, Union consuls in Ireland shared the view that their detection and investigation work on Confederate activities was hampered by the weak support from the Irish people for the Union cause. At the beginning of the civil war, nationalists in Ireland regretted the possibility of the break-up of the Union but, as the conflict got underway and news came through of heavy Irish casualties at the battle of Friedricksburg in December 1862 and the New York draft riots in mid-1863, there was a gradual drift of support to the Confederate side.[16] Many of the merchant and administration class were firm supporters of the Confederacy. The Union consuls believed that this opposition hampered their intelligence work and emigration from Ireland to the Union states to enlist or work.

In December 1861, Consul Hammond reported from Dublin that 'there are many influential persons...who sympathise with the secessionists' and that southern recruitment officers were active in Dublin. In Belfast, Young felt 'deep disappointment and regret at the state of public feeling with regard to our affairs in America'. He had expected 'that the people of this country, from their strong dislike of the institution of slavery, would naturally sympathise with the needful struggles of a paternal government for self existence, I am greatly disappointed in this. Most of the papers in this town show strong partiality for the south – magnify insignificant advantages into victories.'[17] Even when there were Union victories in 1862, Young found that the 'people here will hardly allow themselves to believe it'.[18] Along with the newspapers, he identified the 'mercantile class' and the 'Catholic clergy' to be the main supporters of the Confederate cause, while the 'middling and working classes' supported the Union cause. Young wanted to make a public address explaining the Union cause but abided by Seward's instructions not to interfere in political affairs; neither did he wish to give the British government 'cause for his recall'.[19] Hammond had no such qualms and encouraged Seward to launch a propaganda campaign in Irish and English newspapers to gather support for the Union cause.[20]

One consequence of this limited support was that Hammond in Dublin found it increasingly difficult to gather intelligence concerning 'suspicious vessels' from customs officials and instead obtained it from 'the lower classes of the people, those who usually emigrate to the United States' and were waiting at the dockside.[21] Among the people used by John Young in Belfast in May 1862, were his clerk and a US citizen, a Mr Hopkins who was a trader in tea.[22] Patrick Devine's informants in Queenstown in County Cork on the southern coast were 'true and genuine friends of the government' and included people working for the shipping agents and 'rebel' sympathisers James Seymour in Queenstown and Isaac Notter based further along the coast in Crookhaven.[23] By late 1864, Devine's replacement, Edwin Eastman, asked Seward if he could live in Cork city instead of Queenstown because the 'merchants of Queenstown...are all in favour of the southern cause as well as most of the wealthy inhabitants'. The port had 'become a very unpleasant place for a consul to reside'.[24] Not only did Eastman have to cope with the merchants' opposition but he had to counteract the intelligence work of former US consul Robert Dowling, who was appointed Confederate commercial agent in summer 1863. Dowling had set up office in the merchant James Seymour's office in Queenstown and flew the Confederate flag outside it. His purpose was to act as a conduit for information gathered from local merchants and a network of pursers on the Inman-owned steamers trading between Richmond, New York and Queenstown. Subsequently, Dowling transmitted this information to the Confederate ministers in London and Paris. Eastman managed to identify one of Dowling's informants to be a Mr Fearnagh, the purser on the Inman Line and he advised Secretary Seward to have a 'good detective' watch him when he landed in New York on the *City of London* at the end of July 1863.[25] By April 1864, three prominent Queenstown merchants, Messrs Seymour, Scallen and Cummings, were all actively supporting the confederacy and passing on whatever information came their way to Dowling.[26]

By 1862 the idea of a paid intelligence service was circulating among the Union consuls. Young in Belfast, who believed that 'southern men' had been 'actively at work' in the city, wrote to Secretary Seward in August 1862 asking for funds 'to employ a private observer at our discretion...From the general public we can learn little' because their sympathy lay with the 'accursedly bad cause'.[27] In the following year West, who operated between the Galway and Dublin consulates, suggested to Seward that one individual be paid to co-ordinate the intelligence activities of all consuls in Ireland.[28] The requests were unsuccessful. But Young did not give up. In 1864, after Seward asked all consuls for information about persons selling vessels as blockade-runners or selling munitions of war to the south, Young wrote again to Seward, 'The only possible plan of knowing what may be going on here would be to pay a secret agent. About 75 dollars per annum would do this but you are aware that I have no such fund at my disposal. I think, however, that I ought to have such a fund and that it would pay itself fifty times over.'[29] Clearly, he felt that his sources of information were insufficient but that greater effort would bring better results Finally, Seward established a 'secret service fund'.[30] Some of the people used in Britain and Ireland were dockhands, workers in shipyards, unemployed sailors, dock masters, Lloyds' register agents, customs inspectors, ships' captains, crews and private detectives.

The Union intelligence network failed to stop the building and departure of the *Florida* and *Alabama* in 1862 but Consul Dudley and Minister Adams prevented the departure of the gunboat *Alexandra*, built by William Miller of Liverpool, and two turreted ironclad rams, built by Laird and sons in Birkenhead. These warships never reached the Confederate navy but Bulloch and other confederate agents continued to place orders in British and French shipyards.[31] However, due to the systematic intelligence gathering and the persistent diplomacy, only five European-built warships became active Confederate vessels. So some new vessels were built and delivered to the Confederates but most were not. The last delivery, the CSS *Shenandoah*, built on the Clyde river in Scotland, was still attacking

Union ships in the Pacific Ocean in late June 1865 when its captain learnt of the defeat of all the other Confederate forces. No ships were recorded as having been built in Ireland for the Confederacy but newly built ships came into Queenstown for supplies during trial runs. Also, vessels were bought in Ireland for Confederate use as blockade-runners.

INFORMATION ABOUT CONFEDERATE PURCHASING OF VESSELS AND CARGOES

Immediately after the Union naval blockade was installed in April 1861, the Confederate government resorted to using a variety of methods to export its cotton and tobacco and import war supplies. The principle blockade-running routes were to and from Bermuda, Nassau and the southern ports of Wilmington, Charleston and Savannah. Initially, the Confederate government permitted privately owned vessels to run the blockade and make significant profits. In May 1861, Union consuls were instructed by Secretary Seward to gather intelligence and information about, first, vessels sold as blockade-runners and, second, the nature of any assistance given to such vessels.[32] But before May 1861, Henry Hammond in Dublin reported to Seward, Adams and Dudley that the steamer *Herald* that travelled between Dublin and Liverpol had been sold to Cunard, Wilson and Company in Liverpool for the 'service of the rebels'. Subsequently, the steamer 'very suddenly' left Dublin at night for an unknown port. Hammond learnt it had gone to Liverpool 'to fit out as a "privateer" or to take cargo and then try to run the blockade'. The steamer was 'well-known' in Europe because of its swiftness in making journeys and Hammond felt that if 'the rebels have bought her they may do much mischief with her'. He could not find out its destination because there was 'silence' in Dublin among the mercantile classes. Adams and Dudley confirmed that the *Herald* was receiving a cargo in Liverpool for Bermuda where it was expected to try and break the blockade. The *Herald* left Liverpool for Charleston on 15 February but had to stop into Falmouth four days later because of severe weather. Hammond hoped that this delay would give the Union's blockade squadron time to capture it when it eventually arrived off the Confederate seaboard. He reported on 1 March that it was heading for Savannah and under full steam would make one and half miles in one hour.[33] Eventually it penetrated the Union naval blockade, which was leaky at this early stage of the war.[34]

In the following year, 1862, private efforts continued on behalf of the southern government to purchase ships and run the blockade. Young in Belfast reported on 7 May that the *Adela*, a small swift steamer operating between Belfast and Scotland, was bought by a Mr McDowell, formerly of New Orleans and residing in Dublin, from a Mr Malcolmson who lived in Waterford and that it would be put into service on behalf of the southern Confederacy. Immediately, Young sent word to Hammond in Dublin. And, on the following day, Hammond had learnt that the *Adela* was ready to run the blockade with English goods and to bring out cotton. Young's agents were busy with other business and he found it 'nearly impossible' to find out more information, 'my enquiries were met universally by negatives'. Consequently, he employed a Mr Hopkins, a tea trader, who boarded the *Adela* in Belfast on the pretext that he wanted a passage on the vessel. Hopkins learnt that the vessel would be departing immediately; he could not learn the destination but Young believed it to be Bermuda. Eventually the *Adela* was captured by the Union side and Young welcomed the news in August 1862.[35]

Union naval victories in April and May 1862 off the New Orleans and Norfolk coasts greatly increased the effectiveness of the Union blockade of the southern coastline and reduced revenue for the Confederate states from the sale of cotton. But this did not affect the efforts of blockade-runners and the detection efforts of the Union consuls. In November 1862, former US consul to Dublin Hugh Keenan informed Seward about the arrival of the *Eagle* in Belfast port. It had carried passengers up and down the river Clyde in Scotland but was being refitted in Belfast to carry contraband cargo into the southern states. Young's agents learnt from the crew that gunpowder was brought from London for the *Eagle* and that it would leave Belfast in early November for Madeira and Nassau with a final destination of a creek or river near Charleston in South Carolina. Young spent two nights outdoors himself watching the vessel in case the gunpowder was taken on board. The vessel finally left Belfast in early December 1862 and bad weather forced it into Dublin port before heading to Queenstown to take on coal. A week later, Hammond in Dublin circulated details about its colour, insignia and design. He felt that the only reason the southerners purchased it was because of its speed and he had learnt that its captain had offered very high wages to obtain a pilot familiar with the Confederate coastline but had failed.[36] In December 1862, Hammond reported that there were 'parties now in Dublin trying to buy other steamers and schooners...to use in evading the blockade'.[37]

Despite a stronger blockade, in 1863 there was evidence of continued Confederate success. In March, the *Fanny Lewis* arrived in Queenstown from Wilmington, North Carolina, 'having run the blockade' with a cargo of cotton resin and pitch to be discharged at Liverpool.[38] Hugh Keenan reported in June on the *Heroine* that was purchased by 'rebel' agents in Belfast and was being fitted out to run the blockade.[39] Two months later, the Confederate diplomatic representative, James Mason, arrived in Dublin. William West surmised that they might be about to commission two ironclad Clyde-built steamers then in Kingstown harbour as blockade-runners for the southern government.[40] Much of this early trade was in the hands of private blockade-runners until 1863, when there were shortages of vital supplies in the southern states. Cargoes destined for the south were trapped in foreign ports and, when Confederate leaders discovered that some of these cargoes did not contain vital supplies for the military and civilian population but lucrative luxury goods, there was a change in policy.

Beginning in 1864, the southern government instituted its own system of blockade-runners. More than one hundred vessels were bought either solely by the government, or in partnership with private companies, to carry government cargo. West reported in November 1864 that thirty-six new steamers had left the Clyde within the last nine months to run the blockade.[41] But many of the Confederate ships turned out to be 'unfit, unlucky or untimely' and none were successful.[42] Nevertheless, this new Confederate policy led to more detailed instructions being issued by Seward to Union consuls in early 1864. Now they would report 'any persons who may have given aid to the rebellion by furnishing blockade-runners or munitions of war'.[43] The directive had little relevance to consuls in Ireland as most had continuously reported on blockade-running but it became more detailed from this time onwards. On 28 April 1864, Young indicated that Belfast had not been 'heavily implicated' in blockade-running. Since 1861, four vessels were sold out of Belfast to run the blockade and two were sold purely for profit not political motivation. But he could not give more detailed information because he had 'few friends'.[44]

Yet, not all the information on the blockade-runners was accurate or indeed reported. In 1861 Hammond in Dublin learnt that a vessel owned by V. O'Connor, a tobacco merchant who had lived in Richmond, Virginia, was going to run the blockade with a cargo of porter but instead it went directly to New York, where the cargo was promptly seized. Eastman in Queenstown discovered the invalidity of one of his own reports dated 8 June 1863, which stated the *Smoker* was intended for 'the southern confederacy'. Four days later, he reported that it had legitimate business with the Mexican government.[45] In late 1865, Eastman was instructed by Secretary Seward to find proof that Irish manufacturers had traded with the 'rebel' government during the war. Seward believed that blankets and army clothing, manufactured in Cork and Limerick factories, were delivered to the southern states along with arms. But absence of any proof of payment meant that the Union government could not 'touch' either the contractor or manufacturers.[46] Then on 29 October 1864, West in

Dublin, acting on information from Minister Adams in London, reported the arrival of the blockade-runner *Evelyn* at Foynes port on the river Shannon on Thursday 27 October. Adams had signalled that it would take on arms and clothing. The supply of army clothing came from the Limerick Clothing Company owned by Peter Tait. The vessel also took on coal and left on 28 October. West believed that the arms must have been hidden inside the bales and cases but he had no proof as the Customs officials did not conduct an internal search of the cargo and the Limerick consular agent, M.R. Ryan, had no other source of information.[47] Neither did Eastman find any further information about payments to Tait or report on his other vessels.[48]

USE OF CONSULAR INFORMATION

What happened to all the consular reports, despatches, rumours, affidavits, vessel descriptions, drawings of vessels and maps about Confederate naval activity sent by Union consuls to the State Department? When consuls first collected the information, they evaluated it for usefulness, immediately sent relevant parts to neighbouring consuls and then turned it into a coherent despatch. The latter was sent to the Secretary of State, other consuls and, in the case of Ireland, Adams in London. From 1861 to 1866, Frederick Seward, assistant secretary of state, was responsible for sending and receiving consular despatches.[49] His officials collated the consular intelligence and transmitted a printed report to the naval forces. This process could take as much as three weeks as most of the communication was by mail and was sent on scheduled steamship routes. In addition the Union North Atlantic Blockading Squadron printed bulletins for circulation to their commanders. This meant that a Union commander off the Carolina coast might know the name and description of a new blockade-runner before it had arrived in the area.[50]

This intelligence system, particularly the information received from the consuls in Irish and British ports, expanded from one where a few individual consuls such as Hammond, West, Young, Devine and Eastman worked on their own and paid privately for information, into an intelligence operation employing agents also. Much to Eastman's satisfaction, more than half of the twenty-five steamers that called at Queenstown in 1863 and that he reported as possible blockade-runners were captured by the Union navy.[51] In the following year, he sent reports on thirty-eight blockade-runners and was instructed to report by telegram on every steamer arriving and departing from Queenstown. Also in 1865, Queenstown became a Consulate Despatch Agency for the Union, which placed Eastman at the centre of a network whereby he received and passed on intelligence on the movement of 'rebel' vessels from Union consuls Horatio J. Perry in Madrid, Thomas Dudley in Liverpool and John M. Jackson in Halifax, to the State and War Departments.[52] Although some consular stations used the telegraph to send important messages, its use was not widespread because the State Department considered it no more safe than the written report and it was expensive.

CONCLUSION

For the consuls on the ground in Ireland and elsewhere, the civil war years had been diflcult. In September 1864, Young in Belfast finally ventured that the 'few true friends of America here are now in good spirits'. It was not until a Union victory was almost assured that West, based in Galway and Dublin, reported in January 1865 'a wonderful change in public opinion'.[53] But these few hundred mostly untrained employees helped to defeat the efforts of the Confederate government to build, buy and equip ships for military and economic purposes. The consistent gathering of intelligence combined with Minister Adams' diplomacy in London denied the Confederate states these vital resources. The end of the war reduced the consuls' intelligence activities but the legacy of the war continued in other ways, with consuls seeking pensions, bounties and back pay for relatives of deceased soldiers and sailors, along with knowledge of the where-abouts of missing soldiers and sailors on both sides.

NOTES

1   This article is a work in progress and part of a wider study on the origins and concerns of the US consular service in Ireland between 1790 and 1913. The historiography on the American civil war is extensive. The following have been consulted: Clement Eaton, *A History of the Southern Confederacy* (New York); D.P. Crook, *The North, the South and the Powers, 1861–15* (New York, 1974).
2   Kevin J. Foster, 'The diplomats who sank a fleet: the Confederacy's undelivered European fleet and the Union consular service', *Prologue: Quarterly of the National Archives and Records Administraion*, 33, 3 (2001), p. 182.
3   The first representative of the US government appointed as US consul in Dublin was William Knox in 1790.
4   Charles Stuart Kennedy, *The American Consul: A History of the United States Consular Service, 1776–1914* (Westport, CT, 1990), pp. 127, 129. National Archives and Records Administration (NARA), General Records of the Department of State, Record Group 59 (hereafter S/D), Consular Despatches, Despatches from US consuls in Cork (hereafter Despatches from), 1800–1906, vol. 4, roll 4, T196, Devine to Seward, 30 June 1861; ibid., Despatches from Cork, 1800–1906, vol. 5, roll 5, T196, Eastman to Seward, 8 July 1863.
5   NARA, S/D, Despatches from Londonderry, 1798–1906, vol. 2, roll 2, T216, McGinn to Seward, 28 September 1861; ibid., Despatches from Galway, 1834–63,

vol. 1, roll 1, T570, West to Seward, 10 July 1861.

6 During the civil war, Union consuls were required to report on the arrival and departure of Union ships from Irish ports and an additional duty was to assist with recruitment for the Union forces under the guise of promoting emigration to the Union States. The controversy surrounding the visit of the USS *Kearsarge* to Queenstown on 2 November 1863 will be examined in the wider study.

7 NARA, S/D, Diplomatic Instructions of the Department of State 1801–1906, M77, roll 76, RG59, Seward to Dallas, 27 April 1861.

8 Foster, 'The diplomats who sank a fleet', p. 182.

9 NARA, S/D, Despatches from Cork, 1800–1906, vol. 5, roll 5, T196, Circular, 30 July 1862

10 Ibid., Devine to Seward, 5 August 1862.

11 Ibid., Hill to Devine, 15 August 1862; ibid., Young to Seward, 16 August 1862.

12 Ibid., Despatches from Galway, 1834–1863, vol. 1, roll 1, T570, West to Seward, 16 August 1862.

13 Timothy Collins, *Transatlantic Triumph and Heroic Failure: The Story of the Galway Line* (Cork, 2002), p. 122.

14 Foster, 'The diplomats who sank a fleet', p. 185.

15 Ibid., p. 185.

16 Toby Joyce, 'The American Civil War and Irish nationalism', History, Ireland, 4, 2 (1996), pp. 38–9; Kerby A. Miller, *Emigrants and Exiles: Ireland and the Irish Exodus to North America* (New York, 1985), p. 364.

17 NARA, S/D, Despatches from Dublin, vol. 3, roll 3, T199, Hammond to Seward, 3 December 1861; ibid., Despatches from Belfast, 1798–1906, vol. 2, roll 3, T368, Young to Seward, 30 October 1861.

18 Ibid., vol. 2, roll 4, T368, Young to Seward, 14 May 1862.

19 Ibid., vol. 2, roll 3, T368, Young to Seward, 30 October 1861; ibid., roll 4, T368, Young to Seward, newspaper cutting, Young to Seward, 14 August 1862.

20 Ibid., Despatches from Dublin, 1790–1906, vol. 3, roll 3, T199, Hammond to Seward, 22 January 1862.

21 Despatches from Dublin, 1790–1906, vol. 3, roll 3, Tl99, Hammond to Seward, 5 June 1862.

22 Ibid., Despatches from Belfast, 1798–1906, vol. 1, roll 4, T368, Young to Seward, 2 May 1862.

23 Ibid., Despatches from Cork, 1800–1906, vol. 5, roll 5, T196, Devine to Seward, 17 July 1862; ibid., Notter to Seward, 3 February 1863; ibid., Despatches from Cork, 1800–1906, vol. 6, roll 6, T196, Eastman to Seward, 4 May 1864.

24 Ibid., Despatches from Cork, 1809–1906, vol. 6, roll 6, T196, Eastman to Seward, 4 May 1864.

25 Ibid., vol. 5, roll 5, T196, Eastman to Seward, 11 July 1863.

26 Ibid., vol. 6, roll 6, T196, Eastman to Seward, 4 May 1864.

27 Ibid., Despatches from Belfast, 1798–1906, vol. 2, roll 3, T368, Young to Seward, 30 October 1861; ibid., vol. 1, roll 4, T368, Young to Seward, 20 August 1862.

28 Ibid., Despatches from Dublin, 1790–1906, vol. 4, roll 4, T199, West to Seward, 21 August 1863.

29 Ibid., Despatches from Belfast, 1798–1906, vol. 1, roll 4, T368, Young to Seward, 20 April 1864.

30 Foster, 'The diplomats who sank a fleet', p. 187.

31 For further see ibid., p. 181.

32 Ibid., p. 190.

33 Ibid., Despatches from Dublin, 1790–1906, vol. 3, roll 3, T199, Hammond to Seward, 12, 14, 21 February 1862; ibid., Hammond to Seward, 1 March 1862.

34 Ibid., Despatches from Dublin, 1790–1906, vol. 3, roll 3, Tl99, Hammond to Seward, 11 December 1862.

35 Ibid., Despatches from Belfast, 1798–1906, vol. 2, roll 4, T368, Young to Seward, 7, 14 May 1862; ibid., Despatches from Dublin, 1790–1906, vol. 3, roll 3, T199, Hammond to Seward, 8 May 1862; ibid., Henry B. Hammond to Seward, 22 July 1862; ibid., 22, 29 May 1862; ibid., Despatches from Cork, 1800-1906, vol. 5, roll 5, T196, Young to Seward, 16 August 1862.

36 Ibid., Despatches from Dublin, 1790–1906, vol. 3, roll 3, T199, Keenan to Seward, 7 November 1862; ibid., roll 4, T368, Young to Seward, 4 November 1862; ibid., Hammond to Seward, 4 December 1862; ibid., Hammond to Seward, 11 December 1 862.

37 Ibid., Despatches from Dublin, 1790–1906, vol. 3, roll 3, T199, Hammond to Seward, 4 December 1862.

38 Ibid., Despatches from Cork, 1800–1906, vol. 5, roll 5, T196, Eastman to Seward, 14 March 1863.

39 Ibid., vol. 5, roll 5, T196, Keenan to Seward, 20 June 1863.

40 Ibid., Despatches from Dublin, 1790-1906, vol. 4, roll 4, T199, West to Seward, 21 August 1863.

41 Ibid., vol. 4, roll 4, T199, West to Seward, 9 November 1864.

42 Foster, 'The diplomats who sank a fleet', p. 190.

43 NARA, S/D, Despatches from Belfast, 1798–1906, vol. 4, roll 4, T368, Young to Seward, 20 April 1864.

44 Ibid., vol. 4, roll 4, T368, Young to Seward, 20 April 1864.

45 Ibid., Despatches from Cork, 1800–1906, vol. 5, roll 5, T196, Eastman to Seward, 8, 12 June 1863.

46 Ibid., vol. 6, roll 6, T196, Eastman to Seward, 7 December 1865.

47 Ibid., Despatches from Dublin, 1790–1906, vol. 4, roll 4, Tl99, West to Seward, 29 October 1864.

48 The *Evelyn* was one of three ships used by Tait to transport uniforms to the Confederate forces. One of the last blockade-runners to reach the North Carolina coastline before the war ended in May 1865 was the Right Honourable Thomas Connolly (1823–76) on board the CSS *Owl* captained by Captain John Maffitt 'the prince of the privateers'. See further: Nelson D. Lankford, *An Irishman in Dixie Thomas Connolly's Diary of the Fall of the Confederacy* (Columbia, SC, 1988).

49 John Findling, *Dictionary of American Diplomatic History* (Westport, CT, 1980), p. 439.

50 NARA, S/D, Despatches from Belfast, 1798–1906, vol. 4, roll 4, T368, Young to Seward, 20 April 1864.

51 Ibid., Despatches fiom Cork, 1790–1906, vol. 6, roll 6, T196, Eastman to Seward, 14 January 1864.

52 Ibid., vol. 6, roll 6, T196, Eastman to Seward, 20 June 1865.

53 Ibid., Despatches from Dublin, 1790–1906, vol. 4, roll 4, Tl99, West to Seward, 7 January 1865.

Irish intelligence and British war
planning, 1910–14

Keith Jeffery

One of the most important individuals concerned with British war planning in the years immediately preceding the outbreak of the First World War was the Irish-born Henry Wilson, who between August 1910 and August 1914 was director of military operations in the British War Office, where his responsibilities covered war planning and the collection of intelligence. The particular way in which Wilson saw his role and performed his duties provides us with an instructive case study in how military intelligence can influence strategical planning for prospective war in two main aspects. First, there is the process by which potential adversaries are identified; and, second, there is the development of detailed military plans, both on a grand strategic basis and an tactical/operational level. This case study will also provide an illustration of how an able and articulate officer could 'sell' his own conclusions regarding these decisions to his political masters. It will further allow us to consider how various aspects of the intelligence process, or 'cycle' – collection, analysis and distribution – operated in pre-First World War Britain, as well as permitting a brief assessment of the relationship in this case between government (theoretically in charge of policy making) and the 'intelligence community' (such as it was in those years).

   Henry Wilson was one of the ablest officers of his generation. After successfully completing the two-year staff college course in 1893, he served in the intelligence department of the War Office for three years as the army's youngest staff officer.[1] He was brigade-major of the 4th Light Brigade in the Boer war before moving to the staff of Lord Roberts, the commander-in-chief in South Africa. Apart from a year of regimental duty in 1902–3, he enjoyed a series of War Office jobs until he was appointed commandant of the staff college at Camberley from 1907 to 1910 before moving back to the War Office. 'He had undoubtedly the nimblest intelligence amongst the soldiers of high degree', wrote Lloyd

George in his war memoirs. 'He had also a lucidity of mind and therefore of expression which was given to none of his professional rivals.'[2] Bonar Law described Wilson (to his face) as 'the cleverest man in England'.[3] He was arguably the most important staff officer in the British army during the first quarter of the twentieth century and, with his political skills and ability to explain and articulate strategical and military matters to non-specialists, provided a key link or conjuncture between the military and civil political sectors of government at a crucial stage in the emergence of a democratic state in Britain.

Wilson's opportunities to influence British war planning before 1914 were greatest during his tenure as commandant of the staff college (1907–10) and as director of military operations (1910–14). Throughout these years, and earlier, he was devoted (though not unreservedly so) to the Anglo-French alliance which developed strongly after the *entente cordiale* of 1904. But even before this his Francophile leanings were apparent. 'I have for many years advocated friendship with the French as against the Germans', he reflected in July 1903. There was, he thought, 'no legitimate cause to quarrel with the French, on account of their not wanting Colonies owing chiefly to no overflow population'. The Germans, on the other hand, 'who have an increasing population & no political morals *mean* expansion & therefore aggression'.[4] By the time he arrived at Camberley, the alliance with France was well established, and the possibility of Britain becoming involved with the French in a war against the Germans was widely accepted.

In 1908 and 1909 he set the senior division at the college an exercise called the 'Belgian Scheme', 'a study of operations involving the employment of the British Expeditionary Force on the Continent'. The scenario involved worsening relations between France and Germany, and an assumption that Germany would 'violate Belgian neutrality if such a step will assist her ultimate designs against England'. The students were instructed to provide for the cabinet a memorandum setting forth the views of the general staff 'as to the most effective means of employing the British Expeditionary Force, when its mobilization is completed'.[5] This exercise, while strikingly prescient, was also politically very sensitive. One member of Wilson's teaching staff recalled that the scheme 'came to the ears of some M.P.'s and questions were asked in the House [of Commons] whether we were to be permitted to hatch malicious plots against the harmless, peace-loving Germans'.[6]

While he was commandant of the staff college, Wilson began going on a series of trips to the continent, during which he explored the Low Countries and the Franco-German frontier from the Channel to Switzerland. Between 1907 and 1910 he went on two staff college battlefield tours and took side trips along the frontier on his way to

Switzerland for skiing holidays. Apart from visits to Paris, and some other shorter trips, in 1911–13 he went annually to Belgium and eastern France: for three weeks in October 1911; one week in February–March 1912; and two weeks in August 1913.

We get a flavour of these trips from the entries in the very detailed diary he kept for over forty years. In August 1908, with two colleagues, he set off south from Namur in southern Belgium, travelling by train and bicycle. 'Splendid roads & perfect country for troops', wrote Wilson. They had some trouble getting into a hotel at Dinant sur Meuse 'as they thought we were tramps without luggage [it had been sent on by rail]. Luckily Rawley [Wilson's army colleague Henry Rawlinson] had written to me here, & when they found I was a General all was smiles.' Along the way he made notes about the topography and, further south, near Mézières in the Ardennes, he estimated that it would be difficult country for the French to defend.[7] In December on his way to Switzerland for a skiing holiday he inspected the fortifications around Belfort in Alsace.[8] In August 1909, again travelling by train and bicycle, he went from Mons in Belgium into France, and then down the French frontier nearly to Switzerland. The following spring he motored from Rotterdam into Germany, and worked his way along the German side of the frontier. At St Vith, just north of Luxembourg, he noted a new railway station '& 9 sidings', and at Bitberg a little further south, 'a new double line running west with many sidings'.[9]

In June 1910 Wilson moved on to become director of military operations (DMO), a job he held until August 1914, and which gave him the responsibility to prepare plans for the deployment and use of the British army abroad. As he was also director of military intelligence, he was, therefore, both supplier and customer of intelligence. By the time be became DMO, moreover, he was fully convinced that the British strategic orientation should be at the side of France vis-à-vis Germany, and was also formidably well informed (or apparently so) about the practical consequences of this policy stance.

In the wake of the Agadir crisis in the summer of 1911, which raised the spectre of war between France and Germany, Wilson's potent combination of conviction and intelligence had a significant influence on British policy making. Early in August 1911, at the request of the chief of the imperial general staff, Sir William Nicholson, Wilson prepared an extremely important paper 'on the pros & cons of our joining with France in a war with Germany'.[10] The paper carefully articulated Wilson's own belief that 'we *must* join France', and was adopted by Nicholson as embodying the views of the general staff as a whole.[11]

Wilson began with a classical statement of British strategy, the 'axiom' that 'the policy of England is to prevent any Continental

Power from attaining a position of superiority that would allow it to dominate, and dictate to, the rest of Europe'. he then moved on to the two British policy options in the event of Germany 'in pursuance of a policy of domination', attacking France: first 'England remains neutral'; and, second, 'England becomes the active ally of France'. In the event of British neutrality, Germany would win, and become dominant in Europe, so it was 'impossible for England to remain neutral'. Moving on to consider England as an 'active ally', Wilson asserted that, with British support, the disparity in numbers between the opposing armies would crucially be reduced and that 'the numbers of the opposing forces at the decisive point would be so nearly equal during the opening and early actions of the war that it is quite possible for the Allies to win some initial successes which might prove invaluable'. Furthermore, perhaps 'the most important consideration of all' was that the moral effect on the French of British intervention 'would be of incalculable value'.

The most striking and dramatic part of Wilson's argument related to the deployment of the expeditionary force and was plausibly backed up with a detailed analysis of French and German mobilisation. If both countries mobilised at the same time, by the thirteenth day the Germans would have 57 divisions and the French 63 along the frontier. By the seventeenth day, however, the Germans would have 96 as against the French 66. But geographical factors had also to be taken into account. Here Wilson, of course, could speak with personal authority. He argued that only about half of the 230-mile frontier was 'passable', and 'in the 110 miles of open frontier there are not more than 17 or 18 through roads' which the Germans could use. Asserting that it was practicable for only three divisions to use each road, 'we find that the Germans cannot employ more than 51 to 54 Divisions' in the opening phase of the war.[12] This was his key point. 'The very marked superiority in German numbers' could not 'be brought into play at the commencement of the campaign', and this, in turn, enhanced the importance of the rapid deployment of the British force. 'The early intervention of our six Divisions', he wrote, 'would be more effective than the tardy presence of double their number', and thus Britain must mobilise at *exactly* the same moment as France. Although conceding that the decision for war, and the date and hour of mobilisation, lay with the politicians, he portentously concluded it to be 'essential that the Secretary of State for War should be fully aware of the difference it will make to the course of the campaign whether we mobilize early or late. It is scarcely too much to say that the difference may be that of victory and defeat.'

The secretary of state, Richard Haldane's, response was to have Wilson argue his case at a meeting of the Committee of Imperial Defence (CID), which had been set up in 1902 to co-ordinate defence planning. This meeting turned out to be of extraordinary importance in the evolution of British strategic planning before 1914. As Zara Steiner has observed, it was the only time the CID 'actually reviewed the over-all pattern of British strategy before 1914'.[13] Wilson's paper was circulated in advance, as was one by Sir Arthur Wilson (the first sea lord), which Henry Wilson dismissed as 'one of the most childish papers I ever read about the use of our Exped. force in a Continental war. Absolutely hopeless. It appears that 5 Div. are to guard the east coast & one Div. is to land in Germany! I never heard such a thing.'[14]

Chaired by the prime minister (Herbert Asquith), the CID meeting was attended by Haldane, Winston Churchill (home secretary), Sir Edward Grey (foreign secretary), Reginald McKenna (first lord of the admiralty) and David Lloyd George (chancellor of the exchequer). William Nicholson, Sir John French (inspector-general of the forces) and Wilson represented the War Office; Sir Arthur Wilson and Alexander Bethell (director of naval intelligence) the Admiralty. Beginning at 11.30 in the morning, the War Office batted first. Nicholson left Wilson to put their case. 'I had all my big maps on the wall', wrote Wilson, '& I lectured for $1^3/4$ hours. Everyone very nice. Much questioning by Winston and Lloyd George, especially.' After a break for a late lunch, Arthur Wilson led for the Admiralty. 'It soon became apparent', recalled Churchill, 'that a profound difference existed between the War Office and the Admiralty view.' Insofar as any coherent navy plans existed at all, they depended on the traditional enforcement of a maritime blockade on the enemy, coupled with the limited use of the army for raids on the German North Sea coast. Asquith called the navy's half-baked plans 'puerile' and 'wholly impracticable'. But Churchill's 'profound difference' was one of style as well as substance. In the 'battle of the Wilsons' the admiral was no match for the general, and Henry Wilson carried the day as much through the 'remarkable brilliance' (Maurice Hankey's description) of his exposition as the depth and completeness of his plans.[15]

There were gaps and deficiencies in the army's case as put by Henry Wilson. But the navy's side was put so badly and incompetently by Arthur Wilson that it obscured any weaknesses the army plans might have had. Asquith (who was not particularly keen on the idea of a 'continental commitment') had to agree that 'in principle the General Staff scheme is the only alternative', though he wanted it in the first instance to be limited to the despatch of only four divisions.[16] The 23 August meeting was important, not so much (as some have argued) because this was the moment when the commitment to France was made. This had been agreed by 1906, and military planning had proceeded accordingly. Yet the CID meeting was a moment when Henry Wilson could have *lost* the case (as his naval namesake did). Wilson's brilliance as a lecturer, with his evident mastery of facts, figures and the geography of the Franco-German frontier – dominating the 'intelligence environment' – carried him through, and left an indelible impression on his audience of politicians. Arthur Wilson's incompetence, by contrast, ensured that thereafter no-one seriously considered any alternative to the military continental commitment, which, from now on, was 'the only game in town'.

One of the people whom Wilson most impressed was Winston Churchill, at thirty-seven the youngest member of the cabinet. Although as home secretary he had no responsibility for strategic matters, he was mustard keen to be involved, and seems to have talked his way on to the CID. Churchill was concerned about what Keith Wilson has called the 'Belgian option', and wanted to explore the choices and opportunities available to the British army, not just alongside the French, but the Belgians as well.[17] At the 23 August meeting, Wilson had stated that the expeditionary force would concentrate around Maubeuge on the Franco-Belgian frontier. The assumption was that in an invasion of France the German forces would only cross Belgian territory south of the river Meuse. Pressed by Churchill, Wilson had argued that there were three reasons why the Germans would not extend their right wing any further north. First, to do this they would have to infringe Dutch neutrality in the 'Maastrict appendix'. Second, they would need to divert too many troops to reduce the Belgian fortresses at Liège, Huy and Namur. Finally, while the Belgians would most likely accept 'the violation of their southern provinces, they would almost certainly fight if the Germans were to invade northern Belgium as well'.[18]

Prompted by Lloyd George, who considered that co-ordinated Anglo-Belgian operations should be encouraged, Churchill came to Wilson's office and stayed for three hours discussing the possibilities. Over the next fortnight or so, the two men had several more meetings, and Wilson also had private sessions with both Grey and Lloyd George.[19] What emerged from this was broad agreement between Wilson and Churchill on the high importance of securing, if possible, a British alliance with Belgium which could underpin Anglo-Belgian military operations on the flank of an invading German force. But Wilson's support for a Belgian alliance provoked a sharp reaction from both Haldane and Nicholson. Haldane told Churchill that Wilson was 'a little impulsive. He is an Irishman &, while good, knows little of the Belgian Army.'[20] This was certainly over dismissive. It was, of course, precisely Wilson's job to know about the Belgian army. In January 1911 he had visited Brussels, dined with members of the Belgian general staff and motored across the southern part of the country, from Namur to Luxembourg, with Colonel Tom Bridges, the British military attaché in Brussels.[21] Nicholson was no more enamoured than Haldane of this 'fresh proposal', which would, he claimed, 'involve a radical change in our scheme for supporting France'.[22] Nicholson, moreover, suppressed a lengthy paper by Wilson on 'the political and military situation in Europe', which argued the potential high value of Anglo-Belgian military action on the German flank.[23]

What is interesting about this discussion is that, while we find Haldane and Nicholson supporting the 'pure' British commitment to France, Wilson is arguing for a more flexible, and less exclusively French, position. This, in turn, might modify the easy assumptions of some historians, including, for example, Paul Kennedy, about Wilson's apparently simplistic and unvarying 'devotion to all things French'.[24] Zara Steiner characterises Wilson as 'a one-man propaganda team for the Anglo-French connection', and the underlying supposition in her study of British diplomacy before the First World War is that Wilson was an uncritically pro-French and rather malign influence on British decision making.[25] In the light of the 'Belgian option' evidence, moreover, Gerhard Ritter's magisterial and categorical assertion that Wilson was 'a man, who may without reservation be described as wholly in thrall to French aims and ideas', is wrong.[26]

One reason why Wilson (who was still only a brigadier general) received such flattering attention from senior politicians during the summer of 1911 was the apparent quality of the information he possessed. Politicians are often attracted by the ostensibly intriguing world of intelligence. Throughout his career, Churchill, for one, found secret sources to be seductive, and we have at one stage of the Agadir crisis a snap shot of the 'sexiness' of raw intelligence and an illustration of how readily Churchill responded to 'hot' intelligence provided by Henry Wilson. On 4 September Wilson had heard from an agent in Belgium called Charrier (who had been turned back at the German frontier) that two German divisions had been deployed in Malmédy just across the border. Wilson thought this 'ominous'. Another report described how the Germans were buying up extra stocks of wheat. Late that evening at home he received a letter from Major Twiss (an officer in M.O.2) in Bavaria 'describing the present warlike temper of the German people'. Wilson was sufficiently alarmed by the cumulative effect of these pieces of information that he telephoned Churchill at the Café Royal, where he was having dinner with Sir Edward Grey. Churchill and Grey, in their turn, were concerned enough to call in at Wilson's house at eleven o'clock and stay on discussing the situation until after midnight.[27]

Over the years 1910–14 Henry Wilson was not just gathering information, but also making operational plans, perhaps an inappropriate conflation of responsibilities, especially bearing in mind Wilson's sometimes fervent support for the Anglo-French alliance. He was also quite dependent on the French, especially Ferdinand Foch and Joseph Joffre. He had first met Foch in 1909 when he was commandant of the staff college and Foch was his opposite number at the head of the école supérieure de guerre. The two men got on famously and became life-long friends. Joffre, too, who became chief of staff of the French army in 1911, was notably amicable. In September 1911, for example, Colonel Victor Huguet, the French military attaché in London (and another important close contact), invited Wilson to a meeting with the French general staff to review plans for Anglo-French co-ordination in the event of a German invasion. 'They were most cordial & open', wrote Wilson in his diary. 'They showed me papers & maps, copies of which they are giving me, showing the concentration areas of their northern army. Intensely interesting.' The French also discussed where they would like the British expeditionary force to concentrate, and told Wilson of a 'Kriegspiel' which the German general staff had run in Berlin in 1905, 'a copy of which, with v. Moltke's remarks, was in their possession'. By the end of the meeting Wilson reckoned that he 'was in possession of the whole plan of campaign of their northern armies'.[28]

Wilson's knowledge of the strategical possibilities accompanying a German attack on France, therefore, was informed not only by his own familiarity with the terrain of the Franco-German frontier zone, and his central role in British war planning, but also by extremely privileged access to French intelligence and war planning. The willingness of the French to share this material was no doubt enhanced by their perception of Wilson as a useful and eloquent proponent of the Anglo-French alliance at the highest levels of British decision making, and was designed to copper-fasten the British commitment in the event of a Franco-German war. Indeed, the completeness of Wilson's own planning for the mobilisation of the expeditionary force and the co-ordination of these plans with the French meant that his work had a decisive impact on British policy when war did break out in August 1914. Writing in the early 1930s, Basil Liddell Hart argued that 'the very completeness of the preparations sponsored by Henry Wilson decreed the manner and direction in which the power of Britain should be used'. Furthermore, 'that decree was made absolute by the omission of any alternative arrangements'.[29]

This privileged access to the French planning proved to be a double-edged sword. In a sense, the intelligence provided from Paris was so good, and apparently so complete, that it was tempting simply to take it at face value. Wilson (who was undoubtedly flattered by the French) was perhaps less critical than he might have been, which led him into making too-easy assumptions about what would happen in the event of a German invasion of France. A weakness in Wilson's planning (and one which reflected French thinking) was his assumption about the direction of the expected German thrust through Belgium. The

Germans, less concerned than Wilson assumed about violating Belgian neutrality, were able to subdue the great Belgian forts with overwhelming firepower, and in the event swept further north than anticipated, catching the French and British off-balance and contributing materially to the near-catastrophic retreat from Mons.

A further point about Wilson's personal intelligence gathering is that its ostensibly primitive basis – the senior officer responsible for military intelligence himself bicycling along the Franco-German frontier collecting information – actually added to its persuasiveness, if not also its veracity. When Wilson was, for example, discussing the number of roads along which the invading Germans would have to travel, he could look his audience of politicians in the eye and say: 'I know about this; I've been there myself.' And this might be enough to disarm or deflect all but the most determined critic, as was evidently the case in August 1911. Nevertheless Wilson was not some 'one man band' forcing a policy on the country which it would not otherwise have adopted. His general strategic assumptions and attitudes were shared by most of his army colleagues and, certainly after August 1911 (if not also before), by the most influential men in the government.

The result of this was that, in terms of British planning for a continental war, after August 1911 there was no 'plan B'. Possibly the government was most to blame for not being more specific about what was actually being considered and perhaps it should have demanded alternative studies about the possible deployment of the expeditionary force in the event of it being sent to the continent. The 'tasking' of both the planning process, and the intelligence gathering upon which it rested, was at fault, principally because, once the fundamental decision to go with the army strategy was made in August 1911, this was left in the hands of the War Office itself, where Henry Wilson and his colleagues saw no reason to explore alternatives. Paul Kennedy has remarked on the 'narrowly departmental nature' of British strategic assessment and operational planning, 'due to the existence of an entrenched rivalry between the two armed services'.[30] While this was certainly a factor, it was by no means the only one. If the United Kingdom was to make any meaningful contribution which would help prevent France being rapidly overwhelmed by a German assault, a substantial military commitment alongside the French, as the army envisaged, was a much more realistic option than the airy naval notions of a limited amphibious landing somewhere on the north-east German seacoast, which Admiral Wilson had raised at the August 1911 CID meeting.

Henry Wilson was a successful 'policy entrepreneur', with forceful and articulate views, apparently backed by good intelligence. His success in persuading his political masters to back the army case in 1911 illustrates that 'experts' (military, intelligence or other) can significantly influence the policy-making process, not just when their views coincide or confirm the politicians' general disposition, but also when there might be a policy vacuum or gap, when decision makers are uncertain what to do. Such was the case, not only in 1911 but also in July–August 1914. In the latter instance, faced with the effective alternatives of either implementing Wilson's carefully constructed scheme for the mobilisation and deployment of the expeditionary force alongside the French army, or postponing intervention on the continent, at the possible cost of a French defeat, the cabinet understandably took the first option, though at first holding back one of the expeditionary force's six divisions.

Wilson had argued in August 1911 the importance of the six British divisions, and how they could tip the balance in favour of the forces opposing the Germans. Three years earlier Winston Churchill (then president of the board of trade) had anticipated this argument. Criticising the size of Haldane's proposed expeditionary force, he asserted that 'some nice adjustment', of a comparative handful of British troops, would in fact be irrelevant in a full-scale conflict with Germany on the continent – a 'peril of first-class magnitude'.[31] Perhaps so. And perhaps Henry Wilson's statistical sleight of hand, with which he so impressed the CID, was actually irrelevant to the real issue, which in the first instance was not how many British soldiers could be deployed alongside the French, but whether they would be deployed at all. Ferdinand Foch understood this point only too well, and (according to Huguet) said to Henry Wilson: 'After all it doesn't matter what you send us, we only ask for one corporal and four men, but they must be there right at the start. You will give them to me and I promise to do my utmost to get them killed. From that moment on I will be at ease since I know that England will follow them as one man!'[32]

So, more or less, it was to be. Once even part of the expeditionary force was engaged against the Germans in August 1914, the United Kingdom was effectively committed to continuing the alliance with France and seeing the struggle through to the end. As much as anything else, this was the result of Henry Wilson's 'victory' in the 'battle of the Wilsons' at the CID in August 1911, and what the case of Henry Wilson demonstrates for British war planning is the impact which a potent combination of intelligence and policy preference had in the hands of an outstandingly articulate, plausible – and Irish – protagonist.

NOTES

1   Information about Wilson is taken from my biography, *Field Marshal Sir Henry Wilson: a Political Soldier* (Oxford, 2006), upon which I have drawn extensively for this essay, and my entry on Wilson in H.C.G. Matthew and Brian Harrison (eds),

Oxford Dictionary of National Biography (60 vols, Oxford, 2004).

2   David Lloyd George, *War Memoirs* (Odhams edn, London, n.d. [1938]), ii, pp. 1687–8.

3   Diary of Sir Henry Wilson (hereafter 'Wilson diary'), 27 Apr. 1916 (Wilson papers, Imperial War Museum, quotation from which is by permission of the trustees of the museum).

4   Wilson diary, 6 July 1903.

5   Senior division 'Belgian scheme' notes, Nov.–Dec. 1908 (Wilson papers, HHW 3/3/17 (i)).

6   Sir George de S. Barrow, *The Fire of Life* (London, n.d. [1942]), p. 115.

7   Wilson diary, 11, 14 Aug. 1908.

8   Ibid., 29 Dec. 1908.

9   Ibid., 3–11 Aug. 1909; 26–9 Apr. 1910.

10 Ibid., 11 Aug. 1911.

11 Wilson's draft, dated 12 Aug. 1911, is in the Wilson papers, HHW 3/5/13; copies of the general staff memorandum, 'Military aspect of the continental problem', dated 15 Aug., are in TNA, CAB 4/3/2 and 38/19/47.

12 Wilson's calculations of the numbers of French and German divisions has been sharply criticised by Ernest R. May, giving the impression that the figures were 'cooked' to support the argument in favour of military intervention (May, 'Cabinet, Tsar, Kaiser: three approaches to assessment', in May (ed.), *Knowing One's Enemies: Intelligence Assessment before the Two World Wars* (Princeton, 1984), pp. 11–17). Edward W. Bennett's detailed and devastating critique of May, however, suggests that Wilson's figures were not seriously out of line (Bennett, 'Intelligence and history from the other side of the hill', *Journal of Modern History*, 60 (1988), pp. 324–9).

13 Zara S. Steiner, *Britain and the Origins of the First World War* (London, 1977), p. 200.

14 Wilson diary, 21 Aug. 1911.

15 Ibid., 23 Aug. 1911; CID, 114th meeting, 23 Aug. 1911 (TNA, CAB 2/2/2); Winston S. Churchill, *The World Crisis 1911–1914* (London, 1923), p. 58; Asquith to Haldane, 31 Aug. 1911 (quoted in Samuel R. Williamson Jr, *The Politics of Grand Strategy: Britain and France Prepare for War, 1904–14* (Cambridge, MA., 1969), p. 193); Lord Hankey, *The Supreme Command 1914–1918* (London, 1961), i, p. 79. Col. Hankey was secretary of the CID.

16 Asquith to Haldane, 31 Aug. 1911 (quoted in Williamson, *The Politics of Grand Strategy*, p. 193).

17 See Keith M. Wilson, *Empire and Continent: Studies in British Foreign Policy from the 1880s to the First World War* (London, 1987), pp. 126–40.

18 CID, 114th meeting, 23 Aug. 1911 (TNA, CAB 2/2/2).

19 Wilson diary, 28, 31 Aug., 4-5, 12–14 Sept. 1911.

20 Wilson to Churchill, 29 Aug.; Haldane to Churchill, 31 Aug. 1911 (TNA, ADM 116/3474). Haldane was a Scot.

21 Wilson diary, 27–8 Jan. 1911.

22 Nicholson to Churchill, 2 Sept. 1911 (TNA, ADM 116/3474).

23 'Appreciation of the Political and Military situation in Europe', 20 Sept. 1911 (Wilson papers, HHW 3/5/18a). Nicholson's successor as Chief of Imperial General Staff, Sir John French, had this paper printed and circulated to the CID in April 1912.

24 Paul Kennedy, 'Great Britain before 1914', in May (ed.), *Knowing One's Enemies*, p. 191.

25 Steiner, *Britain and the Origins of the First World War*, p. 197, and passim. This assumption remains the same in the second edition of this work, by Steiner and Keith Neilson (London, 2003).

26 Gerhard Ritter, *The Sword and the Scepter: The Problem of Militarism in Germany*, ii,

The European Powers and the Wilhelminian Empire 1890–1914 (Coral Gables, FL, 1970), p. 71.

27 Wilson diary, 4 Sept. 1911. For Churchill's attitude towards secret sources, see Christopher Andrew, 'Churchill and intelligence', *Intelligence and National Security*, 3 (1988), pp. 181–93; and David Stafford, 'Churchill and intelligence: his early life', in K.G. Robertson (ed.), *War, Resistance and Intelligence: Essays in Honour of M.R.D. Foot* (Barnsley, 1999), pp. 151–68.

28 Wilson diary, 29 Sept. 1911.

29 Basil Liddell Hart, *Foch: Man of Orleans* (Penguin edn, Harmondsworth, 1937), i, p. 69.

30 Paul Kennedy, 'Great Britain before 1914', in May (ed.), *Knowing One's Enemies*, p. 195.

31 Winston Churchill, 'A note upon British military needs', 27 June 1908 (TNA, CAB 37/94/89; quoted in Williamson, *The Politics of Grand Strategy*, pp. 99–100).

32 General Huguet, *Britain and the War: A French Indictment* (London, 1928), p. 26.

The IRA, intelligence and Bloody Sunday, 1920

Anne Dolan

On 6 May 1931 Lord Banbury of Southam entertained the House of Lords by reading lengthy passages from *With the Dublin Brigade*, Charles Dalton's recently published memoir of the Irish fight for independence.[1] Like many of his fellow peers, Banbury was outraged by its content, outraged that a book about murder and rebellion in Ireland had been published at all. That it had been published in London, that it could be bought for a mere two shillings and six pence, that it might fall into the hands of impressionable, rebellious Indians made it that much more sinister still. Indeed, Lord Danesfort, inspired presumably by Banbury's recitations, asked 'Can anything be more pernicious, degrading and criminal than that a self-confessed criminal should publish in this country a justification of one of the basest murders that have ever taken place in Southern Ireland?'[2] Danesfort was referring to Bloody Sunday, or at least Charles Dalton's part in that morning's murder of fourteen men the IRA said were spies. It was the description of this particular morning that infuriated the lords the most. In their opinion the book should be immediately banned and its author arrested if he ever set foot on English soil. The British government was ordered to take 'the powers' in the 'South of Ireland' to task, to 'induce them to take steps against a man who glories in having murdered defenceless gentlemen'.[3] Given that the Free State had rewarded Dalton by making him an adjutant, and eventually a colonel, for, among other things, his part in murdering 'defenceless gentlemen', Banbury's faith in the British government's powers of persuasion seemed quite blind indeed.[4] An English peer's idea of an 'infamous ruffian' was clearly officer material to the Irish army and an Irish minister for defence, but then it would be difficult to find an Irish minister who wouldn't be considered an infamous ruffian himself. When the secretary of state for the colonies, Lord Passfield, rose to remind the noble lords of the king's amnesty for Irish political offences up to the truce, that by his reading of such lengthy passages into the parliamentary record Banbury had given the book more publicity than it ever deserved, the scolded peer and his supporters sat down.[5] The complaint had been made, noted and forgotten, and nothing was done about the book.

The Home Office and the Dominions Office were notified of Banbury's question a little over a month before. Dutifully the book was bought and read, then dismissed. It was not 'a valuable contribution to the literature of the period'.[6] Admittedly it was considered a pity that the book had ever been written; it was better to dwell on the 'happier relations', on the 'spirit of goodwill' established with the old adversary since.[7] Banbury's question was the real problem; it just brought attention to a book that few enough English people would ever notice let alone consider reading. The question just prodded a sleeping dog that both ministries were quite content to let lie. But as the book passed from one senior civil servant to another, as letters went from the Dominions Office to the Home Office and back again, one rather off-hand comment suddenly seems quite telling indeed.

> Possibly... Lord Banbury is under the impression that the writer is identical with a well-known Sinn Feiner of the same name whereas as a matter of fact he is quite an insignificant person who was a mere boy at the time the incidents referred to took place and the main interest of the book is the insight it gives into the minds of these wild young men – Dalton commenced his career as a rebel at 16...[8]

Though the letter manages to make Dalton sound like a hardworking junior clerk who could go far if he applied himself in his chosen profession, this letter epitomises just how much the British government misunderstood the IRA. Yes, Dalton was a mere seventeen-year-old boy on Bloody Sunday morning; yes, he may have been something of a 'wild young man', but they were quite mistaken to think he was an insignificant person. Charles Dalton may not have shot anyone on the morning of 21 November 1920 but he was directly responsible for the deaths of three officers and the wounding of three more at 28 and 29 Upper Pembroke Street.[9] He was the one intelligence officer assigned to this boarding house where the IRA believed the day's most important targets lived. He was also behind the killing of two other officers because he had learned they had moved from Pembroke Street to Upper Mount Street the night before.[10] This mere boy had been behind the murder of five British officers; to have read his book where he admits to this, to still consider him 'an insignificant person', was a very strange response indeed.

Though he liked to be called an intelligence officer, Charles Dalton was a spy. He may not have been a spy in any traditional sense; he had no formal military training, he was no master of disguise, he had no distinguished foreign service and he was just about old enough to be a watcher or a tout. He was not officer material; he was not the stuff we imagine that the British secret service was made of. And therein lies the problem, at least for the British forces in Ireland from 1919 to 1921. Charles Dalton was quite a high-ranking intelligence officer in the IRA. He was a senior figure compared to the majority of the men, women and children who watched and whispered and told small, often inconsequential things. IRA intelligence was a rather indiscriminating breed. It came from places that the British never thought to look. It was amateur and awkward; it was people just going about their daily lives. If someone of Charles Dalton's seniority was considered insignificant, then the British never really understood IRA intelligence at all. Brigadier General Crozier, commandant of the Auxiliary Division of the Royal Irish Constabulary, came to the same conclusion, albeit from a rather different point of view. In terms of Dublin Castle's perception of Michael Collins:

> I was sorely disappointed with the impression the Intelligence Department had arrived at regarding this will-o'-the-wisp who had been represented as a 'cowardly, cringing, sneaking assassin', of the dago type. Collins's make up, his cheery optimism, his smile and frank expression and his clear eyes must have been misunderstood in Dublin Castle where they kept nothing like him.[11]

Admittedly Crozier seemed to have developed something of a soft spot for Collins if this rather romantic portrayal of him is to be taken at its word. But this was perhaps the real problem of Collins in terms of British intelligence. It was not the man's actual activities or talents, but more this type of insidious, sloppy mythology that Dublin Castle among others invested so much time in creating around him that possibly provoked so much concern. Yes, as director of intelligence he was ultimately responsible for much of the IRA's activities, but by depicting him as some sort of criminal mastermind, almost magically orchestrating every stroke, he was credited or blamed, according to your preference, with much that was realistically beyond his knowledge or control. The strength of the spotlight on him just made the shadows all the safer for his army of minions to carry on their arguably more damaging work.

Bloody Sunday has been called 'a spectacular coup by Michael Collins'.[12] It might be more appropriate to think of it as a coup for the men and women who watched and waited, who deciphered false names, who made sense of torn scraps of paper, who took the risk of befriending British officers, who gambled with their lives and, maybe in their more religious moments, with their immortal souls, when they went into those oft-watched houses and hotels on Bloody Sunday morning and kept on shooting until fourteen men were dead. When Kate McCormack queried why her son, a nephew of the late bishop of Galway and a cousin of Michael Davitt, had been shot in the Gresham Hotel on 21 November, when she asked Richard Mulcahy to exonerate him of the charge of being a British spy because 'he was thoroughly Irish in his education and upbringing', Collins was prodded to reveal the real limits of his powers on Bloody Sunday morning.[13] He advised Mulcahy to respond to this woman in the following terms:

> With reference to this case, you will remember that I stated on a former occasion that we had no evidence that he was a Secret Service Agent. You will also remember that several of the 21st November cases were just regular officers. Some of the names were put on by the Dublin Brigade. So far as I remember McCormack's name was one of these. In my opinion it would be as well to tell Mrs McCormack that there was no particular charge against her son, but just that he was an enemy soldier.[14]

There was little comfort for Kate MacCormack in this response, especially since she had been living on the charity of her daughter-in-law's family since her son's death, but it is a particularly valuable letter in terms of establishing, or rather minimising, Collins's role.[15] Bloody Sunday was a Dublin Brigade operation, and it would be simply foolish to go on looking for the hidden hand of Collins when he admits himself that it was only ever discretely there. We might be better served by looking at those overshadowed minions if we really wish to know how Bloody Sunday was brought about.

In many senses these minions have conspired to make it more difficult to understand. Some hierarchy of horror had been grossly breached on Bloody Sunday morning. It was one thing to gun down a man in cold blood in the street. It was quite another to barge into his bedroom, to shoot him where he lay, in front of his wife, within hearing of his child. That nine of the men killed wore only their pyjamas seemed to tip the scales of horror even further still.[16] There was the added indignity of not even being properly dressed. It was for these reasons that Larry Nugent was so insistent in his statement to the Bureau of Military History that it was not murder, that 'it was an act of war duly carried out under orders ... [that] the life of every IRA man in Dublin was at stake';[17] why Frank Thornton kept insisting, even at lectures to young army cadets in 1940, that 'that morning was one of the most critical ones in the history of our movement', that, as he said, 'all jobs were executed' even when they were not.[18] The dead men were the 'cream of British Military Intelligence', spies 'disguised as civilians...liable to the death penalty' like any others of their kind.[19] The participants proclaim with dreary repetition that it needed to be done, that they had to be stopped; that they were all spies, that there were no mistakes. 'The British Secret Service was wiped out on the 21st November 1920'; it was a stunning victory for IRA intelligence.[20] That was the story and the brutality of the day meant that most of the men involved were going to stick to it.

Most who have written about Bloody Sunday since have stuck to it too. Tim Pat Coogan was happy to recount the participants' traditional version of events: 'The sounds of Dublin's mass bells were suddenly punctuated by staccato bursts of shooting as Collins' men crippled the entire British Secret Service operation in Ireland'.[21] And Tom Bowden has done more than most to confirm that each dead man was the spy the IRA claimed him to be. Even Captain McCormack, whom we have already seen Collins exonerate, was condemned by Bowden because he was staying at the Gresham Hotel.[22] The Gresham was apparently too expensive for a retired Royal Army Veterinary Corp man to stay in without dipping into the coffers of British intelligence. He had also just come from Egypt, a hot-bed of British espionage, and, besides, Bowden was unable to find him in the army lists, ergo he must be a spy.[23] James Doyle, the manager of the Gresham, knew that this could not be the case. He remembered that the man rarely left the hotel unless he was going to the races, and Doyle admonished Collins for the killing after the truce; he was haunted by the sight of the body, by the limp hand still holding the copy of the *Irish Field* he had been reading in bed.[24] Bowden's only proof against Leonard Wilde, the other man killed in his room at the Gresham, was that he too was missing from the army lists.[25] At least Archbishop Clune had the good grace to provide some evidence against him, confirming that he was a British spy known to have been thrown out of Spain.[26] Apart from the obvious exceptions, the two auxiliaries, Cadets Carniss and Morris, shot that morning in Northumberland Road as they went for reinforcements, and apart from Thomas Smith, the landlord at Morehampton Road, and John Caldow, the visiting brother-in-law of the officer killed at the same address, the morning's ten other victims are at once easier and more difficult to decipher. Captain Fitzgerald in Earlsfort Terrace, Lieutenants Ames and Bennett in Upper Mount Street, Lieutenant McMahon in Lower Mount Street, Captains Baggally and Newbury in Lower Baggot Street, Captain MacClean in Morehampton Road, and Major Dowling, Captain Price and Colonel Montgomery in Pembroke Street, they were all the secret service men, the 'hush-hush men', the court-martial officers, the soldiers, the husbands, the fathers, the brothers, the sons, possibly all of the things that the IRA, the press, the government, the army and their wives claimed them to be. Some were just easier to call spies than others. Some were shot for no other reason than that they came down the stairs at the wrong time, because they got in the way or they put up a fight, some because they were shot by nervous killers too eager to get the shooting done. Much of the problem with Bowden's approach and, indeed, with the few others who have bothered to pay any close attention to Bloody Sunday morning, is that they cannot have one myth without the other: there can be no spectacular IRA intelligence coup without a dastardly Cairo gang.

Whether there was such a gang, and whether they were dastardly or not, is a matter perhaps best left to the *Record of the Rebellion in Ireland* and the *Report of the Intelligence Branch of the Chief of Police*, the two documents recently released by the Public Records Office and the Imperial War Museum, and edited and contextualized by Peter Hart.[27] But documentary evidence from the British archives is hardly necessary to disprove the legend that Bloody Sunday wiped out the British secret service in Ireland. Events in Ireland, not least the IRA's intention to assassinate sixty spies in and around Grafton Street a few days before the truce, bear witness to the continued strength of the British intelligence network in Ireland. That most IRA intelligence men spend sizeable portions of their Bureau of Military History statements cursing the illusive Igoe gang diminishes the legend; that others concede that most of the 'jobs' on Bloody Sunday were bungled or postponed or never carried out, undermines it further still.[28] But without reducing it all to the level of 'my spies are better than your spies', in terms of the officers killed on Bloody Sunday morning, there is a certain amount of truth in the rather callous remark which Churchill made when he heard about their deaths. They were 'careless fellows' who 'ought to have taken precautions'.[29] This could be interpreted as a further diminution of the capabilities of IRA intelligence, or it could be understood in the way Churchill possibly meant it: that these men were bad at their jobs and got what they deserved; that they were aware, as one contemporary put it, that 'the penalty of secrecy has always been death'.[30] But I think there is another way to interpret this. They were 'careless fellows' because they seemed to have no real idea of just what they needed to be careful about. They made basic, simple mistakes. They lived in boarding houses and hotels but never checked if their owners, or the staff in them, were known members of Sinn Féin or the IRA. They threw their notes in wastepaper baskets, not burning them or even eating them, like we expect all the best spies to do. They did not bother to disguise their English accents and they wore, what one maid described as 'West-End suits of clothes', tailored garments that stood out a sartorial mile beside Switzer's or McBirney's best.[31] 'Fellow-lodgers reported nocturnal wanderings', the comings and goings that seemed curious because the curfew was not seen to apply.[32] And above all they had far too much money for men who sometimes pretended to be IRA volunteers on the run.[33] Almost like Douglas Duff, who began his career as a Black and Tan, unable to 'believe that the kindly, lovable Irish folk that I had known so well had become the dastardly murderers that they were represented to be', these men did not seem to have a sense of the extent of the danger they were in.[34] The 'lovable Irish folk' may still have seemed lovable, but Maudie who brought your clean shirts and folded down your bed, and emptied your wastepaper basket, had a boyfriend now and he was in the IRA. And this boyfriend brought Maudie to meet his friend, and though this friend may have been a 'mere boy' of seventeen, he knew how to follow you and identify you and get you killed in your bed.[35] This was the scope and the simplicity of IRA intelligence, and this was what the British forces failed to understand. Bloody Sunday may have been a particularly cruel way to learn, but British agents recognised their mistakes and rarely made them again. After 21 November, landlords and porters and maids could only be loyalists, freemasons and Protestants.[36] The 'lovable Irish folk' had earned the suspicion they possibly, maybe probably, deserved.

It would be convenient to rehearse what are fast becoming platitudes about Michael Collins's spies; to conscript Ned Broy and David Neligan, Sergeant Mannix and James McNamara, even Lily Mernin, to the cause one more time; to hear again how they were the spies in the Castle, spying on the spies and never getting caught. It might be more interesting to wonder why Ned Broy disliked David Neligan so much, why he thought the self-proclaimed 'spy in the Castle' was 'a low type and dangerous', who never did any of the things he said he did at all.[37] But I would rather look instead at the men and women who have received very little attention; the men and women who possibly made Bloody Sunday quite as shocking as it was. Take Maudie, for example. Charles Dalton explained meeting her thus:

> I was instructed by the Deputy Director of Intelligence to contact a girl who had reported to a Volunteer about some strange residents who were occupying the block of flats in which she was a maid. I met her in this Volunteer's home over a shop in Talbot St. I think his name was Byrne. I questioned the girl, whose name was Maudie. She described the routine of the residents of the flats, and it would seem from her account that they followed no regular occupation but did a lot of office work in their flats. I arranged with her to bring me the contents of the waste-paper baskets. When these were examined we found torn up

documents which referred to the movements of wanted Volunteers, and also photographs of wanted men...I last met Maudie on the Saturday evening, 20th November 1920, at our rendezvous, and she told me that all her "boarders" were at home, with the exception of two who were changing their residence that night to Upper Mount Street.[38]

Maybe Maudie the maid, rather than Charles Dalton, caused the deaths of five men and the wounding of three more. In his memoirs, but not in his Bureau statement, Charles Dalton recounts a meeting with Maudie, alias Rosie, after Bloody Sunday had taken its toll.

The minute she saw me she burst into tears. This greatly surprised and distressed me. Putting my arm around her, I asked her what was the matter. This only caused her to cry more convulsively, so that for a while she could not speak to me at all.

"Oh, why did you shoot them?" she sobbed out at last. "I thought you only meant to kidnap them".

"But, Rosie", said I, "surely you know we are at war, and that these men were shooting our fellows?"

"I know", she said, still crying, "but it was dreadful"...

"...I was so upset I did not leave the house for days. You see, I felt I had had a hand in it, and I couldn't bear my thoughts, and at last I felt I must speak to someone. So I went to a friend of mine who was a priest and I told him everything...He was very nice to me. He told me I needn't blame myself at all. He said that ye were fighting with your backs to the wall. 'A defensive war', that is what he called it. He said the English had no right to be here at all. 'Our boys must defend themselves', he said, and a lot more which I did not understand."[39]

With all the sobbing, and the guilt, and the absolution, and not being able to understand, it might seem unfair to blame this 'country girl' for five men's deaths.[40] It might even be unfair to privilege her over Broy and Neligan. Whatever their differences, they were proven spies who continued to risk their lives for their chosen cause. But without Maudie, and there were others like her, IRA intelligence remains in the ranks of its senior operatives, overstating the case of those who have become the predictable cast of IRA informants and spies. Without Maudie there is no sense of where the bulk of IRA intelligence came from; no sense of the ordinary and the everyday that made it the unpredictable and underestimated force that British intelligence initially failed to reckon with.

Whether Maudie knew what she was doing remains a matter between her and her rabid republican priest, but the same could not be said for Frank Saurin's wife. She went to whist drives run by the Auxiliaries in Dublin Castle. Each time she got an officer to walk her out to the tram and paraded him up and down so that her husband could see what he looked like, so that Saurin could remember him when the time came for 'extermination'.[41] There was no mention of what else Mrs Saurin had to do to get her chosen officer to walk her to the tram, or what she had to do while the tram took its time arriving. There is possibly more to be discovered about the role of women in IRA intelligence than the emphasis on postmistresses and typists, or on Lily Mernin's carbon copies Mernin sat with Frank Saurin in hotels and restaurants pointing out officers or detectives she thought needed to be shot.[42] Dan Breen mentioned 'The lady prostitutes [who] used to pinch the guns and ammunition from the Auxiliaries or Tans at night, and then leave them for us at Phil Shanahan's publichouse [*sic*]. I might add that there was no such thing as payment for these transactions, and any information they had they gave us.'[43] You could say Dan Breen was just an earthy exception to the rule of chaste and pure republicans, but there was a horrid hierarchy of morality, breached for Margaret Browne when she knew that Tom Cullen was off to fraternise with ladies of ill repute. This troubled her more than carrying Cullen's gun for him to and from a killing, more than watching him clean it in her flat before he went to cause someone else to die.[44]

While the prostitutes will probably remain largely unrewarded for their services to IRA intelligence, the debt to the men and women whom Frank O'Connor called 'the real fighters...[the] postmen, telephone operators, hotel porters, cipher experts' was repaid, eagerly and in full.[45] Even Joe Dolan, in the midst of claiming credit for precisely '75% of the information' needed for Bloody Sunday, acknowledged that 'I got all the information I needed from the staff of the hotels I visited'.[46] 'We used to go round to maids and boots in the different hotels and get information from them.'[47] Frank Saurin admitted having contacts in 'Jammets, The Wicklow, The Shelbourne, Fullers, The Moira, The Central', and the list could go on. Indeed, he called the telephonist at the Shelbourne Hotel one of his agents and got her to listen in on all the calls.[48] But the hotels and restaurants themselves proved just as important as the men and women who worked in them. That certain restaurants became known as meeting places for British intelligence officers suggested another sign of their carelessness. It was just foolhardy to assume that IRA spies of the 'cowardly, sneaking...dago type' did not have the money or the good manners to frequent the same establishments. Frank Thornton and Liam Tobin, left their rooms in Crowe Street, their hive of intelligence hiding behind the facade of Donoghue and Smith Manufacturing Agents, and lunched in La Scala every day like any other respectable men.[49] But it was in Kidd's Buffet, or Kidd's Back as it was known, on

Grafton Street, that Frank Thornton, Tom Cullen and Frank Saurin became British secret service touts. Frank Thornton recalled in his Bureau of Military History statement that 'We were introduced in the ordinary way as touts and eventually became great friends of men like Major Bennett, Colonel Aimes and a number of other prominent Secret Service Officers.' Thornton proudly recalled how, over a drink or a lunch or whatever Kidd's Buffet had to offer, these secret service men asked him if he knew those fellows Thornton and Cullen and Tobin; how he wanted the ground to open and swallow him; that it was all terribly risky and exciting; and that clearly the British had no idea what they looked like. Neither Thornton, Cullen, Saurin or Tobin were so eager to mention what kind of information they had to give to gain Ames's and Bennett's trust. No one has bothered to ask that, particularly when Thornton was so emphatic in the same Bureau statement that 'we bred no informers' in the IRA.[50] And heaven forefend that he might have been one himself, however much in the service of the cause. But whatever information he did give Ames and Bennett, they took it with them to their graves on Bloody Sunday morning. Being careless about your choice of drinking partner also caused McMahon's death. He was suspected of killing John Lynch in the Exchequer Hotel, but it was foolhardy to get drunk and maudlin and to tell the first girl you met in a bar.[51] Like Maudie, she too had a boyfriend in the IRA and McMahon joined Ames and Bennett and 21 November's eleven other dead.

Someone like Edward Kelliher came on the next rung down the intelligence ladder. Sent by his company commander to meet with Cullen or Thornton in October 1920, he was told what intelligence work involved, and then recounted with pride that 'I was to be known as "Agent 102"'.[52] And he did the simple sifting, the laborious dirty work that his lowly place in the pecking order suggested.

> I had to report to No. 3 Crow St. each morning and there I was given copies of practically all the papers that came into the country to read. Other agents were similarly engaged. I was told to watch carefully for deaths or marriages of any relatives of the British military serving in the country, the idea being to try and locate the private addresses of the members of the forces concerned. Another duty there was to censor captured mails and make a note of anything that would be of value from the intelligence point of view.[53]

Kelliher also followed suspected spies, admitting losing most of them, but was still trusted to point out men to be shot. And then Kelliher in turn had his spies. People who noted down car registration numbers, a billiards marker in the Kildare Street Club who listened in, a policeman who only told the names of men he saw imprisoned: all just noting simple things they saw or heard in the course of their work. Prior to Bloody Sunday there were sympathetic Dublin metropolitan policemen who did the same. They told of houses on their beats where lights were on when they should have been off. They told nothing else, nothing to draw suspicion on themselves, just enough to begin an observation of a possible address. Some information came by chance. For instance, no one in the IRA knew what Alan Bell, the elderly accountant coming uncomfortably close to the coffers of the Dáil Loan, looked like, at least not until the *Irish Independent* published his photograph and sealed his fate.[54] But generally in the case of Bloody Sunday, chance played a rather minimal role. Bloody Sunday depended more on people like Sean Hyde. Hyde was a boarder in 22 Lower Mount Street. He watched and he listened and he befriended Lieutenant McMahon. He went then and he told Liam Tobin all. Tobin knew that 'Hyde was in great danger', that 'he suffered from his nerves', but 'I was callous, and I wanted to drive him to the end'.[55] Hyde was as expendable as McMahon himself.

Pieced together, all this information made Bloody Sunday morning. Showing 'these whores, the British... that Irishmen can turn up on time', beginning all of the attacks at nine o'clock intensified the shock, made it the 'grim *coup de théâtre*' it has been called since.[56] But it was a coup that came with quite a high price. Even without considering the afternoon's reprisals at Croke Park, that morning cost the IRA Dick McKee and Peadar Clancy, two of the most important figures in the Dublin Brigade. It brought internment in earnest and precipitated what Peter Hart has called 'the worst setback yet for the rebels at the hands of British intelligence'.[57] The day itself brought a poor yield of enemy papers and some of the more important targets were not where they were supposed to be, or they were just simply missed. In Pembroke Street Charles Dalton was confused about which officer was which and had to 'get the hell out' before he could 'search the bloody room'.[58] Yet it was shocking and frightening and appalling enough for the British treasury to pay the men's widows the highest pensions allowed, for the British government to bring the corpses to Westminster Abbey, but there was something more shocking about the deaths fought out however fairly or unfairly at Kilmichael a week later, about the burning of the Liverpool docklands that suggested the kind of war the IRA might choose to wage on Britain's economic heart.[59] Bloody Sunday just alerted Britain to Ireland's real capacity for treachery. No one, not even the maids and the porters, could be above suspicion anymore. War in Ireland was now a question of whether you could trust Christopher Foley, the waiter from the hotel across the road who brought your lunch into Dublin Castle. War in Ireland was now a question of whether Christopher Foley was going to poison you or not.[60]

NOTES

1 House of Lords, Parliamentary debates, 6 May 1931, vol. 80, cols. 1036–44.
2 Ibid., col. 1042.
3 Ibid., col. 1040.
4 Michael Hopkinson, *Green Against Green: The Irish Civil War* (Dublin, 1988), p. 226.
5 House of Lords, Parliamentary debates, 6 May 1931, vol. 80, cols. 1040–1.
6 Memorandum by C.H.P. [?], 9 April 1931, TNA, HO 144/14997.
7 Memorandum by Sir E. Harding, 6 April 1931, TNA, DO 35/459/9; House of Lords, Parliamentary debates, 6 May 1931, vol. 80, col. 1041.
8 Letter from C.S. Markbreiter to Sir Harry Batterbee, 14 April 1931, TNA, DO 35/459/9.
9 Charles Dalton, Bureau of Military History, Dublin (BMH) Witness Statement (WS) 434, Military Archives, Dublin.
10 Charles Dalton, in Ernie O'Malley notebooks, UCDA, p17b/122(22).
11 Brigadier-General F.P. Crozier, *Ireland for Ever* (Bath, 1932), pp. 221–2.
12 Robert Kee, *Ireland: A History* (revised edn, London, 1995), p. 187.
13 Kate MacCormack to Richard Mulcahy, 23 March 1922, Collins Papers, A/0535X, NLI microfilm POS 917.
14 Michael Collins to Richard Mulcahy, 7 April 1922, ibid.
15 Kate MacCormack to Richard Mulcahy, 20 June 1922, ibid.
16 Anonymous, *An Officer's Wife in Ireland* (London & Dublin, 1994), p. 70.
17 Larry Nugent, BMH WS 907.
18 'Account of IRA intelligence by Captain Frank Thornton to Army units', 1940[?], Military Archives, Dublin, A/0800/IV.
19 Donal O'Kelly, 'The Dublin scene: war amid the outward trappings of peace', p. 29, and Piaras Béaslaí, 'Fourteen British officers and agents executed in Dublin on "Bloody Sunday"', in *With the IRA in the Fight for Freedom: 1919 to the Truce* (Tralee, n.d.), p. 117.
20 'Account of IRA intelligence by...Thornton...', Military Archives, Dublin, A/0800/IV.
21 Tim Pat Coogan, *De Valera: Long Fellow, Long Shadow* (London, 1993), p. 190. This was echoed by David Neligan in Kenneth Griffith and Timothy O'Grady (eds), *Ireland's Unfinished Revolution: An Oral History* (Colorado, 1999), p. 176, and by Frank Gallagher in *The Four Glorious Years* (Dublin, 1953), p. 243.
22 Michael Collins to Richard Mulcahy, 7 April 1922, Collins Papers, A/0535X, NLI microfilm POS 917.
23 Tom Bowden, 'Bloody Sunday – a reappraisal', *European Studies Review*, 2,1 (January 1972), pp. 38–9.
24 James Doyle, BMH WS 771.
25 Bowden, 'Bloody Sunday', p. 39.
26 James Doyle, BMH WS 771.
27 Peter Hart (ed.), *British Intelligence in Ireland, 1920–21: The Final Reports* (Cork, 2002). Hart concludes (p. 11) that the morning's shootings were based on 'imperfect' information, that 'some of those shot had nothing to do with spying or trials'. He further argues that the shootings precipitated 'the worst setback yet for the rebels at the hands of British Intelligence', with more frequent and more successful raids and round-ups by the British forces as a direct result.
28 See, for example, C.S. Andrews, *Dublin Made Me* (Dublin, 1979), p. 155.
29 Rex Taylor, *Michael Collins* (London, 1970), p.106.
30 J.M. Nankivell and S. Loch, *Ireland in Travail*, (London, 1922), p. 102.
31 David Neligan, BMH WS 380.
32 Ibid.

33 Laurence Nugent, BMH WS 907.
34 Douglas V. Duff, *Sword for Hire: The Saga of a Modern free-companion* (London, 1934), p. 55.
35 Charles Dalton, BMH WS 434.
36 David Neligan, BMH WS 380.
37 Ned Broy, Ernie O'Malley notebooks, UCDA, p17b/98(22).
38 Charles Dalton, BMH WS 434.
39 Charles Dalton, *With the Dublin Brigade (1917–1921)* (London, 1929), pp. 116–17.
40 Ibid., p. 102.
41 Frank Saurin, BMH WS 715.
42 Ibid.
43 Dan Breen, BMH WS 1,739.
44 Marie Cruise-O'Brien, *The Same Age as the State* (Dublin, 2003), p. 56.
45 Frank O'Connor, *The Big Fellow* (Dublin, 1991), p. 119.
46 Joe Dolan, BMH WS 663.
47 Ibid.
48 Frank Saurin, BMH WS 715.
49 Frank Thornton, in Ernie O'Malley notebooks, UCDA, p17b/100(121).
50 Frank Thornton, BMH WS 615; Frank Thornton, in Ernie O'Malley notebooks, UCDA, p17b/100(120).
51 See, for example, Béaslaí, 'Fourteen British officers', p. 117.
52 Edward Kelliher, BMH WS 477.
53 Ibid.
54 Joe Dolan, BMH WS 663.
55 Liam Tobin, in Ernie O'Malley notebooks, UCDA, p17b/100(111).
56 T. Ryle Dwyer, *Big Fellow, Long Fellow: A Joint Biography of Collins and de Valera* (Dublin, 1998), p. 140; Alvin Jackson, *Ireland 1798≠1998* (Oxford, 1999), p. 249.
57 Hart, 'Introduction', *British Intelligence in Ireland*, p. 12.
58 Charles Dalton, in Ernie O'Malley notebooks, UCDA, p17b/122(22); summary of evidence in the case against James Greene, evidence of the medical officer, Dublin, NLI, Michael Noyk papers, MS 36,221/2.
59 TNA, T161/84/6495 Award of pensions at highest rates of gratuities to widows of officers murdered in Ireland; Peter Hart, *The IRA and its Enemies: Violence and Community in Cork, 1916–1923* (Oxford, 1998), p. 21; Thomas Jones, *Whitehall Diary, vol. III: Ireland 1918–1925*, ed. Keith Middlemas (Oxford, 1971), p. 41.
60 Notes made by Christopher Foley concerning his membership of the Republican movement during the war of independence, the civil war and, subsequently, NAI, Private Accessions 999/637.

Intelligence and Anglo-Irish relations, 1922–73

Eunan O'Halpin

In June 1973 the British ambassador to Ireland 'told the Taoiseach that H[er] M[ajesty's] G[overnment] were not conducting espionage activities against the Government of the Republic and had never done so'.[1] This assurance was offered in the wake of two cases which suggested the contrary. These were the court convictions of a Garda sergeant, Michael Crinnion, together with a man who claimed to work for the British Ministry of Defence, for handling Irish security documents, and the imprisonment of the Littlejohns, armed robbers who maintained that they were agents of British intelligence. These matters had caused acute difficulties for the government of Jack Lynch, and they lent weight to charges that Britain was conducting secret intelligence operations in Ireland.

This paper explores the accuracy of the ambassador's unequivocal statement, addressing a significant but understudied aspect of Anglo-Irish relations over an extended period. What efforts did the British government make to acquire intelligence on Irish affairs or covertly to influence events, were such activities the product of political direction or of low-level intrigue, and were they ever directed against the Irish state? Was any effort made to weigh up the potential costs against the likely benefits? And how did the Irish state react to evidence of British intelligence activities possibly directed against its interests?

In recent years intelligence has moved from being a largely unavowed element of Anglo-Irish discourse to being a very public one, as can be seen in the work of the Independent International Commission on Decommissioning and the International Monitoring Commission (IMC).[2] The weight to be placed on their conclusions depends on the material underpinning them: the two commissions have clearly used assessments from British and Irish security sources, and possibly from the security and intelligence agencies of other states.[3] If such agencies are dispassionate, well informed, apolitical servants bent only on securing the pure, distilled truth, well and good. This is the image often portrayed by intelligence professionals, who argue that their agencies are simply the stoic bearers of 'uncomfortable truths which governments would prefer not to but need to hear' (a close paraphrase of the words of a former MI6 chief).[4] Examination of the historical record does not always present them in such an uncomplicated and virtuous light.

Thanks to the liberalisation of public records policy over the last decade, a good deal of material is now available on the intersection between intelligence activity and policy in Anglo-Irish relations. It is possible to explore the impact of intelligence gathering and assessment, and to an extent other forms of intelligence activities, on decision making in Anglo-Irish relations at the highest levels up to 1974.

This discussion concentrates on the impact of intelligence collection and other covert activities on British policy making in two discrete periods, that is the Second World War – the Emergency in neutral Ireland – and the first years of the recent Northern Ireland troubles. The intelligence activities of any state are defined by national interests and capabilities, not by ethical considerations. Britain, for all her relative decline, remains a nuclear power, a permanent member of the UN Security Council, and a country with worldwide interests and responsibilities. It is consequently inevitable that intelligence has played a far more central role in her policy system since 1922 than in Ireland's. But we should remember that in the Irish state's early years, the army collected intelligence in Britain on Irish republicans, and for a time ran agents in Northern Ireland.[5] Furthermore, as became clear during the 1970 Arms Crisis, in 1969 army and Garda officers were sent incognito to collect information on conditions in Northern Ireland, and one officer developed close links with the IRA with calamitous political consequences.[6]

SECRET INTELLIGENCE AND ANGLO-IRISH RELATIONS
1922–1945

British intelligence interest in the new state was conspicuous by its absence after 1922. During the civil war, there was some sharing of information on republican activities outside Ireland, but only on an ad hoc basis. No British agency attempted to collect intelligence for political, security or military purposes in Ireland. Aside from occasional contact between Scotland Yard and the Irish Special Branch – the British passed on to Dublin miscellaneous intelligence on Irish radical contacts with international communist organisations and the like – there were no arrangements for liaison on security (whereas the security service MI5 had representatives in the other dominions).[7] The Royal Ulster Constabulary (RUC) kept a limited watch on Irish affairs, but solely in terms of the republican threat.

De Valera's accession to power in March 1932 caused alarm, because little was known about his intentions. It produced an immediate intelligence response. British codebreakers started reading Irish diplomatic cables, although they soon switched their attentions elsewhere. The secret service MI6 also established a 'limited information service'.[8] This produced periodic reports on political conditions which were little more than gossip. No attempts were made to suborn Irish officials or to interfere in Irish politics.

When the Second World War began Britain consequently had no worthwhile Irish intelligence. As a result of an Irish initiative, however, the foundations of an understanding on security existed: MI5 and the Irish army intelligence directorate G2 had been in contact for over a year and had already worked successfully on one case of German espionage. This 'Dublin link' was to prove crucial throughout the war, providing a means by which the British and Irish security authorities could co-operate to detect and counteract Axis intelligence gathering in Ireland. It served both Britain and Ireland well, and at times operated to moderate the more extreme impulses of Mr Churchill. MI5 maintained that it was crucial not simply in security terms but in wider Anglo-Irish relations, and the value of effective liaison was repeatedly adduced in debate about how best to deal with the security dangers posed by Axis diplomats in Dublin.[9]

In the early months of the Emergency, G2 pointed out that it was counterproductive to encourage people resident in Ireland to collect intelligence for Britain, as this inevitably came to Irish attention and diverted energies from the serious business of investigating pro-German activities.[10] Such amateurish espionage had other consequences: it was alarmist reports about political conditions and German activities in Ireland which prompted MI6 to suggest an offer of possible eventual Irish unity in return for participation in the war.[11] MI6 also established a limited counterintelligence operation in June 1940, tasked with the surveillance of Axis diplomats and pro-Axis elements. It was penetrated within months and, as it did not directly threaten Irish interests, G2 decided to keep tabs on it rather than shut it down.[12]

Early in 1941 the irregular warfare organisation SOE (Special Operations Executive) proposed the establishment of 'stay behind' groups in Ireland to carry out sabotage and provide intelligence in the event of a German invasion.[13] The British army in Northern Ireland told SOE that this could be done only through co-operation with selected officers of the Irish army, to whom the creation of such groups should be entrusted. The proposal was ultimately blocked, despite a direct plea to Churchill, not because it might compromise existing security co-operation, but because it might reinforce Irish resolve to stay out of the war unless attacked. SOE appointed one Irish agent, primarily to spread 'whispers' (rumours) and to plan sabotage in the event of a German invasion, but MI5 and MI6 soon succeeded in forcing his withdrawal lest his activities jeopardise MI5's 'valuable liaison' with the Irish.[14] The spreading of 'whispers' in Ireland was afterwards left to British diplomats – for a time the press attaché John Betjeman was involved despite his ignorance of 'operational whispering' – and to casual contacts.[15] Such 'whispering' was generally aimed at Axis targets: Dublin was useful because, as in other neutral capitals like Lisbon, Stockholm and Berne, diplomatic missions could be expected to pass on any rumours to their home countries. It was not intended to influence domestic Irish politics. Black propaganda was, however, the one intelligence weapon which wartime Britain used actively to damage Irish interests. SOE and other agencies systematically fabricated and circulated rumours designed to discredit Irish neutrality.[16] In the United States, the American Irish Defense Association (AIDA), whose members included academics, priests, journalists and trade unionists, made the case for Irish support for Britain against Nazi tyranny. Secretly controlled by SOE, it was one element in a concerted British drive to manipulate American opinion against Irish neutrality.[17] Towards the end of the war, SOE put forward an elaborate deception scheme, the 'Casement Plan', designed to lower German morale by spreading tales that the Nazi leaders were planning to flee to a comfortable retirement, not in sunny Argentina as the Foreign Office suggested, but in damp, dismal Ireland. In the face of strong Foreign Office objections on grounds both of credibility and of policy, SOE's Major General Gerald Templer, an Ulsterman, fought hard to keep Ireland as the supposed bolthole, although he was eventually overruled.[18]

For most of the war British codebreakers could read Irish and other diplomatic traffic to and from Dublin.[19] The key exception was important: the German diplomatic code was broken only in December 1942, and the first traffic then tackled was Berlin/Dublin – in addition to cable traffic, the German legation possessed a secret transmitter which was used intermittently to send messages until the Irish government forced its handover in December 1943.[20] Decodes were crucial to British policy on Ireland. They disclosed the material which foreign missions in Ireland, neutrals as well as Axis, were relaying about Britain's war effort and military plans, as well as instructions from the Axis capitals to their Irish missions. The decodes also allowed London to study the evolution of Irish–Axis relations, particularly in respect of consistent Irish pressure on the Germans to eschew intelligence gathering. The British Representative, Sir John

Maffey, was 'put in the picture' about this codebreaking success, on the personal decision of the head of MI6.[21] Irish diplomatic traffic, by contrast, was useful mainly in providing a neutral perspective on conditions and opinion in Europe: there is almost nothing bearing on high policy in the five hundred or so Irish decodes traced.

Churchill saw a considerable number of Irish messages related to Ireland among his daily selection of decoded military and diplomatic traffic.[22] This sometimes caused difficulties. During the build up to Operation Torch – the Allied landings in Vichy-controlled Morocco – in October 1942, Guy Liddell of MI5 noted

> a report on Ireland which is being sent...to the P[rime] M[inister]. The latter has become alarmed by one of the telegrams by the Italian representative in Dublin which appeared to him to indicate leakage of information. In actual fact the information that has been obtained...is of little consequence. Much of it has been inaccurate.
>
> I told Viv[ian of MI6] that I thought the report which had been put up...gave away too much about our relations with Dan [Bryan of G2]...I thought this could be said verbally to the Foreign Secretary.[23]

In April 1943, MI5 needed the support of MI6, the Joint Intelligence Committee (JIC), the Dominions Office and the deputy prime minister Clement Attlee to dissuade Churchill from ordering a precipitate *démarche* about the clandestine German Legation radio in Dublin. Churchill acquiesced only with considerable bad grace: 'It is our duty to try to save these people from themselves...there seems to be a very strong case for doing what is right and just and facing the usual caterwaul from the disloyal Irish...in the Dominions'.[24] He continued to declaim against Irish neutrality, while the intelligence agencies continued to husband their constructive relationship with Dublin. Five days after D-Day, Liddell noted that Churchill still 'seems to have three bad bees in his bonnet', one of which was Ireland.[25]

While many intelligence issues relating to Ireland were discussed at the political level in London, in Dublin security policy and operations, and most crucially Irish co-operation with Britain, were handled by a handful of senior officials – Joseph Walshe and Fred Boland of the Department of External Affairs, and the heads of G2 (Liam Archer until July 1941, and thereafter Dan Bryan). There was minimal ministerial involvement, although security co-operation operated with the general blessing of the taoiseach and minister for external affairs de Valera.

The same was true of Garda/RUC links. There is almost no trace in the available Irish records of any dealings between the two police forces. British records are somewhat more forthcoming, although the RUC inspector general, Sir Charles Wickham, on whom London came greatly to rely, told the Northern Ireland government as little as possible about his wartime dealings with the Garda. He also had unorthodox political views. By October 1944 he was

> heartily sick of the Northern Irish politicians. Partition has now become the battle cry that keeps both Dev[alera] and Sir Basil Brooke in office. If they had not got the border they would probably both lose their jobs. He would like to see a united Ireland and thinks that if there had been one Irish Government it would have joined us in the war.[26]

THE COLD WAR AND ANGLO-IRISH SECURITY RELATIONS

During the Cold War Ireland was happy to supply both London and Washington with information about suspected communist activities and to accept related material in exchange. The roots of such co-operation were both ideological and pragmatic – Ireland was strongly anticommunist, while, the more forthcoming Irish security officials were, the less likely that the Western allies would start spying in Ireland. In 1952 Liddell told Dan Bryan that 'They have laid the foundations of something really worthwhile', and there is other evidence of close links.[27] But there was seldom more to deal with in Anglo-Irish security liaison than could be discussed 'over a good lunch' a couple of times a year.[28] The gentlemanly pace of liaison changed only with the Irish decision to establish diplomatic relations with the Soviet Union in 1972, a development which alarmed prime minister Edward Heath, concerned that Dublin could become a centre for Soviet clandestine activities against Britain. In a personal message to Jack Lynch he cited the testimony of a recent KGB defector, Oleg Lyalin, on Soviet discussions with Irish communists about aid for the Official IRA, and offered 'assistance to your people in the technical fields associated with the control of such subversive activities'.[29]

Within the postwar British intelligence community there were people who knew something of Ireland for the simple reason that they were Irish themselves: Sir Philip Vickery was a graduate of Trinity College Dublin who had spent over twenty years working on Indian intelligence, including the study of Irish–Indian radical links, before joining the Commonwealth Office; Brigadier Bill Magan, who ran each of MI5's four directorates in succession between 1953 and 1968, and was for a time responsible for liaison with G2, hailed from County Meath, where his parents lived until their deaths in the 1960s; Dick Craig, a senior MI6 officer in the 1960s, came from west Cork and had studied at Trinity; and another Trinity man, Air Marshal Sir Harold Maguire from Clare, served on the JIC from December 1964 until he retired as chief of the Defence Intelligence Staff a decade later.[30] But the Ireland of their childhoods had long gone.

With the limited exception of IRA activities during the 'Border campaign' of 1956–62, the entire island of Ireland slipped beneath Whitehall's intelligence radar between 1945 and 1969, at least as reflected in the records of the JIC. The JIC is at the apex of British intelligence tasking and assessment, the forum in which foreign policy considerations in the widest sense – including trade, financial and economic questions – are addressed through the prism of intelligence analysis. The JIC chair was customarily held by the Foreign Office, and between 1967 and 1973 the chairmen successively were Sir Denis Greenhill, Sir Edward Peck and Sir Stewart Crawford. These were also the Foreign and Commonwealth Office officials with overall responsibility for Irish matters. Christopher Ewart Biggs, murdered by the IRA shortly after his appointment as ambassador to Ireland in 1976, served on the JIC from 1966 to 1970, chairing a 'Working Party on Intelligence Priorities and Resources' in 1967.[31] The point is not to argue that these officials were secret spymasters, but rather to emphasise how integrated had become the process of intelligence assessment with wider policy considerations.

The prospect of IRA attacks in Northern Ireland and Britain timed to coincide with the 50th anniversary of the 1916 Rising was raised by the Northern Ireland prime minister in December 1965, citing RUC intelligence on IRA preparations in the Republic of Ireland. During a meeting on trade questions with prime minister Harold Wilson, the imperturbable taoiseach Sean Lemass, himself a former IRA assassin, said 'he thought reports about the IRA tended to be exaggerated but this did not mean that he was taking them lightly'.[32] The JIC then began to consider 'the IRA threat', discussing it on no less than eight occasions between January and April 1966. The RUC anticipated 'incidents to be modeled on EOKA terrorist activities...attacks on individuals rather than sabotage of installations'.[33] The JIC endorsed an approach to the Irish, but the results were disappointing: 'there had been little of value derived from the recent meeting...between officials of the RUC and the...Garda', and so the committee recommended an informal approach by the head of the Belfast Ministry of Home Affairs to his opposite number in Dublin, Peter Berry (who reassured the Northerners about the likely threat).[34] The weight attached to Stormont's warnings is reflected not only in the JIC's deliberations but in the steps taken by the cabinet secretary, Sir Burke Trend. He kept the prime minister fully informed, and personally oversaw precautionary military, police and security arrangements. MI5 concluded that the reason the anniversary passed off virtually without incident was 'the action of the Ulster authorities and the high order of police work there', although Berry maintained that no concerted IRA action had been planned in either jurisdiction.[35] The JIC also briefly discussed

> communist influence in the IRA...There was in particular a professor at Trinity College, Dublin, who had a communist record and was well versed in communist techniques ... The IRA had flirted with communism on several occasions...but had always had to eject communist elements...[as] the IRA relied on the support of members of the Roman Catholic Church.[36]

Once the threat of IRA action disappeared, so too did Ireland. In 1967 and in the first half of 1968 the JIC considered contributions and assessments on all manner of perils, real and imaginary, from Soviet military intentions in a general war to the emergence and implications of the 'Black Power' movement. As part of a drive to make greater use of intelligence capability across the span of government – the 'economic departments' were urged to set clear priorities – the JIC's plans for 1969 included an assessment of the value to Britain of the European Free Trade Area, and a study of 'EC Agricultural Unit of Account in Relation to a Change in Parities', possibly the dullest intelligence document ever commissioned.[37] Of Ireland north or south there was not a mention. It was only in early 1969 that an 'Ulster Working Group' was established to consider the growth of political unrest in Northern Ireland.

1968–1974

In June 1968 the British ambassador in Dublin, Sir Andrew Gilchrist, was placed under increased Garda protection. He thought 'there is some smoke but...extremely little likelihood of fire'.[38] Gilchrist was no stranger to danger: captured by the Japanese in Singapore in 1942, he ended the war in SOE working with resistance groups in Thailand. Trouble followed him: in Iceland, his embassy was attacked by fishermen; and, while ambassador to Indonesia, he stood armed inside the embassy chancellery as rioters attempted to break in. At the time British troops in Borneo and Brunei were fighting a border war with Indonesian infiltrators, and in 1965 the pro-Moscow leader Sukarno was overthrown in a coup. Gilchrist was not overjoyed to be posted to Dublin:

> I had hoped for promotion and am disappointed at not getting it. Quite honestly I thought I had earned it – and earned it not

merely on the basis of sufferings endured (a minor point, qualifying one to be put decently out to grass) but of success achieved. Indonesia...has been quite a major preoccupation for the government, not just a third-rate backwater. I went out there under the worst possible auspices and have now left it at a point where the prospects for a peaceful solution (and an enormous saving of cash for HMG) are better than they have ever been. I have seen our worst enemies killed or put in gaol or deprived of power.

While 'I have nothing against Dublin...I am a poor man with three expensive teenagers'.[39] Despite the tedium of endless haggling about cheese quotas and cattle exports, Gilchrist's sense of humour reasserted itself. He described his first meeting with President de Valera and the minister for external affairs Frank Aiken, who called to his Sandyford residence, 'Glencairn'. De Valera remarked that

> You...have buried...at Glencairn the grave of Strongbow's horse.
> A.G. G[ilchrist]: I didn't even know Strongbow *had* a horse.
> Aiken: This is all news to me. Where did your information come from, Mr President? Where is the grave?
> De Valera: It is either near or in Glencairn – it is spoken about in old legends, recorded in some publication of one of the Gaelic societies.
> A.G. G.: I shall make every effort to follow this up [I very *nearly* said: "And when we *do* find the horse's grave, we'll ask for it to be dug up and returned to England in return for Casement": but I am growing discreet with advancing years].[40]

Shortly afterwards the commonwealth relations secretary George Thomson (who had fond memories of his honeymoon spent in Dublin) assured Gilchrist that 'Dublin had been intended as a well-deserved rest' and that he would get more 'active employment before too long'.[41] How right he was.

Gilchrist's social contacts reflected his old intelligence interests:

> the three Irishmen with whom I can talk most freely & frankly about Irish politics are all moderate men, and they know very well what side they are on. They are General Collins-Powell, Mr David Neligan, & Mr Erskine Childers.[42]

Collins-Powell was a nephew of Michael Collins, and had been involved in secret military liaison with the British during the Emergency. Neligan had, as his 1968 memoir put it, been *The Spy in the*

Castle, a policeman who had worked for Michael Collins during the War of Independence, and who became a controversial head of the Garda Special Branch. Erskine Childers' father had written *The Riddle of the Sands*, by far the best Edwardian spy novel, before serving as a naval intelligence officer during the First World War and then committing himself to Irish separatism, which led to his eventual execution during the civil war.[43] Gilchrist's confidantes were, in short, people who knew a thing or two about conspiracy, intelligence and subversion.

Given his experience and associates, Gilchrist might have seemed the ideal man to have in Dublin when serious trouble broke out. He had, after all, seen this kind of thing before, and as a result of the assassination scare was on good terms with the head of the Garda Special Branch, chief superintendent John Fleming.[44] He took the opportunity to prepare a dispatch on the IRA which noted its marked move to the left. While the IRA's political support was negligible, the question of partition remained a shared grievance with the mainstream political parties, although most ministers 'have their emotions under control and are working for that *détente* with Northern Ireland and for rapprochement with Britain which form an essential accompaniment to their programme of social and economic progress'. They were, however, not inclined to take vigorous action against the IRA for fear of stoking up public sympathy: 'it is better on the whole for the Government to endure a little discomfort and disorder and humiliation and to hope that the IRA will not go too far'.[45]

Gilchrist was as surprised as anyone by events after 1968.[46] Dublin was not Djakarta, and so far from calling for covert action against the Irish state, in August 1969 he suggested the 'immediate suspension of the Stormont constitution (and of Ulster representation at Westminster)' and the creation of a 'Constitutional Assembly to work out a fair system other than numerical majority-rule-democracy under which the province could have peace'.[47] He also, according to his own notes, told the JIC that the Lynch government needed to 'be strengthened & encouraged to deal with [the] IRA problem'.[48] The JIC had concluded in June that 'the potential for disorder in Northern Ireland comes from the inter-action of three distinct groups: the Irish Republican Army (IRA), the civil rights movement, and the Paisleyites', who were 'ultra Protestants'. It also identified growing communist influence on the IRA, and Trotskyite infiltration of the civil rights movement.[49] Gilchrist's analysis of the political constraints on resolute Irish government action against the IRA, in particular popular feeling about the treatment of northern nationalists and the operation of the Special Powers Act, did not persuade all his JIC listeners. It was suggested that 'the power of the IRA...and its influence over the Irish Government might not be so great as described...the Government might be overstating the IRA menace to justify an unhelpful attitude towards us over Northern Ireland', although 'there was no doubt that the IRA contained a hard core with a single-minded extreme outlook comparable with that of the Mafia'. Since the introduction of British troops in support of the civil authorities in Northern Ireland, 'liaison with the Garda...our main potential source of information on the IRA...had dried up altogether, and it was unlikely to be reopened in the foreseeable future' either on government instructions 'or as a result of the initiative of individual Garda officers'. The JIC suggested that 'sources such as journalists should be tapped', and observed that 'there was much information readily available in public houses where a great deal of unguarded conversation took place', although they did not indicate how such material was to be gathered or by whom. More significantly, they agreed that Gilchrist should receive the committee's assessments on Northern Ireland as a matter of course. They also invited him to keep them informed on 'future developments in the Republic of Ireland relating to the IRA'.[50]

Within a few months, Northern Ireland had become a standard item on the JIC's agenda: following the August disturbances, it was discussed at eleven successive meetings. The ad hoc Ulster Working Group was replaced by an Ulster (sometimes also described as 'Ireland' and 'Northern Ireland') Current Intelligence Group, and the first of many efforts were made to improve, streamline and make secure the flow of intelligence between Belfast and London, and between different agencies operating in Northern Ireland. The search for effective intelligence arrangements was to be a drearisome feature of the next decade.[51] In December 1970 a 'longer term assessment' to cover the period up to the end of 1972 was commissioned from the JIC for a ministerial working party, the first evidence of the use of the central intelligence assessment machine to look at wider considerations.[52] Preparation of this paper dragged on for months: in August 1971 it was decided to exclude 'a forecast of the economic outlook', although 'it should...include an assessment of the future effectiveness of the security forces, including the RUC, and of the sort of political reforms that the Protestants might accept'.[53] A further draft assessment on the possible impact of direct rule circulated in November 1971 was

> controversial in parts. It is certainly unlike any other JIC appreciation that I have seen...In one sense, the document is a rather depressing one. It suggests that direct rule may not help us to separate the Catholic population from the IRA; that once direct rule is imposed we shall have to go very quickly towards our long term solution or the situation will rapidly deteriorate; and

that unless the Republic is closely associated with, and approves of, the constitutional arrangements, they have little chance of success. This may reflect the Foreign Office background of its author, but there is something in what is said.

The draft assessment – 'a poor thing but our own – at least in the sense that we commissioned it'- ran into considerable criticism.[54] It was eventually abandoned after 'Bloody Sunday' in January 1972 completely changed Anglo-Irish politics. The draft gave consideration to the likely reaction in 'The Republic', concentrating entirely on Jack Lynch's position:

> Lynch would probably be prepared to support Direct Rule... provided it could be presented as a new start and provided the Republic could be seen to have a continuing and influential role ... His freedom of manoeuvre has been reduced by what is seen as his failure so far to influence Her Majesty's Government in the smallest degree.[55]

This is the first substantial rumination on Dublin's future role to be found among JIC papers following Sir Andrew Gilchrist's discussions with the committee of September 1969. His difficulties in convincing London of the destabilising impact on Irish politics of events in Northern Ireland largely arose from the fact that in 1969 the Foreign Office scarcely knew where Ireland was. As an official put it in 1970,

> "The Republic of Ireland" was...a non-subject until 1969. Certainly there was no Whitehall structure to cope with the strains that arose. Unlike the traditionally great themes of Europe, the Middle East, the Soviet bloc etc., there is virtually no corpus of knowledge and experience within the Office.[56]

By the time Gilchrist departed from Dublin in March 1970, his voice carried little weight in Whitehall. In retirement he passed on a letter from a Dublin friend, commenting that 'the prediction of a "Greek" authoritarian phase is plausible' – this following the sensational revelation of Irish efforts to import weapons for possible use by nationalists in Northern Ireland, the Arms Crisis which rocked Jack Lynch's government and saw two ministers unsuccessfully prosecuted.[57] On this the permanent under-secretary at the Foreign Office minuted: 'I do not intend to encourage any further correspondence of this kind – you only need *one* Ambassador in a small country like Ireland.'[58]

Gilchrist was succeeded by John Peck, who had to come to grips with Irish affairs just as the Arms Crisis broke in May 1970. A less colourful figure than Gilchrist, he too fell out of favour in London. When he retired in February 1973, his valedictory dispatch stated that 'Dublin should be an ambassador's last post. Nothing that he has learnt in his career will be wasted. Much that he learns... would be irrelevant anywhere else.'[59] While he had maintained good relations in Dublin at a very difficult and confused time, he was criticised for failing to visit Northern Ireland and for not grasping the importance of border security. His last dispatch

> played down, but has not concealed, the differences between the Department and himself on the extent to which HMG should feel satisfied with the Irish Government's performance, and the extent to which our pressure for more action was justified or wise.[60]

The Foreign Office took care to ensure that Peck's successor, Arthur Galsworthy, was better briefed on security issues: before he even reached Dublin he attended a succession of meetings in London and Belfast with civilian, military and intelligence figures.[61]

It is clear from British records that between 1969 and 1973 Whitehall saw the political stability of the Lynch government as a *sine qua non* for progress on Northern Ireland. The resolution of the Arms Crisis was regarded as strengthening Lynch and vindicating his generally realistic approach to Northern issues. It is hard to reconcile the thrust of British policy towards Ireland in those years with a secret aim of destabilising the Irish state or of bringing about Lynch's downfall in favour of a more amenable regime.

By the autumn of 1970, it was agreed in Whitehall that part of the solution to the violence in Northern Ireland lay in persuading the Irish government to deal more firmly with the IRA along the border. It was universally believed that the Irish were not doing remotely as much as they should to prevent cross-border IRA attacks, or to prevent the theft of explosives for bomb making. These considerations became a defining element of British policy. British preoccupation with border security, and with documenting Irish inadequacies, developed partly in response to the Irish government's increasing interest in the problems of the nationalist community in Northern Ireland, particularly in respect of human rights abuses after the introduction of internment in August 1971, a measure which the defence secretary initially believed had 'lanced the boil of terrorism'.[62] There is, however, no evidence that London believed that the half-hearted Irish approach to border security was intended to extract political concessions. Rather, it was thought that Lynch shied away from resolute security action against the IRA essentially for fear of splitting his Fianna Fáil party. This was something which London also feared, as shown by prime minister Heath's decision to block a proposal for covert aerial mapping of the border precisely because it could create internal party difficulties for Lynch.[63]

This is what makes the decision to spy on the Garda Security Section (C3) so strange. Was it a reflection of high-level British unease at the inadequacy of information provided by the Irish, or a blunder by an overenthusiastic field officer? Was the operation cleared with the JIC or with ministers? A former British official, when questioned about the logic of penetrating a force with which co-operation was ongoing, commented, somewhat ruefully, 'insurance'.[64] Having suborned Sergeant Crinnion, the British government then made the cardinal error of feeding back to Dublin much of the intelligence obtained from him. In November 1972 a detailed dossier on IRA border activists was presented to Lynch. The foreign secretary told Heath:

> What we must seek from the Irish is an undertaking that an under-standing attitude at the top will be matched by a positive instruction to all subordinate officials and military units that action against the IRA should be vigorous. This is notably lacking at present. It is also desirable to obtain agreement on continuing consultation between the security forces on both sides of the border.[65]

The Irish smelt a rat. Foreign minister Patrick Hillery told Peck that the material

> we passed to the Irish Government about IRA activities had frequently been of low quality, but had suddenly shown such a marked improvement that it could only have come from one source and this had put their security service on the trail...He then said that...the Taoiseach had been on the phone to him to convey his deep personal dismay and shock...The British action in penetrating the...Gardai displayed such a lack of confidence that it completely undermined the very hopeful new relationship and the plans for practical co-operation that were being developed between him and the prime minister. Dr Hillery added that politically Mr Lynch was now out on a limb. The IRA, who were practically broken, would now take on a new lease of life and quote we are right back to square one unquote.[66]

Peck could deny all knowledge of this British operation with a straight face, because no one had told him about it in advance. There were serious consequences: the Foreign Office gloomily accepted that it would be impossible to exert any further pressure about border security until the controversy died down.[67]

Of almost equal embarrassment were the Littlejohn brothers, two English career criminals who robbed a Dublin bank in 1972. When arrested in Britain on foot of an Irish warrant, and in an ironic play on Irish republicans' use of the same principle of international law, they fought against extradition on the grounds that their alleged offence was essentially political: they claimed they had gone to Ireland with the covert blessing and support of the British government, as part of a scheme to discredit the IRA and to collect intelligence. There were elements of truth in their story: at a minimum, British officials knew of their intentions, had asked them to pass on any information which they might pick up, and had omitted to warn Dublin that these criminals were heading to Ireland to ply their trade.[68]

The available records suggest that British policy from 1969 to 1973 was emphatically to support the Lynch government, if only for fear of what might replace it. Lynch was, as Harold Wilson, now in opposition, remarked to Edward Heath in October 1971, 'the best prime minister – or rather taoiseach – that we have', and shortly before the February 1973 election Heath felt Lynch 'has been doing well from our point of view'.[69] Yet London was favourably surprised by the election of the Cosgrave coalition: the new taoiseach was determined to confront the IRA, the minister for defence was helpful on border security and the foreign secretary deemed his new Irish opposite number Garret FitzGerald 'quite good but very Irish'.[70] The records also indicate that from 1969 onwards security policy and operations relating to Northern Ireland were closely monitored by the JIC and by No.10 Downing Street.[71] The Littlejohn and Crinnion affairs consequently present a problem for historians of Anglo-Irish relations: were they aberrations, at odds with general policy on intelligence activities concerning Ireland since independence? Alternatively, are they evidence of the operation of a twin-track approach in the 1970s and 1980s? By the mid-1970s, the Irish army director of intelligence was in London 'every three or four weeks' for discussions with MI5 and the army on republican and loyalist paramilitary activities, and Garda/RUC and Metropolitan Police contacts were even more extensive.[72] Yet deepening co-operation was, allegedly, paralleled by covert intelligence activity designed to pressure Dublin into stronger measures against the IRA.[73] A recent judicial inquiry into Ulster loyalist paramilitary killings in Ireland between 1972 and 1976 was unable to reach a definitive conclusion about charges of British collusion because of London's refusal, despite assurances of assistance from prime minister Blair, to grant access to original RUC, army and intelligence records.[74] It may be some time before historians can make a useful contribution to that debate, although the available evidence indicates that since 1922 Britain has generally protected her security interests more effectively through co-operation with the independent Irish state than by clandestine operations against it.

NOTES

1 Thom (British Embassy, Dublin) to White (Foreign Office), 4 Sept. 1973, TNA, London], FCO 87/204.
2 The IMC was established in 2003 by an international agreement of the British and Irish governments to monitor the normalisation of security operations, and paramilitary observance of terms of the Good Friday Agreement of 1998. Three of its four members have extensive experience of security matters.
3 In a press conference of 26 September 2005 televised on the BBC, General John de Chastelain of the International Commission stated that they had had access only to 'assessments' of the British and Irish security forces about republican weapons stocks, not to 'operational intelligence'.
4 Speaking at a confidential seminar of the British Study Group on Intelligence, London, in 1996. Broadly, MI6, the secret intelligence service, is responsible for foreign intelligence. MI5, the security service, deals with security, counter-intelligence, counterespionage and counterterrorism within the United Kingdom.
5 Eunan O'Halpin, *Defending Ireland: The Irish State and its Enemies since 1922* (Oxford, 1999), pp. 53–8.
6 For a circumspect summary of the crisis, see O'Halpin, *Defending Ireland*, pp. 308–11. The late Captain James Kelly, who became a successful serial litigant, threatened proceedings despite the fact that I had deliberately relied on his own sworn testimony. I am very grateful to Eugene Davy and to Paul O'Higgins SC for their advice in that moment of peril. Justin O'Brien, *The Arms Trial* (Dublin, 2000), argues that Lynch and the minister for defence Jim Gibbons knew far more about the arms importation scheme than they afterwards maintained.
   The Foreign Office had under consideration the British military attaché's plan to bring Irish officers on fact-finding tours of Northern Ireland at the time that the crisis broke. Foreign Office to British Embassy, Dublin, 23 Apr., and reply, 6 May 1970, TNA, FCO 33/1085.
7 As an example, see Machtig (Dominions Office) to Walshe (Department of External Affairs), 19 Nov. 1931, relaying a report of a Soviet arms shipment believed to be intended for the IRA, TNA, DO 121/77.
8 Eunan O'Halpin (ed.), *MI5 and Ireland, 1939–1945: The Official History* (Dublin, 2002), p. 20.
9 *The Security Service 1908–1945: The Official History* (London, 1999), pp. 277–86.
10 O'Halpin, *Defending Ireland*, p. 226. The observation was offered to the newly appointed British naval attaché.
11 Liddell diary, 4 June 1940, TNA, KV4/186. On the British offer, see Paul Canning, *British Policy towards Ireland, 1921–1941* (Oxford, 1985), pp. 272–87.
12 Interview with Colonel Dan Bryan (1900–85), director of intelligence, 1941–52, 1983.
13 SOE war diary, 30 Jan. 1941, TNA, HS 7/212; Eunan O'Halpin, '"Toys" and "whispers" in "16-land": SOE and Ireland, 1940–42', *Intelligence and National Security* 15, 4 (Winter 2000), pp. 1–18.
14 'C' (Stewart Menzies, head of MI6) to Gladwyn Jebb of SOE, 24 Apr. 1941, TNA, HS8/305.
15 The term is used in an SOE memorandum. D/Q to AD/P, 27 Feb. 1942, TNA, HS 6/305.
16 SOE war diary, 19 Mar. 1941, TNA, HS 7/214. In August 1941 the newly formed

Political Warfare Executive took over the manufacture of 'whispers', although their distribution outside the United Kingdom remained SOE's responsibility. There is a limited amount of material related to Ireland in lists of 'whispers' circulated for approval in 1941–2 in TNA, FO 868/69. See also Eunan O'Halpin, 'Hitler's Irish hideout: a case study of SOE's black propaganda operations', in Mark Seaman (ed.), *Special Operations Executive: a new Instrument of Warfare* (London, 2006), pp. 201–16.

17 Reports on the work of AIDA are in the SOE records at TNA, HS 8/56–60.

18 SOE Council minutes, 22 Dec. 1944, TNA, HS 8/201.

19 Diplomatic decodes for the war years, mainly in monthly folders, are in TNA, HW 12/243–331.

20 Information from Sir Harry Hinsley, the official historian of British intelligence in the Second World War, 1991.

21 Vivian (MI6) to Stephenson (Dominions Office), 13 Apr. 1943, TNA, DO 121/184. Immediately after the war Maffey caused consternation in MI6 when he suggested that de Valera be shown some decodes of Hempel's clandestine traffic in order to emphasise how dangerous the radio link had been to both Irish and Allied interests. TNA, DO 121/89.

22 These are in TNA, HW 1.

23 Liddell diary, 24 Oct. 1942, TNA, KV 4/190.

24 Churchill to Attlee (dominions secretary and deputy prime minister), 5 May 1943, TNA, DO 121/84.

25 Liddell diary, 11 June 1944, TNA, KV 4/194.

26 Liddell diary, 4 Oct. 1944, TNA, KV 4/194. On Wickham see O'Halpin, *Defending Ireland*, p. 207.

27 Liddell to Bryan, 26 Mar. 1952, UCDA, Bryan papers, P 71/427.

28 Private information from a British official involved.

29 Foreign Office to Bridges (Downing Street), 29 Feb., and Foreign Secretary to Peck (Dublin), conveying text of Heath to Lynch, 1 Mar. 1972, TNA, PREM 15/1046. Lyalin, who had already been suborned by the British, defected after his arrest for drink driving. His job was to make arrangements for sabotage and subversion in the UK and Ireland in the event of war. His disclosures contributed to the expulsion of 105 Soviet personnel from Britain in October 1971. A month earlier Wilson told Heath that during a recent visit to Moscow he had managed to disabuse Soviet foreign minister Kosygin of his illusions about the nature of the Northern Ireland conflict and hoped that this might influence Soviet policy. Note of discussion between Heath, Wilson and James Callaghan, 18 Oct. 1971, TNA, PREM 15/485.

30 Sir Philip Vickery (1888–1982) ran Indian Political Intelligence (IPI) from 1925 until its absorption into MI5 following Indian independence in 1947. He served in the Commonwealth Relations Office until 1965. William Magan, who retired from MI5 in 1968, is author of *An Irish Boyhood* (Edinburgh, 2002), *The Story of Ireland* (Shaftesbury, 2000), *Middle Eastern Approaches: Memoirs of an Intelligence Officer* (Salisbury, 2001) and *Soldier of the Raj* (Norwich, 2002). JIC minutes, 10 Dec. 1964, TNA, CAB 159/42,

31 Confidential annex to JIC minutes, 29 June 1967, TNA, CAB 159/47.

32 Downing Street to Home Office, 13 Dec. 1965, TNA, PREM 13/49.

33 JIC minutes, 10 Feb. 1966, TNA, CAB 159/45. EOKA was a Greek Cypriot terrorist group with which the IRA had some contact.

34 JIC minutes, 24 Feb., and 17 Mar. 1966, TNA, CAB 159/45; O'Halpin, *Defending Ireland*, p. 302.

35 JIC minutes, 21 Apr. 1966, TNA, CAB 159/45.

36 JIC minutes, 21 Apr. 1966, TNA, CAB 159/45. I have redacted other details in the document which clearly identify this person.

37 Memorandum by Sir Dick White, undated, circulated with JIC(B) (69) (SEC), 3 Feb., and JIC (B) minutes, 21 Apr., and JIC (B) minutes, 16 May 1969, TNA, CAB 188/3.
38 Gilchrist to FO, 27 June 1968, TNA, FCO 23/192.
39 Gilchrist to ?, 6 May 1966, Churchill College Archives (CCA), GILC 14B.
40 Extracts of draft report of conversation, 27 Feb. 1967, CCA, GILC 14B. The remains of Sir Roger Casement, executed for treason in Pentonville Prison in 1916, were exhumed and returned to Ireland in March 1965.
41 Gilchrist note, 7 Oct. 1967, CCA, GILC 14/C.
42 Draft dispatch to FCO, 30 Jan. 1969, CCA, GILC 962/14A.
43 David Neligan, *The Spy in the Castle* (London, 1968); for a recent study of Childers see Jim Ring, *Erskine Childers* (London, 1996). Erskine Childers TD was minister for post and telegraphs in the Lynch government. He represented a border constituency, Cavan-Monaghan.
44 Gilchrist to Hunt (Foreign and Commonwealth Office), 4 July 1968, TNA, FCO 23/192.
45 Memorandum by Gilchrist, 5 July 1968, TNA, FCO 23/192.
46 On the first years of the crisis see especially Ronan Fanning, '"Playing it Cool": the response of the British and Irish governments to the crisis in Northern Ireland, 1968–9' in *Irish Studies in International Affairs*, 12 (2001), pp. 57–85.
47 Personal letter, Gilchrist to Greenhill, 5 Apr. 1970, CCA, GILC 14B.
48 Undated notes, 1969, CCA, GILC 14B. Gilchrist had previously attended a JIC meeting while ambassador to Indonesia. JIC minutes, 1 Oct. 1964, CAB 159/42.
49 The Ulster Working Group included a senior RUC Special Branch officer, an innovation which raised eyebrows in MI5 (private information). JIC minutes, 16 June 1969, TNA, CAB 186/3.
50 JIC (69), 38th meeting, 18 Sept. 1969, TNA, CAB 185/9.
51 The partly redacted minutes of JIC meetings up to 1975 are now open to research in the National Archives in the series CAB 185. JIC memoranda are available only up to 1969, again with some redactions. The papers of the Ulster Working Group and its successor the Ulster Current Intelligence Group are not open to research, although some material can be found in Foreign Office and Prime Minister's Office records. In a valedictory report of 12 Jan. 1972, the outgoing JIC secretary, 'one of the sharpest critics of the intelligence arrangements in Northern Ireland in the past', was able to report considerable improvements. Trend to Gregson, enclosing a copy of the secretary's report, 21 Jan., and Heath's direction that 'the points are followed up', 25 Jan. 1972, TNA PREM 15/998.
52 Annex to JIC minutes, 31 Dec. 1970, TNA, CAB 185/4.
53 JIC meeting, 19 Aug. 1971, TNA, CAB 185/7.
54 Trevelyan (Home Office) to Woodfield (Home Office), 5 Jan. 1972 and 30 Nov. 1971, TNA, CJ 4/280.
55 Draft 'assessment of the probable effects of Direct Rule in Northern Ireland', undated, prepared by Anthony Wood of the Cabinet Office Assessment Staff, TNA, CJ 4/280.
56 White to Crawford, 23 Sept. 1970, TNA, FCO 33/1214.
57 Gilchrist to Greenhill, 6 June 1970, CCA, GILC 14B. The Dublin friend in question was probably the writer and one-time American intelligence officer Constantine Fitzgibbon.
58 Minute by Greenhill, undated, on Gilchrist to Greenhill, 6 June 1970, TNA, FCO 33/1214.
59 Peck to Foreign Office, 15 Feb. 1973, TNA, FCO 87/209.
60 Minute by White, 15 Mar. 1973, TNA, FCO 87/209.
61 Foreign Office to Northern Ireland Office, 24 Jan. 1973, TNA, FCO 87/209. Among those scheduled to meet Galsworthy was Frank Steele of MI6, widely credited with developing the lines of contact with the Provisional IRA which ultimately

contributed to the ceasefires of the 1990s.

62 Note of meeting on security with Northern Ireland ministers, 1 Oct. 1971, TNA, PREM 15/472.

63 Gregson (private secretary to the prime minister) to Ministry of Defence, 21 Oct. 1971, TNA, PREM 15/495.

64 Private information.

65 Foreign secretary to prime minister, 23 Nov. 1972, TNA, FCO 73/143.

66 Peck to Foreign Office, 21 Dec. 1972, TNA, FCO 87/48.

67 White to Crawford, 3 Jan. 1973, TNA, FCO 87/247.

68 Heath, who was on a visit to Canada when the Littlejohn affair became public, took a close interest in how it was handled. Trend (in Canada) to Dunnett, Ministry of Defence, 6 Aug., and Downing Street to Ministry of Defence, 7 Aug. 1973, TNA, FCO 87/204 and 205. Garret FitzGerald, *All in a Life: An Autobiography* (Dublin, 1991), p. 204 points out that Heath did warn Lynch after Littlejohn's arrest, that they had some contact with security officials.

69 Prime Minister's Office to Northern Ireland Office, 22 Jan. 1973, TNA, FCO 87/187.

70 Note of discussion between Heath, Wilson and James Callaghan, 18 Oct. 1971, TNA, PREM 15/485; British ambassador, Dublin, to Foreign Office, reporting discussions with Cosgrave, 13 Apr., and on discussions with defence minister Donegan, 18 Apr. 1973, TNA, FO 87/247; note by Alec Douglas-Home on report by British ambassador, Dublin, on talks on the Littlejohn affair with Dr FitzGerald , 12 Aug. 1973, TNA, FO 87/204 .

71 See Cabinet Office to Prime Minister's Office, 23 Sept. 1970, TNA, PREM 15/474, on new arrangements to ensure 'up to date' intelligence on Northern Ireland.

72 'Report of the Independent Commission of Inquiry into the Dublin and Monaghan Bombings', p. 13, and 'Mr Justice Henry Barron's statement to Oireachtas Joint Committee, 10 Dec. 2003', in House of the Oireachtas Joint Committee on Justice, Equality, Defence and Women's Rights, *Interim Report on the Report of the Independent Commission of Inquiry into the Dublin and Monaghan Bombings* (Dublin, 2003). See the obituaries of Commander John Wilson of the Metropolitan Police Special Branch, who was credited with greatly improving relations with both the RUC and the Garda Síochána during the 1970s, in *The Daily Telegraph*, 27 Feb., and *The Newsletter*, 28 Feb. 2006.

73 As was alleged in John M. Feehan, *Operation Brogue: A Study of the Vilification of Charles Haughey Codenamed 'Operation Brogue' by the British Secret Service* (Dublin, 1984). Less easy to dismiss are the allegations of collusion by members of the security forces in Northern Irish loyalist attacks after 1972. See Don Mullan, *The Dublin and Monaghan Bombings* (Dublin, 2000).

74 'Report of the Independent Commission', as in note 72 above.

Research for this chapter was partly funded by the Arts and Social Sciences Benefactions Fund, and by the Institute for International Integration Studies at Trinity College Dublin. I am also grateful to W.K. White, CMG, for his comments provided at short notice and at an awkward time for him.

IMPERIAL POWER AND GLOBAL CONFLICT: ANCIENT ROME TO THE CONTEMPORARY WEST

Trajan's Parthian adventure: with some modern caveats

Rose Mary Sheldon

A leader of an empire decides to invade Iraq. He has inadequate intelligence and underestimates the resistance of the locals, but he believes his overwhelming military might will bring him a swift victory. His mighty army overruns the area between the Tigris and the Euphrates, but no sooner does he occupy the area than a massive insurgency arises, made up of various ethnic and religious groups. What began as a simple conquest for glory and dominance now becomes bogged down in deadly fighting as the once-victorious commander-in-chief now desperately searches for an exit strategy.

This scenario could just as easily be 113 CE or 2003 CE. Both ancient and modern attempts to invade Iraq have been plagued with the same problems. These problems are caused by inadequate intelligence gathering, both strategic and tactical, and have resulted in long drawn out wars that have been costly in both money and manpower, ultimately leading to no real gain, either political or military, at the end of the fighting.

Trajan's Parthian adventure has stumped scholars for at least two centuries. The times, the places, and even the purpose of Trajan's campaign are obscure.[1] The evidence is scattered, fragmentary and much of it is of inferior quality. What has occupied classical scholars is the close dating of the coinage and the unravelling of Trajan's titles on coins and inscriptions.[2] For military and intelligence historians, however, the concern is what can happen to a well-trained army and an imperial commander with ambitions in Iraq when an insurgency strikes after the initial campaign of shock and awe.

All of Rome's Parthian campaigns had one thing in common: Roman armies never subdued Parthia, they simply overran it.[3] The Parthian empire was too large, and its strong native cultures too

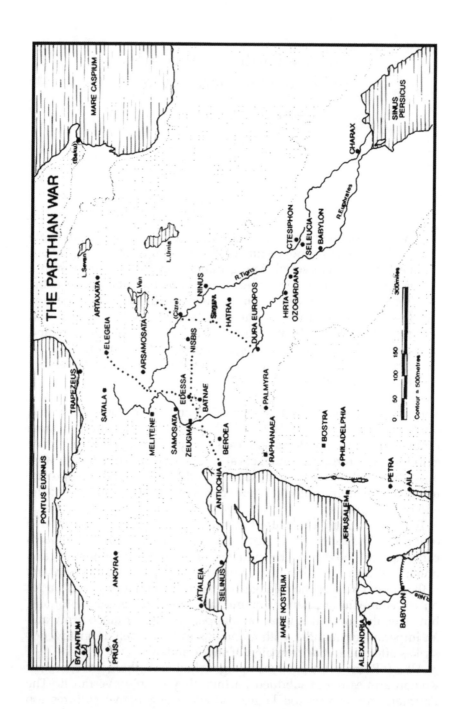

strong, for long-term integration into the Roman cultural and political spheres. Even with the feudal structure of the Parthian government and their constant internal squabbling, they were still strong and resilient enough to prevent the successful annexation as new Roman provinces. With a large, powerful imperial army, it was possible for the Romans to overrun a great deal of territory; but the problem then becomes, what does one do with it? Because if the native population decides you are going to leave, you eventually will.

THE STATUS QUO BROKEN

At first glance, Trajan's attack on Parthia seems unnecessary since he had the diplomatic solution to the problem right in the palm of his hand. The two powers had agreed to terms negotiated by Augustus and confirmed under Nero. The ruler of Armenia was to be nominated by Parthia, but Rome alone had the power to approve the choice and effect the installation. This arrangement had worked well for eighty years. On the surface at least, it seems that Parthia broke the pattern. In 113, the Parthian king, Osroes, who had recently succeeded his brother Pacorus, deposed the Armenian ruler Exedares, the younger son of Pacorus, in favour of Exedares' older brother Parthamasiris.[4] That Parthia should now abrogate the agreement, especially during the emperor's *quindecennalia*, could have been seen by the Romans as an affront to the dignity of the emperor.

There is evidence, however, that Trajan already had a Parthian campaign on the agenda long before the affair in Armenia, and that the Parthian choice of rulers was the result of Trajan's actions and not the other way around.[5] Such a suggestion is not unlike that from critics who accused George Bush of having an Iraqi campaign on the agenda long before 9/11. Perhaps it is not impossible that the Parthians made the move in order to choose an Armenian king who was more likely to be able to mount a defence against a pre-emptive strike by the Romans.[6]

WAS TRAJAN PLANNING AN INVASION?

Trajan's precise motives in attacking Parthia have been much discussed, but the argument of Dio Cassius still remains valid.[7] Trajan annexed Armenia as an extension of his policy in Dacia and Arabia, and his primary motives were his passion for glory and the expansion of Roman power. Planning for both Trajan's and Bush's eastern wars started early. The evidence for premeditation on Trajan's part comes in five groups of events:[8]

1) Trajan's general, and soon to be the next emperor, Hadrian was given command of the eastern provinces from April 112, a commission perhaps connected with the logistical preparations for a war with Parthia. The preparations must have begun the previous year at the very latest.[9] It has also been suggested that Julius Quadratus Bassus, appointed to command Cappadocia about this time, was charged with organising the northern armies in readiness for an eastern campaign.[10]

2) Military themes characterised the coins minted in 111/12–13, announcing the emperor's imminent departure on campaign. For example, towards the end of 111, Trajan issued a series of coins with FORT(una) RED(ux) (May fortune return you safely), which some think heralds an impending imperial journey overseas.[11]

3) Towards the end of 111, a series of coins was issued commemorating Trajan's deification of his father, Ulpius Traianus, *triumphator* over the Parthians when he was governor of Syria. His father was one of the few Roman generals to receive triumphal decorations for an eastern campaign.[12]

4) Probably not coincidentally, the Via Egnatia, the main route from Italy to the eastern provinces via the Greco-Balkan peninsula, was ordered to be restored in the course of 112. It was a substantial undertaking. One milestone records that work was necessary on the entire 250 mile long route, from Dyrrachium in the west to Acontismaa in the east, because the road had long been neglected.[13]

5) Nabataean Arabia was organised into a province in 106 to keep the southern border safe.[14]

When these activities are considered together they suggest preparations for an eastern campaign. The public inscriptions and coinage have been seen as an attempt to prepare the national will towards recognising and approving Trajan's familial duty to subordinate Rome's last remaining enemy.[15] The fact that active hostilities did not actually break out until the spring of 114, after Parthia had twice offered a diplomatic solution, only serves to confirm the thesis that the war was premeditated as early as 111, and merely awaited a suitable and felicitous *casus belli*. Trajan was conveniently delivered a motive by the intervention of the Parthian king into the Armenian succession. Whether there were WMDs or not, Trajan was going to invade Iraq.

Trajan's use of the Armenian succession as a pretext for war seemed specious even to the Roman historian and senator Dio Cassius because Rome and Parthia had, in effect, agreed on the candidate. The only bone of contention was the actual coronation, which had offended Trajan's sense of dignity. But slights to dignity, denting of image, or challenges to power do play a part in decisions to go to war.

George Bush referred to Saddam Hussein as 'the guy who tried to kill my dad'.[16] Such factors could then, as they do now, result in violent and quite unnecessary armed conflict in place of reasoned diplomacy. There was no strategic need for a war with Parthia at this time. The treaty between the two powers had worked thus far to the advantage of both sides, and none of the admittedly few and fragmentary sources even hints that Parthia was making threatening moves against Rome.[17] On the contrary, the Parthian kings were most often distracted by their own dynastic struggles, and appear to have preferred peaceful co-existence with Rome. Instead, it was the megalomania of successive Roman *viri militares* prompting expeditions across the Euphrates, abrogating existing agreements in the process, which usually brought about confrontation between Parthia and her imperious neighbour. This is not to say Trajan was a pathological warmonger, but we cannot rule out the possibility that Trajan wanted to follow up his Dacian success, and the dedication of his Forum and Column, with an eastern campaign to conquer what all other conquerors had failed to take – except Alexander. Those senatorial advisors who argued against such a policy may have suffered.[18]

THE PREPARATIONS OF 113

Trajan left Rome in the autumn of 113 on the sixteenth anniversary of his adoption by Nerva.[19] He travelled to Brundisium, then by ship to Corinth and overland to Athens. He was met by an embassy from Osroes, who proposed that, since Exedares was 'satisfactory to neither the Romans nor the Parthians, Parthamasiris should be allowed to retain the Armenian throne'.[20] Osroes suggested that the solution of the problem was for Trajan to offer Parthamasiris the royal diadem, as had been the practice since Nero's time. Trajan ignored him and refused to discuss the matter; he also refused to accept any of the gifts sent to him by Osroes. The embassy was sent packing with the words that 'friendship and diplomacy were determined by deeds, not words' and that Trajan would review the matter after he arrived at his forward base in Syria.[21] Dio saw this as further confirmation that Trajan had already decided on war.

Trajan crossed the Aegean to Ephesus, travelled overland to Aphrodisias, and continued by ship along the coast of Asia Minor to Seleucia-in-Pieria, the seaport of Antioch and the principal base and imperial residence for the campaign.[22] Hadrian met him late in December and they entered Antioch on 7 January 114.[23] The passes in Armenia reach altitudes of 6,000 feet and were probably still blocked with winter ice and rock falls.[24] While Trajan was waiting for the spring thaw, he entered into diplomatic negotiations with the kingdoms of the border marches. He received an embassy from Abgarus of Osrhoene, who balked at coming in person (in the hope of remaining neutral) and instead sent gifts and a message of friendship. Another embassy was sent from Osroes to receive Trajan's decision on the terms proposed in Athens. As George Bush refused to believe Saddam Hussein's claim that he had no WMDs, Trajan refused any peace overtures from Osroes.[25]

THE CAMPAIGN OF 114

In the spring, Trajan left with his army for Satala, his campaign base for the 114 campaign year. He travelled to the fortress of Zeugma, headquarters to the Legio IV Scythia. From Zeugma he probably followed a route along the right bank of the Euphrates eiver as far as Samosata, the base of the Legio VI Ferrata.[26] From Samosata, the easiest route north for a large army was directly across the Malatya Daglari to Melitene and its fortress, at this time garrisoned by the Legio XII Fulminata.[27]

Peace overtures continued to arrive. Trajan received a letter from the Armenian pretender, Parthamasiris, suggesting that the *fait accompli* of his own enthronement be accepted and that he should come to Trajan and be formally presented with the Armenian royal diadem. Trajan considered this letter peremptory in tone because Parthamasiris had the audacity to sign it as 'King of Armenia', a status not yet recognised by the Romans. Trajan did not even deign to reply.[28] A second, more conciliatory letter was brought for the emperor's consideration. This one left out the royal title and asked that the governor of Cappadocia, Marcus Julius Homullus, be empowered to open negotiations on behalf of Trajan. The emperor would not agree to this, but instead dispatched Marcus Junius' son to verify the terms being offered by Parthamasiris.[29]

Trajan continued on the second leg of his journey by crossing the Euphrates for the route via the Elazig Pass to the southern Armenian city of Samosata (Palu), which was now occupied without resistance.[30] He continued north through the Pülümur Pass, crossed the Euphrates again, probably at Eriza. A day's march from there brought him to Satala, the headquarters of the Legio XVI Flavia Firma, where he arrived late in May of 114.[31] At Satala Trajan had assembled the greatest concentration of Roman legions ever known. Seven legions from the eastern armies were present in full or slightly reduced strength.[32] There were contingents from the Danubian armies, some of whom had travelled overland from the Balkans by way of Ancyra (Ankara) in the winter of 113/14.[33] Logistical supplies had been sent from Tomis along the coast of the Black Sea by water to Trapezus and then overland through the Zigana Pass to Satala.[34] Trajan thus had eight fully supplied legions totalling 80,000 men.

After receiving the homage of local kings, Trajan advanced into Armenia.[35] His destination was the Armenian capital Elegeia, 110 miles east of Satala and 180 miles west of Parthamasiris's capital at Artaxata. Parthamasiris and the leading Armenian nobility were supposed to meet Trajan at Elegeia, but they arrived late, claiming they were held up by bands of Exidares' supporters.[36] Not a good tactical move under the circumstances. Coming before Trajan seated upon his throne, Parthamasiris removed his diadem and laid it at the emperor's feet in confident expectation it would be returned. Trajan left it on the ground, whereupon his soldiers declared him *imperator* for having deposed a monarch without striking a blow.[37] Parthamasiris' retainers were told they were now Roman subjects and as such would remain in camp. Parthamasiris himself was escorted by Roman troops outside the city walls, where he was promptly murdered.[38]

Roman armies now swarmed over Armenia. Lucius Quietus descended the River Araxes and destroyed the Mardi, then garrisoned the area near the Caspian Gates south of Lake Van, which controlled access to the Bitla Pass.[39] A second unit under C. Bruttius Praesens, legate of the VI Ferrata, operated in the Armenian highlands, where his men adopted the native snowshoes to get around as they campaigned late in the year in wintry conditions.[40] The Romans used the same tactics that had proven successful in other mountainous areas. They advanced up the valleys of navigable rivers, occupied key points at their head and systematically isolated the mountain masses by a network of roads and forts drawn round them on every side. By the end of 114, all of Armenia had been consolidated, and it was declared a Roman province with L. Catilius Severus as its first governor.[41] Trajan remained at Elegeia for the summer receiving delegations, and he may have also been developing a network of permanent garrisons in the Caucasian hinterland.[42] On account of these military successes in the summer of 114, the Roman Senate voted Trajan the title Optimus, which he formally adopted into his nomenclature. With a successful first year of campaigning behind him, Trajan spent the winter of 114/15 at Elegeia or Artaxata.[43]

MESOPOTAMIAN CAMPAIGN OF 115

In the spring of 115, Trajan began his Mesopotamian campaign. He marched south with this army over the central Taurus Mountains to consolidate the territory between the Euphrates and the Upper Tigris. Permanent garrisons were left at opportune points along the way to secure the regions. We are told he travelled with his men on foot, fording rivers and that he used his time during this unopposed advance to practise manoeuvres and marching dispositions.[44] By mid-summer, Trajan had reached Upper Mesopotamia and was ready to annex it.

From what little detail we have, Trajan was planning to take Mesopotamia with a large-scale pincer movement. One part was led by Lusius Quietus, who had finished subduing the Mardi, and now moved south into Adiabene and then advanced into eastern Mesopotamia. Trajan himself skirted Osrohene and set about the reduction of the western part of the territory.[45] Trajan took Batnae and then occupied the main strategic centre, Nisibis, which he used as his own base.[46] Abgarus VII of Osrohene found himself surrounded on three sides and made the best of the situation. On the approach of the Romans, King Abgarus, prompted by his son Arbandes, offered homage to Trajan to make amends for not doing so the year before. Trajan met Abgarus outside his capital at Edessa (Sanliurfa). With the Romans in full force before him, Abgarus had little choice but to come over to the Roman side. He sent out gifts, weapons and troops to Trajan as a sign of fealty; Trajan returned them. Nevertheless he pardoned the King, granted Osrohene the status of protectorate, and left it autonomous for the time being.[47]

The two sides of the pincer movement met as Trajan joined Lusius Quietus in Adiabene. Lusius was allowed to possess the Scenite Arab town of Singara and from there move down to Hatra and possibly even Libana, with a corresponding thrust down the Euphrates to Dura Europas. This completed the occupation of northern Mesopotamia.[48]

The intensity of the fighting during this period can be gauged by the fact that Trajan received five imperial salutations between Autumn 114 and December 115. Trajan dispatched a laurelled letter to the Senate on 21 February 116 announcing annexation of both Armenia and Mesopotamia. Shock and awe had succeeded. Coins were minted announcing the territories as 'subjugated to the power of Rome'. Trajan was voted the title of Parthicus, and prayers were offered for his safety.[49] Trajan garrisoned Edessa and returned to Antioch for the winter of 115/16, where he nearly lost his life in a devastating earthquake. He lived out of doors in the hippodrome to protect himself from collapsing roofs.[50]

THE TIGRIS CAMPAIGN OF 116

Early in 116 Trajan marched out of Antioch for the Tigris on his third campaign against the Parthian confederation. He could have taken the two new provinces, organised and garrisoned them, and just gone home, but this would not have sufficed for his imperial designs on Parthia. Perhaps he was lured on by the seemingly total lack of Parthian resistance and the opportunity for acquiring more war booty.[51]

Trajan struck hard across the Tigris at the Jewish kingdom of Adiabene. To reach the capital, Arbela, he had to cross the Tigris, which he achieved by using prefabricated pontoons brought by wagon. These had been built the previous winter at Nisibis, which had lots of wood available from the forests of Mt Massius (Tur Ab'din) north of the city. The river was eventually crossed, but with some difficulty because of fast water and, no doubt, fighting Adiabenians. Trajan's troops crossed in the vicinity of the modern city of Cizre, and at least part of the province was taken.[52] The occupation of Adiabene was probably the occasion for Trajan's twelfth imperial salutation.[53] It is believed by some that he formed the territory into the new province of Assyria. Others believe that most of Adiabene remained in enemy hands, and thus no 'Adiabene capta' coins were struck.[54]

The army moved west and occupied Edessa. Most accounts try to bring Trajan back from Adiabene by the most expeditious route so that he could take command of the second force. Trajan marched at the head of a force down the Euphrates to Dura Europus, where another army, supported by a supply fleet, awaited him. They proceeded down the western bank of the Tigris as far as Babylon, meeting no opposition on the way. Dio says there were civil conflicts which kept the Parthians busy.[55] Trajan was accompanied by a river fleet on the Euphrates; Arrian lists fifty ships. The largest craft was the emperor's flagship decorated in gold, with the emperor's name on the sails.[56]

Trajan intended to cross the Tigris and attack Ctesiphon, south of modern Baghdad.[57] He chose not to use the artificial canal called Naharmalcha (Royal River) which ran from the area that is now Fallujah to the Tigris some distance south of the point where Seleucia and Ctesiphon faced each other on opposite banks of the river. The canal may have not been functional, and at one point Trajan contemplated cutting a canal between the Tigris and the Euphrates at Sippar. Since the Euphrates flowed at a higher level than the Tigris, however, he feared that one river would drain and flood the other. He elected instead to have his fleet dragged overland by means of capstan devices and rollers.[58] Trajan took Seleucia on the west bank and then crossed the Tigris unopposed and entered the city of Ctesiphon without a fight.

Osroes and his entourage had fled, leaving behind his daughter and his golden throne to be captured by the emperor.[59] Trajan's army saluted him as *imperator* and he established his right to be acclaimed Parthicus. Trajan issued coins with the legend PARTHIA CAPTA.[60] The capture of Ctesiphon marked the official culmination of Trajan's third campaign and of the war. And yet, during the entire time, Trajan had not once encountered any resistance from King Osroes or his cavalry. Osroes had used traditional tactics against his enemies; he withdrew over the Zagros Mountains in the face of a superior force.[61]

Using ships from the Euphrates fleet, Trajan sailed down the Tigris to the Persian Gulf. After nearly losing his life in a tidal bore, the emperor eventually arrived at Spasinu Charax (Basra) located at the river's mouth. We are told that Trajan arrived there just in time to see a merchant ship sailing for India, and he publicly lamented that he was no longer young enough to follow in Alexander's footsteps.[62] This episode signalled the end of Trajan's aggressive drive through Parthia. He dispatched another laurelled letter to the Senate, announcing his accomplishments, and erected a statue that marked the limit of his advance. He left his ships behind, with the intention of a future campaign eastwards. The Senate voted him a triumph over as many nations as he wished, and he achieved his thirteenth imperial salutation. More coins were issued with the legend FORT(una) RED(ux), wishing the emperor a safe return to Italy.[63]

THE UPRISING

When he arrived back in Babylon, however, Trajan discovered that a widespread rebellion had broken out in northern Mesopotamia. His capture of Ctesiphon had galvanised the Parthians, who now put aside their internal differences and incited a widespread insurgency. With the Romans overextended and the commander far from the centre of action, Osroes' brother Mithridates began recapturing large tracts of Roman territory.[64] When Mithridates was killed in an equestrian accident his son, Sanatrukes, continued to incite pro-Parthian resistance. Sanatrukes was also nominated by the Parthians as king-in-exile of the Armenians in place of Parthamasiris.[65]

Sanatrukes seems to have been able to organise a rebellion in many places simultaneously. He co-ordinated it at a time when Trajan had advanced too far and too quickly without making sure he had sufficient resources to consolidate his gains. This took advance planning, suggesting he had been watching Trajan's advance very closely. Trajan had absented himself from the lower Euphrates without properly securing his perimeters.[66] There were Parthian invasions of both Mesopotamia and Armenia: many occupied towns drove out or massacred their Roman garrisons. Osrhoene rebelled, while Trajan himself was threatened by the revolt of Seleucia and the prospect of all of Babylonia following its lead.

Trajan ordered three divisions against the rebels. His best general, Lusius Quietus, recovered Nisibis and a number of cities including

Edessa, which he sacked and burned; he was promised a consulship in the following year.[67] A force, under the joint command of two legates, Erucius Clarus and Julius Alexander, captured Seleucia and burned it. Trajan himself joined this group. The three commanders then went on to defeat a Parthian host somewhere in the vicinity of Ctesiphon, after which Sanatrukes was killed.[68]

Armenia was threatened by a Parthian army under Sanatrukes's son Vologaeses.[69] The situation must have been critical for, when an armistice was offered in return for part of the territory, Trajan quickly agreed and granted him a portion of Armenia in exchange for peace. In an effort to avoid further insurrection in Babylon and perhaps to assert some authority over Vologaeses, Trajan went to Ctesiphon and appointed as king of Parthia Parthamaspates, son of Osroes. He personally crowned him with a royal diadem, after which Parthamaspates did obeisance to Trajan in the traditional manner in full view of the assembled population, confirming his subordinate status.[70] The status of Parthamaspates was advertised on coins issued late that year bearing the legend REX PARTH [IC]US DATUS, 'A king is given to the Parthians'.[71]

Trajan had to justify his action to the Senate because some thought he was abandoning Roman territory, and indeed he was. His reply encapsulates the problem of having inadequate strategic intelligence:

> So vast and infinite is this domain, and so immeasurable the distance that separates it from Rome, that we do not have the compass to administer it. Let us then [instead] present the people with a king who is subject to Rome.[72]

The irony is, this was the eastern policy already in place when he began the unnecessary war. With both Parthia and a major part of Armenia restored to client-kings, Trajan hurried north to recover what he could of Mesopotamia. Trajan besieged Hatra, the caravan city in revolt, which controlled the central route from Nisibis to Ctesiphon. The area had neither water in the surrounding desert nor timber or fodder for a besieging army. The Roman army was plagued by flies, which swarmed over their food and water and brought discomfort and even disease to the troops.[73] Still Trajan persisted with the siege. He even managed to breach the defences with a cavalry charge using his own *equites singulares*, during which his distinctive 'majestic grey head' attracted the attention of the Hatrian archers. They missed him but hit a trooper in his escort.[74] When winter set in, and they had to contend with sudden cloudbursts, hailstorms and thunderstorms in addition to their other troubles. Trajan lifted the siege, and returned west to Antioch.[75]

THE JEWISH REVOLT

Trajan's troubles increased when the Greek-speaking Jews of the diaspora began a separate, bloody revolt. It would seem that religious tensions between the Jewish and pagan communities flared into open riot and there was widespread destruction of pagan shrines by the Jews.[76] It is not clear whether the Jewish revolt began as part of the Parthian *revanche* or separately. The canonical date for the revolt is 115–17: it started in Cyrene, in North Africa, although at least one scholar has suggested it started in Mesopotamia and spread west.[77] Were the Jews incited by the Parthians? Did the Jews see the Romans as 'on the ropes' and decide it was a good time to strike out for independence? Whatever the case, the revolt was very bloody and Trajan had to expend more manpower to put it down.[78] Marcus Turbo was dispatched to Alexandria to help subdue the disturbances.[79] Renewed fighting between Greeks and Jews continued even after the Roman intervention.[80]

Daily news arrived of fresh uprisings across Trajan's *imperium*.[81] Parthamaspates, the Roman appointee to the Parthian throne, was fighting a civil war. Faced with more Jewish revolts throughout the East, Armenia already lost, and the fate of Mesopotamia hanging in the balance, Trajan decided to return to Rome and celebrate his Parthian triumph. He appointed Hadrian to the overall command of the armies in the East.[82] In the summer of 117 Trajan boarded his royal yacht at Seleucia- in-Pieria when the climate was favourable for sea travel. Sick and in his sixty-third year, Trajan became paranoid and began to think his illness was due to poison.[83] As his ship coasted along the rough shores of Cilicia, Trajan's condition worsened. The ship pulled into the nearest harbour, Selinus, where he took to his bed and died.[84]

Hadrian immediately abandoned the eastern campaign. He justified his action by quoting the dictum of Cato, that those who could not be subject should be made free.[85] Trajan's more aggressive officers were replaced or died under suspicious circumstances, including A. Cornelius Palma, C. Avidius Nigrinus and Lusius Quietus, governor of Judaea.[86] They probably resented Hadrian's policy of giving back territory they had fought hard to conquer. All the territory east of the Euphrates was immediately relinquished, as was the Syrian pre-desert. Dura Europas was abandoned before 30 September 117.[87]

ROME'S IMPERIAL FOLLY

Trajan was a great general and no fool. He did not blunder into Parthia as Crassus had done, losing three legions and their standards. Trajan did not go into Armenia with poor logistical support like Mark

Antony. Plague did not strike his army, as happened under Lucius Verus. Yet, by the end of the campaign, he had nothing to show for it. Many scholars portray the invasion as a success, but there is as much reason to believe Trajan was pulling himself out of a situation that was degenerating daily. Dio, in his justly famous passage, said that conquering Mesopotamia was a constant source of war that became a great financial burden to the Roman economy. This seems borne out by Trajan's actions as well as Hadrian's.[88]

It is not enough just to overrun a country, create a great deal of destruction, steal what you can, and leave. If you wish to acquire territory and create provinces that are viable entities, then you must stay behind and do the work of province building. Once you destroy a regime, you are, by definition, in charge of internal security. Rebels can come out of the woodwork with knives and stab you in the kidney in any crowded market place. The clean-up job is expensive and time consuming. It becomes your job to pacify the countryside, quell urban rioting, and keep millions of Parthians (or Shi'ites) happy.

ROMAN GRAND STRATEGY

The idea that Rome went into Parthia to rectify borders or create a 'scientific frontier' is incorrect, and the image of the Romans as expert military strategists in the modern sense of the word is illusory. This has been argued quite convincingly by Susan Mattern, Benjamin Isaac and John Mann.[89] To attribute Roman success to superior insight or expertise, to some science of war or administration, is a trend contradicted by the ancient sources themselves, which say glory and honour were a Roman commander's main motivation. Certainly one sees this in the case of Trajan's Parthian adventure. Modern historians wish to see the Romans as expert strategists tracing defensible borders and buffer zones on the well-plotted topography of Europe and Asia. They believe that the Romans could, as we can, evaluate the political and military strengths and weaknesses of their enemies, collect intelligence, track enemies and allocate financial resources to meet their strategic goals. This idea is a chimera.[90]

Roman foreign policy was much simpler than that. Maintaining image and achieving 'national honour' were their most important policy goals and, according to this view, Roman strategy was coherent over a remarkable period of time. In a world where the technology and intelligence necessary for our modern types of military strategy were lacking, their approach was quite effective. They operated on the principle that status and security depended upon one's perceived ability to inflict violence. In the arena of international relations, Rome did not play a complex geopolitical chess game, as Americans do now, but what we do share is a competition for status, with much violent demonstration of superior prowess, aggressive posturing and terrorizing of the opponent. The value that the Romans attached to honour, which was maintained by conquest, terror and retaliation, is the only way to explain their repeated and futile attempts at expanding their empire at the expense of Parthia and their seemingly disproportionate investment of force, money and manpower in trying to retain territories that ultimately could not be held. Each time the Romans failed in Parthia, a conquest there simply became more attractive to upcoming glory-seekers and fortune hunters.

Even Edward Luttwak, creator of the Roman grand strategy myth, had to admit that there were no permanent borders on the eastern frontier of the Roman empire. The political boundary of the empire was irrelevant as a concept, and the military boundary was never organised as a line of defence.[91] The forces in the East were mostly used as a police force that quelled rebellions and enforced the collection of tribute. That is why all the garrisons were in cities and not in the desert along some imaginary line in the sand. Luttwak wrote that the system of imperial security on the eastern front was based on three elements: 1) a chain of client states, 2) the buffer state of Armenia, and 3) the four strong legions in Syria. Rome had all these in place when Trajan took office. How did trying to absorb 1) and 2) and getting a large part of 3) killed make Rome safer? Even Luttwak admits the frontier that Trajan inherited was much neater than the one the Julio-Claudians had to defend. Luttwak justifies Trajan's behaviour by saying the frontier was 'highly unsatisfactory' because it could not support the 'substantial forces needed to meet any high-intensity threat'. But there *were no high-intensity threats*. If anything, Parthia was weaker and more divided than ever when Trajan invaded. The Parthians had never been expansive at the expense of the Romans. Luttwak himself admits that Trajan's Parthian war was not 'a limited border-rectification offensive, nor is it usually considered to have been a purely rational enterprise entirely motivated by strategic considerations'.[92]

THE EMPEROR AS DECISION-MAKER

Observers both ancient and modern question whether one president or one emperor can be responsible for starting a war. In the Roman case, the emperor's decisions were paramount. Those who wish to absolve Trajan of guilt for an unnecessary war argue that the individual contribution of emperors to foreign policy was over-estimated, but: if not the emperor, then who?[93] Modern democracies can impinge somewhat on their governments; the Roman people could not. Individual rulers dictated frontier policy, not the empire's citizenry as a whole and not the Senate. There was only the emperor and his whims. It was the ambition of Roman emperors and not the collective fears of its people that led to constant interference in the politics of Armenia and Parthia. That collective fear, real or imagined, merely showed Rome's leaders where best to win the honour and glory for themselves. The decision to start this war was that of Trajan and his generals, as America's war with Iraq was the brainchild of the Bush administration.

SHOCK AND AWE

In a recent article Robert Tomes suggests that the US military was no more prepared for the kind of war it had to fight in Iraq than were the Romans.[94] Both used shock and awe to subdue a perceived enemy.[95] The point is to defeat an adversary so thoroughly that you shatter their confidence and they roll over. However, Tomes points out that such concepts are not well attuned to fighting a counterinsurgency war in a terrain such as Iraq, which depends upon both intelligence gathering and adaptive military organisations.[96] The US had expectations of a much quicker conclusion to the Iraq war. Obviously, so did Trajan.

History records few examples where foreign powers waging counterinsurgency warfare won decisively or even achieved their envisioned long-term results. The US Army general who opined 'any good soldier can handle guerrillas' vastly underestimated the task.[97] General Maxwell Taylor also fell into this trap when he said 'any well-trained organization can shift the tempo to that which might be required in this type of situation'.[98] The Romans did not have the manpower necessary to occupy Mesopotamia and put down all the insurgencies, and even the Americans are having a difficult time of it. The attractive notion of a violent but brief conflict may be as chimerical for the Americans as it was for the Romans. Eliot Cohen wrote that 'an intellectual comprehension of the demands of small wars does not necessarily translate into the implementation of the policies required to wage it [sic] successfully'.[99] Students of small wars and counterinsurgencies are not impressed with contemporary US military thought and its fascination with precise air strikes and the reduced need for 'boots on the ground'. The realities of counter-insurgency warfare continue to rub against mainstream US military thought and defence planning. Intelligence is the critical enabler. Comprehensive information about the environment must be gathered and analysed. The operational intelligence effort must remain flexible, adapting to the situation as it develops. If the Americans could not succeed, how much more difficult was it for the Romans with so many fewer men and no high-tech equipment. Some now argue that Saddam's last official orders included planning for protracted opposition to any new government, and insurgency warfare against foreign troops. Could this also have been Osroes' last order? Trajan was able to withdraw back to his own boundaries with seemingly no permanent damage to the Roman empire. It remains to be seen whether the Americans will be as lucky.

NOTES

References to classical authors are by author, short title (where applicable), book, chapter, verse. The particular edition used by the author is cited on first reference to a source.

1   On Trajan's Parthian war, see F.A. Lepper, *Trajan's Parthian War* (Oxford, 1948); J. Bennett, *Trajan Optimus Princeps* (Bloomington, IN, 2001); N.C. Debevoise, *A Political History of Parthia*, (Chicago, 1938); J. Guey, *Essai sur la guerre parthique de Trajan* (Bucharest, 1937); C. S. Lightfoot, 'Trajan's Parthian war and the fourth century perspective', *Journal of Roman Studies*, 80 (1990), pp. 115–26; R. P. Longden, 'The wars of Trajan', *Cambridge Ancient History*, 11 (1936), pp. 236–52; R.P. Longden, 'Notes on the Parthian Campaigns of Trajan', *Journal of Roman Studies*, 21 (1931), pp. 1–35; R. Paribeni, *Optimus Princeps* (2 vols, Messina, 1926-27); R. Hanslik, 'M. Ulpius Traianus', in A. Pavly and G. Wissowa, *Real-Encyclopädie der klassischen Altertumswissenschaft* (Stuttgart) [hereafter *RE*], Supplement 10, col. 1035–1102.

2   On the coin evidence, see G.G. Belloni, *Le Monete di Traiano* (Milano, 1973); P.L. Strack, *Untersuchungen zur römischen Reichspragung des zweiten Jahrhunderts* (3 vols, Stuttgart, 1931), vol. I. On the chronological problems, see T. Frankfort, 'Trajan Optimus – recherche de chronologie', *Latomus*, 16 (1957), pp. 333–4; J. Guey, 'Le problème chronologique que soulève la guerre de Trajan contres les Parthes', *Acàdemie des inscriptions et belles-lettres, Comptes rendus des séances*, 1934, pp. 72–4.

3   G. Wylie, 'How did Trajan succeed in subduing Parthia where Mark Antony failed?', *Ancient History Bulletin*, 4 (1990), pp. 37–43 sets up a false analogy.

4   Exedares in Dio 68.17.3: Cassius Dio, *Dio's Roman History*, ed. E. Cary (9 vols, Cambridge, 1954); Axidares in Arrian *Parthica* fr.38 (translation of the fragments of Arrian can be found in Lepper, *Trajan's Parthian War*).

5   On premeditation, see J. Guey, *Essai*, p. 27; Paribeni, *Optimus Princeps*, ii, p. 281; Lepper, *Trajan's Parthian War*, pp. 164–90.

6   G. Rawlinson, *The Story of Parthia* (New York, 1893), p. 299.

7   M. College, *The Parthians* (New York, 1967), p. 53, and others discuss Trajan's frontier policy as a rude and costly interruption of a process of careful and economical stabilisation which had been begun by the Flavians and to which Hadrian wisely returned. Lepper (*Trajan's Parthian War*, pp. 106, 191–204) disagrees. On contemporary Roman criticism of Trajan's Parthian campaign, see W.C. McDermott, 'Homullus and Trajan', *Historia*, 29 (1980) p. 118.

8   M. Danner, 'The secret way to war: the Downing Street memo', *New York Review of Books*, 52, 10 (9 June 2005), p. 70 shows that an invasion of Iraq was already being discussed by the Bush Administration by 21 November 2001 when the President ordered the Secretary of Defense Donald Rumsfeld to look at what it would take to remove Saddam Hussein.

9 Hadrian's appointment to the assignment is substantiated by a single documentary source: Dio, 89.1.1. The possibility that Hadrian was appointed as interim governor is reasonable. There is a *lacuna* in the Syrian *fasti* between L. Fabius Justus, whose term of office ended 111/12 and C. Julius Quadratus Bassus, appointed 114/15. See Werner Eck, 'Jahres- und Provinzialfasten der senatorischen Statthalter...', *Chiron*, 12 (1982), pp. 353–7; E. Mary Smallwood, *Documents Illustrating the Principates of Gaius, Claudius and Nero* (London, 1967), p. 108.

10 R.K. Sherk, *Aufstieg und Niedergang der römischen Welt* [hereafter *ANRW*] 2,7 (1980), p. 1006.

11 Bennett, *Trajan*, pp. 183–4; Strack, *Untersuchungen*, I, pp. 215–16.

12 Strack, *Untersuchungen*, I, pp. 199–202; Belloni, *Le Monete di Traiano*, p. 14.

13 Smallwood, *Documents*, p. 415 on the milestone. See also M. Fasolo, *La Via Egnatia, I* (Rome, 2005), pp. 1–9; F. O'Sullivan, *The Egnatian Way* (Harrisburg, PA, 1972), p. 136.

14 Dio 68.14 says Trajan appropriated the Nabataean kingdom at or about the time of the Second Dacian War, which means either 105 or early 106, See G.W. Bowersock, *Roman Arabia* (Cambridge, MA, 1983), p. 79. Both Eutropius and Festus speak of Trajan forming Arabia into a province but the claim is usually treated as a *post eventum* reference to the earlier assimilation of Nabataean Arabia in 106.

15 America, on the other hand, had town meetings with Condoleezza Rice and UN briefings with Colin Powell, *St. Petersburg Times*, St. Petersburg, FL, August 8, 2003, p6A. On 10 October 2004 Rice, appearing on *Fox News Sunday*, defended the invasion of Iraq, citing the need to topple Saddam Hussein and saying the debate over WMDs was irrelevant: CNN.com.

16 CNN, Friday, 27 September, 2002.

17 B. Isaac, *Limits of Empire* (Oxford, 2000), pp. 22–3, has argued that there is surprisingly little evidence for believing Parthia ever sought open conflict with Rome.

18 Junius Homullus may have done so and this cost him the governorship of Armenia *maior* to Catilius, McDermott, 'Homullus and Trajan', p. 119.

19 The chronological problem is discussed in Lepper, *Trajan's Parthian War*, pp. 28–30.

20 Dio 68.17.3 E (Cary translation).

21 A similar arrogance was displayed by the Romans in the spring of 53 BCE when the Parthians demanded the reason for Crassus' unprovoked invasion and were told he would tell them the causes when the Romans reached Seleucia, Plutarch *Crassus* 17–18: *Plutarch's Lives*, with an English translation by Bernadotte Perrin (London, 1920–8).

22 D. van Berchem, 'La port de Séleucie de Piérie et l'infrastructure lofistique des guerres parthiques', *Bonner Jahrbücher des Rheinischen Landesmuseums in Bonn und des Vereins von Altertumsfreunden im Rheinlande*, 185 (1985), pp. 47–87. The route from Athens to Seleucia in Pieria is generally confirmed by Dio 68.17.2–3.

23 John Malalas, *Chronographia* 2.272: For a discussion of Malalas' dates, see M.I. Henderson's review of Lepper's *Trajan's Parthian War*, in *Journal of Roman Studies*, 39 (1949), pp. 122–4.

24 See V.W. Yorke, 'A journey in the valley of the Upper Euphrates: Part I, The Journey', *The Geographical Journal*, 8, 4 (1896), pp. 325, 333.

25 Arrian *Parthica*, fr.33.

26 Bennett, *Trajan*, p. 192. For the military dispositions in the area, see J. Crow, 'A review of the physical remains of the frontiers of Cappadocia', in P. Freeman and D. Kennedy (eds), *The Defense of the Roman and Byzantine East*, BAR International Series 297 (2 vols, 1986), I, pp. 79–81, 84.

27 Melitene commanded the southern approaches to the Caspian Gates. On the legionary fortress there see T. B. Mitford, 'The Euphrates frontier', *Studien zu den Militärgrenzen Roms (SMR)* II (Cologne-Bonn, 1977), pp. 504-5.

28 Dio 68.19–20; Bennett, *Trajan*, p. 192 and n. 42.

29 Dio 68.19.1; Bennett, *Trajan*, p. 192; Marcus Junius Homullus was the governor who commanded the XVI Flavia Firma, T.B. Mitford, 'Cappadocia and Armenia Minor: historical setting of the Limes', *ANRW*, 2, 7 (1980), p. 1196. Homullus' son was serving under his father as *tribunus laticlavus*, Anthony Richard Birley, *Hadrian: The Restless Emperor* (London, 1968), p. 69.

30 Dio 68.19.2 refers to 'Arsamosata'. This has been the object of considerable discussion. Arsamosata is not on the direct route between Antioch and Satala. Mitford, 'Cappadocia and Armenia Minor', p. 1196, thinks a march to Arsamosata is geographical nonsense; he suggests it should read 'Samosata'. Cf. Louis Dilleman, *Haute Mesopotamie orientale et pays adjacent*, (Paris, 1962), pp. 277ff; M.G. Angelli-Bertinelli, 'I romani oltre l'Euphrate', *ANRW*, 2/9, 1 (1976), pp. 12–13, n. 49. For the route from Melitene eastwards into Armenia and then from Arsamosata through the Pülümur Pass into the valley of the Upper Euphrates, see Lightfoot, 'Trajan's Parthian war', p. 117; Bennett, *Trajan*, p. 192.

31 The legion XVI Flavia Firma had spent the winter of 113/14 in Ankyra: Arrian *Parthica*, fr.85; *L'Année Epigraphique*, 1950, p. 66.

32 See Mitford, 'Cappadocia and Armenia Minor', pp. 1196–8, for a listing of the legions epigraphically or otherwise attested in the Parthian war. Bennett, *Trajan*, p. 192; Debevoise, *Parthia*, pp. 220–1. On Satala and the Euphrates frontier, see Mitford, 'Euphrates frontier', pp. 501–10.

33 The reinforcements from the Danubian provinces marched some 475 miles through difficult country in about seven weeks: Birley, *Hadrian*, p. 69; Bennett, *Trajan*, p. 192; Sherk, *ANRW*, 2, 7 (1980), pp. 1196–8; Smallwood, *Documents*, p. 215, whose content Bennett thinks is 113/14.

34 Mitford, 'Euphrates frontier', p. 502.

35 Anchialus, ruler of the Heniochi, and Machelones of the Coruh Nehri are mentioned in Dio 68.19.2; Bennett, *Trajan*, p. 194, n. 46. See Eutropius, *Breviarum* 8.3: *The breviarum ab urbe condita of Eutropius* ed. H.W. Bird (Liverpool, 1993); Festus 20 – Festus Historicus, *The breviarum of Festus*, ed. John W. Eadie (London, 1967), p. 139. Trajan appointed a new ruler to the Iberi and Albani. Julianus of the Apsilae was confirmed in his kingdom, Sherk, *ANRW*, 2, 7 (1980), p. 1198.

36 Arrian, *Parthica* frs.38–40; Bennett, *Trajan*, p. 194.

37 Dio 68.19.2–20 describes the main events at Elegeia: Sherk, *ANRW*, 2, 7 (1980), p. 1198.

38 On the death of Parthamasiris, see Arrian *Parthica* fr.40; Fronto, *Princ. Hist.*, 18: *The Correspondence of Marcus Cornelius Fronto with Marcus Aurelius…* , ed. C.R. Haines (Cambridge, MA, 1962); Sherk, *ANRW*, 2, 7 (1980), p. 1198; Bennett, *Trajan*, p. 194. On the REX PARTHUS coins which show on the reverse the humiliation of Parthamasiris at Elegeia, see Strack, *Untersuchungen*, no. 209; Harold Mattingly et al., *The Roman Imperial Coinage* [hereafter *RIC*] (10 vols, London, 1923–94), no. 312; Lepper, *Trajan's Parthian War*, p. 46.

39 Debevoise, *Parthia*, p. 224; Dilleman, *Haute Mesopotamie*, pp. 98–9 locates the Mardi among the mountains south and west of Artaxata in the foothills of Mt. Ararat. See Sherk, *ANRW*, 2, 7 (1980), p. 1198; Birley, *Hadrian*, p. 70.

40 Dilleman, *Haute Mesopotamie*, p. 278. Bennett, *Trajan*, p. 194. The snowshoes incident is recorded in Arrian, *Parthica*, fr.85; *L'Annee Epigraphique*, 1950, p. 66. Melitene at 3,000 feet has a month of snow. Satala at 6,000 feet has snow from December to March. See Mitford, 'Euphrates frontier', p. 503, on the suffering of Corbulo's army in the same area.

41 Debevoise, *Parthia*, p. 225; Sherk, *ANRW* 2, 7 (1980), pp. 1026, 1199, n. 87. On the Roman establishment in Armenia, see M.L. Chaumont, 'L'Armenie entre Rome et L'Iran', *ANRW* 2, 9 (1976), pp. 138–9; Crow, 'Review', pp. 80–1.

42 Bennett, *Trajan*, p. 194. Arrian reports that the kings of three tribes along the Pontic coast – the Lazi, the Abasci and the Sanigae – all received their authority from

Rome. On the Black Sea coast, see Isaac, *Limits of Empire*, pp. 42–50.

43 Dio 68.23.1: the Senate votes Trajan the title of Optimus. The arguments over the date of this event are summarised by Lepper, *Trajan's Parthian War*, pp. 34–9, especially Table 1. The winter of 114/15 at Elegeia or Artaxata is obscured by the Dio/Xiphilinus account. The Mesopotamian campaign then begins in 115, including the events which lead to Trajan receiving the title Parthicus, which the *Fasti Ostienses* firmly dates to 115, Bennett, *Trajan*, p. 195.

44 Dio 68.23.1–2.

45 These movements are inferred from his known activities around Lake Van and the events described in Dio 68.22.2. His success was rewarded by his adlection into the Senate as praetor. Dio 68.32.5; Bennett, *Trajan*, p. 195 and n. 64.

46 Arrian *Parthica* fr. 54–6; Dio 68.23.2; Eutropius *Breviarum*, 8.3; Festus 20; Bennett, *Trajan*, p. 196. On the importance of Nisibis, see J. González, 'La Guerra Pártica de Trajano', in J. González (ed.), *Imp. Caes. Nerva Traianus Aug.* (Sevilla, 1993), p. 154.

47 Arrian *Parthica* fr. 42–8 says there was a faction in Edessa that objected to the reappointment of Abgarus. Arrian also adds the details about Arbandes wearing gold earrings. Cf. Dio 68.21; Lepper, *Trajan's Parthian War*, pp. 93–4.

48 On these events see Dio 68.22.1; Lepper, *Trajan's Parthian War*, pp. 208–9; Bennett, *Trajan*, p. 196. On the extent of the new province of Mesopotamia, see Lepper, *Trajan's Parthian War*, pp. 141–8.

49 A fragment of the *Fasti Ostienses* first published in 1934 gives a virtual fixed point for Trajan being voted the title Parthicus in February 116, Lepper, *Trajan's Parthian War*, pp. 39–43.

50 For a description of the earthquake see Dio 68.24–25. Lepper, *Trajan's Parthian War*, pp. 65–87 discusses the problems with the chronology and Malalas' dating, as does Longden, 'Notes', pp. 3–5; Bennett, *Trajan*, p. 196.

51 Even Lepper, *Trajan's Parthian War*, p.129, notes that Trajan had accomplished so much in 115 that one begins to wonder why he went on in the following year to attack Adiabene and Ctesiphon at all.

52 Dio 68.26.1 for the pontoon bridges built at Nisibis. He notes at 68.26.2 that the crossing was dominated by the Gordyaean Mountains, so the location of the crossing is at Cizre. Lightfoot, 'Trajan's Parthian war', p. 120, does not believe the story. Arrian, *Parthica* fr.7. Cf. J.G. Taylor, 'Travels in Kurdistan', *Journal of the Royal Geographical Society*, 35 (1865), p. 56.

53 Trajan's twelfth salutation can be dated to 20 February–9 December 116; Lepper, *Trajan's Parthian War*, pp. 44–5.

54 Eutropius, *Breviarum*, 8.3; not all scholars are convinced such a province existed. For those who think it did, see Longden, 'Notes', pp. 13–14; Henderson, 'Review', p. 125; David Magie, *Roman Rule in Asia Minor* (Princeton, 1950), p. 608; Dilleman, *Haute Mesopotamie*, pp. 288–9; College, *Parthians*, pp. 54–5; Chaumont, 'L'Armenie', *ANRW*, 2, 9, p. 140; A.D.H. Bivar, 'The political history of Iran under the Arsacids', in E. Yarshater (ed.), *Cambridge History of Iran. 3, 1: The Seleucid, Parthian and Sasanian Periods* (Cambridge, 1983), p. 496; Debevoise, *Parthia*, p. 230. For dissenters, see A. Mariq, 'Hatra de Sanatroup', *Syria*, 36 (1959), p. 254; Lightfoot, 'Trajan's Parthian wars', pp. 121–4; Lepper, *Trajan's Parthian War*, pp. 152–3. There is no celebration of the foundation of an Assyria Provincia on the Trajan coinage. While there is a name for the governor of Armenia, there is no record of any Roman official appointed to Assyria. There is no trace of Roman occupation around Djebel Singara in the second century. If there was a province in Assyria, it was so transitory it left no trace in contemporary records.

55 Dio 68.26.

56 Arrian, *Parthica* fr. 67.

57 Lepper, *Trajan's Parthian War*, p. 133; on Naharmalcha see F.H. Weissbach, 'Naharmalcha', *RE*, 16.2 , columns 1440ff.

58 Arrian *Parthica* fr.67.

59 Hadrian later restored the daughter, c. 128, and at the same time promised to return the throne, but failed to do so. Antoninus Pius later refused a direct request for it, *Scriptores historiae Augustae*, [heraffter *SHA*] ed. David Magie (3 vols, Cambridge, MA, 1921–32), *Hadrian* 13.8; *Antoninus Pius* 9.7; Bennett, *Trajan*, p. 199.

60 PARTHIA CAPTA coins: Belloni, *Le Monete di Traiano*, p. xxxvi, Title *Parthicus*, Dio 68.28.2-3. This should be the twelfth salutation. See Lepper, *Trajan's Parthian War*, pp. 44–5 for the problems.

61 Bennett, *Trajan*, p. 199.

62 Dio 68.29; Bennett, *Trajan*, p. 199. On the province of Characene and Charax, see J. Black, 'The history of Parthia and Charactene in the second century AD', *Sumer*, 43, 1–2 (1984), pp. 230–4; Lepper, *Trajan's Parthian War*, p. 10.

63 On the thirteenth imperial salutation, see Bennett, *Trajan*, p. 199; on the statue marking his advance see Jordanes, *Rom*, 268: *The Gothic History of Jordanes*, ed. C.C. Mierow (Princeton, 1915). The statue was apparently still standing in 569 when recorded by John of Ephesus in his *Ecclesiastical History*, Bennett, *Trajan*, p. 285, n. 83; Lepper, *Trajan's Parthian War*, p. 14. More coins were issued with the legend *fortuna redux*, Henry Cohen, *Description historique des monnaies frappés sous l'Empire romain* (Paris & London, 1880–92), pp. 157, 158, 159, 160. Strack, *Untersuchungen*, pp. 454, 459.

64 Dio 68.30-32 and 75.9; John Malalas 11.273-20-74.

65 Mitford, 'Cappadocia and Armenia Minor', p. 1199.

66 On securing perimeters, see Bennett, *Trajan*, pp. 199–200.

67 Dio 68.32.5. The end of Abgarus' reign and presumably the fall of Edessa can be closely dated to between 6 June 116 and 1 July 117. See Lepper, *Trajan's Parthian War*, pp. 92–5, but this still does not tell us when the Parthian *revanche* began, as Bennett, *Trajan*, p. 285, n. 88, points out.

68 Bennett, *Trajan*, p. 200.

69 Vologaeses II: Bennett, *Trajan*, p. 200; Dio 68.31; Debevoise, *Parthia*, p. 237.

70 Bennett, *Trajan*, p. 200 and n. 89.

71 H. Mattingly et al., *Coins of the Roman Empire in the British Museum* (London, 1932–62) (*BMC*), 1054. Belloni, *Le Monete di Traiano*, pp. xxxv, xxvi, 48; *RIC* 310, 311, 312, 66; RIC 667, 668. Strack, *Untersuchungen*, 476; Cohen, *Description*, 328.

72 Bennett, *Trajan*, p. 200.

73 Dio 68.31.4.

74 Dio 68.31.3.

75 Bennett, *Trajan*, p. 201; Dio 68.32.

76 M. Pucci ben Ze'ev, 'Greek attacks against Alexandrian Jews during Emperor Trajan's reign', *Journal for the Study of Judaism*, 20 (1989), pp. 31–48. On the evidence from papyri, see A. Fuks, 'The Jewish revolt in Egypt (A.D. 115–117) in the light of papyri', *Aegyptus* 33 (1953), pp. 131–58.

77 T.D. Barnes, 'Trajan and the Jews', *Journal of Jewish Studies*, 40 (1989), pp. 145–62.

78 We are told that in Cyrene 220,000 Greeks and Romans perished and had their flesh eaten, and their entrails used to make belts. There is more documentation for destruction of property than there is for atrocities, especially in Cyrene. See Fuks, 'Jewish revolt', p. 156, and S. Applebaum, 'The Jewish revolt in Cyrene in 115–117 and the subsequent re-colonization', *Journal of Jewish Studies*, 2 (1951), pp. 177–81.

79 Dio says Trajan sent Lusius 'among others'. Turbo was prefect of the Misenum fleet. On Marcus Turbo's prefecture in Egypt see Fuks, 'Jewish revolt', p. 152.

80 Fuks, 'Jewish revolt', p. 153.

81 Insurrection in Mauretania, *SHA Hadrian* 5.9; Roxolani and Iazyges, *SHA Hadrian*, 6.6; British brigands, *SHA Hadrian* 5.1; signs of rebellion in Judaea, *SHA Hadrian*, 5.1; Bennett, *Trajan*, pp. 201–2. M. Mary Smallwood, 'Palestine A.D. 115–118', *Historia*, 11 (October 1962), pp. 500–10, discusses the unrest in

Palestine, the possibility of a revolt and Lusius Quietus' being sent there to quell the uprising.

82 Trajan suffered a stroke which led him partially paralysed. The symptoms suggest congestive heart failure brought on by hypertension. Certainly, marching through the Anatolian mountains and crossing the Arabian desert at sixty years of age did not help.

83 At the same time, his wine and table steward and taster, M. Ulpius Phaedimus, contracted similar symptoms and died; he was only 28: Dio 68.33.2ff. For an attractive if unproveable theory concerning the events surrounding the death of Trajan and Phaedimus and the matter of Hadrian's succession, namely that Trajan was assassinated and Phaedimus murdered to assure silence, see Paribeni, *Optimus*, 2.310, no. 16; Ronald Syme, *Tacitus* (Oxford, 1958), p. 240, n. 7; Bennett, *Trajan*, p. 202; *SHA Hadrian* 4.7.

84 Dio 68.33.3; Bennett, *Trajan*, p. 202. The date of his death is not certain, but it was before 11 August 116.

85 SHA *Hadrian* 5.1–5 on Hadrian abandoning the eastern conquests. The speech by Cato was supposedly given in the Senate in 167 BCE after the defeat of Perseus, the last king of Macedonia, at Pydna; see Livy XIV 17–18: Livy, *Ab urbe condita*, ed. B.O. Foster et al. (14 vols, London, 1961). Tacitus *Annals* 1.11 on the non-expansion of the empire: Tactitus, *The Annals*, ed. J. Jackson (3 vols, Cambridge, 1956).

86 On the plot to kill Hadrian hatched by these four generals and their condemnation by the Senate see SHA *Hadrian* 7.2-3; Bennett, *Trajan*, p. 203.

87 *SHA Hadrian* 5.3, 9.1; Bennett, *Trajan*, p. 203. Dura Europas was abandoned before 30 September 117, Smallwood, *Documents*, p. 53; Bennett, *Trajan*, p. 203; M. Rostovtzeff, 'Parthian foreign policy', in *Cambridge Ancient History* I (Cambridge, 1965), p. 108. (Rostovtzeff modified his views in a later article, making the abandonment of Dura take place in two stages: 'Kaiser Trajan und Dura', *Klio* 31 (1938), pp. 285–92; Lepper, *Trajan's Parthian War*, 148–9.

88 Dio 68.3.2-3. Longden, 'Notes', pp. 27–8, believed Trajan had no original intentions of annexing Mesopotamia.

89 S. Mattern, *Rome and the Enemy*, (Berkeley, 1999), pp. 21–2; Isaac, *Limits of Empire*, pp. 5–6; J. Mann, 'Power, force and the frontiers of the empire', *Journal of Roman Studies* 69 (1979), p. 90. Mitford, 'Cappadocia and Armenia Minor', p. 1196, says Trajan annexed Armenia for 'strategic reasons' but he never clarifies what the strategy was except for annexation in the name of defence.

90 On grand strategy a chimera, see Isaac, *Limits of Empire*, pp. 373–4.

91 E.N. Luttwak, *The Grand Strategy of the Roman Empire* (Baltimore, 1976), p. 3; yet he follows Lepper in describing the defence of a 'Chaboras-Singara line'. Lepper, *Trajan's Parthian War*, p. 120, himself points out that, if 115 was spent consolidating a line that was to become the permanent eastern frontier, none of the literary sources took note of the fact.

92 Luttwak, *Grand Strategy*, p. 108.

93 Lepper, *Trajan's Parthian War*, p. 106.

94 Robert R. Tomes, 'Schlock and blah: counter-insurgency realities in a rapid dominance era', *Small Wars and Insurgencies*, 16,1 (March 2005), pp. 37–57 at p. 40, on whether the US force was large enough, and pp. 48–52 on the intelligence requirements.

95 The term 'shock and awe' derives from two main sources in military thinking: rapidity in operations and overwhelming military superiority. H. Kullman and J.P. Wade introduced the term into defence discourse with a widely read chapter in their monograph *Shock and Awe: Achieving Rapid Dominance*, (Washington, D.C., 1996); see also H.K. Ullman and J.P. Wade, *Rapid Dominance*, (London, 1998).

96 Tomes, 'Schlock and blah', pp. 52–5.

97 Army chief of staff George Decker, cited in Tomes, 'Schlock and blah', p. 39.
98 Ibid., p. 39.
99 Ibid., p. 39.

Indian Political Intelligence (IPI): the monitoring of real and possible danger?

Kate O'Malley

Indian Political Intelligence, or IPI, was formally established in 1921 as a consequence of the development of Indian nationalist activities at the turn of the century. The collection of IPI records, housed in the British Library, was released as a result of the British 'Open Government' policy of the late 1990s (the Waldegrave initiative), and it comprises some 770 or so files. There has not been extensive study of the record carried out nor is there a publication available detailing the contents of the IPI files. The collection provides a rich source of material spanning several decades of intelligence gathering. It should also be noted that much material available in the IPI files is more than likely contained in numerous as yet unreleased files of the Security Service (MI5) and the Secret Intelligence Service (MI6 or SIS), as IPI's role was essentially a 'catch-all' co-ordination of information about anything relating to India and to Indians within the empire and relied heavily on MI5 and SIS reports to supplement its data.

This paper will show how the monitoring of Indian nationalists' activities throughout Europe and America by IPI revealed radical contacts previously less evident to the British authorities. As Indian elite activists fled their country for Europe or America, they arrived in a geographical arena more conducive to practical collaboration with fellow anti-imperialist conspirators. It will show how IPI files document the gradual development of an international contra-imperialist nexus which the British government gradually became aware and apprehensive of, as its repercussions were not immediately discernible to them. It will also demonstrate how, early on, IPI successfully monitored the activities of dangerous individuals (like Subhas Chandra Bose) who potentially posed a threat to the empire. This paper seeks to support a more general argument about British intelligence in the interwar period, that is, that an analysis of IPI material indicates that an over emphasis was placed on monitoring the actions of communist or Bolshevik suspects and organisations at the expense of other perhaps more menacing threats to empire, such as the development of right-wing organisations, radical nationalism and anti-imperialist nationalist alliances of a non-communist variety. This is hardly surprising, as Christopher Andrew has noted how agent penetration of the Communist Party of India (CPI) seems to have been extensive and British intelligence reporting on Indian communism prolific. The British intelligence services' reports on communism, which frequently quoted intercepted Comintern and Communist Party of Great Britain (CPGB) communications, have since become a major source for both Marxist and non-Marxist historians of Indian Communism.[1]

Rozina Visram's thoroughly researched *Asians in Britain* is arguably the only book that records the activities of Indians in Britain in any great depth.[2] While Visram's work fills a long vacant void in Indian historiography, it covers a vast span of four hundred years and a lack of further material in this vein means that, in detailing the conduct of those who were politically active in the twentieth century, her work fails to address the deeper implications that the mere existence of such radicals at the very heart of the empire had on British policy making. This is especially significant in relation to the development of British security and intelligence policy as the Indian independence movement was gaining momentum. The importance of using IPI material in the documentation of the Indian nationalist movement abroad becomes all the more significant given the nature of the collection. IPI material and India Office files can be found side by side, while most other intelligence and security material in the UK national archives have been removed from various series. Therefore the way in which IPI influenced policy making is clearly visible. To date the history of the Indian nationalist movement abroad has focused largely on personalities, the standard approach has been commemorative and individual subjects have been treated largely in isolation from political developments.[3] The IPI collection, which contains many personal files of the better-known individuals based in the UK and Europe, facilitates a more holistic approach to the movement and crucially, as noted, the information is presented to the researcher in the context of both British security and India policy. It should also be pointed out that IPI has particular Irish links, as for most of its existence it was headed by a Trinity College Dublin man, Sir Philip Crawford Vickery, who was seconded to it from the Indian police during the First World War and who became its chief from 1926 until its closure in 1947 (when India became independent, and IPI was absorbed as a section in MI5).[4] Another key IPI officer was Sir Charles Tegart, also a Trinity man, who refused the headship of the organisation in 1923 and instead became chief commissioner of the

Calcutta police.[5] These Irish links merit attention when information about Irish nationalists presents itself in IPI records, and they raise the question of the impact of these officers' own Irish loyalist backgrounds on their analysis of the potential threat that Indian revolutionary activity generally, and Indo-Irish collaboration more specifically, could provide.

Why was IPI, which was essentially a separate and non-avowed intelligence agency, although it worked closely with MI5, SIS and the Scotland Yard Special Branch, established at all? In the wake of the unpopular partition of Bengal in 1905 one of the most surprising features of the Indian revolutionary movement for the British was the speed of its growth, and an even more alarming feature was the emergence of revolutionary centres abroad. By 1907 Indian revolutionary groups could be found in London and Paris. In London a group of Indian students set up 'India House' in Highgate and began publishing *The Indian Sociologist*. Some began military training. One of the more famous Indian activists associated with India House was Veer Savarkar, who later became the President of the hard-line Hindu *Mahasabha* group, which was implicated in Gandhi's murder in 1948.[6] In Paris, Indians who had established the revolutionary centre there were also suspected of dispatching explosives and revolvers to India. Among the activists there at this time were Sarat Chandra Bose, brother of Subhas, and Madam Cama, both of whom had established contact with the Irish nationalist Maud Gonne MacBride. By the eve of the First World War the British authorities were alarmed to discover that Indian radicals were also active in the United States and Canada. This group became k own as the revolutionary Ghadr Movement; its figurehead was Lala Har Dayal, who in 1914 sought German support for the liberation of India. Richard Popplewell has documented the activities of the Ghadr movement and British monitoring of them from 1904 to 1924 in his book *Intelligence and Imperial Defence*, but at the time of publication the IPI files remained closed.[7]

As a result of this increase in international activity, IPI was provisionally established through the secondment in 1909 of John Wallinger from the Indian Police to the India Office.[8] His brief was to watch Indian nationalists throughout Europe but also to co-ordinate the activities of a non-declared operation against Indians on the Pacific coasts of North America, which was run under the cover of the Canadian Immigration Department. The Delhi Intelligence Bureau (DIB) continued to run operations there in India. That same year, 1909, an Indian student, Madan Lal Dhingra, shot dead Sir William Curzon Wyllie, the political aide-de-camp of the Secretary of State for India, Lord Morley, on the steps of the India Office in London, and in 1912 there was an unsuccessful attempt on the life of the Viceroy Lord Hardinge. As Popplewell succinctly put it: 'in the period 1907 to 1917 the Raj faced a serious threat from Indian revolutionaries; this threat was a major stimulus to the growth of British intelligence operations on a global level'.[9] This also provided the impetus for the formation of IPI. Viewed from this standpoint IPI has a contemporary resonance of great significance, as the recent 'war on terrorism' has seen Western governments, especially Britain, similarly seek to confront trans-national threats that evaded traditional national-based intelligence strategies.

In 1915 the demand increased for the monitoring of Indian national-ist activity in the aftermath of the outbreak of the First World War and Philip Vickery joined Wallinger, who in the meantime had managed to recruit the writer Somerset Maugham as an agent. Maugham subsequently used Wallinger as 'R' in several short stories.[10] Vickery was charged with expanding and developing the network and in 1919 was deployed to the US and Canada, where he ran operations for five years. It was an enormous responsibility for someone so young; he was 29. By 1921 IPI had been formally established and had expanded throughout Europe and America. Back in India, however, the fledgling agency was not without its critics. To the annoyance of the Government of India, London, rather than Calcutta, Delhi or Simla was to remain the clearing house for all intelligence relating to India right up until independence. In 1922 the Home Department of the Government of India even suggested to the India Office that IPI be merged with SIS. The response was unequivocal and also throws light on some other difficulties that the existence of IPI threw up for the British Intelligence services, as well as the importance that the India Of fice placed on its new separate agency:

> The suggestion that the IPI might be amalgamated with the SIS is not practicable or likely to result in economy... SIS is not allowed to work in the United Kingdom or the United States of America, where IPI *must* have agents. Difficulties of housing in London would be raised; and differences in direction and policy as between the objects of the SIS and those of the IPI might easily cause friction between the Foreign Office and this office.[11]

Sir Cecil Kaye of the Home Department (and father of the writer M.M. Kaye) was not convinced and noted:

> I must admit that I feel rather sceptical regarding both the India Office arguments: and am inclined to doubt whether, if they could really be examined in detail, from this end, they would hold water. As it is, of course, they cannot be challenged.'[12]

After the First World War IPI's activities were concentrated on the

Communist threat, on suspect Indian subversives and, as the introduction to the catalogue itself states, 'to a lesser extent on mainstream Indian nationalism'. A quick breakdown of the percentage of files relating to various topics shows that 'Personal Files' encompass 17 per cent of the overall collection, but larger than that again are files devoted to 'Communism' in all its various guises, which amounts to 20 per cent of the collection. Other topics include, for example, 'Islam and the Kalifat Movement' (1.9 per cent), 'North America' (5.6 per cent) and 'Indian National Congress' (which amounts to only 2.2 per cent). Even more surprisingly, what IPI describe as 'Revolutionary and Terrorist Activities' comprises only 3.5 per cent and 'Arms Smuggling' only 2.8 per cent. With the later rise of and threat supplied by Subhas Chandra Bose and his Indian National Army (INA), even though Bose himself was monitored closely from an early stage, this seems with hindsight to be quite an anomaly.

Throughout IPI's existence files detailing harmless organisations and suspects, most of whom spent their time on or around platforms in Hyde Park, can be found alongside more serious subjects. Many of these files make quite mundane reading but some can be, perhaps unintentionally, quite humorous. The details contained in most of these files were more than likely supplied to IPI in the form of Special Branch reports. For example, in 1928 an Irish woman, Mrs Ayres, who was affiliated with the Indian Freedom League run by Ali Mohammed Khan was reported as being 'an undoubted rapid revolutionary' who was 'understood to have severely assaulted with her heavy knobbed umbrella someone who insulted Khan when the latter was speaking from the League's platform'.[13] In a file detailing the activities of London Student Unions that had a large number of Indian members in 1933, it was noted how 'on the occasion of the table tennis match held on Thursday the 26th January between Indian and Irish students, no anti-British political discussion took place'.[14] Vickery also referred to the *Hindustan Times* journalist Chaman Lal as 'Chaman Lal of Basil Blackett fame', in order to differentiate him from another Indian of the same name, the left-wing swarajist Diwan Chaman Lal. This was a reference to an incident in 1928 when ' in a fit of nationalist ardour [Lal] threw his attache case from the press gallery of the Legislative Assembly in Delhi on to the head of the late Sir Basil Blackett, the finance minister'.[15] However, although Patrick French has similarly observed how 'many of the IPI files on individual suspects are stunningly innocuous, students, businessmen, writers and scientists were all watched', I would disagree with his assessment that it was 'often for the most trivial of reasons'.[16] One of the main reasons why people such as Mrs Ayres and London-based Indian students were being watched in the late 1920s and 1930s was because many of them, innocently enough, became involved in an organisation that a lot of people interested in Indian independence throughout Europe were joining, the League Against Imperialism (LAI).

The LAI was initiated by the well-known Berlin-based communist Willie Munzenburg, in the wake of a new departure by the Comintern which allowed for collaboration between communists and nationalists in colonial regions.[17] By the late 1920s many left-wing figures throughout Europe had joined the organisation, many of whom were not communists, like the Irish republicans Frank Ryan and Donal O'Donoghue. Most notably during his time in Europe in the 1920s Jawaharlal Nehru had endorsed the LAI and attended one of its general meetings, and Albert Einstein had become a member. The British intelligence services were baffled as to how the LAI had managed to '(enlist) the sympathies of some prominent pacifist writers and men of learning'.[18] Nonetheless, any Indian LAI member was now considered a suspect subversive by IPI and there are twenty large files detailing the organisation's activities from 1924 until its demise in the late 1930s. The LAI files disclose considerable unease on the part of IPI with the activities of left-wing Indian activists in Britain, Ireland and the Continent. Apprehensions existed about their exact relations with established Communist Parties and their possible contacts with Moscow. Although the Comintern made increased efforts to incorporate into its doctrines strong aspects of anti-imperialism in an effort to win over nationalist revolutionaries in the colonies, in the case of Indian and Irish activists, national liberation was too strong a inherent principle to simply leave by the wayside. On the whole, apart from Shapuri Saklatvala, M.N. Roy and Virendranath Chattopadhaya, each of whom had their own separate files, many of those Indian activists who became involved with the LAI and were being monitored by IPI were not communists. They were either unaware of its communist origins or were motivated from an anti-imperialist, nationalist perspective, with communism, allowing for its contemporary popularity, proving a suitable vehicle for a means to an essentially nationalist end. What the authorities were slow to realise was that this organisation provided a much needed service, namely an opportunity for anti-imperialists of a variety of political back-grounds and from around the world to meet and exchange ideas.

The outbreak of the Second World War resulted in increased activity by IPI, worried that Indian radicals would use 'Britain's difficulty as India's opportunity', as the Irish had in 1916, and indeed as Subhas Chandra Bose would try to do with the support of the Axis powers.[19] A booklet entitled 'Suspect Civilian Indians on the Continent of Europe' was issued every two months, with extra attention being given to those active in Vienna or Berlin suspected of establishing links with the Nazis.[20] Throughout the war Indians resident in the UK were also monitored and given extra attention. This included many journalists and Indian sympathisers who were considered dangerous by virtue of their espousal of anti-British opinions. In the early 1930s an Indian law student named Dowlat Jayaram (D.J.) Vaidya arrived in London and was given an introduction to the CPGB in the UK on account of the interest he had taken in labour and communist activities in Bombay.[21] Vaidya's IPI file is quite sparse until the outbreak of the war, by which time informants were submitting regular reports on his activities. This surveillance was primarily as a result of his nascent career as a journalist with *Life* and *Time* magazines, where he was in charge of their Eastern Department, but was also attributable to his past associations with the LAI and his liaising with another Indian activist based in London who later became a very significant figure, Krishna Menon.[22]

It appears that during the war, Vaidya's office telephone was being tapped, a fact which throws light on both IPI's increased wartime remit as well as more general concerns over wartime censorship and the publication of pro-Indian independence propaganda. An unexpected interception regarding the Irish republican Geoffrey Coulter came to light in 1942. Coulter had been arrested several times in the 1930s and was an assistant editor of *An Phoblacht* as well as a left-wing cohort of prominent activists Frank Ryan and Peadar O'Donnell.[23] IPI had reason to believe that Coulter was *Life* magazine's correspondent in Ireland and telephone calls to him from the magazine's editor, the American journalist Stephen Laird, were being noted and passed onto IPI when Coulter was in the process of submitting a piece relating to pro-Indian Irish sentiment in the wake of the failed Cripps mission.[24] Laird had informed him how he was 'anxious to say something about the Irish reaction to this India business', to which Coulter responded that 'study of the Irish newspapers discloses practically no quotation of foreign comment unfavourable to Congress or to Gandhi. Opinion here is 90% pro both.'[25] Laird expressed how he thought it was the opposite with regard to the British press and was delighted to hear such reports, but he none the less asked that, in his piece, Coulter would 'elaborate that statement about Irish opinion being 90% pro-Congress. Don't make it as flat as that.'[26] Laird clearly thought that there were many Irish parallels that could be drawn upon to illustrate the gravity of the Indian situation:

> I am going to present the line that this may be an Easter 1916 for India and draw the parallel between the Moslem Hindu set-up and the North and South. Of course, the newspapers here are playing it all down and taking the line that it's pretty nearly over and has all been a flop, but so was Easter 1916 at first.[27]

Less then two weeks later Vickery had duly acquired further information about Coulter for his colleagues in IPI as upon receiving the telephone conversation transcriptions they were curious to find out more. This new information threw remarkable light on this somewhat obscure figure in the Irish republican movement, and was acquired and verified in a very short space of time.

> In June 1932 COULTER was a member of the I.R.A. and had been assistant editor of "AN PHOBLACHT" ... [he] was assisting the Irish Revolutionary Worker's Party, though he was not a member... he was obviously left-wing I.R.A. but in November 1933, the Eire High Commissioner reported that he had "now disaffiliated himself from his Communist activities" ... since 1933 little has been learnt about his political activities, but he has incurred some suspicion because he has worked in Eire under Erland ECHLIN, first for "Time" and then for "Newsweek". Erland ECHLIN is an American, of pro-German sympathies who is now interned... the view of the Security authorities regarding Coulter is at present that he is "a good journalist, who will try to spread news whether it is discreet to do so or not, and who generally has more sympathy with the left than with the right".[28]

Vickery went on to note how there was nothing on record to show that Coulter was interested in India but in his opinion it was 'certainly a subject which would appeal to a man with an I.R.A. background'. Throughout his career at IPI Vickery, as an Irishman, appears to have gotten great pleasure in locating precise and up-to-date information about any Irish names and figures that appeared on file from time to time. He often overwrote and corrected any misspellings or inaccuracies relating to Ireland in other people's reports, and he always availed himself of the opportunity to show his true colours as a loyal Irish servant to the Crown, something revealed in his last note regarding Coulter: 'curiously enough, or perhaps not so curiously, since many "Irish patriots" are not Irish, Coulter is an Englishman. He has been many years in Ireland.'

A great deal of information about both Irish and Indian radical activities was gleaned by tracing the activities of the Indian journalist D.J. Vaidya and those close to him. In fact one of his associates, V.K. Krishna Menon, was of particular interest to IPI during the war. In some cases IPI attempted to create communist leanings where there were none and this is particularly evident from Menon's file. Menon had been based in London since the 1 920s and ran the India League. As late as 1940 IPI said of Menon that he was known to have regularly 'taken the advice of the leader of the Communist Party... his views were undistinguishable from those of Moscow (and) he went to great pains to impress these views on Nehru.'[29] Vickery added, however, that he thought Menon was 'not a Marxian Communist, having neither the brain needed to work out Marxian dialectics for himself, nor the type of character which would enable him to accept spoon-feeding from those who have'.[30] A few years later Menon would be designated as India's first High Commissioner in London and it is of interest to note that IPI continued to keep Menon's file open even as the transfer of power was approaching. An India Office report admitted that while 'the target set for IPI' was altering, it was 'essential to be aware of the activities of such persons as Krishna Menon and of other persons of even more dubious record'.[31]

It is possible that some more threatening Indian radicals slipped through the net or were at least not given due attention during this period as they lacked communist credentials One such person who was a considerably dangerous individual based on the continent was the drugs and arms trafficker Henry Obed. Obed travelled from Lucknow to Europe and based himself in Hamburg in 1922. When ousted by the authorities there, he set up shop in Antwerp, under the cover of a curious animal import and export business. He was an elusive character with neither the Belgium nor British authorities ever able to find proof of his suspected criminal activities. IPI had in fact lost track of him in the late 1930s. Interestingly, and much to the British authorities' discomfort, when he did show up it was in Cork in July 1940 along with two Gerrnan South African accomplices. They were in possession of 'a quantity of explosives, – two suitcases containing eight incendiary bombs and five canisters of explosives – and also £800 in cash'.[32] He was imprisoned and did not leave Ireland until 1947 as his release was complicated due to his Indian and therefore British citizenship. As he had not been found guilty of any crime in Europe or India he could not be extradited. It was noted on his IPI file how his continued 'presence in Eire is an embarrassment to us and… if we miss this opportunity we may find it difficult to shift him later.'[33]

IPI can be credited with having tracked and detailed the movements of another dangerous individual, Subhas Chandra Bose, whose actions during the Second World War were to prove much more worrying than Obed's. In the 1920s the DIB and IPI reports relating to Bose were short and concise and very much lead one to believe that the British authorities did not take very seriously Bose and his volunteer force of khaki-clad students established in Calcutta in the early 1920s. Gradually, as the years passed, there was a significant change in attitude towards Bose. As he made his way through Europe and received the extended attention of many of its leaders, IPI reports about him became longer, more detailed and acquired an overwhelmingly sober tone. On his jaunt as a roving ambassador for Indian independence in the 1930s his every move was noted and an almost obsessive account of his travels and networking is on view in his substantial IPI files, second only in size to those belonging to the leading Indian communist M.N. Roy.

The formation and eventual workings of IPI were a vital addition to the British intelligence services in a time of increased concern, when anti-imperial activity was no longer a problem just in India or Ireland but had escalated to a global level. It not only shed light on the nature of ostensibly communist organisations and networks and the apparent threat that these posed to law and order in the colonies, but it led to the authorities becoming more aware of less easily discernible radical contacts that had been established in the shape of, among other things, Indo–Irish and, during the Second World War, Indo–Axis collaboration. This has been merely a glimpse into some of the fascinating, sometimes entertaining and always insightful, material available in the Indian Political Intelligence collection. There is an abundance of subjects, people and countries included in its scope. The collection has been open to research now for coming up to ten years and, although a few general histories of India published since have used a fraction of the material available here, it seems quite an anomaly in Intelligence historiography that an overall study of this absorbing collection has yet to be carried out.

NOTES

1   Christopher Andrew, *Secret Service* (London, 1985), pp. 324–38.
2   Rozina Visram, *Asians in Britain: 400 Years of History* (London, 2002).
3   Peter Heehs, *Nationalism, Terrorism, Communalism: Essays in Modern Indian History* (Oxford, 1998), p. 1.
4   Born in County Fermanagh in 1890, Vickery studied Modern Languages at Trinity College Dublin and joined the Indian Police Service in 1909. He was sent to America and Canada to carry out surveillance of Indian radicals in 1919 and remained there until 1926, when he returned to London and took over IPI. He remained there until its closure in 1947. He worked in the Commonwealth Relations Office from 1952 to 1962, and died aged 97 in 1987.
5   Born in County Derry in 1881. Tegart was educated at Trinity College Dublin and joined the Indian Police Service in 1901. Appointed Commissioner of Calcutta Police in, 1926, he, retired from the Indian Police Service in 1931 served on the Council of India, 1931–7 was offered the post of inspector general of the Palestine Police in 1937 but declined and instead accepted a short-term post to organise the police force to combat terrorism there. Tegart controversially worked in Ireland for the British intelligence services during the Second World War; he died in 1946.
6   For further reading see Vidya Sagar, *Savarkar: A Study in the Evolution of Indian Nationalism* (London, 1967).
7   Richard Popplewell, *Intelligence and Imperial Defence: British Intelligence and the Defence of the Indian Empire, 1904–1924* (London, 1995).
8   British Library [hereafter BL], Oriental and India Office Collections [hereafter OIOC], India Office Records [hereafter IOR], Indian Political Intelligence files

[hereafter IP&J/12] catalogue introduction notes.

9 Popplewell, *Intelligence*, p. 1.

10 Somerset Maugharn, *Ashenden* (London, 1928) and *Ashenden: or the British Agent?* (London, 1934)

11 Ferrard to O'Donnell, 23 Aug. 1922, Home Department Political, 12, 1922 Poll, Indian National Archives. My thanks to Deirdre McMahon for this reference.

12 Ibid.

13 Extract from Scotland Yard report, 28 Nov. 1928, BL, OIOC, IOR, L/P&J/I 2/258 .

14 Extract from Scotland Yard report, Jan. 1933, BL, OIOC, IOR, L/P&J/12/42.

15 IPI note on Chaman Lal, 30 Aug. 1946, BL, OIOC, IOR, L/P&J/12/470. By this stage Blackett had died in a road accident in Germany aged just 53 .

16 Patrick French, *Liberty or Death: India's Journey to Independence and Division* (London. 1997), p. 99.

17 Jean Jones, 'The League Against Imperialism', *The Socialist History Society Occasional Paper Series No. 4.* (London, 1996), p. 4.

18 Secret unsigned report on Munzenburg, 29 Sept. 1930, TNA, records of the Security Services KV2/772.

19 For further reading on the career of Subhas Chandra Bose see Mihir Bose, *The Lost Hero* (London, 1982). A revised edition ofthis book, which utilises material on Bose contained in the IPI collection, was published this year in India but at the time of writing is not available in the English language. Information from Eunan O'Halpin.

20 French, *Liberty*, p. 121 and see various files dating from the Second World War in BL, OIOC, IOR, L/P&J/12 category.

21 History sheet of Dowlat Jayararn Vaidya (no date but ends c. 1942), BL, OIOC, IOR, L/P&J/12/478.

22 Born in Calicut in 1897, Menon joined Annie Besant's Home Rule movement in India before travelling to England in 1924. He became general secretary of the India League in 1929 and established a strong friendship with Nehru in the 1930s. During this time he was an active Labour Party member. Following the transfer of power he was appointed High Commissioner to the UK, 1947–52, and became India's first Ambassador to Ireland, 1949. Elected to the Upper House of the Indian Parliament, in 1953, he entered the Cabinet as a Minister without Portfolio in 1956–7, and served as Minister for Defence in, 1957. He resigned from the Congress Party in 1967 and, died in 1974.

23 For further information on these and other left-wing republicans in Ireland at this time see Richard English, *Radicals and the Republic* (Oxford, 1994).

24 Recently declassified US documents show that Laird had in fact been a Soviet spy since the 1930s and provided Soviet agents with information during the 1940s. See John Earl Haynes and Harvey Klehr, *Venona: Decoding Soviet Espionage in America* (London, 1999).

25 Transcribed telephone conversation, London to Sutton, Dublin, 14 Aug. 1942, BL, OIOC, IOR, L/P&J/12/478.

26 Ibid.

27 Ibid.

28 Vickery to Silver, 29 Aug. 1942, BL, OIOC, IOR, L/P&J/12/478.

29 Fact sheet of V.K. Krishna Menon, 10 June 1940, BL, OIOC, IOR, L/P&J/I 2/323 .

30 Ibid.

31 French, Liberty, p.267.

32 Vickery to Silver, 20 July 1940, BL, OIOC, IOR, L/P&J/12/477.

33 Price to Moore, 11 Apr. 1947, BL, OIOC, IOR, L/P&J/12/477.

Stalin and foreign intelligence during the Second World War

Geoffrey Roberts

During the Second World War Stalin had at his disposal a vast and highly productive foreign intelligence apparatus. In November 1944 Soviet security chiefs Beria and Merkulov reported to their boss that in the past three years they had sent 566 illegal operatives to work abroad. These illegals ran a network of 1,240 agents and informants. This network had supplied 41,718 different pieces of intelligence material, including 1,167 documents of a technical-industrial character, half of which had already been utilised in domestic production.[1]

Among Soviet sources abroad were the famous 'Cambridge' spy ring of Philby, Burgess, Maclean, Cairncross and Blunt, who provided documents from the Foreign Office, the Cabinet Office and the Bletchley Park decryption centre. There was also an extensive network of political, economic and military informants in the United States, including sources working at the highest levels of the Roosevelt administration.[2] In Europe there were various Soviet intelligence rings, including several in Germany. There is even a suggestion that Soviet intelligence penetrated the top levels of German military intelligence and the Gestapo.[3] Closer to home, the NKGB[4] bugged foreign embassies in Moscow and its codebreaking operations enabled it to read much of the diplomatic traffic coming in and out of the Soviet capital.[5]

As well as these espionage activities there was the ground-level intelligence and counterintelligence war that the Soviets waged against Germany on the front line. According to a recent study the Soviets employed 175,000 operatives in this covert war with the Germans.[6] Among the well-attested successes of the Soviets were deception operations covering up every major Soviet military offensive on the Eastern Front, including the decisive counterattacks at Moscow in 1941, Stalingrad in 1942 and Kursk in 1943.

The Soviet Union had the benefit of extensive intelligence sharing with its British and American allies during the war. Particularly important was information received on the German order of battle, on German breaking of Soviet codes and a limited amount of information from Enigma decrypts – although the British never revealed to the Russians the extent and success of their deciphering operations. This intelligence sharing increased in quantity and quality after the Tehran summit of Churchill, Roosevelt and Stalin at the end of 1943. In 1944 the Soviets co-operated with the British in a deception operation to convince the Germans that an Anglo-Soviet invasion of Norway was imminent, whereas the actual plan of the Red Army was to attack and encircle Army Group Centre in Belorussia.[7]

The general outline of Soviet intelligence activities during the Second World War has been known for some time and in recent years has been filled out by further revelations from defectors[8] and by the release of British and American decrypts of Soviet signals. These sources have been supplemented in post-Soviet times by official publications containing a great number of intelligence documents from the Russian archives. In the mid-1990s the FSB – the Russian organisational successor to the KGB – published a multi-volumed history of Soviet foreign intelligence operations. Included in the volumes were copies of Cabinet and foreign office documents provided by Soviet spies in Britain.[9] Even more useful for historians has been the publication of a series of volumes of documents on Soviet intelligence activities at home and abroad during the Second World War. The six volumes published so far, covering the 1939–42 period, contain 1,249 Soviet documents as well as hundreds of explanatory notes and a good number of 'trophy documents', that is, intelligence documents from foreign sources captured by Soviet forces during the war.[10] Perhaps the greatest success of Soviet foreign intelligence during the war was the industrial and scientific espionage that penetrated the Manhattan Project. A multivolume collection of documents on the Soviet atomic project now provides many details of the intelligence procured by the Soviets and about how this information was assessed and utilised by Soviet scientists.[11]

What use did Stalin make of the vast quantities of intelligence presented to him during the war? At first sight Stalin's general attitude towards spies and espionage suggests that he might have taken it very seriously indeed. Soviet politics and society in the Stalin era were characterised by what James Harris has called 'spymania'.[12] Before the Second World War Stalin believed that foreign spies and saboteurs were ubiquitous and threatened the very foundations of the Soviet system, or would do if their nefarious activities continued unimpeded. Arguably, it was fear of the spy factor that drove much of Stalin's determination to root out the 'enemy within' in the great purges of the 1930s. Stalin and the system he presided over was also obsessed with secrecy and went to great lengths to control the flow of public information and to keep confidential what the leadership was saying and doing in private – even though most of what they were up to was apparent from a reading of the Soviet press.[13] But while Stalin perceived foreign spies as a great danger, particularly when linked to saboteurs and internal opponents of his regime, he was very suspicious of his own people engaged in espionage abroad. Stalin's closest confidant for most of his career in power was V.M. Molotov, Soviet prime minister in the 1930s and foreign minister in the 1940s. Molotov's attitude to spies was:

> I think that one can never trust intelligence. One has to listen to them but then check them. The intelligence people can lead to dangerous situations that it is impossible to get out of. There were endless provocateurs on both sides. That is why one cannot count on intelligence without a thorough and constant checking and double checking. People are so naive and gullible, indulging themselves and quoting memoirs: spies said so and so, defectors crossed the lines…[14]

Stalin's low opinion of spies was evident in a post-mortem discussion of the Soviet-Finnish war in April 1940: 'you do not have a spy's soul', he told I.I. Proskurov, who was in charge of military intelligence during that war, 'you have the soul of a very candid man… . A spy should be full of poison and gall; he must not believe anyone.' Later in the same discussion Stalin said that 'intelligence is not only keeping a secret agent in disguise someplace… Intelligence is working with clippings and reprints. This is pretty serious work.' On the other hand, at a meeting with Winston Churchill in Moscow in August 1942 Stalin proposed a toast to military intelligence officers: 'Spies… are like friends who honourably serve their own people…. Spies were good people who selflessly serve their country. Whenever they fall into enemy hands nobody would envy their fate'.[15]

In the literature on Stalin and foreign intelligence during the Second World War two stereotypes prevail. Firstly, there is the official view of the Russian/Soviet security apparatus contained in the FSB history and in various other publications produced with the FSB's co-operation and authorisation. These texts represent the Soviet foreign intelligence apparatus as a formidably efficient organisation that supplied Stalin with an enormous amount of top-quality documents, summaries and assessments and kept him well informed and well armed on vital matters of foreign, military and security policy. This official literature also contains a good sprinkling of epic accounts of the heroic exploits of Soviet spies in the service of the socialist motherland, including foreign recruits such as the Cambridge Five.

The problem with this representation of Stalin's relationship to Soviet intelligence material is that it is difficult to assess its validity without access to the full range of intelligence briefings given to Stalin, not just the FSB's selected highlights, which invariably feature the accurate material but omit the misinformation and misassessments transmitted to the Soviet leader. One thing is certain, however: during the war Stalin did not have the leisure to read that many intelligence reports. The thousands of intelligence documents and summaries presented to Stalin formed only a small stream of a veritable flood of material that swept through his office during the war years. There were thousands of diplomatic reports and equally large numbers of documents on economic questions, internal security matters and party issues. Stalin's General Staff produced daily briefings for him on the military situation at the front and drafted innumerable orders and directives for his signature. The State Defence Committee chaired by Stalin adopted 9,971 resolutions between 1941 and 1945. Of these Stalin personally signed 2,256. In many hundred of instances he drafted, dictated or heavily corrected the resolutions himself.[16] Stalin also had to keep up with the Soviet propaganda war. He oversaw the work of the Soviet Information Buro and supervised the contents of the Soviet press very closely, also keeping an eye on what was appearing in foreign newspapers.[17] From Stalin's appointments diary we know that he spent much of the war not reading but in meetings with his generals, his political associates and with a stream of visiting foreign dignitaries.[18] Another large chunk of his time was taken up with telephone and teletype conversations with his commanders on the front line.

Presumably Stalin found some time to read the more important and interesting intelligence documents or at least listen to briefings on their contents from Beria, Molotov and others. But it is difficult to pin down what he actually read or heard about or took notice of. For example, he may well have paid attention to the extensive documentation from his spies in Britain that detailed Anglo-American discussions in 1942 about their commitment to open a Second Front in France – documents that showed they intended to renege on their commitments to the Soviets and postpone the operation until 1943 or 1944.[19] But Stalin received similar briefings from his diplomats in London and Washington, and he could have drawn much the same conclusions from a close reading of the allied press. In his dealings with his allies on the Second Front issue Stalin betrayed no sign of any inside knowledge and acted as if he believed that his continuing political pressure on this matter could secure an early opening of the Second Front, notwithstanding the fact that the secret documentation at his disposal clearly indicated otherwise.

The second stereotype about Stalin and foreign intelligence – one very common in western literature on the subject[20] – is that Stalin was a political paranoid who distrusted the intelligence provided to him, preferred to act as his own intelligence analyst and frequently cowed his intelligence services into reporting to him what he wanted to hear. This particular stereotype is based mainly on Stalin's mishandling of Soviet foreign intelligence on the eve of the German attack on Russia in June 1941. Often cited as the classic example of intelligence failure, 22 June 1941 is an important case study of Stalin's use and misuse of intelligence. The different phases of the controversy about Stalin's failure to respond to warnings of a German surprise attack – which began with Khrushchev's 'secret speech' to the 20th party congress in 1956 – have generated a lot of documentation, including materials from Russian military archives. It is one of the very few episodes in the history of Soviet foreign intelligence about which it is possible to come to some definite, evidence-based conclusions.

That Stalin had good intelligence on both German intentions and preparations for a major attack on the Soviet Union is beyond doubt. This intelligence came from multiple sources: from spy networks in various counties, from signals intelligence, from border recon-naissance and from political and diplomatic sources. Contrary to the assertion that Stalin's subordinates told their boss what he wanted to hear, this intelligence was generally reported to him in a straight-forward manner. Everything Stalin wanted to know about Hitler's intentions and preparations for war could be gleaned from the evidence made available to him by intelligence sources. However, the intelligence flowing into Stalin's office was multidimensional, and complicated by a number of factors. The other pattern that could be discerned in the intelligence picture – a false one, it turned out – was that in summer 1941 a peace scenario was unfolding in Soviet-German relations, not a war scenario.

For a start there were the signals emanating from the Soviet-Japanese neutrality pact of April 1941. Moscow and Tokyo had been talking for 18 months about signing a Soviet-Japanese treaty that would commit the two sides to neutrality and non-aggression and resolve various territorial and jurisdictional disputes. The final negotiations took place during the course of a European tour by Matsuoka, the Japanese foreign minister, in March–April 1941. Matsuoka visited Moscow in March and again in April, having just been to Berlin to talk to Hitler. Matsuoka did not know that Hitler intended to make war on Russia and in his conversation with Stalin on 12 April he gave no hint that he thought any major trouble was brewing in Soviet-German relations.[21] If Hitler was bent on war, Stalin must have reasoned, he would surely have steered his Japanese ally away from such a pact. Japan's willingness to sign a neutrality pact could be seen as a positive signal from Berlin as well as from Tokyo.

Then there was the role played by the German ambassador in Moscow, Schulenburg, an advocate of the eastern orientation in German foreign policy and a firm believer in long-term alliance with Russia. In mid-April 1941 Schulenburg returned to Berlin for consultations. When he met Hitler on 28 April the Führer complained bitterly about recent Soviet foreign policy actions, particularly Stalin's decision to sign a friendship treaty with Yugoslavia just before Germany invaded the country in early April 1941. Schulenburg defended the Soviet Union's behaviour during the Yugoslav treaty episode, pointed to a number of subsequent friendly gestures by Stalin and tried to persuade Hitler that the Soviet leader 'was prepared to make even further concessions'.[22] Although the meeting with Hitler concluded on an indeterminate note, Schulenburg returned to Moscow in early May with deep forebodings about the future of German–Soviet relations. In a series of meetings with the Dekanozov, the Soviet ambassador to Germany, who was home on leave from Berlin, Schulenburg tried to prod the Soviets into a major diplomatic initiative to ease tensions in Soviet–German relations. At the first meeting on 5 May Schulenburg gave Dekanozov a fairly accurate report of his discussion with Hitler, highlighting the Führer's concerns about the Soviet–Yugoslav treaty episode. But Schulenburg was more concerned about reports of a coming war between Russia and Germany and said that something had to be done to blunt the edge of these rumours. Dekanozov asked what could be done but Schulenburg would only say that they should both think about it and meet again for further discussion. At the second meeting on 9 May Schulenburg proposed that Stalin send a letter to Hitler professing the Soviet Union's peaceful intentions. Dekanozov suggested a joint Soviet–German communiqué, and Schulenburg thought this was a good idea, too, but action had to be taken quickly. At their third and final meeting on 12 May Dekanozov reported that Stalin had agreed to a joint communiqué and to an exchange of letters with Hitler about the rumours of war but that Schulenburg should negotiate the actual texts with Molotov. At that point Schulenburg drew back from this personal initiative, saying that he had no authority to conduct such negotiations.[23]

Schulenburg's initiative was purely personal, but he was, after all, the German ambassador and he had just returned to Moscow from Berlin having met and talked to Hitler. Stalin could be forgiven for interpreting his approach to Dekanozov as an informal but official sounding. This interpretation also fitted with the growing perception in Moscow that there was a split in German ruling circles between the advocates of war with the Soviet Union and those who favoured further co-operation with the USSR. In this light Schulenburg's sounding could be read as evidence of the activities of a peace party in Berlin. The 'split theory', as Gabriel Gorodetsky has called it, had circulated in Moscow in one form or another since Hitler came to power in 1933 and reflected Marxist dogma about the division in German capitalism between economic groups that favoured eastern territorial expansion and those that preferred to trade with the Soviet Union. Moscow's predisposition to believe in the existence of 'hawks' and 'doves' in Berlin was reinforced by many Soviet intelligence reports, including those submitted by a Gestapo double agent who had infiltrated one of Moscow's spy rings in Germany.[24]

Another event that served to underline the split theory was the dramatic flight of Hitler's Deputy, Rudolf Hess, to Britain on 10 May 1941. Hess flew to Britain on a personal mission to broker a peace deal between Britain and Germany. In Moscow one spin put on the affair was that Hess's aim was a peace that would pave the way for an Anglo-German alliance against Bolshevik Russia. A more optimistic reading was that Hess's defection was further evidence of the split between those who wanted war with Russia and those who still saw Britain as the prime enemy. Most important, Hess's defection coloured Stalin's view of the many intelligence reports on the coming German attack that were now crossing his desk. Were the reports accurate or were they rumours circulated by those who wanted to precipitate a Soviet–German war? Stalin's thinking in this regard was not far wrong. The British did use the Hess affair to sow discord in Soviet–German relations by circulating rumours that he was on an official mission to form an Anglo-German alliance against Russia.[25] The irony was that when the British became convinced that Germany was about to invade Russia and attempted to warn Stalin of the danger, they were not believed by the Soviets. At meetings with Maisky, Soviet ambassador to London, on 2, 10, 13 and 16 June 1941 British officials gave him chapter and verse on German troop movements along the Soviet frontier.[26] Maisky duly reported this information to Moscow but it had little impact.

In this uncertain situation Stalin used his own reasoning to assess Hitler's likely intentions: it did not make sense for Germany to turn against Russia before Britain was finished off. Why fight a two-front war when the Soviet Union self-evidently posed no immediate danger to Germany? In May 1941 Stalin told the graduating cadets of the Red Army academies that Germany defeated France in 1870 because it fought on only one front but had lost the First World War because it had to fight on two fronts. This rationalisation was reinforced by the assessment in some of the intelligence reports presented to him. For example, on 20 March 1941 General Filip Golikov, the chief of Soviet military intelligence, presented a summary of reports on the possible timing and course of military action against the USSR. Golikov concluded, however, that 'the most likely date for the beginning of military action against the USSR is after victory over England or after the conclusion of an honourable peace with Germany. Rumours and documents that war against the USSR is inevitable in the spring of this year must be considered as disinformation emanating from English or even, perhaps, German intelligence'.[27] Golikov's subsequent reports to Stalin, however, presented the information on the concentration of German (and Rumanian) forces along the Soviet border in a much more balanced manner.[28] On 5 May, for example, Golikov reported that the number of Germans divisions concentrated on the Soviet border had in the past two months increased from 70 to 107, including an increase in tank divisions from 6 to 12. Golikov further pointed out that Rumania and Hungary had between them about 130 divisions and that German forces along the Soviet border were likely to increase further following the end of the war with Yugoslavia.[29]

Another persistent source of warnings about German preparations for war with the USSR were two highly placed Soviet spies in Germany: 'Starshina', who worked in the headquarters of the Luftwaffe and 'Korsikanets', an economist in the German economics ministry. Between them they sent dozens of reports to Moscow containing evidence of the coming German attack.[30] On a report from 'Starshina' dated 16 June 1941 Stalin wrote to his intelligence chief, V.N. Merkulov: 'perhaps you can send your 'source' from the staff of the German air force to go fuck his mother. This is not a 'source' but a disinformer'.[31] As Gabriel Gorodetsky says, Stalin's outburst was not so much a signal of disbelief as a sign that he was getting rattled by all these reports of a coming German attack, and feared they might be true.[32]

Another stream of warnings came from the Far East. Richard Sorge was a Soviet spy in Tokyo, working under the cover of a German journalist. His main sources of information were the German ambassador and the German military attaché in Tokyo, whom he had befriended. Sorge's reports were based on the expressed opinions of these two sources and they did not prove to be wholly accurate. Early reports from Sorge suggested Germany would invade the USSR only after finishing off Britain. When he started to report that the Germans would invade Russia before the end of the war in the west, his first predicted date for the attack was May 1941. As late as 17 June 1941 Sorge was reporting that the military attaché was not sure whether there would be war or not. On 20 June, however, Sorge reported, that the ambassador thought that war was now inevitable.[33]

Closer to home there were the reports being submitted by Dekanozov from Berlin. Again, there was an element of equivocation in them. On 4 June he reported on widespread rumours of an imminent Soviet–German war, but also stories that there would be a rapprochement between the two countries on the basis of Soviet concessions to Germany, a spheres of influence deal and a promise from Moscow not to interfere in European affairs.[34] On 15 June Dekanozov cabled Moscow that the Danish and Swedish military attachés believed that the concentration of German forces on the Soviet border was no longer a demonstration designed to extract concessions from Moscow but part of the 'immediate preparation for war with the Soviet Union'.[35] He did not, however, make it clear that he shared these views.

Adding to the uncertainty was the extensive disinformation campaign waged by the Germans, which was designed to explain away the massive concentration of their forces along the Soviet border. The Germans began by asserting that the military build-up was a defensive measure. Then they put it about that their build-up in the east was a ruse to lull the British into a false sense of security. Another story was that the German divisions were there not to invade but to intimidate the Soviets into economic and territorial concessions. One of the most prevalent rumours was that even if Hitler did attack he would first present an ultimatum to Stalin – an idea designed to cover up the unannounced surprise attack that the Germans were actually planning.[36]

After the event it was easy to identify which reports were true and which were false and to see through the equivocations of many of Stalin's sources. At the time, however, there was room for at least a little doubt, particularly about the timing of the German attack. Stalin's calculation in summer 1941 was that Hitler would not attack just yet and that evidence suggesting otherwise could be explained by the split theory or by the machinations of British intelligence. At the same time Stalin could not afford to discount the possibility of war in the short term. Stalin was never foolhardy; while he might disparage foreign intelligence as false reporting by stupid spies or agent provocateurs the evidence of the German military build-up from Soviet border reconnaissance was just too weighty to ignore. Stalin might hope, even believe, that Hitler would not attack, but the evidence was clear that the German dictator *might* be planning to attack, and soon. Stalin responded to this possibility by the continuation and, indeed, acceleration of his preparations for war, including a massive build-up of Soviet frontline forces:

- in May-June 800,000 reservists were called up
- in mid-May 28 divisions were ordered to the western districts of the USSR
- on 27 May these districts were ordered to build field command posts
- in June 38,500 men were sent to the fortified areas of the border districts

- on 12–15 June the districts were ordered to move forces to the frontier
- on 19 June, district HQs were ordered to move to new command posts. Orders were also issue to districts to camouflage targets and disperse aircraft.[37]

By June 1941 the Red Army had over 300 divisions, comprising some 5.5 million men, of whom 2.7 million were stationed in the western border districts.[38] On the night of 21–22 June this vast force was put on alert and warned to expect a surprise attack by the Germans.[39]

But still the question remains: why didn't Stalin order a full-scale advance mobilisation of Soviet forces, if only as a precautionary measure? One part of the answer is that Stalin did not want to provoke Hitler into a premature attack. 'Mobilisation means war' was a commonplace of Soviet strategic thinking. It derived from Russia's experience during the crisis that led to the outbreak of the First World War. Tsar Nicholas II's decision to mobilise the Russian army as a precautionary measure in July 1914 had provoked, it was believed, a German countermobilisation and hence the escalation of the 'July Crisis' into a European war. Stalin was determined not to repeat that mistake. Besides, he did not think it mattered much if Hitler was able to spring a surprise attack because according to Soviet military doctrine the outbreak of hostilities with Germany would be followed by a period of two to four weeks during which both sides would mobilize and concentrate their main forces for battle. In the meantime, there would be tactical battles along the frontier and penetrations and incursions by mobile forces probing for weaknesses and preparing the way for major outflanking movements. In any event, the decisive battles, as in 1914, would be fought a few weeks after the outbreak of war.

Taking into account all the complexities in the intelligence picture it could be argued that Stalin's misreading of the intelligence was wrong but understandable: a case of 'military disaster as a function of rational political calculation'.[40] But the deeper point concerns the failure of military doctrine and preparedness. Stalin was confident that Soviet defences would hold and there would be time to mobilise and prepare counteraction in the event of German attack. What neither he nor the Soviet high command anticipated was an immediate main force attack by the Germans that would crumble Soviet defences and disrupt plans for counteroffensive action. Stalin did not so much misread the intelligence as deliberately ignore it because he thought the costs of the Germans mounting a successful surprise attack when Soviet forces were not fully mobilised would not be too high and that the prize of a prolongation of peace until 1942 was worth the risk of getting caught on the hop. 22 June 1941 is an example not so much of intelligence failure as failure of strategic vision. It may be a cliché, but Stalin and the Soviet generals really were preparing to fight the last war again.

Another classic case study of Stalin's handling of foreign intelligence during the Second World concerns the battle of Moscow of autumn 1941, specifically his decision to transfer Soviet divisions from the Far East to defend the Soviet capital. The story often told here is that intelligence on Japanese intentions in the Far East enabled Stalin to take this critical decision, which helped save Moscow and bought time for the preparation of the Red Army's decisive counteroffensive in front of the Soviet capital on 5 December 1941. The successful Soviet defence of Moscow was, without doubt, the first great turning point of the Eastern Front campaign and if intelligence and the Far Eastern divisions did play the role attributed to them, it was a very important contribution to the outcome of the whole of the Second World War.

The hero of the hour – in Western and Soviet literature alike – was once again Richard Sorge. In September–October 1941 Sorge supplied information to Moscow which indicated Japan had decided on southern military expansion, which would bring the country into conflict with the United States, rather than a northern strategy of expansion from China into the eastern USSR. But, as in the case of Sorge's warnings about the German attack on the Soviet Union, the intelligence picture is a little more complicated than this simple story suggests.

Sorge's initial reports from Tokyo, again based on his contacts in the German embassy, indicated that the Japanese *would* join in the German attack on the Soviet Union. It was only after the evident failure of the German invasion that the Japanese began to change their minds about attacking Russia and Sorge's reports from September 1941 onwards reflected this new view.

Sorge was not the only source of Soviet intelligence on Japan's intentions; the Soviets had broken the Japanese diplomatic code and it may well be that this was as important a source to Stalin as Sorge's reports. Also available to Stalin were reconnaissance reports and analysis of the signals traffic of Japanese forces in Korea and Manchuria, which indicated that the Japanese were not preparing an attack in the Soviet direction, at least not in the immediate future. But Stalin could not be certain of the value of any of this intelligence for the simple reason that the Japanese themselves remained divided until almost the last moment about what course of military action to pursue. It was only when the Japanese attacked Pearl Harbor on 7 December – well after the critical phase of the battle of Moscow – that Stalin could be sure about Japan's immediate intentions. Even so,

Stalin remained concerned about a possible switch in Japanese policy. Substantial Soviet forces remained stationed and on alert in the Far East throughout the war and were periodically issued with directives from Moscow about action in the event of a Japanese attack.[41]

In terms of the impact of the transfer of the Far Eastern divisions on the outcome of the Moscow battle, their importance has been greatly exaggerated by those wishing to highlight the role of Sorge and the intelligence factor. Fourteen divisions were transferred from the Far East in autumn 1941. Nine of these divisions, including two tank and one motorised division, served on the Moscow front. This may seem a lot but during the course of the battle of Moscow the Soviet high command raised ten new reserve *armies* and deployed nearly one hundred additional divisions for defensive and offensive action in front of the Soviet capital. In Soviet military literature and memoirs the reinforcements from the Far East are mentioned but not generally highlighted. The Soviet high command's capacity to raise huge reserve armies to defend the Soviet capital while conducting a ferocious defensive battle all along the Eastern Front is rightly seen as the decisive factor in halting and then turning back the tide of the German invasion.

A more clearcut case of intelligence directing and helping to determine the outcome of an important battle is Kursk in summer 1943, but the intelligence that mattered to Stalin and his high command was not the strategic information supplied by Soviet spies or high-level codebreakers. Much more important was the frontline tactical intelligence which identified the location of German formations, their strength and their deployment patterns.

The hero (or anti-hero) of this intelligence tale is John Cairncross, who worked at the Bletchley Park deciphering centre and in May 1943 provided information from Enigma decrypts which indicated an impending major German offensive in the Kursk region. On the basis of this information the Soviet high command issued a series of alerts to their army commanders about an imminent German attack.[42] The German attack came in early July and the Soviets were ready and waiting. The Red Army was able to absorb the massive German armoured thrust and then launch a devastating counteroffensive. Kursk was the last major strategic operation launched by Hitler on the Eastern Front.

Long before the reports from London based on Cairncross's information came through, the Soviet General Staff had concluded that the Kursk salient would be the site of major German action in the near feature. Indeed, it was obvious that the Germans would attempt to pinch out this bulge in the Soviet defensive line with a view to strengthening their own defensive position on the central sector of the Eastern Front, which would give them a chance of regaining the strategic initiative at some point in the future. The General Staff decided as early as April 1943 – before the German plans had even been formulated – that they would stay on the defensive in the Kursk sector, aiming to absorb any German attack, and then go on the counteroffensive. What the Soviets needed to know was precisely when the German attack would come and, equally, the details of how the operation would be implemented. The problem with the Cairncross intelligence was that it warned of an attack that didn't come. These premature warnings encouraged some Soviet generals to advocate a pre-emptive strike. That Stalin held his nerve and remained on the defensive until the Germans attacked may indicate a certain level of confidence in the intelligence provided by Cairncross, or it may just show he had decided to stick to the General Staff's predetermined plan. Moreover, the foreign intelligence did not tell the General Staff what they needed to know in order to plan and implement their projected counteroffensive. That crucial data was provided by air reconnaissance, patrols, prisoner interrogations, partisan reports and analysis of signals traffic by German frontline units. This tactical intelligence was far more important to Soviet military planners than general alerts of a coming German attack in the Kursk area, although Cairncross did provide some important details, particularly about Luftwaffe dispositions and operations. As far as Stalin was concerned, it is doubtful that he had time to engage with detailed frontline intelligence, although the fact that the two sources – foreign and tactical – converged in their predictions about German action might have reinforced his inclination to remain on the defensive.[43]

The most famous and dramatic success of Soviet foreign intelligence during the war was the acquisition of atomic secrets from the Manhattan Project, although the debate continues as to how important the information was to the Soviet bomb project. Western analysts tend to argue that the Soviets stole the atomic secret from the British and Americans, while the Russians contend that their scientists would have succeeded in making their own bomb anyway. Perhaps the best guess is that the data secured from the Manhattan Project speeded up production of the Soviet bomb by two-to-three years and thus advanced the date of the first Soviet test from the early 1950s to 1949.[44] As has often been said, the biggest secret of the A-bomb was that it was possible at all; and that information became public knowledge in August 1945. A related controversy concerns which Western scientists supplied the Soviets with atomic secrets, with the NKGB intelligence operative, Pavel Sudoplatov, claiming that as well as those that were caught many other top names involved with the Manhattan Project – Oppenheimer and Fermi, for example – were passing information.[45]

Stalin was told about the bomb by Truman at the Potsdam conference in July 1945, following the successful Trinity test in New Mexico. According to Truman, Stalin displayed no emotion when told that the Americans had a new weapon which they intended to use against the Japanese. Other Western observers at Potsdam report much the same lack of reaction, but according to Marshal Zhukov Stalin decided immediately to speed up the Soviet bomb project.[46] However, it was not until a few weeks later – on 20 August – that Stalin issued a formal directive establishing a special committee, chaired by Beria, to manage the Soviet bomb project.[47] This was after the American A-bombing of Hiroshima and Nagasaki had helped precipitate the Japanese surrender on 14 August (the other shock factor was the Soviet declaration of war on Japan on 8 August). Even so, it is not clear that Stalin fully appreciated the significance of the military revolution augured by the A-bomb. In public the Soviets consistently downplayed the military importance of the Bomb, until they acquired one for themselves. In private, Stalin told Gomulka, the Polish communist leader, in November 1945 that 'war is not decided by atomic bombs, but by armies'.[48] In a sense Stalin was right; the real nuclear revolution was yet to come with the development in the mid-1950s of thermonuclear bombs and the reliable and accurate long-range missile technology with which to deliver them.

This treatment of Stalin's use and misuse of foreign intelligence during the Second World War illustrates some of the classic issues that have emerged from intelligence history. It is always easier to assess the value of intelligence after the event than at the time, when the intelligence picture might seem to decision-makers to be much murkier than it appears in retrospect. Like all political leaders Stalin had not only to assess the intelligence, but also to calculate the impact of his own actions, including the possibility that his use of the information might precipitate the very events predicted by it. From the historian's point of view the great difficulty of intelligence history is disentangling the impact of intelligence on decisions and action from that of other influences that might well have been even more important. This difficulty is compounded by the propensity of intelligence agencies to keep secret the totality of the information generated by their spies and analysts. During the Eastern Front war the intelligence that mattered most was not the sexy, high-level strategic information supplied by spies or cryptanalysts but the low-level, local intelligence of the battle zone. Even having knowledge of the greatest secret of the war – the Manhattan Project – only became important and usable when the atomic bomb was successfully tested and deployed. The limitation of intelligence is that it can predict actions but not consequences. This point is illustrated by Stalin's failure to act on intelligence of the coming German attack in June 1941.

What Stalin needed to know was what was going to happen as result of the attack – a task that proved beyond all the resources of Soviet intelligence.

NOTES

1   V.V. Poznyakov, 'Sovetskiye Razvedytelnye Sluzhby v Stranakh Zapada v gody Vtoroi Mirovoi Voiny, 1939–1945'. I am grateful to Professor Poznyakov for giving me a copy of his paper.
2   E. Mark, 'Venona's Source 19 and the 'Trident Conference' of May 1943: Diplomacy or Espionage?, *Intelligence and National Security* 13, 2 (1998), pp. 1–31.
3   R.W. Stephan, *Soviet Counterintelligence against the Nazis, 1941-1945* (Lawrence, KS 2004), pp. 109–10.
4   The NKGB – *Narodnyi Komissariat Gosudarstvennoi Bezopastnosti* – the People's Commissariat of State Security – was responsible for espionage and counterintelligence operations against non-military targets, The GRU – *Glavnoe Razvedyvatel'noe Upravlenie* – the Chief Intelligence Administration – was responsible for espionage against military targets. The NKVD – *Narodnyi Komissariat Vnutrennikh Del* – People's Commissariat of Internal Security – was responsible for domestic security. See ibid., appendix A.
5   D. Kahn, 'Soviet Comint in the Cold War', *Cryptologia*, 22, 1 (1998). I am grateful to the author for a copy of this paper.
6   Stephan, *Soviet Counterintelligence*, p.191.
7   B.F. Smith, *Sharing Secrets with Stalin: How the Allies Traded Intelligence, 1941–1945*, (Lawrence, Kansas, 1996).
8   For example, C. Andrew and V. Mitrokhin, *The Mitrokhin Archive* (London, 2000).
9   *Ocherki Istorii Rossiiskoi Vneshnei Razvedki*, vols 3–5 (Moscow, 1997–2003).
10 *Organy Gosudarstvennoi Bezopastnosti SSSR v Velikoi Otechestvennoi Voine*, vols 1–3, (Moscow, 1995–2003). Each of these volumes is published in two parts, so there are six books in all.
11 *Atomnyi Proekt SSSR: Dokumenty i Materialy* (3 vols, Moscow, 1998–2002).
12 J. Harris, 'Stalin's Spymania and the Great Terror', paper presented to the Soviet Industrialisation Project Series, University of Birmingham, November 2004.
13 M. Harrison, 'Secrecy under Stalin: the case of the Defense Industry', in M. Harrison (ed), *Guns and Rubles: the Defense Industry in the Stalinist State* (forthcoming).
14 Cited by G. Gorodetsky, *Grand Delusion: Stalin and the German Invasion of Russia* (London, 1999), p. 53.
15 Cited by O.A. Rzheshevsky, 'Winston Churchill in Moscow (1942)', paper presented to the Anglo-Russian Seminar on Churchill and Stalin, Foreign and Commonwealth Office, London, March 2002.
16 U. Gor'kov, *Gosudarstvennyi Komitet Oborony Postanovlyaet (1941–1945)* (Moscow, 2002), p. 80.
17 The press summaries prepared for Stalin may be found in RGASPI [Rossiiskii Gosudarstvennyi Arkhiv Sotsial'no-Politicheskoi Istorii: Russian State Archive of Social-Political History], F.71, Op.10, D.237–238. These generally concentrated on what was being said about Stalin and the Soviet Union in the allied press.
18 The records of Stalin's appointments diaries, which record who he saw, when and for how long, were published in *Istoricheskii Arkhiv* in the mid-1990s.
19 *Organy Gosudarstvennoi Bezopastnosti SSSR v Velikoi Otechestvennoi Voine*, vol. 3, book 2 (Moscow, 2003) documents 1005, 1022, 1024, 1031, 1037, 1041.

20 For example, C. Andrew and J. Elkner, 'Stalin and Foreign Intelligence', in H. Shukman (ed.), *Redefining Stalinism* (London, 2003).

21 *Dokumenty Vneshnei Politiki*, vol. 23, book 2, pt. 2 (Moscow, 1998), document 772.

22 R. J. Sontag & J. S. Beddie (eds), *Nazi-Soviet Relations* (New York, 1948), pp. 330–2.

23 *Dokumenty Vneshnei Politiki*, vol. 23, book 2, pt. 2, documents 814, 823, 828. In connection with these meetings there is an oft-told story that Schulenburg actually warned Dekanozov that Hitler was going to attack and asked him to pass this information to Stalin. One source of this story is the memoirs of Stalin's trade minister, Anastas Mikoyan, *Tak Bylo* (Moscow, 1999), p. 377. Dekanozov's reports show that this story is entirely without foundation. Indeed, since Schulenburg's purpose was to help improve Soviet–German relations it would have been extraordinary if he had told Dekanozov that he thought Hitler was going to attack Russia. See Gorodetsky's treatment of this episode, *Grand Delusion*, pp. 211–7.

24 Gorodetsky, *Grand Delusion*, pp. 181–6.

25 Ibid., ch. 12

26 *Vestnik Ministerstva Inostrannykh Del SSSR*, 30 April 1990, pp. 77–8.

27 *1941 god*, vol. 1 (Moscow, 1998) document 327.

28 *1941 god*, vol. 2, documents 393, 413, 472, 525, 528.

29 *Organy Gosudarstvennoi Bezopastnosti SSSR v Velikoi Otechestvennoi Voine*, vol. 1, book 2 (Moscow, 1995), document 201.

30 Ibid., document 273. This is a tabulation of the reports these two sources submitted in the period September 1940–June 1941.

31 Ibid., document 251.

32 Gorodetsky, *Grand Delusion*, pp. 296–7.

33 *1941 god*, vol. 2, documents 488, 513, 514, 566, 567, 590; *Sovetsko-Yaponskaya Voina 1945 goda: Istoriya Voenno-Politicheskogo Protivoborstva Dvukh Derzhav v 30–40-e gody* (in the series Russkii Arkhiv) (Moscow, 1997), documents 14, 148, 150, 151, 152, 154. Sorge was arrested and executed by the Japanese in 1944. This article's questioning of the value of the intelligence he supplied to Moscow is not meant to denigrate in any way the courage he showed in serving the communist cause.

34 *Dokumenty Vneshnei Politiki*, vol. 23, book 2, pt. 2 (Moscow, 1998), document 853.

35 *Vestnik Ministerstva Inostrannykh Del SSSR*, 30 April 1990, pp. 76–7.

36 B. Whaley, *Codeword Barbarossa* (Cambridge, MA, 1973), ch. 7; D.E. Murphy, *What Stalin Knew: The Enigma of Barbarossa* (New Haven, 2005), ch. 17.

37 L. Rotundo, 'Stalin and the Outbreak of War in 1941', *Journal of Contemporary History*, 24 (1989), pp. 277–99 at p. 283.

38 *1941 god* vol.2, document 550.

39 Ibid., document 605.

40 G. Roberts, 'Military Disaster as a Function of Rational Political Calculation: Stalin and 22 June 1941', *Diplomacy & Statecraft*, 4, 2 (1993).

41 On Sorge and the battle of Moscow: V. Gabrilov and E. Gorbunov, *Operatsiya "Ramzai"* (Moscow, 2004), ch. 9. A number of Sorge's reports are reproduced in *Sovetsko-Yaponskaya Voina 1945 goda: Istoriya Voenno-Politicheskogo Protivoborstva Dvukh Depzhav v 30-40-e gody* (Moscow, 1997), series Russkii Arkhiv.

42 V.V. Korovin, *Sovetskaya Razvedka i Kontrrrazvedka v gody Velikoi Otechestvennoi Voiny* (Moscow, 2003), pp. 113–122.

43 T.P. Mulligan, 'Spies, Ciphers and "Zitadelle": Intelligence and the Battle of Kursk, 1943', *Journal of Contemporary History*, 22 (1987), pp. 235–60.

44 See D. Holloway, *Stalin and the Bomb* (London, 1994).

45 P. Sudoplatov, *Special Tasks* (London, 1995), ch. 7.

46 www.dannen.com/decision/potsdam.html. These web pages contain extracts from the different accounts of Stalin's reaction to being told by Truman about the Bomb.

47 A copy of this document may be found in the Volkogonov Papers, Library of Congress Manuscripts Division. Also in *Atomnyi Proekt SSSR*.

48 Conversation between Gomulka and Stalin 14 Nov. 1945 in *Cold War International History Project Bulletin*, 11 (winter 1998).

'Let's make it clear that we'll get him sooner or later': British covert action against Nasser's Egypt in the aftermath of Suez

Robert McNamara

Recent historical research has demonstrated that at times the British could be just as ruthless in protection of their imperial interests as any other country, even during an era of retreat from empire. This essay explores one of Britain's most fraught postwar international relationships – that with Nasser's Egypt. Its emphasis is on the less documented post-Suez 1956 period and it demonstrates the willingness of the Conservative governments of Harold Macmillan (prime minister 1957–63) and Alec Douglas-Home (prime minister 1963–64) to use top secret covert action to foil what they considered an implacable foe of British interests in the Middle East. It also assesses why the policy failed.

ANGLO-EGYPTIAN RELATIONS 1882–1956

Egypt, due to its geographical position adjacent to the Middle East and straddling one of the main arteries of the British Empire, the Suez isthmus, was of vital strategic importance to Britain. The construction of the Suez Canal in 1867 greatly increased its importance. When internal disorder and nationalist feelings threatened British imperial and financial interests in 1882, Britain militarily occupied Egypt. As a result Britain maintained a major military presence in Egypt until 1956. Anglo-Egyptian relations can be divided into a number of distinct phases. Between 1882 and 1922, Britain operated a veiled protectorate, in which British officials, most notably Lord Cromer, operated in the background, ruling Egypt with a hidden hand. Nominal independence was granted in 1922 and Egypt became a monarchy. However, British forces remained in Egypt. This was confirmed by the 1936 Anglo-Egyptian agreement, which granted Britain extensive base rights until 1956. Meanwhile British ambassadors, most notably Miles Lampson, carried on interfering in Egyptian internal affairs, particularly during the Second World War, when Egypt was a major theatre of operations.

After 1945 violent nationalist agitation against the British base was allowed to flourish by the Egyptian government. This culminated in the Egyptian government in 1951 abrogating the 1936 agreement and demanding an immediate British withdrawal. This resulted in serious Anglo-Egyptian clashes in late 1951 and early 1952, which severely destabilised the monarchy and helped pave the way for a military coup in July 1952. By 1954, Colonel Gamal Abdel Nasser had emerged as the leading figure in the new regime. Nasser successfully negotiated a British military withdrawal from Egypt in that year. However, the determination of Britain to maintain a leading role in Middle Eastern affairs – because of its oil and continued strategic importance – through the maintenance of other military bases in the region and a new regional military alliance, the Baghdad Pact agreed with Iraq, Turkey, Iran and Pakistan in February 1955 destroyed any hope of an Anglo-Egyptian rapprochement and ushered in a twelve-year Anglo-Egyptian cold war. The problem was that Colonel (from 1956 President) Nasser was determined to pursue a pan-Arabist (Arab unity) agenda. This required the removal of British influence in the Middle East. Nasser deployed propaganda and subversion to attack his Arab enemies and Britain. His demagoguery and ability to rouse the masses of the Arab street filled British ministers with fear. They became convinced that Nasser was a clear and present danger to British interests and had to be 'destroyed'.

SUEZ[1]

By March 1956, Anthony Eden, Britain's Conservative Prime Minister (1955–7) was determined that Nasser be removed. The preference was to do this in co-operation with the United States. However, Nasser's nationalisation of the Anglo-French owned Suez Canal Company in July 1956 convinced Eden that a military solution was necessary. In the analogous fantasy of Eden and other members of his Conservative government Nasser was a throwback to Hitler and Mussolini and the canal was the Rhineland in 1936. This was the time, according to this reasoning, to strike the enemy before he became too strong. A huge Anglo-French expeditionary force was gathered in Malta for a full-scale invasion of Egypt to regain the canal and topple Nasser. However, a legitimate *casus belli* proved frustratingly difficult to find. Then in October 1956, British ministers and officials, including Foreign Secretary Selwyn Lloyd, conspired with French and Israeli leaders and concocted perhaps the most famous war-plot of the twentieth century. The plan, implemented between 29 October and 6 November 1956, involved an Israeli attack on Egypt, which would trigger an Anglo-French intervention ostensibly to keep the peace but in reality to regain the Suez Canal and topple Nasser. The invasion was a military success to a point in that Anglo-French forces seized part of the canal before a ceasefire was accepted and Israel achieved complete military success in its Sinai campaign. The operation was a complete political disaster, however, thanks to American opposition. By the end of 1956, the Anglo-French force was humiliatingly forced to withdraw under huge American political and economic pressure. Soon after, in January 1957, Eden was forced to resign as Prime Minister.

THE MACMILLAN STRATEGY

Harold Macmillan, the most enthusiastic supporter of Suez in the Cabinet, replaced Eden. This meant the reduction or the elimination of President Nasser of Egypt's influence in the Arab world remained the central tenet of British strategy in the aftermath of Suez.[2] However, instead of engaging in reckless plots with the Israelis and the French, the central focus of Macmillan's strategy was ensuring the Americans join an anti-Nasser crusade.

President Eisenhower (US president 1953–61), who had strongly opposed the Suez operation, introduced his Eisenhower Doctrine in January 1957. This aided Macmillan's strategy of forging an Anglo-American anti-Nasser coalition. The doctrine, with its emphasis on providing support for Nasser's conservative Arab enemies, alienated Nasser and radical Arab nationalism. They felt that the United States was intervening to prevent the success of the pan-Arab cause. Nasser's hostility towards the Americans in the first half of 1957 brought them around to the British way of thinking about Nasser.

Macmillan was still determined to overthrow Nasser. 'Let's make it clear that we'll get him sooner or later', he told a shocked Eisenhower at the March 1957 Anglo-American summit in Bermuda.[3] Macmillan had not lost his enthusiasm for covert action against Nasser. At the same meeting Eisenhower noted in his diary that the British spoke of

> the existence of a secret Egyptian plot for executing a coup to dispose of Nasser. They apparently thought we knew a great deal about it and wanted us to make some public statement against Nasser in the hope that this would encourage the dissident Egyptians. Manifestly anything the British said against Nasser would only make him stronger in the area.[4]

THE SYRIAN CRISIS

In the late summer and early autumn of 1957 the United States, convinced that the radical government of Syria was about to turn the country into a Soviet satellite, encouraged the conservative Arab states and Turkey to take action to topple it. Macmillan saw the opportunity to restore Anglo-American co-operation on policy making in the Middle East. More dubiously, he appears to have hoped that an Anglo-American backed Iraqi-Jordanian attack on Syria might have the effect of bringing Nasser into a conflict with Iraq, the United States and Britain. A rerun of Suez, this time with the promise of American support, briefly appeared to be within his grasp.

The Americans were concerned that Syria was about to turn into a base for communist subversion in the Middle East, especially after the expulsion in August 1957 of three American diplomats accused of plotting to overthrow the regime.[5] American Secretary of State John Foster Dulles wrote to Macmillan soon after, suggesting that the increasingly troublesome Syrian regime merited the use of covert action by her neighbours, including Britain's closest ally Iraq. Macmillan, desperate to be at the centre of American planning in the Middle East, was delighted to be able to help. It was agreed that a Syrian Working Group would be established with the aim of sharing intelligence and to co-ordinate military and political action in Syria.[6] Eisenhower and Dulles attempted to mobilise Syria's neighbours against her. Deputy Secretary of State Loy Henderson was despatched to Istanbul to meet with representatives from Turkey, Iraq and Jordan to urge them to take action, including if necessary military action, against Syria.[7]

Macmillan was enthusiastic about the plan. In a letter to Dulles on 28 August – in which he discussed the possibility of an operation to drive the Communists out of Syria – he urged such an operation should be 'undertaken by Syria's Arab neighbours, led if possible by Iraq'. However, Macmillan foresaw problems in finding a reasonable *casus belli*.[8] Dulles, Macmillan noted, was now advocating measures that a few months ago he would have denounced as 'immoral'.[9] The British Ambassador to the United States, Harold Caccia, was more cautious towards the plan, warning Macmillan that 'if anything goes wrong, you may be sure that Mr Dulles will place the blame elsewhere'.[10] He further warned, 'In American eyes the use of force by others is justifiable in almost any circumstances when it can be shown to be directed against communism; but that conversely when the connection cannot be clearly shown, there are almost no circumstances in which they can be counted on to support it'.[11] On 6 September, the British Cabinet discussed the crisis. Macmillan informed its members of the substance of his correspondence with Dulles, warning of the dangers of reticence and emphasising the benefits of once more acting in concert with the United States in the Middle East.[12] As a result, the British Cabinet, on 10 September 1957, endorsed a memorandum that the Americans planned to send to the Turks and the Arab states, which outlined the circumstances in which they would back an attack on Syria.[13]

ANOTHER SUEZ?

Macmillan and other ministers became increasingly intrigued about the possibilities that might emerge from Egypt's response to an Iraqi attack on Syria. The Syrian crisis was the main focus of a meeting in New York between Lloyd and Dulles on 16 September, but Lloyd seemed most interested in what the United States would do if the Egyptians blocked the Suez Canal in response to allied action in Syria. Dulles replied that the US 'should use force to the degree necessary to secure the reopening of the Canal'.[14] On 21 September Dulles told Lloyd that Egyptian military action in support of the communist cause in the Middle East would see a favourable American response to any request for aid from Jordan or Iraq.[15] Lloyd responded by saying that Britain did not have any obligation to Jordan but as 'regards Iraq, we were by our special agreement under the Baghdad pact under an obligation to go to her assistance if she was attacked. I thought this would apply to an attack by Egypt in the circumstances envisaged, just as much as to an attack by the Soviet Union.'[16]

The Syrian Working Group had reported on 18 September 1957, urging the implementation of a covert plan to attack Syria. The essence of the plan was to incite internal unrest in Syria and create border incidents that would justify an Iraqi-Jordanian invasion. Western intelligence agencies were to be heavily involved in sabotage and the widespread use of propaganda. The final section of the report is the most striking. Its title, 'Elimination of Key Figures', leaves little to the imagination. As Matthew Jones notes, the British and American officials who drafted the report were suggesting the liquidation of those they considered the most troublesome of the Syrian regime.

> In order to facilitate the action of liberative forces, reduce the capabilities of the Syrian regime to organize and direct its military actions, to hold losses and destruction to a minimum, and to bring about the desired results in the shortest possible time, a special effort should be made to eliminate certain key

individuals. Their removal should be accomplished early in the course of the uprising and intervention and in the light of circumstances existing at the time. Those who should be eliminated are Sarraj, Bizri and Khalid Bakdash.[17]

On 23 September 1957, the legal adviser to the Foreign Office, Gerald Fitzmaurice, gave his views of the obligations of the British Government to Iraq in the event of an attack by the Egyptians. He concluded that British military action in support of Iraqi offensive action against Syria would be legally dubious.[18] However, a report from a meeting of the Working Group on 28 September 1957 was far more bullish. It noted 'that both United Kingdom and United States Governments would be disposed to act against Egypt, if the Egyptians attacked the Iraqis or Jordanians while the latter were carrying out a policy which had been approved'.[19] Macmillan continued to explore the possibility of war. He wrote to Duncan Sandys, the Minister of Defence, at the end of September 1957 seeking to know what were Britain's military options against Nasser.[20] Sandys gave a short analysis that mainly stressed the deployment of airpower against Egypt.[21]

Macmillan's plans came to naught. The Arab coalition, which was never the most stable, began to have serious doubts about the wisdom of launching a military attack against Syria.[22] A parade of Arab leaders, whom the Anglo-Americans had been depending upon to act against Syria, arrived in Damascus pledging non-aggression. Only non-Arab Turkey showed any willingness to move against Syria. The Syrian Working Group completed its work sometime around the middle of October and it came out in favour of a less expansive policy codenamed 'containment plus', which had more modest goals of protecting pro-Western regimes in the region.[23]

The beneficiary of the crisis turned out to be Nasser. The Egyptian President successfully enhanced his prestige on 13 October when a contingent of Egyptian troops landed in Syria, ostensibly to protect Syria from Turkish attack.[24] Nasser took the opportunity to increase his influence in Syria at the expense of his Arab enemies but also at the expense of his erstwhile allies: the Soviets and their communist allies. The latter policy led to a rapprochement with the Americans, who began to view Nasser as possible tool against the Syrian communists. At the end of October 1957 Dulles and Eisenhower expressed interest in improving relations with Nasser without telling the British.[25] Nasser contacted the American Embassy to reassure them of his anticommunism.[26] The Americans replied that they would welcome action designed to impede the communist threat to the security of Syria and the entire Middle East and 'wish to avoid impeding any Egyptian efforts to bring about change in the region'.[27] Macmillan appeared to be utterly unaware of the American moves towards Nasser. He noted in his diary entry of 19 December that Eisenhower and Dulles 'are now completely converted – too late – and wish devoutly that they had let us go on and finish off Nasser'.[28]

The British lack of insight into the shifting views of the Americans was demonstrated by their reaction to the announcement of Egyptian–Syrian union, the United Arab Republic (UAR), in January 1958. Dulles's initial reaction, with strong backing from Selwyn Lloyd, was to promise support for any initiative from Iraq and Jordan to stop the union.[29] On his return to Washington, more informed opinion in the State Department changed the Secretary of State's mind.[30] Lloyd appears to have dusted down the 'Preferred Plan' of the Syrian Working Group and plotted covert action again. Nuri al-Said, the Iraqi Prime Minister and Britain's most reliable Arab ally, proposed much the same ideas. Once Dulles's change of views became known, Nuri's plans became in the words of Macmillan 'dangerously vague'.[31] Indeed, Nuri's Arab Union scheme (a union between Iraq and Jordan to oppose the UAR), with its need for Kuwaiti oil, became as much of a threat to British interests as Nasser.[32]

THE COLLAPSE OF THE MACMILLAN STRATEGY

In the summer of 1958, Macmillan's post-Suez strategy collapsed. In spite of strong British urging, the United States refused to contemplate joint military action to support President Camille Chamoun of Lebanon against Nasser-backed rebels. Chamoun was illegally attempting to extend his Presidential term. The Americans organised a deal with Nasser involving the peaceful replacement of Chamoun with General Fuad Chebab. This seemed to have resolved the crisis until the Iraqi monarchy was toppled on 14 July 1958. Eisenhower and Dulles, convinced that Nasser was behind the Iraqi revolution, now decided to act. American Marines landed in the Lebanon, though the replacement of Chamoun went ahead. Macmillan wanted a wider operation to restore order in the Middle East, an option that was rejected by the Americans on practical and political grounds. British troops were successfully deployed to Jordan to shore up the monarchy but, with Iraq now ruled by militant Arab nationalists, Britain's position in the Middle East was now gravely weakened. Coming to terms with Nasser was now forced on a reluctant British government. As a result a more accommodating policy towards Arab nationalism and President Nasser was endorsed at the start of 1959.[33] It was the logical consequence of events since the Suez Crisis.

For a couple of years after the Iraqi revolution, British policy makers appear to have believed that the new oil discoveries in North Africa and Nigeria had diminished the importance of the Middle East. In the final analysis, access to oil on reasonable terms was all that Britain cared about. There was a growing British disinterest in the region in 1959–62, the years that mark the high-water mark of the Anglo-Egyptian détente. In the summer of 1961 the Egyptians and British co-operated in solving the Kuwait crisis. The break up of the UAR (October 1961) did cause some tension but this was resolved in the early months of 1962. President Kennedy's policy of détente with Nasser carried Britain along in the slipstream. At the same time, the impetus had gone out of Arab unity.

THE YEMEN CIVIL WAR AND THE COLLAPSE OF THE ANGLO-EGYPTIAN DÉTENTE

The opportunity for Nasser to regain the initiative in the Arab world returned in September 1962 when pro-Nasser elements in the Yemen armed forces overthrew the absolute ruler Imam Badr in September 1962.[34] Imam Badr was able to flee to the mountains and rally tribal support against the coup. The Saudi Arabian monarchy and Jordan supported the Imam's attempt to overturn the coup. In response, the president of the newly proclaimed Yemen Arab Republic (YAR), Brigadier Sallal, appealed to Cairo for military aid. Nasser deployed thousands of Egyptian troops to the YAR.[35] A bitter civil war ensued that was to cause thousands of casualties. The war resembled, if anything, the Soviet campaign in Afghanistan (1979–89) where a well-equipped modern army found itself being frustrated by a primitive army driven by fanatical religious zeal.

The British government most certainly did not welcome the revolution, for it brought a regime of Nasser-influenced republicans to the borders of their South Arabian protectorates and the British base at Aden. Aden's military and strategic value had been minor until the 1950s but now it was the key base for interventions in the Gulf (such as the 1961 Kuwait operation) and as a staging post covering the route to Britain's defence responsibilities in the Far East.[36] Tensions soon emerged between the Foreign Office and the Colonial Office about what the British attitude to the new regime should be. The Foreign Office was anxious that Britain would not upset Nasser.[37] Macmillan was deeply concerned.[38] The Americans had no wish to see their investment in bilateral relations with Egypt thrown away over such a marginal interest as the government of Yemen. Their problem was that America's key regional allies Saudi Arabia, Britain, Israel and Jordan saw the Yemen intervention as a revival of Nasser's pan-Arab ambitions and a threat to their regimes and interests.[39] The Americans proposed an end to Jordanian and Saudi support for the Royalists in return for the phased withdrawal of Egyptian forces. Consequently, the British Foreign Secretary, Lord Home, now advised Macmillan that the time had come to recognize the republican regime in Yemen.[40]

Eventual recognition of the new regime in the Yemen would have been the likeliest outcome if it were not for the arrival on the scene of the maverick Conservative MP, Lieutenant-Colonel Neil McClean. On a tour of the Middle East in the autumn of 1962, in October he was granted an audience with King Saud of Saudi Arabia. The king warned McClean that the intervention in a Yemen was part of wider plot by Nasser in which the Soviets were involved, so Saud requested that the British withhold recognition and provide air support to the Royalists. He also expressed a wish to restore diplomatic relations, which had been broken at the time of Suez.[41] Philip De Zulueta, Macmillan's private secretary, was particularly impressed by this communication. He pointed out to Macmillan that the minus of losing relations with Yemen would be more than made up for by restoration of ties with the Saudis.[42]

The Colonial Office under Duncan Sandys was implacably opposed to recognition despite a successful American negotiation on 21 November 1962 of a disengagement plan for Yemen.[43] The British Governor of Aden, Charles Johnston, was not placated by the plan, which was 'too obviously slanted in Egypt's favour...'.[44] The Colonial Office warned that recognition would make it more difficult 'to give countenance to still more assistance to Royalist attempts to overthrow Sallal'.[45] The Americans went ahead and recognised the YAR on 19 December 1962, leaving Britain the only Western power not to have recognised the new republic. The Foreign Office, especially Harold Beeley, the ambassador in Cairo, were certain that the issue would eventually have a catastrophic effect on Britain's relations with the Arab world.[46] The Egyptians, who had been displaying uncustomary patience over the British decision on recognition, were now convinced that the British were once again supporting the conservative forces in the Middle East.[47] The non-recognition party remained in the ascendant in Whitehall. On 10 January 1963 the Cabinet, after consideration of pro-recognition and anti-recognition papers, rejected recognition once more. This ended the matter, sparking a growing Anglo-Egyptian antagonism.[48] Interdepartmental conflict continued within the British government between the Foreign Office (who wanted détente) and, particularly, the Colonial Office (who wanted to strike back at Nasser).[49] The Americans presciently warned that the consequences of non-recognition would be that Nasser would now initiate an 'aggressive policy against Aden'.[50]

A period of relative British disinterest in the Middle East was coming to an end.[51] In spite of the new policy and the failure to recognise Yemen, Anglo-Egyptian relations did not deteriorate as quickly as might have been expected. Instead it was the Americans and their carefully cultivated relationship with Nasser that ran into difficulties as disengagement after disengagement agreement broke down and pro-Nasser regimes seized power in Iraq and Syria in the spring of 1963.[52] Jordan's King Hussein tottered on his throne as a result of pro-Nasser rioting.[53]

COVERT ACTION

In June 1963 a National Liberation Front (NLF), committed to the liberation of South Arabia, was established in S'ana in North Yemen under Egyptian patronage. With Egyptian and Yemeni patronage, it began to plan a guerrilla war against the British base in Aden. At the same time allegations of chemical warfare were being made against the Egyptians.[54] Hopes that the poison gas allegations would embarrass Nasser were dashed when a War Office investigation of bomb fragments proved nothing. This incident merely irritated the Egyptians but what concerned them far more was the steady stream of supplies to the Royalists through the British-protected territory of Beihan. Some of this had come from Saudi Arabia to avoid UN monitoring but much of it was being sourced from Aden with the co-operation of the High Commissioner for the South Arabian Federation, Kennedy Trevakis, who replaced Charles Johnston in 1963.

Trevakis believed that a Nasserite victory in Yemen would endanger the base facilities at Aden. Contrary opinion, he argued, overlooked the 'human instinct to exploit success, and the compelling attraction which Aden would have to both the Egyptians and the Republicans'.[55] Trevakis pursued with the full acquiescence of his boss, Duncan Sandys, a highly secret covert plan to undermine the Egyptian position in Yemen.[56] An arms supply operation to the Royalists, beginning sometime in the spring of 1963, was master-minded by Trevakis's aide-de-camp (ADC), Flight Lieutenant Anthony Boyle, with the co-operation of ex-SAS servicemen – including the unit's founder, David Stirling – and French mercenaries.[57] It would seem that the operation was acquiesced in by senior British ministers. Nigel Fisher, Parliamentary Under-Secretary of State for the Colonies, recalls Macmillan authorising 'very substantial help to the Royalists'.[58] Colonel McLean, who appears to have been the linkman with the mercenaries, was closely associated with the Minister for Aviation, Julian Amery. Who, as Macmillan's son-in-law, was hardly likely to have been operating without some sort of approval from the top.[59] Clive Jones's recent work has revealed just how close was the relationship between ministers and mercenaries. McClean and another ex-British soldier, Colonel David Smiley, who was acting as an adviser to the Royalists, sent a steady stream of reports accusing Egypt of atrocities, including chemical warfare, as well as urging increased aid from Britain to the Royalists.[60] Amery, Smiley and McClean had all served in the Special Operations Executive in the Balkans in the Second World War and were firm believers in the value of irregular operations and covert action.

The end of 1963 saw the assassination of President Kennedy and the resignation of Macmillan. The new Prime Minister, Alec Douglas-Home (formerly Lord Home) and the new President, Lyndon Johnson, did not enjoy the close relationship of their predecessors.[61] The new Foreign Secretary, R.A.B. Butler, was to find himself aligned against the Prime Minister, the Colonial Secretary, Duncan Sandys, and the Minister of Defence, Peter Thorneycroft, over what to do with Nasser. Upon acceding to the premiership, Douglas-Home ordered a review of British policy towards Yemen. The Foreign Office and Colonial Office were, for once, in agreement that the present stalemate in Yemen suited British interests. The only question was whether Britain needed 'to do anymore at the moment to keep the situation on the boil'.[62]

There were increasing signs that an Egyptian-backed campaign against British rule in South Arabia was taking shape. In the last months of 1963, there was increasing guerrilla activity in the Radfan region of the Federation of South Arabia, as well as numerous politically motivated strikes in Aden. Most spectacular was the attempted assassination of High Commissioner Trevaskis on 10 December 1963. He was leaving for a conference in London to discuss development plans when a grenade injured fifty bystanders and killed Sir George Henderson, one of his chief advisers.[63]

CONFRONTATION, 1964

Frank Brenchley, the Head of the Arabian Department at the Foreign Office, informed the American Embassy of 'accumulating evidence' that the YAR/UAR was about to step up subversion in the South Arabian Federation. There was, he claimed, a 'long list of intelligence reports submitted from Aden indicating YAR/UAR [were] arming more Radfan tribesman and ... also reports that Yemeni terrorists plan [to] infiltrate into Aden, ostensibly as refugees from Yemen, with mission of eliminating Aden VIPs'. There were further alarming reports of increased movements of UAR troops to the southern part of Yemen 'which could mean direct Brit–UAR military confrontation in that area.'[64]

On 22 February 1964, Nasser used the opportunity provided by comments of Douglas-Home in Canada, defending Suez, to launch a major attack on British Middle Eastern policy and demanded that British 'bases in the Middle East must be liquidated'.[65] Libya subsequently requested Britain leave its base there immediately after Nasser's speech.[66] Within British government circles there was mounting frustration with Nasser over Egyptian air attacks on the Federation. In retaliation, senior ministers ordered an RAF attack on the Yemenese border fort at Harib.[67] The Americans were intensely annoyed by the British action.[68]

The British, though, were more concerned about the mounting evidence of YAR/UAR-backed subversion in the Federation. Trevakis, on 16 April, reported 'reliable information' that the Egyptian commander-in-chief in the Yemen was endeavouring to organise a campaign of terrorism and sabotage in Aden. A document captured by the British and purportedly written by the YAR Chief of Staff concerned the smuggling of twelve High Explosive bombs for use against senior Federation and Aden officials.[69] Douglas-Home wanted to respond vigorously. The objective of British policy in the Yemen, he wrote, should be to secure the withdrawal of the UAR influence from the Yemen, or tie up their troops in stalemate. He was not sure that Britain had 'exhausted all the possibilities open to us as regards both attributable and unattributable action'. He suggested that Britain's options 'should be set down, preferably in ascending order of "intensity" – so that we can take definite decisions on how far we are prepared to go'.[70]

Douglas-Home, Sandys and Thorneycroft, influenced by Tory backbenchers, urged a more aggressive policy, while Foreign Secretary Butler was more moderate.[71] Thorneycroft, the Minister of Defence, proposed much bolder measures to deal with the cross-border threat. He argued that it was 'important to tackle these activities at their source'. He recommended:

> a) Tribal revolts should be covertly organised in those areas adjacent to the Federation from which subversive activities are being launched. b) Deniable action should be taken to sabotage intelligence centres and kill personnel engaged in anti-British activities (including the Egyptian intelligence HQ at Taiz. c) Covert anti Egyptian propaganda in the Yemen should be intensified.[72]

Butler was sent to Washington tasked with the mission of converting the United States to an anti-Nasser crusade.[73] He told his hosts that his presentation would have been more radical if he were 'in the hands of the extremists in the Cabinet'.[74] Robert Komer, an assistant in the National Security Council, considered the British were 'grossly over reacting' and advised President Johnson to warn the British off their plans.[75] Butler failed to persuade President Johnson but was more encouraged by the attitude of Secretary of State Rusk, who had told him privately that they were 'squaring up to an assessment of their position vis-à-vis Nasser'.[76] Nasser also tried to influence the Americans. He told the American ambassador in Cairo, John Badeau, that he had 'completely reliable and convincing evidence' of British arms, money and military support to Yemeni dissidents flowing across the Southern border and 'because of this our men are being killed and I cannot accept this, hence my attack on the British'.[77]

The American refusal to support any vigorous countermeasures caused a rethink in London. Douglas-Home noted that 'whether we like it or not, we have to face the fact that the escalation of the Aden–Yemen trouble always rebounds to Nasser's advantage and not to ours, since it always rallies to him popular support, not least in the Aden itself'.[78] Consequently, on 8 May the Defence and Overseas Policy Committee decided to defer a decision on the supply of arms to the Royalist cause.[79] Emotions in Britain, however, were heightened by rumours of the beheading of two British soldiers in the Radfan and this prevented the Labour opposition from being too critical of Douglas-Home. This was rather fortunate as the secret support for the Royalists was exposed when correspondence belonging to Trevakis' ADC, Flight Lieutenant Boyle, was captured by the Egyptians and published on 1 May in *Al-Ahram*. It was subsequently republished in the *Sunday Times*, causing the government considerable embarrassment.[80] The revelations may have further undermined the Prime Minister's confidence in covert means of getting at Nasser.

However, coming to terms with Nasser was easier said than done. The Radfan, the most troublesome area of South Arabia, exploded into rebellion in early May. It was estimated that two hundred Egyptian-trained guerrillas were leading some five hundred NLF rebels. The guerrillas, according to Frank Brenchley, were equipped and uniformed and led by obviously trained officers on a scale not before encountered. The British Ambassador, Harold Beeley, was to speak to Nasser, warning him that the British knew what he was up to but offering compromise.[81] Meanwhile, on 28 May the Colonial Secretary authorised the supply of certain quantities of both arms and money to Yemeni Royalists.[82] This was combined with a deployment of British forces in Aden to Radfan in order to crush the revolt. They were tied down in counter-insurgency operations for much of the rest of 1964. By tying down the Aden force and preventing it from being deployed elsewhere, with the Radfan rebellion the NLF and the Egyptian Intelligence service removed a good deal of the *raison d'être* for the base.[83]

After an announcement from Sandys that Britain would, subject to assurances about the base, grant independence to South Arabia by 1968, Nasser told the diplomatic correspondent of the *Observer*, Robert Stephens, that he would be willing to accept a British staging post at Aden and suggested this might be a means of resolving the confrontation.[84] The Defence Secretary, Peter Thorneycroft, was in no mood for compromise. His assessment of 13 July 1964 was that in 'the foreseeable future the only threat to our control [of South Arabia] will come from President Nasser'. He urged that negotiating with Nasser could not take place until Britain had strengthened her own position and weakened his. To achieve this he recommended 'a sharp increase in deniable support in terms of both arms and money for the Royalists...'.[85] Oliver Wright, the Prime Minister's Private Secretary, was sceptical: 'We are on collision courses [UK and Egypt]; would it not be worthwhile seeing if we could not reverse the engines a bit before we actually collide?'. The only solution was political. Wright considered that it was 'a fundamental mistake' not to have recognised the YAR and that the government had been acting on 'consistently bad advice' from Aden. Britain, he said, 'should recognise that Nasser has been able to capture most of the dynamic and modern forces in the area while we have been left, by our own choice, backing the forces, which are not merely reactionary (that would not matter so much), but shifty, unreliable and treacherous'.[86]

Unfortunately, a change in British policy was not going to be easy as Nasser was determined to end the Yemen war and strengthen his hand against the new Saudi Leader, King Faisal, before the Second Arab Summit scheduled for September. To this end, the summer of 1964 saw a massive UAR offensive against the Yemeni Royalists. Kenneth Strong, the Director General of Intelligence at the Ministry of Defence, warned that 'If we do not help Faisal to provide the Royalists with enough aid to enable them to continue the struggle, he will almost certainly decide to come to terms with Nasser before the Royalists collapse.' Strong's assessment was 'that covert British assistance should be given to the Royalists'.[87] Douglas Home supported this and expressed a wish 'to make life intolerable for [Nasser] with money and (arms?)'. Indeed on 22 July 1964 a Joint Action Committee was established by a decision of the Defence and Overseas Policy Committee. This was to look at co-ordinating measures between the three Whitehall Departments on what to do in Yemen and South Arabia.[88]

Frank Brenchley laid out British policy to the Americans. He explained that the Saudis had never stopped supplying weaponry to the Royalists and indeed much of this aid had been channelled through British protected territory in South Arabia, namely, the state of Beihan, which was out of sight of the UN Observer mission. Brenchley said that the British had never urged the Saudis to halt supplies and would not do so now. Furthermore, he 'did not think that British Ministers were prepared [to] jettison their policy decision of not letting Yemeni Royalists go down the drain'.[89] Subsequently, the British Ambassador to Saudi Arabia, Colin Crowe, was instructed to tell Faisal of continued British support in the campaign against Nasser.[90] Other anti-Egyptian activity continued. At the beginning of September 1964, the Colonial, Defence and Foreign Secretaries, as well as the Prime Minister, authorised the supply of weaponry to Royalists for an operation in the Yemen city of Taiz.[91]

CONCLUSION: THE DANGERS OF COVERT ACTION

The Labour party under Harold Wilson won a narrow victory in the November 1964 general election. Wilson and his government had little interest in covert action and the activities of Trevakis appear to have ceased soon after. Indeed, he was replaced in early 1965. However, the Egyptian-backed guerrilla campaign against the base became increasingly violent. It soon became clear that in terms of both security and economics it was too costly for Britain to hold. In spite of fears that Nasser would claim it as a victory, it was decided at the end of 1966 to withdraw by 1968 without keeping the base or making a defence agreement with the Federation of South Arabia.[92] Whatever political gains Nasser made were soon dissipated by his catastrophic defeat in the June 1967 Arab–Israeli war. The Israeli victory was made easier by the presence of thousands of Egyptian troops in Yemen. Yemen had blown back on Nasser as well.

If the maintenance of British power in the Middle East was the aim of British covert action against Nasser, it can be viewed as an unambiguous failure. If it had the narrower aim of making life uncomfortable for Nasser, it was more successful, but it might be argued that it was hardly worth the price. British support for the Yemeni Royalists against the Egyptian-backed Republicans almost certainly encouraged Nasser to go after British interests. The evidence would suggest that British actions certainly speeded up the process and the violence in the Yemen eventually spread and consumed the British base at Aden.

British ministers were too ready to use covert, deniable action against Egypt. Considering how obsessed they were with 'lessons of the past', particularly the idea that Nasser was a throwback to the fascist dictators of the 1930s, it is surprising that they never looked at previous British covert plans against Nasser (such as Syria in 1957) and saw how they too came to nothing and may in part have contributed to the fall of the pro-British Iraqi regime in 1958. Indeed, the Syria and Yemen crises demonstrate the dangers of covert action and how it can blow up in the faces of its instigators.

NOTES

1 For the crisis, K. Kyle, *Suez* (New York, 1991); W. Scott Lucas, *Divided We Stand* (London, 1991); W.R. Louis and Roger Owen (eds), *Suez 1956, the Crisis and the Consequences* (Oxford, 1989); David Carlton, *Britain and the Suez Crisis* (Oxford, 1988).

2 For post-Suez British policy in the Middle East see Robert McNamara, *Britain, Nasser and the Balance of Power in the Middle East 1952–67* (London, 2003); Nigel John Ashton, *Eisenhower, Macmillan and the Problem of Nasser* (New York, 1996); Ritchie Ovendale, *Britain, the United States and the Transfer of Power in the Middle East* (Leicester, 1996).

3 *Foreign relations of the United States* [hereafter *FRUS*] *1955–57, vol. 27: Western Europe* (Washington, D.C., 1995), document 239, 21 Mar. 1957; TNA, PREM 11/1838, British Minutes of 1st Plenary Session of the Bermuda conference, 21 Mar. 1957.

4 *FRUS 1955–57, vol. 27*, document 271, 21 Mar. 1957. For speculation about the British plots see J. Bloch and P. Fitzgerald, *British Intelligence and Covert Action* (Dingle, 1983), p. 126.

5 Most accounts suggest that they were indeed plotting against the regime: P. Seale, *The Struggle for Syria* (Oxford, 1965), p. 294; A. Rathmell, *Secret War in the Middle East: The Covert Struggle for Syria* (London, 1995), p. 139; D. Little, 'Cold War and covert action', *Middle East Journal*, 44, 1 (1990), p. 71; Charles Yost, *History and Memory* (New York, 1980), pp. 236–7.

6 A. Horne, *Macmillan 1957–86* (London, 1989), p. 42.

7 *FRUS 1955–57, vol. 13, Near East: Jordan and Yemen* (Washington, D.C., 1988), document 373, Miner-Dulles, 26 August 1957.

8 Horne, *Macmillan 1957–86*, pp. 41–2.

9 Harold Macmillan, *Riding the Storm* (London, 1971), pp. 277–8.

10 Horne, *Macmillan 1957–86*, p. 42.

11 Caccia to Hoyer Millar, 10 Sept. 1957, cited in William Roger Louis and R. Robinson, 'The imperialism of decolonisation', *Journal of Imperial and Commonwealth History*, 22 (1994), pp. 505–6, endnote 140.

12 TNA, CAB 128/140 Cabinet Conclusions (57) 64, 1, 6 Sept. 1957

13 TNA, CAB 128/140, Cabinet Conclusions (57) 65, 1, 10 Sept. 1957. The British copy is in TNA, PREM 11/2119, Syria Memo, 10 Sept. 1957, Top Secret.

14 TNA, PREM 11/2119, record of communication between Secretaries Lloyd and Dulles, 16 Sept. 1957, Top Secret

15 TNA, PREM 11/2521, New York – Foreign Office [hereafter FO], No. 1533, For Prime Minister from Secretary of State, T402/57, 21 Sept. 1957.

16 Ibid.

17 See Matthew Jones, '"The Preferred Plan": the Anglo-American Working Group report on Covert Action in Syria, 1957', *Intelligence and National Security*, 19, 3 (autumn 2004), p. 408.

18 TNA, PREM 11/, FO – New York No. 2376, For Secretary of State, 23 Sept. 1957. Sir Gerald had pointed up the weakness of the government's case for military action during Suez: L. Johnman, 'Playing the role of a Cassandra', in S. Kelly and A. Gorst (eds), *Whitehall and the Suez Crisis* (London, 2000), pp. 46–62.

19 TNA, PREM 11/2521, Washington–Foreign Office, No. 1953, 28 Sept. 1957.

20 The copy in TNA is in PREM 11/2521, PM514/57. Macmillan's biographer had access to the Macmillan papers, which are still not available for research. Horne, *Macmillan 1957–86*, p. 45.

21 TNA, PREM 11/1899, Sandys–Macmillan, Note by COS, Possible British action to support Iraq against attack by Egypt, 1 Oct. 1957, Top Secret.

22 Seale, *Struggle for Syria*, pp. 303–4; D.W. Lesch, 'Nasser and an example of

diplomatic acumen', *Middle East Studies*, 31, 2 (April, 1995), p. 365; Rathmell, *Secret War*, p. 142.

23 TNA, PREM 11/2521, Morris (Washington) for Hood and Hayter, Working papers XVII & XIX, 11 Oct. 1957. Completed drafts were contained in telegrams around this time, e.g. TNA, PREM 11/2521, Lloyd–Macmillan No. 2084, Prime Minister's Private Telegram /455/57, 15 Oct. 1957.

24 This is discussed in Lesch, 'Nasser and an example of diplomatic acumen', pp. 367–8.

25 *FRUS 1955–57, vol. 13*, document 392, 4 Nov. 1957; document 398, 13 Nov. 1957.

26 *FRUS 1955–57, vol. 13*, document 420, 11 Dec. 1957.

27 *FRUS 1955–57, vol. 13*, document 421, 12 Dec. 1957.

28 Macmillan Diary, 19 Dec. 1957, cited in William Roger Louis, 'Macmillan and Middle East Crisis of 1958', *Proceedings of the British Academy*, 94 (1996), p. 214.

29 This is quoted from the British account of the meeting in TNA, FO 371/134386 VY10316/10, Lloyd (Ankara, no. 195) – Lord Privy Seal Butler, 28 Jan. 1958.

30 *FRUS 1958–60,vol. 13: Arab-Israeli Dispute, United Arab Republic, North Africa* (Washington, D.C., 1992), document 194, 8 Feb. 1958.

31 Macmillan, *Riding the Storm*, p. 504

32 USNA Memcom White House, 9 June 1958, MCT MC/5, CF120, Macmillan Talks Miscellaneous, Box 150.

33 TNA, CAB 134/2230, OME, 1st meeting, 16 Jan. 1959.

34 See Fred Halliday, *Arabia without Sultans*, (Harmondsworth, 1974), pp. 90–104. The background is in Edgar O'Balance, *The War in the Yemen* (London, 1971), pp. 10–35.

35 T. Y. Hasou, *The Struggle for the Arab World* (London, 1985), p. 139.

36 See Lord Lloyd's statement to the Aden Legislative Council in 1956, cited in Phillip Darby, *British Defence Policy East of Suez* (Oxford, 1973), p. 211. Also Colonial Secretary Lennox-Boyd's 1958 comments on Aden's importance to Commonwealth defence, in A.N. Porter and A. Stockwell (eds), *British Imperial Policy and Decolonisation, 1938–64, vol. 2: 1951–64* (London, 1989), pp. 495–6.

37 TNA, PREM 11/3877, New York to FO, No. 1431, 27 Sept. 1962, Johnston (Aden)–Colonial Office (CO), 3 Oct. 1962; *FRUS 1961–63, vol. 18: Near East 1962–63* (Washington, D.C., 1995), document 76, 9 Oct. 1962.

38 TNA, PREM 11/3877, Macmillan to Thorneycroft, PM M271/62, 6 Oct. 1962.

39 *FRUS, 1961–63, vol. 18*, document 79, 12 Oct. 1962.

40 TNA, PREM 11/3877, Home to Macmillan, PM62/139, 25 Oct. 1962.

41 TNA, PREM 11/3878, Aden No. 934 to SOS Colonies Sandys, 26 Oct. 1962 and Parkes (Amman) to FO No. 1206, 1 Nov. 1962.

42 TNA, PREM 11/3878, De Zulueta to Macmillan, 7 Nov. 1962.

43 TNA, PREM 11/3878, Sandys to Macmillan 38/62, 10 Nov. 1962; *FRUS 1961–63 , vol. 18*, document 96, 12 Nov. 1962.

44 TNA, PREM 11/3878, Johnston to SOS Colonies No. 1076, 13 Nov. 1962.

45 TNA, PREM 11/4356, Prime Minister's Note, 12 Dec 1962, Top Secret.

46 TNA, PREM 11/4356, Beeley to FO, 17 Dec. 1962.

47 TNA, PREM 11/4356, Cairo–FO, No. 11, 6 Jan. 1963.

48 TNA, CAB 139/112, (63).3, Memo by the SOSFA, 10 Jan. 1963.

49 TNA, CAB 128/38, Cabinet Conclusions, 10 Jan. 1963; TNA, PREM 11/4357, Johnson to Sandys, No. 155, 8 Feb. 1963.

50 *FRUS 1961–63, vol. 18*, document 156 and note 3, 347.

51 See the following documents: TNA, CO 1055/61, Luce (Bahrain) to Roger Stevens, B1052/3/G, 17 Jan. 1963; TNA, CO1055/61, Stevens to Luce, 8 Feb. 1963; TNA, FO 371/ 172 872, VG 1051/7, Beith addressed to Chancery, 6 Mar. 1963.

52 See Douglas Little, 'The New Frontier on the Nile', *American Historical Review*, (1990), pp. 521–4.

53 Z. Shalom, *The Superpowers, Israel and the Future of Jordan 1960–63* (Brighton, 1999),

p. 48; and U. Dann, *King Hussein and the Challenge of Arab Radicalism*, (Oxford, 1989), pp. 129–34, for the rest of the crisis.

54 TNA, CAB 128/38, Cabinet Conclusions 43, 27 June 1963. The issue was raised in Cabinet twice but the minutes are not very discursive. TNA, CAB 128/38, Cabinet Conclusions 46, 11 July 1963 and Cabinet Conclusions 47, 18 July 1963; diary entry for 16 Aug. 1963 in Harold Macmillan, *At the End of the Day* (London, 1973), p. 277. See TNA, FO 371/ 168804, BM1015/363, FO Guidance telegram No. 478; TNA, FO 371/ 168804, BM 1015/365, FO to Bamarko, No. 111.

55 TNA, FO 371/ 168816, BM1024/1/G, Trevakis (Aden) to CO, No. 19, 14 Oct. 1963, Extracts.

56 See Bloch and Fitzgerald, *British intelligence,* pp. 128–30; and Tom Bower, *The Perfect English Spy* (London, 1995), pp. 251–4.

57 Sir Peter De La Billiere, *Looking For Trouble* (London, 1994), pp. 202–11; Clive Jones, *Britain and the Yemen Civil War 1962–65. Minister, Mercenaries and Mandarins: Foreign Policy and the Limits of Covert Action* (Brighton, 2004), pp. 130–5. See also *The Mayfair*

58 S. Smith, 'Revolution and reaction: South Arabia in the aftermath of Yemeni Revolution', in K. Federowich and M. Thomas (eds), *Diplomacy and Colonial Retreat* (London, 2000) p. 201.

59 Bower, *Perfect English Spy*, pp. 251–4.

60 Jones, *Britain and the Yemen Civil War*, p. 101.

61 D.R. Thorpe, *Alec Douglas-Home* (London, 1996), p. 340.

62 TNA, PREM 11/4929, Wright to PM, Meeting with the Foreign Secretary, Colonial Secretary and MOD, 22 Nov. 1963.

63 See Glen Barbour-Paul, *The End of Empire in the Middle East: Britain's Relinquishment of Power in her Last Three Arab Dependencies* (Cambridge, 1991), p. 80; and Karl Pieragostini, *Britain, Aden and South Arabia* (London, 1991), p. 60.

64 USNA, AmEmbassy London to State, 3903, 12 Feb. 1964, POL UK-US Box 2785, DOSCF.

65 See TNA, FO 371/178594, VG1051/15, Transcript of Canadian Broadcasting Company Broadcast, 11 Feb. 1964; TNA, FO 371/178594, VG1051/14, Maitland (Cairo) to R.S. Scrivener, 27 Feb. 1964; TNA, FO 371/178581, VG 1022/2, Cairo–FO, No. 136, 23 Feb. 1964.

66 TNA, CAB 128/38 Cabinet Minutes, 20, No. 3, 24 Mar. 1964.

67 See the account given to US Ambassador Bruce by Frank Brenchley of the Foreign Office, reported in Lyndon Baines Johnson Library [hereafter LBJL], AmEmbassy London to State, No. 4815, 1 Apr. 1964, Yemen Cables, Vol. I., National Security Files [NSF] Country File, Yemen Box 161.

68 USNA, Taiz to State, No. 549, 29 Mar. 1964, Pol 32–1, Aden-Yemen dispute, Box 1866, DOSCF; LBJL, Rusk telcon with Johnson, Citation No. 2931, WH6404.05, Johnson Tapes. Johnson's message is in TNA, PREM 11/4679, FO to Washington, No. 5115, 15 Apr. 1964; LBJL, Komer to McGeorge Bundy, 2 Apr. 1964, NSF Country File, Yemen Memos, Vol. I, Box 161.

69 TNA, DEFE 13/569, Trevakis to CO, No. 355, 16 Apr. 1964; USNA AmEmbassy London to State, No. 5239, 23 Apr. 1964, DOSCF, Pol 32–1, Aden–Yemen dispute, Box 1866.

70 TNA, DEFE 13/569, Home to Butler M39/64, 23 Apr. 1964.

71 USNA, AmEmbassy London to State, No. 5267, 24 Apr. 1964, DOSCF, Pol 32–1, Aden–Yemen dispute, Box 1866.

72 TNA, DEFE 13/569, Thorneycroft to Douglas-Home, 22 April 1964.

73 TNA, FO 371/178583, VG1023/5/G, Following from Butler, Washington to FO, No. 1587, 28 Apr. 1964.

74 LBJL, Memcom, 27 Apr. 1964, UK meetings with Butler, NSF Country File, Box 213.

75 LBJL, Komer to McGeorge Bundy, 28 Apr. 1964, UK meetings with Butler, Sanitised copy, NSF Country File, UK Box 213.

76 LBJL, Memcon between President and Foreign Secretary Butler, 29 Apr. 1964, UK meetings with Butler, NSF Country File, UK Box 213; TNA, PREM 11/4980, Butler to Home, PMPT T122A/64, 29 April 1964.
77 *FRUS 1964–68, vol. 21: Near East Region* (Washington, D.C., 2000), document 341, 8 May 1964.
78 TNA, DEFE 13/569, Home to Butler M49/64, 5 May 1964.
79 TNA, DEFE 13/570, Note for Secretary of State for Defence, 20 July 1964.
80 S. Dorril, *MI6: Fifty Years of Special Operations* (London, 2000), pp. 692–3.
81 LBJL, AmEmbassy London to State, No. 5522, 6 May 1964, NSF Country File, Box 161.
82 TNA, DEFE 13/570, Note for SOS Defence, 20 July 1964.
83 R.J. Gavin, *Aden under British Rule 1839–1967* (London, 1976), p. 346.
84 *The Observer*, 5 July 1964.
85 TNA, DEFE 13/570, Maintaining our Position in South Arabia, Memo by Peter Thorneycroft, 13 July 1964.
86 TNA, PREM 11/4929, Wright to Douglas-Home, 18 July 1964.
87 TNA, DEFE 13/570, Strong note of discussion with Col. McClean, 20 July 1964.
88 Jones, *Britain and the Yemen Civil War*, p. 101.
89 LBJL, London to State, No. 435, 27 July 1964, section one, Yemen Cables, NSF Country File, Box 161.
90 TNA, PREM 11/4929, FO to Jedda, No. 718, 24 July 1964.
91 Jones, *Britain and the Yemen Civil War*, p. 111.
92 Simon C. Smith, *Britain's Revival and Fall in the Gulf* (London, 2004), p. 26.

The Iraq crisis:
intelligence driven or risk driven?

Yee-Kuang Heng

'What has changed that suddenly gives us the legal right to take military action that we didn't have a few months ago?' – David Blunkett, UK Cabinet meeting on Iraq, March 7 2002[1]

The recently revealed doubts of the former British Home Secretary – and close ally of Prime Minister Tony Blair – not only raised eyebrows. It also cut straight to the chase regarding the decision to unseat Saddam Hussein's regime in Iraq. The key operative word here is 'suddenly', underlining the need to inquire into what, if any, fresh evidence or dramatic developments in Iraq actually warranted urgent military action. After all, while certainly a pesky strategic thorn in the sides of Downing Street and the White House, Saddam had been tolerated for more than a decade. To this end, various intelligence dossiers, official and independent, were published in the run-up to invasion. These sought to undertake a process of 'net assessment' of Iraqi intentions and capabilities. It was hoped a so-called 'smoking gun' would be uncovered demonstrating Iraqi fingerprints in the 11 September 2001 terrorist attacks and thus its purported Al Qaeda links. Alternatively, proof had to be provided of Baghdad's reconstituted Weapons of Mass Destruction (WMD) programmes. The latter, especially in nuclear form, Bush Administration officials asserted, could easily be slipped to terrorists. This paper contends that the debates about intelligence and 'net assessment' were certainly crucial. Yet ironically they remained somewhat tangential to the crisis. Britain's pre-eminent strategic thinker Sir Lawrence Freedman has written recently that the crisis was not fuelled by freshly gleaned intelligence.[2] It was striking how little of this there actually was. Taking Sir Lawrence's conclusion a step further, it is suggested here that 'net assessments' too failed to provide the much sought-after 'smoking gun'. What officials were more concerned with in essence was risk-orientated thinking based on the Precautionary Principle.

This paper proceeds as follows. First, the difficulties of intelligence gathering, analysis and historical failures will be raised. This injects some sense of historical circumspection and background into Anglo-American intelligence claims during this Iraq crisis. More specific intelligence issues, documents and processes in the run-up to war will then be discussed. In particular, the concept of 'net assessment' employed in various dossiers from both sides of the Atlantic is examined for its role in driving intelligence analyses. The final section highlights how the ubiquitous postwar official inquiries concluded there was in fact no new evidence to warrant war. The conclusion demonstrates that what was crucial was in fact not 'net assessment' drawing on intelligence breakthroughs. Rather, the searing experience of 9/11 shifted the emphasis towards averting probabilistic risk scenarios and hypothetical catastrophic consequences. This in effect meant incorporating the Precautionary Principle into military strategy and international relations for better or worse.

THE LESSONS OF HISTORY: INTELLIGENCE AS AN ART

If there is one thing that the long and chequered history of intelligence tells us, it is that intelligence gathering and analysis is best described as an Art. Intelligence is not a hard Science. It is very rarely able to provide definitive answers or possess concrete, incontrovertible evidence. As a result there is ample reason for considerable modesty and to a certain extent, scepticism, when it comes to intelligence claims. Various reasons have been cited for this. Intelligence communities are often prone to what is known as collective groupthink. They share the same assumptions and/or succumb to peer pressure and socialising influences. Indeed, this was one of the criticisms levelled at the CIA and other Western intelligence agencies after failures over Iraq. French President Chirac reportedly dissented with his own intelligence agency's view that Iraq held banned weapons. He felt that the intelligence services 'sometimes intoxicate each other'.[3] Intelligence itself is also often full of uncertainties and intangibles, composed of scraps of unreliable information sometimes derived from informants with their own axes to grind. The analyst has to try to reach as balanced and accurate an analysis as possible given these methodological problems. The conclusions reached are never completely right or completely wrong, as the Iraq issue demonstrates. Western intelligence was certainly correct that Saddam intended to restart his WMD programmes once sanctions were lifted. They were wrong with regard to how far he had gone with reconstitution.

It is thus a clear testimony to the difficulties of intelligence analysis that the scrap heap of history is littered with countless examples of failures and debacles. From the twenty-first century right back to ancient times, there have been instances of underestimation, overestimation, complacency or pure ignorance. One need only look from the twentieth century on. Pearl Harbor and its oft-cited contemporary equivalent, 11 September 2001, share some similarities in terms of intelligence inadequacies. The inability to interpret Japanese radar blips correctly and link them to Japanese radio traffic decoded by the US Navy's *Magic* system parallels the failing to connect the dots of the 9/11 conspiracy. In both cases, it was a concoction of pure ignorance, complacency or underestimation of the enemy. Stalin too underestimated the German threat of invasion on the eve of Operation Barbarossa despite unmistakable military signs and warnings from Soviet allies Britain and America. In the Falklands, the British in turn were guilty of intelligence shortcomings and a certain level of complacency. They felt able to have sufficient warning of an Argentine invasion.

Given these notable historical precedents, much more than a pinch of salt should have been taken with the intelligence claims being put forth in the months of debate before the war on Iraq. US Defence Secretary Donald Rumsfeld claimed to have 'bulletproof' evidence of Baghdad's links with Al Qaeda.[4] Other intelligence claims on terrorism by the Administration suggested that one of the 9/11 hijackers, Mohamed Atta, had met with Iraqi intelligence – the Mukhabarat – in Prague. There was also then CIA Director George Tenet's now infamous use of a sports metaphor for the benefit of his fellow sports fan President George W. Bush: intelligence on Iraq's WMD programs was a certainty, a 'slam dunk'. The Administration's leading resident neo-con hawk Paul Wolfowitz told the Council on Foreign Relations in New York in January 2003 that America's case was 'grounded in current intelligence... it is very convincing'.[5] Bush in his January 2003 State of the Union address alluded to an Iraqi procurement network attempting to acquire yellowcake uranium oxide from the African state of Niger: sixteen words that stirred up a hornet's nest of controversy. On the British side, the Blair Government dossier of September 2002 contended that Baghdad's forces could deploy and use WMD within 45 minutes of being given the order to do so.

As Lawrence Freedman once again points out, the historical record demonstrates that only very rarely have Britain and America gone to war based supposedly on intelligence. War was mostly in response to a clear-cut provocation. The question then is really to what extent did intelligence debates propel the coalition to war? This is especially pertinent in light of recent leaks, in the British press and the American media, of the so-called Downing Street memos. This set of minutes of high-level meetings in Downing Street in 2002 indicated that Sir Richard Dearlove, the Head of MI6, felt that in the US the decision for war had already been taken. The intelligence and facts were 'fixed' afterwards to suit political choices.

INTELLIGENCE AND 'NET ASSESSMENT'

In the intense public debate in the run-up to war during late 2002 – early 2003, there were many so-called intelligence dossiers and reports seeking to assess the security challenges posed by Saddam Hussein's regime. In a sense, the public demand for accountability and transparency was unprecedented. Hitherto confidential and sensitive documents from the UK Joint Intelligence Committee (JIC) report published in September 2002 were available to public access on the Internet. Indeed, it was the first time the JIC had ever released a public document in such a public manner. Similarly, portions of the October 2002 US National Intelligence Estimate on Iraq were declassified. During the May 2005 British election campaign, Tony Blair was even pressured into releasing confidential advice from the Attorney General on the legality of war. The Prime Minister himself advised the public to go read the full legal advice on the Internet and make up their minds. Among the plethora of reports, many were official government documents. Others issued by widely regarded independent think tanks, also weighed significantly in the intelligence debate. Two such reports will now be addressed in greater depth.

One of these was published by the reputable London-based International Institute for Strategic Studies (IISS) in September 2002 and entitled *A Strategic Dossier: Iraq's WMD, A Net Assessment*. This report attempted to appraise Iraq's current WMD capacities as dispassionately as possible. It was lauded by both Tony Blair and senior US officials such as Deputy Defence Secretary Paul Wolfowitz for providing factual and thoughtful analyses of Iraqi capabilities. Across the Atlantic, a second notable document was *Iraqi Warfighting Capabilities: A Dynamic Net Assessment*, authored by Middle East military expert Professor Anthony Cordesman of the Center for Strategic and International Studies (CSIS) in Washington in July 2002. Professor Cordesman cited at length from this report in his testimony that summer to a Congressional panel attempting to evaluate the Iraqi threat more precisely.

What is perhaps most striking from both publications is the use of the concept 'net assessment' explicitly and quite prominently within their titles. Briefly speaking, military organisations and analysts have invested significant resources in net assessments for years.

Sophisticated analytical and modelling tools were often employed. This notion appeared then prima facie to have played a role in the prewar intelligence debates. If so, what did this concept entail? Did it drive intelligence analyses and in turn the resort to war? How significant was it? What are the conceptual problems and assumptions underlying its use?

Unfortunately, and perhaps unsurprisingly, the fields of intelligence and international relations employ many essentially contested concepts. Multiple differing definitions of 'net assessment' exist. Furthermore, the IISS dossier does not supply one nor attempt to define it. It actually uses the term rather loosely and imprecisely. However, stripped down to its bare-bones essentials, the notion implies analysing the ability of a country's armed forces and its particular force postures to perform military missions against enemy forces. The US Department of Defense defines it as the 'comparative analysis of military, technological, political, economic and other factors governing the relative military capabilities of nations'.[6] The key word here is 'relative', and possibly should involve dynamic comparison of interaction of opposing forces in battle scenarios. However, in practice, much of what passed as 'net assessment' during the Cold War was simplistic and static bean-counting of numerical forces staked up against one another.[7]

Calculations: Net Assessment and the Coming of World War Two, is one of the few academic books to address this issue. Williamson Murray and Alan Millet defined net assessment, in its bureaucratic structured manifestation, as the gathering of information about potential enemies, processing and comparing it with one's own strengths and weaknesses, and providing reliable information for decision-makers.[8] Paul Kennedy in his contribution to that book summarised net assessment as a combination of perceptions, processes and final product. Britain, argued Kennedy, before the Second World War had perhaps most closely resembled a sophisticated formal net assessment arrangement. London had effective intelligence organisations and multitiered committees and subcommittees. Yet it is by no means guaranteed that an accurate net assessment translates into the appropriate policy choice. Once again, there have been notable historical failures. For instance, France before the Second World War possessed the necessary information and generally reliable net assessments on the rise of Nazi Germany. Yet Paris lacked political will to confront Hitler. Despite Whitehall's relative sophistication compared to its peer-competitors then, its net assessment efforts were relatively primitive compared to what the US has today. The Pentagon has its very own Office of Net Assessment on the third floor, a secretive but highly influential unit run by the legendary 84-year-old Andrew Marshall. Described as the most influential yet unknown thinker in

America, Marshall has been referred to as the Jedi Master Yoda, and at other times alluded to as the mythical Delphi Oracle. Problematically for an agreed definition of net assessment and its role in the Iraq crisis, the Office of Net Assessment (ONA) did not seem to have played a key part. Its brief and self-defined mission statement was more related to thinking creatively and out-of-the-box on long-term strategic issues and developments.

If net assessment in the bureaucratised form of the ONA kept a low profile, how then did the concept work in practice with regard to the Iraq crisis? In particular, as it was employed in the various dossiers presented, what did it actually reveal about the specific intelligence concerns regarding Iraq and Saddam Hussein? The IISS Strategic Dossier concluded that, based on its net assessment, Iraq did not yet have nuclear capabilities but could possess some checmical and biological weapons. This view was echoed in the US October 2002 National Intelligence Estimate (NIE), and of course the JIC's infamous 45-minute claim. The CSIS report and the IISS both assessed that Saddam certainly desired to retain or reconstitute his WMD efforts. The US NIE went further, suggesting that reconstitution was probably already underway, although the State Department's in-house intelligence and research unit dissented. This was rather unusual for an NIE, which is normally assumed to be a composite of views held by the entire intelligence community.

Nonetheless, despite the dissensions, what can generally be surmised from the emphases of both the CSIS and IISS reports and those of the official dossiers? It was a focus on the motivations driving Saddam, his plans as well as his military capacities. In a nutshell, Baghdad's intentions and capabilities were the core dual components of these intelligence concerns. Therefore US force postures and fielded military capabilities were judged adequate in handling the Iraqi armed forces and its current WMD capacities. The net assessment efforts also very clearly revolved around perceptions of Saddam's decision-making process and intentions. It was assumed that Saddam's WMD programmes were designed to aid terrorists wreak massive destruction on the West. The British Government's dossier of September 2002 thus concluded that Saddam was a pressing danger, founded on an assessment of his capabilities and intentions/plans.[8] In general, intelligence agencies, including those of France and Germany, believed Iraq had retained both WMD capacities and ambitions.

Saddam certainly did pose a tricky security problem. However, the net assessment results based around intentions and capabilities on the whole did not translate into a 'smoking gun', as Cordesman admitted in his Congressional testimony. There was no 'killer fact' that should drive the crisis onward into military confrontation. The US NIE in fact accepted it lacked specific information on Baghdad's WMD programme and capabilities as well as alleged terrorist links. As suggested earlier, it was unusual in presenting quite a few dissenting footnotes and alternative views. The assessments of Saddam's intentions were also wrong in hindsight. Postwar investigations and interrogations indicated his WMD programmes were directed mainly at Iran rather than the West. These strategic realities were unfortunately not captured nor reflected adequately in intelligence analyses produced before the war. So how did intelligence and the net assessment procedures fare?

David Kay summed it up well when he quit as Head of the Iraq Survey Group (ISG) in January 2004, stating that 'we were almost all wrong'. This was a telling statement coming from a man who was previously convinced there were indeed WMDs to be found. Kay's successor Charles Duelfer released the Duelfer Report in October 2004 (updated in January 2005) and concluded no reconstitution effort was underway: there were no WMDs. Intelligence was, however, correct in that Saddam had 'strategic intent' to restart WMD efforts once sanctions were lifted. He had maintained a small scientific pool of intellectual capital and resources while balancing the need for UN cooperation with minimal foreign interference and loss of face.[9] David Kay once again put it very succinctly in his view of the Duelfer Report's key findings: 'future intent but no capabilities did not equal imminent threat'.[10] Iraq, rather than positioning itself to become a major threat with actively growing capabilities matching malicious intent, was actually going down the opposite path and it had stripped its capabilities down to bare essentials. The 9/11 Commission also reported that there was no compelling evidence of the alleged link between lead 9/11 hijacker Mohamed Atta and Iraqi intelligence.[11] By now, even Donald Rumsfeld himself, in a speech to the Council of Foreign Relations in October 2004, had to backtrack from his earlier claim of 'bulletproof' evidence. Rumsfeld conceded that there was in fact 'no hard evidence' of Baghdad's alleged Al Qaeda links.[12]

Across the Atlantic, the flurry of postwar inquiries into intelligence in Britain reached very similar and discomfiting conclusions. Most notably, the Butler Report in July 2004 sought to address three questions: the quality of intelligence about the Saddam regime's 'strategic intent' to pursue WMD and its efforts to achieve a 'break-out capability', as well as assessments of Iraqi production/possession of WMD.[13] Once again, mirroring parallels with its American counterpart, the focus of this high-level inquiry was on how well British intelligence assessed Iraqi intentions and capabilities. (key components of the 'net assessment' effort). It concluded that there was indeed latent strategic intent on Saddam's part to reconstitute sometime in the future but there were no WMD capabilities ready for immediate battlefield deployment, certainly not at 45 minutes' notice as previously claimed.[14]

The Report went on to suggest that the 2002 dossier on Iraqi intentions and capabilities was marred by overstatement and embellishment but had not been wilfully altered by 10 Downing Street. An earlier UK Intelligence and Security Committee report in September 2003 also noted that the 2002 dossier did not sufficiently make clear that Saddam was not considered an imminent or current threat to the UK mainland.[15] All in all, net assessment efforts and a focus on the intentions and capabilities of the Saddam Hussein regime did not yield all the right results.

This might not be surprising given the historical precedents and problems with net assessment highlighted earlier by Murray and Millett. However, given the postwar deluge of official reports in effect rubbishing intelligence claims, did intelligence and net assessment outcomes actually drive the crisis? To be fair, hindsight is always 20/20. The Cabinet Office, back in 2002, had already noted poor UK intelligence on Iraq.[16] Most intelligence agencies, even the French and Germans, did believe Iraq had some WMD stocks squirrelled away. After all, the Senate Committee on Intelligence reported in July 2004 that collective groupthink plagued not only US intelligence but also its allies and the UN agencies involved.[17] The danger was genuinely perceived by the UK intelligence agencies as real and present at the time, given the available information, a view reflected in a House of Commons Foreign Affairs Committee report in July 2003.[18]

But the deeper question that needs to be raised is, rather, was there any new evidence that had come to light to plunge the world into crisis? What had actually changed since 1998, when UN inspectors were booted out amid beliefs, even then, that Iraq was concealing its WMD programmes? What had changed the situation and in such dramatic fashion that war and regime change were the outcome? Indeed, looking back again at the IISS Strategic Dossier, its net assessment efforts were pretty solid until December 1998 as inspectors had access to Iraq.[19] Once inspectors were expelled, its analysis relied on much weaker factual evidence and more on hypothesising. Former British Foreign Secretary Robin Cook, for one, had already noted when the British JIC dossier was released in September 2002 that there was 'so little new material... no new evidence of a dramatic increase in the threat requiring urgent invasion'.[20] Cook, who was in office at the time of the December 1998 crisis, would have been familiar with the most sensitive intelligence materials. Cook's view was hardly unique nor limited to the British political classes.

In Washington, Tony Cordesman, commenting in September 2002, noted that 'the problem you have in analysing any new evidence is that we haven't had any'.[21] According to Cordesman, much of what was presented in the dossiers was public information which had been available for months, and even years in some instances. The White

House paper 'A Decade of Deception and Defiance', designed to outline Saddam's breaches of UN resolutions, was denounced by Cordesman as a 'glorified press release that doesn't come close to the information the U.S. government made available on Soviet military power when we were trying to explain the Cold War'. It qualified in his view only as a 'D-minus' grade.[22]

Postwar official inquiries confirmed this prewar scepticism. The US House of Representatives Intelligence Committee found in September 2003 that the US had 'no fresh evidence' of Iraqi WMD or links with Al Qaeda.[23] Most of what Washington had to go by were outdated assessments and little since 1998, when the inspectors left. Indeed, having no inspectors amounted to what the *New York Times* colourfully described as 'losing your GPS [Global Positioning Systems] guidance'.[24] Analysts were reduced to groping for fragmentary information such as alleged Iraqi interest in uranium from Niger and aluminium tubes. Finally the Butler report concluded there was 'no recent intelligence' that would single out Iraq as of more immediate concern than other states, although Saddam's history of WMD use meant the threat of force was needed to bring about compliance.[25] Intelligence, it suggested, played only a 'limited role' in determining the legality of the war.

Given the sombre conclusions of these high-level official inquiries, if intelligence and net assessment did not provide compelling rationales for war or propel the crisis at heart, what actually did? Paul Wolfowitz suggested in an interview for *Vanity Fair* in July 2003 perhaps bureaucratic reasons. The administration settled on the WMD issue simply because it was the only one the various agencies could agree on. It also seemed a politically acceptable reason for regime change. As Bob Woodward recounts in his insider account of decision-making in the Bush White House, the WMD issue was highlighted among a range of possible concerns because it 'had legs' in the run-up to war.[26] Another possible reason, suggested Senator Carl Levin, ranking Democrat on the Armed Services Committee, was that Saddam was removed on the grounds he had committed a 'thought crime'. Saddam had dared to plan a crime in the future, with future intentions to acquire WMD. Levin complains this was not the stated prewar case for invasion. In fact, this paper suggests that this idea of going to war on a 'thought crime' raises interesting implications. Coupled with the startling and candid admission by Condoleezza Rice in July 2003 that 'the question of what was new after 1998 is not an interesting question',[27] this implies that, in fact, new intelligence about dramatic Iraqi misbehaviour was not central to the crisis. This defies conventional assumptions, given the emphasis which had been placed on intelligence in the lead-up to war. Even more significantly, Donald Rumsfeld's testimony to the Senate Armed Services

Committee in July 2003 revealed that in actual fact 'the coalition did not act because we had discovered dramatic new evidence of Iraq's pursuit of WMD'.[28] What is most illuminating from Rumsfeld's testimony is that existing, even somewhat outdated intelligence and evidence had been simply recast and reinterpreted in 'a dramatic new light'. The 'prism of 9/11' had shaped judgements and heightened appreciation of the vulnerability and risks America faced.

THE PRECAUTIONARY PRINCIPLE GOES TO WAR

Given this information from a very influential Cabinet official in the inner sanctum of the Bush Administration, a very useful contrast and comparison with official assessments and pronouncements on Iraq pre-9/11 can then be made. In March 2001, Secretary of State Colin Powell testified to the Senate Foreign Relations Committee that Saddam did have something to hide but was still not yet a 'full-fledged threat'.[29] Rumsfeld and Wolfowitz's Congressional statements pre-9/11 barely mentioned Iraq. Baghdad was then viewed more as a long-term ballistic missile threat which necessitated National Missile Defence systems, at that time the pet project of the Administration.

In the new post-9/11 light, far from net assessments or any intelligence about new alarming developments inside Iraq proper driving the crisis, it is changes in the mindsets of British and American policy-makers that were more important to the crisis. For instance, President Bush observed that, before 9/11, the focus of discussion was how to revise smart sanctions and tighten up the sanctions regime. However 'the strategic vision of our country shifted dramatically' after 9/11.[30] As Condoleezza Rice put it, Iraq had become 'part of the insecurity we all feel' after 9/11.[31] Consequently, rather than reasoned net assessments based on intelligence about Iraqi or Al Qaeda intentions and capabilities, the debate shifted inexorably towards a concern with vague probabilities of links between the two and resulting catastrophic results. This shift from intentions and capabilities towards probabilities and consequences was indicative of risk-orientated thinking. This overshadowed attempts to weigh up security threats precisely through net assessment exercises. As late as October 2004 it was quite clear that neither WMD nor terrorist links would be found. President Bush doggedly continued to defend the invasion on the grounds of speculative scenarios that Saddam could pass WMD secretly to terrorists without leaving any fingerprints. In the UK, the Butler Report noted that 'what had changed was not the pace of Iraq's prohibited programs, which had not been dramatically stepped up, but tolerance of them following the attacks of 11th September 2001.'[32] Tony Blair's own testimony to the Butler Report indicated clearly that

9/11 was the key factor changing his mindset with regard to rogue states acquiring WMD. The corresponding changed calculation of risks in policy-makers' minds implied that any dissenting intelligence from the JIC or CIA was to a certain extent inconsequential. In such a climate, much of what passed for evidence was not SIGINT (signals intelligence), HUMINT (human intelligence), SATINT (satellite intelligence), but actually RUMINT (rumour intelligence) which seemed to fit the worst-case assumptions swirling around.

What drove the Iraq crisis then were not intelligence net assessments based on dramatic new information. Rather it was speculative hypotheses and taking precautionary action on fears of a post-9/11 Perfect Storm: a possible linking of WMD-armed Iraq and Al Qaeda.[33] Further broken down into more specific 'risk' components, this implied a concern with catastrophic consequences and probabilities. Senior Administration officials were rolled out on Sunday talk shows to warn of possible worst-case outcomes. Condoleezza Rice, for instance, warned on CNN of a nuclear 'mushroom cloud'. Donald Rumsfeld suggested that the penalty for inaction was 'another 9/11'.[34] Rather than taking action on more concrete intelligence and net assessments, Rumsfeld famously advocated acting on 'unknown unknowns', where you don't even know what it is that you don't know with regard to Iraq.[35] The focus had to be on probabilities. This convoluted argument won Rumsfeld the 'Foot in the Mouth' award from the Plain English Campaign. In fact, however, he made crystal clear sense to students of risk and followers of the Precautionary Principle. His subsequent arguments that 'absence of evidence is not evidence of absence' further frustrated people but Rumsfeld came across sounding like a guru expounding the merits of the Precautionary Principle. Given this focus on acting even on vague probabilities, in effect the coalition did not need concrete evidence to act. Furthermore, it appeared that Rumsfeld's philosophy of averting worst-case scenarios by adopting the Precautionary Principle rubbed off onto the head honcho himself. President George W. Bush declared, 'we have every reason to assume the worst and we have an urgent duty to prevent the worst from occurring'.[36]

Assuming the worst and then taking action to prevent it from happening has serious consequences. Worst-case thinking is not historically unprecedented, with Cold War examples of the Bomber and Missile Gaps. However, the nature of elusive security concerns in today's globalised world in contrast to the more calculable material threats posed by the Soviet Union lends itself easily to an increasing focus on risk-orientated thinking. This might well compromise the intelligence community's independent impartial analyses, on which it rightly prides itself. Indeed, there was concern that the intelligence dossiers provided during the crisis without sufficient qualification implied that the intelligence communities came under political pressure to come up with overstated worst-case interpretations of existing evidence, which could undermine the long-established concept of net assessment. The emphasis on probabilities and worst-case consequences might well displace more careful, reasoned appraisal of enemy intentions and capabilities.

NOTES

1 See 'From Memos, insights into Ally's doubts on Iraq war', *Washington Post*, 28 June 2005.
2 L. Freedman, 'War in Iraq: Selling the Threat', *Survival*, 46, 2 (summer 2004).
3 Quoted in Hans Blix, *Disarming Iraq: The Search for Weapons of Mass Destruction*, (London, 2004), p. 128.
4 US Department of Defense news briefing – Secretary Rumsfeld and General Myers, 24 October 2002.
5 'Iraq: What does disarmament look like?', remarks as delivered at the Council on Foreign Relations, 23 January 2003, available at http://www.dod.mil/speeches/2003/s20030123-depsecdef2.html
6 US Department of Defense Directive 5111.11, August 2001.
7 See, for instance, Aaron Friedberg, 'The Assessment of Military Power: A Review Essay', *International Security*, 12, 3 (winter 1987–8), pp. 190-202.
8 Williamson Murray and Allan R. Millett, 'Net Assessment on the Eve of World War II', in Murray and Millett (eds), *Calculations: Net Assessment and the coming of World War II* (New York, 1992), pp. 1–18.
9 Paul Kennedy, 'British "Net Assessment" and the Coming of the Second World War' in Murray and Millett, *Calculations*, pp. 19–59.
10 Steven Ross, 'French Net Assessment', in Murray and Millett, *Calculations*, pp. 136-74.
11 *Iraq's Weapons of Mass Destruction: The Assessment of the British Government*, Executive Summary, London, 24 September 2002, http://www.archive2.official-documents. co.uk/document/reps/iraq/summary.htm
12 *Comprehensive Report of the Special Adviser to the DCI on Iraq's WMD*, Washington, 30 September 2004, with Addenda March 2005, available at http://www.cia.gov/cia/reports/iraq_wmd_2004/ (accessed 11 July 2005).
13 Quoted in 'Bush Administration in denial about lack of Iraqi WMD: Kay', *Agence France Presse*, (7 October 2004, available at http://www.truthout.org/docs_04/100804W.shtml
14 National Commission on Terrorist Attacks Upon the United States (9/11 Commission), Final Report, 22 July 2004, Washington, Ch. 2, p. 66.
15 'An Update on the Global War on Terror with Donald Rumsfeld', Council on Foreign Relations, New York, 4 October 2004.
16 *Review of Intelligence on Weapons of Mass Destruction* [hereafter The Butler Report], (London, July 2004), HC 898, paragraph 473, p.116.
17 The Butler Report, paragraph 397, p. 99.
18 UK Intelligence and Security Committee, *Iraqi Weapons of Mass Destruction – Intelligence and Assessments*, Cm 5972, London, 20 September 2003, p. 26, paragraph 83. Available at http://www.cabinetoffice.gov.uk/publications/reports/isc/iwmdia.pdf
19 See 'From Memos, insights into Ally's doubts on Iraq war', *Washington Post*, 28 June 2005.

20 Senate Committee on Intelligence, *Report on the US Intelligence Community's Prewar Intelligence Assessments on Iraq*, Washington, 7 July 2004, p. 18. http://intelligence.senate.gov/iraqreport2.pdf

21 House of Commons Foreign Affairs Committee, Ninth report, *The Decision to Go to War in Iraq*, 3 July 2003, London, HC813-I, Paragraph 41.

22 Rolf Ekeus, 'Reassessment: the IISS Strategic Dossier on Iraq's Weapons of Mass Destruction', *Survival* 46, 2, (summer 2004), pp. 73–88.

23 From Robin Cook's memoirs serialised in the *Sunday Times*, 5 October 2003.

24 Quoted in United Press International, 'US evidence against Iraq: nothing new', 10 September 2002, available at http://www.upi.com/view.cfm?StoryID=20020910-125706-2015r

25 Quoted in 'Bush's evidence of Hussein misdeeds shows its age', *Washington Post*, 13 September 2002.

26 Dana Priest, 'House Panel skewers intelligence community on Iraq', *Washington Post*, 28 September 2003.

27 For detailed analysis of intelligence estimates on Iraq, see 'In sketchy data, trying to gauge the Iraqi threat', *New York Times*, 20 July 2003.

28 The Butler Report, paragraph 427, p.105.

29 Bob Woodward, *Plan of Attack* (New York, 2004), p. 220.

30 Quoted in 'In sketchy data, trying to gauge the Iraqi threat', *New York Times*, 20 July 2003.

31 Prepared testimony by US Secretary of Defense Donald H. Rumsfeld before the Senate Armed Services Committee, 9 July 2003.

32 Testimony at Budget Hearing before Senate Foreign Relations Committee, 8 March 2001.

33 Joint Press Conference with Prime Minister Tony Blair at the White House, Washington D.C., 31 January 2003.

34 Quoted in David Sanger, 'Debate over attacking Iraq heats up', *New York Times*, 1 September 2002, and also *Avenging Terror*, Channel 4 (UK), 31 August 2002.

35 The Butler Report, paragraph 427, p. 105.

36 Freedman, 'War in Iraq: selling the threat', p. 17.

37 US Department of Defense news briefing- Secretary Rumsfeld and General Myers, 3 September 2002.

38 US Department of Defense (DoD) news briefing – Secretary Rumsfeld, 12 February 2002.

39 President Bush outlines Iraqi threat, Office of the Press Secretary, 7 October 2002.

Index